1000
Great Places to Travel *with kids* in Australia

ANNA CIDDOR

This book is dedicated to all my family, who have shared my explorations of Australia, from my parents, who introduced me to the joys of travel, to the newest member, our precious little Amelie.

Thank you to Heidi Marfurt for her dedicated and inspired editing, to my nieces Sophie and Ariele, who helped me out when time was running short, and to my wonderful daughter Elissa, who designed the outstanding cover, and collaborated with me over the illustrations.

CONTENTS

INTRODUCTION

At the age of eleven, as I was leaving for a holiday with my family, my best friend handed me a gift – a travel journal. The moment I was on board the plane, I excitedly opened the book to the first page and began to record my impressions: the prickly feel of the seat under my bare knees, the fun of the little fold-down table, the basket of lollies the flight steward was offering around... My obsession with travel writing had begun!

1000 Great Places to Travel with Kids in Australia is based on my own travels – both as a child, and as a parent – along with contributions from countless other kids and parents. My original intention was to write a book that covered 100 great places, but I quickly realised 100 would have to expand to 1000... and in fact I ended up including so many that I lost count!

However, this book is far more than a list of places. I've had fun including fabulous facts about the history, oddities and enchantments that make up Australia, as well as tantalising questions and challenges. Why do echidnas snort a lot? Do rainforests really have a lot of rain? Why were the images of the first men walking on the moon broadcast from tracking stations in Australia? As you skim these pages to find places to take your own kids, I hope you are inspired by how much there is to marvel at, and cherish, in Australia.

TIPS FOR TRAVELLING WITH KIDS

Anticipation is half the fun

If possible, get the whole family involved
in planning where to go and what to see.
Explore websites together, read books set
in different locations – I've included a
few suggestions – and find YouTube
videos about the places you are visiting.

Keep them snap-happy

Give the kids the chance to take their own photos – it's amazing how
much this adds to their enjoyment and appreciation of sights and
events. Encourage them to keep diaries or travel blogs and incorporate
these photos. Plan to print a book with their photos and comments
when you get home.

It's not just the destination

When my cousin took her two small kids on a 24-hour bus journey,
she packaged up a tiny, cheap present to give each of them every
hour. This was so successful in keeping them entertained that they
begged to return the same way! You may not be planning such
a long haul, but it just goes to show how a bit of preparation allows
the whole family to enjoy the journey as well as the destination.

To keep car journeys fun:

- Organise the back seat with lap-top tables, convenient rubbish
  bags and a variety of entertainment options that are easy
  to access.

- Make frequent stops.

- Try some family activities such as singalongs, I-spy games,
  and hangman spelling quizzes.

- The free website www.toiletmap.gov.au is a great help for finding
  emergency toilet stops.

Always consider different transport options. When you're in the
planning stages, keep in mind that it can be fun – and more

environmentally friendly – to travel by train instead of by road or air. Trains also give kids more of an opportunity to move around.

The right place at the right time
Kids can be more sensitive to weather extremes than adults. Some destinations have 'off seasons' and I have indicated this in their introductions. If you travel to the north of Australia during the hot, humid season, you may find that all your kids want to do is play in the hotel pool. Likewise, if you travel to Tasmania in the depths of winter, they may be too cold to appreciate anything.

Be aware that school holiday dates vary from state to state; see www.australia.gov.au/topics/australian-facts-and-figures for links to school and public holidays throughout Australia. If you choose to travel during school holidays, not only will you find that most attractions listed in this book run fabulous extra activities, but many places not listed have special kid-friendly activities for a few weeks. Check out what's on offer in historic houses, art galleries and local libraries. Regional tourism websites are a good source of information. The downside of travelling in school holidays is that attractions are usually more crowded at those times and you may need to book accommodation well in advance.

For all destinations, I have tried to include indoor, wet-weather options. Even if these sound enticing, try to keep them in reserve for rainy days and do the outdoor activities while the weather is fine. Make sure everyone brings effective wet-weather gear, though, so if you have a really long run of rainy days, you can plough ahead with outdoor activities.

Sticking together
In your everyday lives you already have techniques in place to minimise the risk of your kids getting lost. When you set off on this new adventure, you may want to add a few extra strategies, such as

supplying the kids with whistles, mobile phones or even tracking devices. In crowded places make sure they have a bit of money, a note with your current address, and your mobile phone number (some people write this on their kids' arms). Plan with the kids what to do if they get separated from you – think of various scenarios where this might happen, such as boarding trains or getting out of lifts.

To keep track of your possessions as you move around, get everyone into the habit of checking carefully to make sure nothing has been left behind before moving on. This applies to restaurants, planes and airport lounges as well as accommodation. Our technique when leaving accommodation is for one adult to take the kids outside with the packed suitcases, while the other pulls all the bedding off the beds to look for cuddly toys or pyjamas, checks the bathroom for clothes left drying and does a quick skim-through of drawers, cupboards and under furniture.

A timetable to suit kids

When you discover all the wonderful things there are to see and do in a place, it is so tempting to get carried away and try to squeeze in too much! You are the best judge of how many 'big' activities your kids can manage in a day – so remember this when you plan each 24 hours.

Pick your favourite activities and then try to plan the best way to enjoy them. For example, if you choose the Penguin Parade at Phillip Island (which is an evening activity), work out if it would be best for your kids to see this as a day trip from Melbourne, or whether it would be better to stay a night or two on Phillip Island. If you choose a bus tour from Melbourne, should the kids have a quiet day first and then take a late tour directly to the Penguin Parade, or would it be better to take a whole-day tour that includes other activities?

Safety

Wherever you go, be alert to warning signs. If a notice warns that a river is infested with crocodiles, or the sea with dangerous stinging jellyfish, then don't swim there!

Be water safe. Try to keep to beaches patrolled by lifesavers, or at least ask locals about swimming conditions before entering the water. Before you go out on a boat, check there are child-sized lifejackets and make sure your kids wear them. In swimming pools, show your children where the shallow end is and keep them under your supervision at all times.

If you travel in summer, find out if any of your planned destinations could be at risk of bushfire. If so, check for fire warnings, updates and emergency procedures.

If you visit a tropical area where mosquito-borne disease is a problem, purchase insect repellent with DEET that is suitable for kids, bring mosquito netting for cots and beds, make sure the kids have loose, light-coloured clothes with long sleeves and pants to wear, and avoid going outdoors at dusk.

I've included some warnings about specific seasonal risks in the brief introductory sections for each location, but once you've chosen where to go, research this more yourself. You may encounter slippery, icy roads in snow-prone areas, or flooding and cyclones in tropical areas. Make sure you find out – and follow – the correct procedures for minimising risks.

Childproof your accommodation

If you have very small kids, check for safety hazards in any place you are staying. Here are a few suggestions:

- Have a few electric socket protectors, portable cupboard locks and corner protectors ready in your luggage. Alternatively, take some masking tape and wadding for improvising.

- Keep doors to balconies and other outside areas locked.

- Move dangerous cleaning fluids to high cupboards.
- Move bunk bed mattresses to the floor if you are concerned about falls.
- Check cot safety – in particular, look for incorrectly spaced bars, loose screws and rough edges.
- Make sure heaters or fireplaces are well guarded.
- Put away slippery rugs.

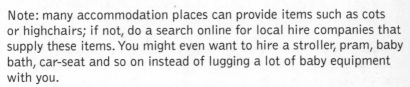

Note: many accommodation places can provide items such as cots or highchairs; if not, do a search online for local hire companies that supply these items. You might even want to hire a stroller, pram, baby bath, car-seat and so on instead of lugging a lot of baby equipment with you.

Sulk-busters

Remember that kids need time out just to relax and have fun. Hire bikes or kayaks, or let them burn off energy at local parks, pools, indoor play centres, beaches and playgrounds (you'll find some of the best ones listed in this book). For some quiet time, visit local libraries to sit and read books together – you might even catch a special activity.

Enforce a strict 'taking turns' policy that applies to everything, from choosing what to watch on the portable DVD player in the car, to where to go for dinner.

Keep fuelled. We all know a hungry or thirsty kid is not much fun. If this means forking out for an over-priced drink at a tourist attraction, remind yourself it will be a much bigger waste of money if the child is grumpy and everyone has a rotten time. Find another opportunity to save money – and try to have snacks and drinks on hand next time.

A wonderful way to stop kids constantly nagging you to buy them things is to give them their own spending budgets and let them make their own decisions. It is interesting to see them learn very quickly not to waste money!

HOW TO USE THIS BOOK

What's included
All over Australia there are magnificent, unique and exciting corners to explore, and I had the difficult task of selecting which ones to include in this book. I made my choices based on 'hot spots' that seemed to have the greatest quantity and variety of family-friendly activities, but I hope this book gives you a taste for adventure so you will go on to explore and discover some more obscure locations on your own.

If you'd like to share your wonderful discoveries and experiences – and maybe see them in a future edition – please email Explore Australia (info@exploreaustralia.net.au).

Who's it for?
Whether you're exploring the state you live in, visiting another part of Australia or visiting from overseas, if you're travelling with kids, this book is for you.

Here you'll find attractions that are exciting, fun and challenging for tiny-tots and teens, and all ages in between. I've hunted for activities to cater for all tastes and obsessions. You'll find dinosaurs, beaches, horseriding, rock climbing, circus classes, kangaroos, sports museums, ghost tours, antenna dishes that talk to the solar system, and much, much more.

If you're looking for inspiration, check out the themed index (p. 606) for the type of attractions that appeal to your kids.

Planning tips

The information provided in this book was checked at the time of writing, but I recommend phoning ahead to confirm details before you travel. If it's something critical that you want to check, don't rely solely on website information, which is often out of date.

Distances and travel times given are approximate and are intended as a guide only. This book is designed to be used in conjunction with a reliable road atlas and city/town maps. Wherever possible, I have tried to list attractions in sub-regions to assist with planning, but be aware that distances in more sparsely populated areas can be vast and travel times vary greatly depending on terrain and road conditions.

Opening times

Most free attractions, such as parks and beaches, are open around the clock every day of the year. Most paid attractions are open daily for at least the hours 10am–4pm, except for major public holidays such as Christmas Day and Good Friday. I have tried to alert you to variations outside these standard hours, but opening times, tour schedules and so on are highly prone to change. As there is nothing more annoying than staring at a locked door after a guide book has told you a place will be open, I strongly urge you to phone ahead for up-to-date operating hours.

If I have listed an attraction as opening early, this means it should be open before 9am, which can be useful for families with early risers!

Note: for many attractions, last entry may be well in advance of closing time.

Accommodation listings

When researching suitable accommodation for families, I looked for places with cooking facilities, a guest laundry and the option of a separate bedroom (and beds) for the kids, as that is what we have always preferred when travelling. Be aware, if you are doing your own research, that accommodation which claims to sleep four (or more) might only offer a double bed for the kids. This is something you'll need to check when you are booking (unless, of course, your kids don't mind sharing a bed). I have tried to make sure that all of the places listed in this book have single bed options available.

Most accommodation places offer a way of getting a cheaper deal than the published rate. You can find these by phoning them or searching the internet. Warning: only book online with websites that you are sure you can trust.

Pricing

For the purposes of this book, I have calculated all prices based on an imaginary family of two adults and two fee-paying children. Most attractions and tours do not charge for infants, but the age category for this varies. Calculations were based on rates quoted at the time of writing – please keep in mind that prices change regularly.

Key to accommodation pricing

Accommodation costs are calculated based on a family staying for a week in shoulder season. Accommodation pricing is categorised as follows:

- budget (below $150 per night)
- mid-range ($150–$300 per night)
- high cost (over $300 per night)

Key to attractions pricing

Entry pricing for a family (see above definition) is categorised as follows:

- free or by donation
- budget (up to $25 per family)
- mid-range ($25–$100 per family)
- high cost (about $100+ per family)

Note: Many attractions (and accommodation places) have discount offers online, often with the added benefit of avoiding queues when you arrive.

Places to eat

Where possible, I've tried to include eateries that offer something unique, as well as being kid-friendly. Some are only open during the day, not for evening meals, so please check opening times (and prices) before you go.

Walking tracks

Most of the tracks chosen for the book are wheelchair accessible, which means they should be fine for pushers or prams – and not be too difficult for small legs to negotiate.

Highlights

With some of my favourite places, there was too much information to fit into a short entry, so I turned these places into 'Highlights' with additional sections called 'Insider Tips', 'Don't Miss' and 'Fabulous Facts'. This also gave me the chance to create Kid Quests – special activities to try out, or intriguing questions to solve, that will hopefully inspire not just the kids, but the whole family. Some of them are answered at the back of the book, but try to resist the urge to peek at the answers till after you have had the fun of solving them for yourselves!

HAPPY TRAVELS!

In this book I have gathered a wealth of wonderful things you can do as a family all around Australia. I hope it inspires you to break from routine, to play and discover together, and create memories that will last a lifetime.

Have fun, and travel safely!

Anna Ciddor

NEW SOUTH WALES

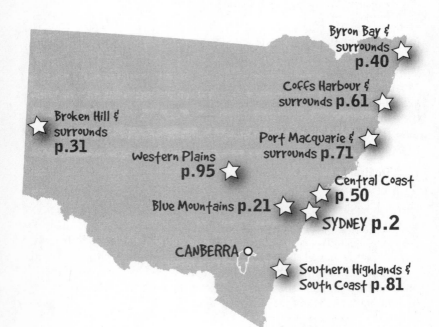

Byron Bay &
surrounds
p.40

Coffs Harbour &
surrounds **p.61**

Broken Hill &
surrounds
p.31

Port Macquarie &
surrounds **p.71**

Western Plains
p.95

Central Coast
p.50

Blue Mountains **p.21**

SYDNEY **p.2**

CANBERRA ○

Southern Highlands &
South Coast **p.81**

FAVOURITES

Jenolan Caves – some of the oldest and most magnificent limestone caves in the world, just west of Sydney *p. 26*

A ferry ride on Sydney Harbour, with the kids excitedly recognising the Sydney Harbour Bridge and Sydney Opera House *p. 6*

Pet Porpoise Pool – get kissed by a seal and play ball with a dolphin at Coffs Harbour *p. 63*

Scenic World – stand on a glass floor 270 metres above a dazzling rainforest ravine in the Blue Mountains *p. 21*

TreeTop Adventure Park – swing like monkeys through the treetops of Ourimbah State Forest *p. 56*

Tropical Fruit World – discover chewing gum fruit, ice-cream bean, chocolate pudding fruit and red dragon fruit (all real)! *p. 44*

Western Plains Zoo – feed giraffes, shake paws with a kangaroo and rub a wombat's tummy *p. 98*

TOP EVENTS

SYDNEY

HIGHLIGHTS

In town

Australian Museum
6 College St, Sydney
(02) 9320 6000;
www.australianmuseum.net.au
MID-RANGE

Imagine standing in a dim, eerie space, smelling the scents of a jungle, hearing ominous growls, when a stampede of giant dinosaurs erupts and charges towards you! With its huge video screens, life-sized models and high-tech interactive displays, the Dinosaurs exhibition makes you feel as if you are really in the dinosaur world.

Kids can also have fun dressing up as dinosaurs or experience the thrill of unearthing and trying to identify a fossil. Nearby is the Search and Discover gallery where they can indulge their curiosity by peering into microscopes and touching the specimens (some of them live!).

INSIDER TIPS

- Watch for temporary exhibits and activities specially aimed at children.

- Kids are welcome to bring their questions, or even real specimens, to the experts in the Search and Discover gallery.

DON'T MISS

- The Indigenous Australians exhibition where kids can sit in a reconstructed cave and listen to recordings of Dreaming stories told by Indigenous Australians.

- Kidspace – your under-5s will love the cubby houses, magnifying glasses for examining insects, animal X-rays on a light table and a human skeleton they can touch. There's even an enclosed baby-friendly space for crawlers.

- Special touch tables around the museum, where kids can touch and examine chosen pieces from the collections. There is generally a staff member on hand to answer any questions.

FABULOUS FACTS

The Australian Museum is Australia's oldest museum, founded in 1827. In the early days, its main aim was to collect and preserve specimens. Unfortunately, the first custodian, William Holmes, was accidentally shot and killed in 1831 while collecting birds for the museum. The 19th-century specimens are now extremely valuable for research because scientists can study how species might have changed over time. The collection has grown to millions of objects, too many to be displayed all at once, so many of them are kept in storage.

Kid Quest

Indigenous Australians used ingenious methods to manufacture tools from natural materials. Look for a drill used to make holes in shells so they could be threaded into necklaces. What is the drill bit made from?

See pp. 640–4 for the answer

Harbour Bridge, Sydney

Harbour Bridge
Pylon Lookout, South East Pylon, Sydney
(02) 9240 1100;
www.pylonlookout.com.au
MID-RANGE
Visit the Pylon Lookout and read the history of the bridge on the way up. If your kids are asking to do the bridge climb but they are too small – they must be 10 years old and 1.2 metres high – then you can take a family walk along the bridge instead. There are walkways on each side, fenced for safety. It takes about 20 minutes to cross on foot, and you can take a train back.

Hyde Park Barracks Museum
Queens Sqr, Macquarie St, Sydney
(02) 8239 2311; www.hht.net.au/
museums/hyde_park_barracks_museum
BUDGET
In the 19th century, thousands of convicts were transported to Australia from Britain. Many worked in labour gangs to build early Sydney and slept at night in the Hyde Park Barracks. In the museum you can find out what it was like to be a convict – what you would have eaten, where you would have slept, how you would have worked. Many items on display have survived until now because rats dragged them to their nests under the floorboards!

Justice and Police Museum
Cnr Phillip and Albert sts, Circular Quay
(02) 9252 1144;
www.hht.net.au/museums
BUDGET
This one's not for the squeamish. In the magistrates court, police charge room and remand cells of the 1890s you'll find artefacts from early-Sydney crimes. Exhibits include death masks of hanged men and the zinc-lined bath where the Pyjama Girl's body was suspended in formalin for 10 years.

Monorail
(02) 8584 5288; www.metrotransport.
com.au/index.php/monorail/guides.html
VARIOUS PRICES
The monorail is not just a method of transport to many tourist destinations – it's an experience in itself.

Museum of Australian Currency Notes
Reserve Bank of Australia,
Ground Floor, 65 Martin Pl, Sydney
(02) 9551 9743 or 1800 300 288;
www.rba.gov.au/museum
Closed weekends, public and bank holidays
FREE

Discover the intriguing history of coins and notes in Australia. Look for holey dollars – the first coins produced in the colony of New South Wales – made by punching the centres out of Spanish dollars. Find out how damaged polymer notes can be recycled into compost bins and house bricks.

Powerhouse
500 Harris St, Ultimo
(02) 9217 0111;
www.powerhousemuseum.com
BUDGET
Powerhouse is a technology museum with lots of interactive exhibits for kids. Look for the piece of rock brought home by astronauts from the moon (which proves the moon is *not* made of cheese) and check out the kids' activities on the website.

Queen Victoria Building
455 George St, Sydney
(02) 9264 9209; www.qvb.com.au
FREE
If your kids enjoy grandeur and splendour, they'll like this wonderfully ornate historic shopping complex which includes a huge Hobbyco toy store. Take tea in the opulent old ballroom, and don't miss the two clocks. The Great Australian Clock shows various Australian history scenes and pastimes, but even more entrancing is the Royal Clock. Be there on the hour to see the trumpeters and all the little figurines enacting scenes from British history.

The Rocks Discovery Museum
Kendall La, The Rocks
(02) 9240 8680; www.therocks.com
FREE
Interactive exhibits and games reveal the story of Sydney from pre-European settlement to the present.

Royal Botanic Gardens
Mrs Macquaries Rd, Sydney
(02) 9231 8111 or
(02) 9231 8125 on weekends;
www.rbgsyd.nsw.gov.au
FREE
The gardens are superb for picnics, but there's so much more on offer here. Attractions include the Wollemi pine, one of the world's rarest plants. Visit the glass pyramid Tropical Centre for an extra cost (budget) to see, smell and touch exotic plants, and don't miss the sensory fountain and sundial at the aromatic Herb Garden.

Powerhouse, Ultimo

Susannah Place Museum

58–64 Gloucester St, The Rocks
(02) 9241 1893; www.hht.net.au
Entry by guided tour only;
check times

BUDGET

Read Ruth Park's novel *Playing Beattie Bow* before you visit, and the kids will be absolutely intrigued to visit The Rocks and explore these 19th-century working class terrace houses. The museum includes a recreated corner store.

Sydney Ferries

13 1500; www.sydneyferries.info

VARIOUS PRICES

This fun mode of transport delivers you to destinations such as Manly and Taronga Zoo, and also offers an economical way to cruise Sydney Harbour and catch iconic views of the Sydney Opera House and Harbour Bridge.

Sydney Opera House, Sydney

Sydney Opera House

Bennelong Point, Sydney
(02) 9250 7111;
www.sydneyoperahouse.com
Check guided tour times

MID-RANGE

Kids always love to see famous places and the Sydney Opera House has to be one of the most recognisably famous places in the world. It's a few minutes' walk from Circular Quay. You can take a guided tour if you wish to see more than the foyer areas. Check the Kids at the House program for special children's shows.

Sydney Tower

Above Centrepoint shopping centre,
cnr Pitt and Market sts, Sydney
(02) 9333 9222;
www.sydneytower.myfun.com.au
Open daily till late

MID-RANGE

Enjoy views from the Observation Deck and swoop all over Australia in the virtual reality Oz Trek ride. Those aged 10 years and over can expose themselves to the elements on the more extreme Skywalk experience.

Darling Harbour

Australian National Maritime Museum
2 Murray St, Darling Harbour
(02) 9298 3777; www.anmm.gov.au

FREE; ENTRY TO SHIPS EXTRA COST

In the submarine exhibit kids will enjoy trying out the bunks, peering through a periscope and playing the sonar operator game, but even better is going out on the wharf and climbing down a ladder into an actual navy submarine, the HMAS *Onslow*. Eyes will widen as they try to picture how sailors managed to live and move around in these cramped conditions. You can also board a replica of Captain James Cook's ship, *Endeavour;* tread the decks of a restored 19th-century tall ship, the *James Craig*; or take part in Action Stations on the destroyer HMAS *Vampire*.

INSIDER TIPS

- Entry to the museum's core exhibitions is free, but it is definitely worth paying for tickets to board at least one of the vessels out on the wharf. Remember to wear sensible closed shoes for clambering up and down ladders on the vessels.

- Be aware that the last boarding of vessels is 50 minutes before closing and there are restrictions: children under 13 must be accompanied by an adult, and children less than 90 centimetres tall are not permitted to board the *Endeavour* replica or the submarine HMAS *Onslow*. Anyone with a fear of confined spaces will want to give the submarine a miss.

- Yots cafe has highchairs, colouring books and a great kids' menu, but take care as the cafe is not fenced off from the water.

- There are sometimes opportunities to sail on one of the ships from the Sydney Heritage Fleet; see www.shf.org.au

DON'T MISS

- Mini Mariners – a special experience suitable for children aged 2–5 years. Be there at 10am or 11am any Tuesday in term time for an interactive gallery tour with a costumed guide, craft

activities, stories and dress-ups. Bookings are essential:
(02) 9298 3655.

■ Kids on Deck fun day – craft activities, stories, games, puzzles
and dress-ups for 5–12 year olds, 11am–3pm every Sunday;
no booking required.

FABULOUS FACTS

HMAS *Vampire* is one of the largest destroyers ever built in Australia
and the last of Australia's big gun ships (Australia's fighting ships are
now equipped with rocket weaponry). Have a look at the anti-aircraft
guns and the three twin turrets housing 4.5-inch guns. There used to be
torpedo launchers and anti-submarine mortars as well. The *Vampire*
served in the Royal Australian Navy from 1959 to 1986. When
Australian troops were sent to fight in Vietnam in the 1960s, the
Vampire escorted them, but never took part in a battle.

Kid Quest
*Navy vessels are usually given names like Sydney
or Brisbane. See if you can find out why this ship is
called* Vampire!
See pp. 640–4 for the answer

Sydney Aquarium
Aquarium Pier, Darling Harbour
(02) 8251 7800; www.sydneyaquarium.myfun.com.au
Open till late

MID-RANGE

Watch your kids' faces as they step inside a transparent tunnel and see
stingrays, sea turtles and 3-metre sharks gliding and diving all around
them. It's an incredible experience to be 'in the water' among these
giant (and dangerous!) sea creatures. Right through this aquarium
are exhibits that will keep the whole family pointing and gasping:
fluorescent coral from the Great Barrier Reef, glowing red jellyfish,
comical little platypus paddling madly, seals that swim around you in a
glass tunnel, clown fish (like Nemo) and strange-looking dugongs.

INSIDER TIPS
■ Pre-purchase your tickets online to bypass the long entry queue.

- At Darling Harbour, watch for the People Mover Trains, trackless electric carriages that chug between the aquarium and various other attractions. Flag down the driver to catch a ride and give tired little legs a rest; www.tonyquirkamusements.com

DON'T MISS

- The chance to get up close to live sharks at the Great Barrier Reef Oceanarium. Take a ride in a glass-bottomed boat and share the water with these fearsome creatures. The 11am ride (more expensive) includes feeding the sharks!

- Talks and feeding times daily – check the timetable before you go.

FABULOUS FACTS

Sydney Aquarium is one of the few places in the world where you can see captive dugongs. Pig and Wuru were both found as orphans. It is thought that dugongs are the origin of the mermaid myth. Dugongs are mammals and their closest living relatives are elephants! In the wild, dugongs eat sea grasses but in the aquarium they are fed on lettuce – each one eats about 80–90 kilograms a day. A baby dugong is called a calf. A mother dugong hugs her calf to her chest with her flipper.

Kid Quest

The Sydney Aquarium has an example of the world's largest living reptile, which can grow to over 7 metres long. See if you can find out what it is.

See pp. 640–4 for the answer

Chinese Garden and Teahouse
Pier St, Darling Harbour
(02) 9240 8888; www.darlingharbour. com/sydney-Things_To_Do-Chinese_ Garden.htm
BUDGET
Kids will be intrigued by this authentic and beautiful garden, and they'll love the chance to hire ornate traditional Chinese costumes (small sizes available). Enjoy a peaceful interlude in the tea house with tea and steamed buns.

Imax screen
31 Wheat Rd, Darling Harbour
(02) 9281 3300; www.imax.com.au

MID-RANGE

This Imax screen is one of the largest anywhere in the world. It screens epic and educational movies, many of them in 3D.

Pyrmont Bridge
Spans Darling Harbour

FREE

Built in 1902, this was one of the first bridges in the world to have an electric swing-span that opened to allow tall ships to sail through. The swing-span still operates at 10.30am, 12pm, 1pm, 2pm and 3pm on weekends and public holidays.

Wildlife World
Aquarium Pier, Darling Harbour
**(02) 9333 9288; www.
sydneywildlifeworld.myfun.com.au**

MID-RANGE

This is the place to see Australian wildlife in a compact environment right in the heart of the city. You'll find all the usual suspects here, plus some more unexpected creatures such as spiders, scorpions, and cockroaches. For an extra fee you can pat a koala and have your photo taken.

Suburbs

Taronga Zoo, Mosman

Taronga Zoo
Bradleys Head Rd, Mosman
(02) 9969 2777; www.taronga.org.au

HIGH COST

Taronga is a zoo which offers wonderful interactive opportunities. In the Backyard to Bush exhibit your kids will set out to explore a couple of ordinary-looking houses and find a worm farm, a frog pond, a possum box, pet lizards, and farmyard animals. They'll let out squeals as they discover slugs in the letter box, mice in the walls, cockroaches under the sink and ants in the sugar bowl. Through playing around, patting the animals, smelling the fragrant plants, exploring a giant underground 'wombat burrow', your kids will discover many ways to live in harmony with the environment.

INSIDER TIPS

- Check the website before you go. You can download a map (also available at the entrance), find out the times for the keeper talks, animal feeding and special shows, and plan your visit in advance.

- The zoo is on a hill. If you arrive by ferry you'll be down the bottom. Catch the free Sky Safari (cable car) to the top of the hill or take the escalators or lift from the food court. Plan your visit so you don't have to climb up and down the hill too much – but if little legs do get too tired, keep your eye out for the trackless electric trains that roam around.

- The busiest times are school holidays, sunny days and weekends. Arrive as early as possible to avoid the crowds and pre-purchase your tickets online so you can bypass the long queue to get in.

- There are various wonderful opportunities available at extra cost. Animal Encounters offer a special experience with your chosen animal. On the Wild Australia Experience tour you prepare delicious titbits like fly pupae, mealworms and frozen mice in the animal kitchen, and then the zoo keeper lets you feed and pat the animals. Check the website for more information.

- If you really like the zoo, consider staying the night! (*See* ACCOMMODATION p. 19.)

DON'T MISS

- The free-flight bird show and the seal show. Be there early for a good view, as seats start to fill 45 minutes before the shows begin.

- The keeper talks – your opportunity to get a really good look at the animals who recognise their keepers and come close, expecting to be fed.

FABULOUS FACTS

Taronga, along with other zoos and wildlife parks, runs insurance breeding programs for endangered animals to make sure they do not disappear entirely. One of the animals on this program is the Tasmanian devil, the largest surviving carnivorous marsupial in the world. The devils eat small mammals, including wallabies, devouring bones, fur and all with their powerful teeth and jaws. Early European settlers eliminated large numbers of Tasmanian devils using traps and poison because they feared the animals were taking their lambs. Now, due to the spread of Devils Facial Tumour Disease, Tasmanian devils are vanishing in the wild altogether.

Kid Quest

Two Australian mammals lay eggs. One is the platypus.
Can you find out what the other one is?

See pp. 640–4 for the answer

Centennial Park

Paddington
(02) 9339 6699;
www.centennialparklands.com.au
Seasonal opening times
FREE ENTRY; VARIOUS PRICES FOR ACTIVITIES

In this surprising bushland setting, less than 5 kilometres from the centre of Sydney, you can enjoy a picnic, go birdwatching or take an evening spotlight prowl with a ranger. The park is also a popular horseriding venue. If you prefer two wheels, there are bikes for hire and even a learners' cycleway.

Entertainment Quarter

Lang Rd, Moore Park
(02) 8117 6700;
www.eqmoorepark.com.au
VARIOUS PRICES

The name says it all: shops, eateries and loads of entertainment options for the kids, including Bubbles of Fun (walk on water inside your own bubble!), bowling, laser skirmish, IMAX and other Hoyts cinemas, bungy and rock climbing, jumping castles, soccer clinics, carousels and plaster-painting studios.

Luna Park

1 Olympic Dr, Milsons Point
(02) 9033 7676; www.lunaparksydney.com
Seasonal opening times
FREE ENTRY; VARIOUS RIDE PASSES AVAILABLE

The huge, toothy-faced Luna Park entrance is one of Sydney's landmarks. Located on the north shore of the harbour, Luna Park is easily accessible by train or ferry. Rides are labelled with relevant height restrictions for children.

Nutcote, Home of May Gibbs
5 Wallaringa Ave, Neutral Bay
(02) 9953 4453; www.maygibbs.com.au
Check opening times; often closed in school holidays

BUDGET

In the early 1900s, author and illustrator May Gibbs created the first children's fantasies based on the Australian bush. Share her stories with your kids before you go, then see if you can find any bush babies or scary banksia men in her garden.

Olympic Park
Sydney Olympic Park Visitor Centre
Cnr Showground Rd and Herb Elliott Ave, Sydney Olympic Park
(02) 9714 7888;
www.sydneyolympicpark.com.au
VARIOUS PRICES

Luna Park, Milsons Point

This is a vast, exciting complex of parks, entertainment venues and sporting facilities. Visit the Aquatic Centre and let your little swimmers try to smash Thorpey's records, or just have fun splashing around in the water playground. Take an interactive tour of ANZ Stadium, one of the world's most technologically advanced stadiums, and go right into the players' changing rooms or have your photos taken on a winners' podium.

Manly

Experience Manly
Manly Visitor Information Centre, The Forecourt, Manly Wharf, Manly
(02) 9976 1430; www.visitmanly.com.au or www.manlyaustralia.com.au
VARIOUS PRICES

Manly is kid heaven: beaches with perfect sand and rockpools, bushwalks around the headlands looking for wildlife, and fun visits to Oceanworld, Manly Waterworks or ghost tours at the Old Quarantine Station (*see p. 15*). The magic begins with a ride on the ferry from Circular Quay. This tubby watercraft with its green and cream paintwork is just like an illustration from a picture book. Your kids will stand on deck waving delightedly at smaller boats bobbing below, and then squeal in excitement when the famous Sydney Opera House and Harbour Bridge loom up huge and impressive beside them.

INSIDER TIPS

- Choose an open deck on the ferry – kids are less likely to get seasick with fresh air in their faces and this is the best vantage point for photos.

- For information about Sydney Ferries, see p. 6.

- Explore the different beaches. The little coves around the harbour side are free of surf and safer for swimming. Little Manly Beach is a favourite for families and has an enclosed pool area. On the ocean side there are long stretches of surfing beaches, as well as the more sheltered Shelly Beach.

- If you're heading into the water, remember to swim between the flags and keep an eye out for warnings about bluebottle jellyfish (also known as Portuguese man-of-wars). Don't be misled by reckless people ignoring the signs; the sting feels much worse than a bee sting.

- There are plenty of eateries, ranging from historic beachside kiosks to restaurants and fast-food outlets, in the attractive shopping strip of the Corso.

- If you plan to do a bushwalk, check out www.visitmanly.com.au beforehand and bring a list of photos of flora and fauna to spot.

DON'T MISS

- The chance to ride a wave – surf lessons are offered by SEA Australia. Bookings are essential: (02) 9907 7650; www.seaaustralia.com.au

- Some wonderful snorkelling opportunities on the harbour side and in Cabbage Tree Bay, the marine reserve between Manly and Shelly beaches. See the Manly Environment Centre website for information on the range of marine life you are likely to spot; www.mec.org.au

FABULOUS FACTS

Sydney Harbour National Park at Manly is home to an endangered colony of long-nosed bandicoots. As you walk the track, see if you can spot any small, conical-shaped hollows in the ground where bandicoots might have been burrowing for food. Bandicoots use their front paws for digging, then snuffle around with their long noses to find insects, earthworms, spiders, plant tubers and roots to eat. You aren't likely to spot any of the bandicoots themselves, as they sleep in nests hidden in the ground under leaves during the day.

Kid Quest

If you go snorkelling, try to spot a weedy sea dragon. These cute sea creatures are closely related to seahorses.

Manly Waterworks

Cnr West Espl and Commonwealth Pde, Manly
(02) 9949 1088;
www.manlywaterworks.com
Seasonal opening times
MID-RANGE

Head to Manly Waterworks for lots of waterslide fun. Note that the minimum height for participants is 120 centimetres.

Oceanworld

West Espl, Manly
(02) 9949 2644;
www.oceanworld.myfun.com.au
MID-RANGE

You can view all sorts of underwater creatures, reptiles and spiders, or even plunge in the water and swim with them at Oceanworld. Snorkel classes for 8–13 year olds are available weekends and holidays, while older kids and parents can go on a shark dive. Check the website for details and restrictions. You can also watch animal shows, movies and fish feeding.

Old Quarantine Station

North Head Scenic Dr, Manly
(02) 9466 1551; www.qstation.com.au/experience/tours.php
Admission by guided tour only; check times
MID-RANGE

The Old Quarantine Station was used from 1835 to 1984 as an isolation area in times of epidemic or for new immigrants suspected of carrying disease. Consequently, it has seen much history and death. Take an evening ghost tour (there's one suitable for families), nature walk or daytime history tour.

Oceanworld, Manly

Special events

Royal Easter Show
Easter
www.eastershow.com.au
This one's an old favourite: two weeks of exciting family fun, with carnival rides, showbags, animal exhibits, a farmyard nursery, fireworks and plenty of live entertainment.

Sydney Children's Festival
Sept/Oct
www.sydneychildrensfestival.com
Bring out the inner artist with two weeks of workshops and activities in music, visual arts, storytelling and theatre. There are lots of free activities including storytelling by popular authors.

Vivid Sydney
Late May–mid-June
www.vividsydney.com
This festival of light, music and ideas features spectacular illuminations of the Sydney Opera House sails.

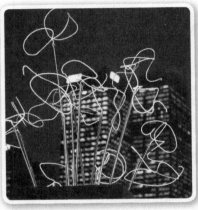
Lights display, Vivid Sydney

Day trips

Cruise with the Riverboat Postman
Brooklyn wharf next to Hawkesbury River Railway Station, Dangar Rd, Brooklyn
(02) 9985 7566;
www.hawkesburyriverferries.com.au
50 km/1 hr north
HIGH COST

Join Australia's last riverboat postman delivering mail, milk, groceries and newspapers to settlements along the scenic Hawkesbury River. Cruises include commentary and depart at 9.30am on weekdays (except public holidays) and take three to four hours.

Elizabeth Farm

70 Alice St, Rosehill
(02) 9635 9488; www.hht.net.au/
museums/elizabeth_farm
20 km/35 min west
Check opening times
BUDGET

Not only is this the oldest surviving house in Australia, it's also one of the most enjoyable to visit. Kids can make themselves at home, trying out the beds and chairs. Elizabeth Farm was built in 1793 by early free settlers John Macarthur and his wife Elizabeth. The Macarthurs imported and bred merino sheep and helped establish the Australian wool industry. There are several other historic houses in the area.

Featherdale Wildlife Park

217–229 Kildare Rd, Doonside
(02) 9622 1644; www.featherdale.com.au
40 km/45 min west
MID-RANGE

Featherdale Wildlife Park offers a very special chance to get up-close and personal with Australian wildlife. Imagine holding and feeding a baby kangaroo! There is also a spectacular crocodile exhibit, an aviary with hundreds of birds, and a nursery of farm animals for your little ones to pat.

Ku-ring-gai Chase National Park

Mount Colah
Kalkari Discovery Centre (02) 9472 9300;
www.environment.nsw.gov.au
30 km/40 min north
Seasonal opening times
BUDGET

Explore the magnificent scenery, visit the Barrenjoey Lighthouse, take a tour of the Aboriginal sites or join in one of the many family activities run by the Kalkari Discovery Centre. There are over 800 Aboriginal sites recorded in Ku-ring-gai Chase National Park, including rock engravings, burial sites, axe-grinding grooves, and middens of shells and animal bones near cave shelters.

Symbio Wildlife Park

7–11 Lawrence Hargrave Dr,
Helensburgh
(02) 4294 1244; www.symbiozoo.com.au
50 km/1 hr south

MID-RANGE

This park has animals from around the world, and offers the chance to feed and cuddle many of them. Daily demonstrations and keeper talks are on offer, and you might want to book a behind-the-scenes tour. Combine your visit with a walk in the nearby Royal National Park or a drive along the magnificent coastline. And take note of the address – it was in this area in 1894 that Lawrence Hargrave (now on the $20 note) made one of the first successful flights in the world, rising 5 metres with the aid of four box kites.

Tobruk Sheep Station

5050 Old Northern Rd, Maroota
(02) 4566 8223;
www.tobruksheepstation.com.au
70 km/1 hr 30 min north
Bookings essential

MID-RANGE

Enjoy an Australian outback experience at this family-run farm on a high plateau overlooking the Blue Mountains. Watch working-dog and sheepshearing demonstrations, learn how to crack a whip or throw a boomerang, and enjoy billy tea and damper around the campfire.

See also Blue Mountains (p. 21), Central Coast (p. 50)

Accommodation

Hyde Park Inn

271 Elizabeth St, Sydney
(02) 9264 6001;
www.hydeparkinn.com.au

MID-RANGE

There are family studios available with a queen bed, two singles and a kitchenette; pay extra and get two separate bedrooms.

Lane Cove River Tourist Park

Plassey Rd, North Ryde/Macquarie Park
(02) 9888 9133 or 1300 729 133;
www.lanecoverivertouristpark.com.au

BUDGET

Enjoy the bushland setting of this lovely tourist park, located within a national park, only 10 kilometres from Sydney. Choose a camping or caravan site, or a three-and-a-half star family cabin with bathroom, reverse cycle air-conditioning, TV and kitchen, linen and towels supplied. The park has a toddler pool, outdoor swimming pool and recreation room.

Quay West
98 Gloucester St, The Rocks
(02) 9240 6000; www.mirvachotels.com
HIGH COST
This five-star luxury apartment hotel with indoor pool is close to the Circular Quay ferries. You can make use of the kitchen and `eat in' or explore the many local eateries. Choose a two-bedroom apartment or make use of the sofa bed in the lounge of the one-bedroom apartment.

Sydney Gateway Holiday Park
30 Majestic Dr, Parklea
(02) 8814 4222;
www.sydneygateway.com.au
BUDGET
This park offers a range of accommodation, including self-contained villas and plenty of ensuite and powered caravan sites

and camping sites. There is a huge heated spa and large resort-style swimming pool which lights up magically after dark. Situated 35 minutes west of the city, it is owned by NRMA Motoring and Services.

Sydney Harbour YHA
110 Cumberland St, The Rocks
(02) 8272 0900; www.yha.com.au
MID-RANGE
This new deluxe youth hostel has family rooms with private bathrooms and is conveniently situated in The Rocks.

Taronga Zoo
www.taronga.org.au/taronga-zoo/plan-your-visit/overnight-stay.aspx
Minimum age 5 years
HIGH COST
For one special night, join the animals at the zoo! Sleep in a luxurious safari-style tent with a view over Sydney Harbour. Everything is provided, including a roast feast and a chance to go behind the scenes with the keepers. You might even feed a giraffe or pat a seal. For more information, see Taronga Zoo (p. 10).

Places to eat

Check out the delights of Chinatown, Darling Harbour, The Rocks and Manly Corso. Most of the tourist attractions have suitable cafes, but for something a bit different try:

Botanic Gardens Cafe
Royal Botanic Gardens,
Mrs Macquaries Rd, Sydney
(02) 9241 2419
Ring up and order a picnic hamper. The kids will love helping you unpack the blanket, cutlery and delicious treats from the picnic basket. Then they can play around you in the gardens while you relax and eat.

Lilies on the Park
Bicentennial Park, Olympic
Park Complex
(02) 9764 9900; www.waterviewvenue.
com.au/cafe-and-kids/index.asp
Before you visit Olympic Park, phone ahead to check what special hands-on activities are on offer at Lilies on the Park. You might want to book in for Kites and Cakes (ages 4 years and over), or Cookies and Craft (ages 2–5 years). Situated in 40 hectares of rolling parklands, this relaxed, family-friendly cafe is open seven days a week 8am–5pm. There's also a takeaway menu, including a kids' lunchbox.

Sydney Harbour Tall Ships
Campbells Cove, The Rocks
(02) 9252 3630 or 1300 664 410;
www.sydneytallships.com.au
Enjoy a barbecue lunch or dinner while sailing Sydney Harbour in an authentic tall ship! You can even help hoist the sails.

BLUE MOUNTAINS

Katoomba is located 120 kilometres west of Sydney and is accessible by train

Year-round day trip or holiday destination

HIGHLIGHTS

Jenolan Caves   *p. 26*

Scenic World   *p. 21*

Three Sisters and Echo Point   *p. 23*

Glenbrook–Katoomba

Scenic World
Cnr Violet St and Cliff Dr, Katoomba
(02) 4780 0200 or 1300 SKYWAY; www.scenicworld.com.au

MID-RANGE

Imagine hurtling in a train down an almost vertical cliff-face or soaring 270 metres above a ravine with only a glass floor beneath you. Scenic World will give you and your kids some of the most heart-stopping moments of your lives, and these experiences are not artificial theme park rides but the real thing! The historic Scenic Railway is the steepest incline railway in the world. It transports you to a World Heritage site: a rainforest valley with ancient ravines and dazzling waterfalls. You can travel up again via the Scenic Cableway, and if you want to view the valley from above, ride the Skyway with its Electro-Sceniglass floor.

INSIDER TIPS

■ For the most exciting trip on the Scenic Railway, try to get a seat in the front car!

■ Don't be put off by rain. Just bring your wet-weather gear and enjoy the scents and colours, the trickle of running water from hidden waterfalls and the sounds of the birds enjoying the rain. There are storm shelters along the path.

■ There are toilets and food outlets at Scenic World, but no toilets in the valley.

■ Weather conditions in the valley can be different from the weather above. Be prepared with wet-weather gear and sunhats!

DON'T MISS

■ The boardwalk through the ancient rainforest in the valley. You can hire an audio guide and there are interpretive signs about plant species and coal mining next to the path.

■ Tasting the pure Blue Mountains water. Make sure you take a bottle of water on your walk, but when you find the Marrangaroo Spring, stop and taste it.

FABULOUS FACTS

Believe it or not, this World Heritage site was actually a coal mine in the late 19th and early-20th centuries! The Scenic Railway was originally built for hauling coal and miners up and down, but hikers in the area began to beg lifts on the train to rest their weary legs. At first, the hikers just sat on a plank inside the coal skip, but after a while mine operators built a 12-seater carriage to use on weekends and public holidays, charging sixpence a ride, and the tourist industry was born.

Kid Quest
Stand on the cafeteria deck and see if you can spot the artificial koala in one of the trees!

Three Sisters and Echo Point

Echo Point, Katoomba
Blue Mountains Visitor Information Centre
1300 653 408

FREE

Three Sisters, Katoomba

You will feel as if you are at the top of the world as you gaze out at hazy, blue-tinged mountains, lush forests and jagged towers of yellow sandstone. On some days, the clouds hang beneath your feet in the valleys. The Three Sisters rock formation in front of you is one of the most photographed scenes in Australia. Encourage your kids to imagine how it would feel to be an explorer or Aboriginal person standing here in the days before the solid, fenced-in viewing platform was built, and read them the legend about the Three Sisters (*see* FABULOUS FACTS *below*) while you are all surrounded by this spectacular setting.

INSIDER TIPS

- There's a gently sloping track that leads from Echo Point to the Three Sisters – you end up actually standing in a niche in one of the rocks.

- If you decide to do a long hike on one of the bushwalking trails, make sure you follow correct hiking procedures such as bringing appropriate basic necessities and registering your planned route with friends.

DON'T MISS

- Exploring the valley – a magical world of waterfalls and rainforest plants. Anyone with loads of energy can descend by the Giant Stairway – about 900 steps. If the return trip is too daunting, follow the Scenic Railway signs (*see* Scenic World p. 21) for a ride up instead; the last train departs at 4.50pm.

FABULOUS FACTS

The legend of the Three Sisters:
Three beautiful sisters, Meehni, Wimlah and Gunnedoo, fell in love with three brothers from a neighbouring tribe, but Aboriginal law forbade

the marriages. When the men went into battle to try to capture their brides, a witchdoctor turned the girls into stone to protect them. Unfortunately, the witchdoctor was killed in the battle and no one has ever been able to reverse the spell.

Kid Quest

Give a shout from Echo Point and see if it really echoes!

Blue Mountains Chocolate Company

176 Lurline St, Katoomba
(02) 4782 7071;
www.bluemountainschocolate.com.au
FREE

Learn about the history of chocolate from interactive displays, and then indulge! Buy and try handmade chocolates, a real hot chocolate or an ice-cream. There are demonstrations of chocolate making on weekday afternoons; bookings recommended.

Everglades Gardens

37 Everglades Ave, Leura
(02) 4784 1938; www.everglades.org.au
BUDGET

Explore the picturesque gardens that surround the historic Art Deco house – you'll find grottos, weeping cherry trees and an area known as Bluebell Wood.

Ghost Tour

Departs from Gearins Hotel, Katoomba
(02) 4751 2622 or 0418 416 403;
www.bluemountainsmysterytours.com.au
Fri and Sat nights
MID-RANGE

For a very different experience of the Blue Mountains, visit cemeteries and historic houses on the 'ghost bus'. Mystery and scenic tours are also available.

Leuralla Toy and Railway Museum

36 Olympian Pde, Leura
(02) 4784 1169;
www.toyandrailwaymuseum.com.au
MID-RANGE

This grand mansion, set in 5 hectares of gardens, contains an intriguing collection of vintage toys including dolls, teddies, lead figures, comics, aeroplanes and working model-railways.

Marked Tree

3 km west of Katoomba on the Great Western Hwy
FREE

In the early years of European settlement, the Great Dividing Range was a barrier to the spread of settlement. Then in May 1813, the famous explorers Blaxland, Wentworth and Lawson found a route across the Blue Mountains. Supposedly, they carved their initials in a tree and today the stump can be seen, sheltered and floodlit, by the side of the highway.

Norman Lindsay Gallery
14 Norman Lindsay Cres, Faulconbridge
(02) 4751 1067;
www.normanlindsay.com.au
MID-RANGE

Norman Lindsay was a famous Australian author and artist. Share his children's picture book *The Magic Pudding* with your kids and they'll have fun exploring his house and grounds, looking at exhibits about the book and studying the ship models he created.

Red Hands Cave and Euroka Clearing
Glenbrook section, Blue Mountains National Park, entrance gate in Bruce Rd, Glenbrook
Glenbrook Visitor Information Centre
(02) 4739 2950 or 1300 653 408;
www.greaterbluemountainsdrive.com.au/glenbrook.php
BUDGET

The Red Hands Cave, accessed by a 6-kilometre return walk, features stencilled Aboriginal hand paintings, now covered with perspex to protect them from vandals. Euroka Clearing is home to a large population of eastern grey kangaroos and is popular for picnics and camping. Camping permits are required and can be obtained from the visitor centre.

Selwood Science and Puzzles
41 Railway Pde, Hazelbrook
(02) 4758 6235;
www.selwoodscience.com.au
Check opening times
MID-RANGE

There's plenty of hands-on fun at Selwood, with puzzles and challenges galore.

Special event

Winter Magic Festival
June
www.wintermagic.com.au
Katoomba puts on a day packed with family activities including clown shows, belly dancing, drumming workshops, music, circus acts and storytelling.

Around the Mountains

Broken Column in Lucas Cave, Jenolan Caves

Jenolan Caves

Jenolan Caves Rd,
Jenolan Karst Conservation Reserve
(02) 6359 3911 or 1300 76 33 11;
www.jenolancaves.org.au
Entry to most caves by guided tour only
MID-RANGE

This is a world right out of a fairytale, a place where giants or fairy princesses might reside. Explore magical caverns with pink and orange formations glowing under invisible lights, eerie tunnels leading into the depths of the earth, and hidden rivers. There is a new wonder around every corner – your children will be enchanted!

INSIDER TIPS

- The approach road to the caves is winding and narrow; some sections are one-way. Check the website for driving instructions.

- Try to arrive early to avoid the crowds. If the closest carpark is full, you will need to park higher up the mountain, which means a very steep walk down (and a steep walk up at the end).

- Each cave tour takes one to two hours. See the website to select the cave/s to visit and find out tour timetables in advance. Check the difficulty level when choosing. Some caves involve climbing up and down hundreds of steps, but there are regular pauses during the tours so you do have time to catch your breath. The one-hour Imperial Cave tour is one of the easiest.

- Your ticket to a guided tour entitles you to the loan of an audio recording (available in a children's version) for a self-guided, self-paced tour of the Needle Cave and Devil's Coach House (*see* DON'T MISS p. 27).

- Adventure-caving tours are available; minimum age 10 years.
- Starting from the upper level carpark, you can take a bushwalk along the Devil's Coach House or Carlotta's Arch track.

DON'T MISS

- The nearby Needle Cave and Devil's Coach House, which are free to enter. If your kids are afraid of the dark, or of enclosed spaces, the Devil's Coach House has huge, open caverns.
- The opportunity to spot platypus in Blue Lake. Start early and walk around the Blue Lake before your cave visit; you might see platypus playing with the ducks. Alternatively, stay overnight at Jenolan Caves House (see ACCOMMODATION p. 30) and look for platypus at dusk.

FABULOUS FACTS

Caves are produced in limestone areas because rainwater passing through soil picks up carbon dioxide from plant roots and acids from decaying vegetable matter, and the solution dissolves the limestone. The Jenolan Caves are some of the oldest and most magnificent limestone caves in the world. They were discovered by European settlers about 150 years ago, but they were known to the Indigenous Gundungurra people for many thousands of years. The Gundungurra believed the underground waters had healing powers.

Kid Quest

When you visit Nettle Cave, see if you can spy any sooty owls lurking in the shadows.

Glow Worm Tunnel

Newnes State Forest, north of Lithgow
(02) 6350 3230 or 1300 760 276; www. lithgow-tourism.com/glowworm.htm
FREE

To find the glow worms, walk through a rocky gorge surrounded by ferns – watch for kangaroos and wallabies – and follow a disused rail track into an old tunnel. Check the website for accurate directions. Carry a torch and take care as there may be water underfoot. At the darkest point of the 400-metre tunnel, look for tiny blue glowing dots on the walls. If you find them, this is a magical experience.

Mount Annan Botanic Garden, Mount Annan

Megalong Australian Heritage Centre
Megalong Rd, Megalong Valley
(02) 4787 8188; www.megalong.cc
MID-RANGE
Visit the heritage farmyard and feed the animals or go on a horseriding adventure. Accommodation is available on site at Megalong Ranch Guesthouse, (*see* ACCOMMODATION p. 30).

Mount Annan Botanic Garden
Mount Annan Dr, Mount Annan
(02) 4634 7935;
www.rbgsyd.nsw.gov.au/annan
BUDGET
This is the Australian native plant section of Sydney's Royal Botanic Gardens. You can see Wollemi pines (some of the world's oldest and rarest trees), wander through a sculpture garden, play in a terrific adventure playground, then eat at the family restaurant *see* PLACES TO EAT p. 30). You might even spot a few free-roaming wallabies and wallaroos.

Mount Tomah Botanic Garden
Bells Line of Rd, Mount Tomah
(02) 4567 3015; www.rbgsyd.nsw.gov.au/
mount_tomah_botanic_garden
BUDGET
Pick up an Adventure Quest for the kids at the entry booth. This will keep your kids entertained for an hour and they'll win a small prize at the end. Mount Tomah is the cool-climate garden of Sydney's Royal Botanic Gardens. It features plants from all around the world.

Zig Zag Railway
Clarence Railway Station, Clarence
(02) 6355 2955;
www.zigzagrailway.com.au
Check website for timetable
MID-RANGE
Travel by steam train over winding tracks constructed in the 19th century – an incredible engineering feat. At special times, you can choose a day out with Thomas the Tank Engine or depart from 'Platform 9 and ¾' of *Harry Potter* fame on the Wizard Express.

En route from Sydney

St Matthews Church, Windsor
Moses St, Windsor
www.hawkesburyweb.com.au/
information/thingsToDo_windsor.asp
FREE
Many familiar names from Australian history lessons are associated with this attractive old church. It was designed by the convict architect Francis Greenway under the direction of Governor Lachlan Macquarie and consecrated in 1822 by Samuel Marsden, the convicts' chaplain. Plaques mark the graves of several First Fleeters (the first convicts sent out to Australia) buried in the cemetery.

See also Featherdale Wildlife Park (p. 17)

Accommodation

Dunns Swamp Camping
Wollemi National Park, Rylstone
NSW National Parks and Wildlife
Service, Mudgee (02) 6372 7199;
www.wildwalks.com/camping-in-nsw-
parks/near-sydney-campsites/dunns-
swamp-camping-ground.html
BUDGET TO MID-RANGE
This camping and picnic area on the banks of the Cudgegong River offers bushwalking, fishing, swimming and canoeing. There are also Aboriginal paintings and you have a good chance of spotting kangaroos, possums, wallabies and wombats. If you want to have a go at camping without the hassle, let the folk from Wollemi Afloat look after you; www.wollemiafloat.com.au

Hatter's Hideout
Secret location, near Bell
(02) 6355 2777; hattershideout.com.au
BUDGET TO HIGH COST
For something very special, you can stay in a luxury lodge with views over the Wollemi Wilderness World Heritage area, or you can even 'rent' a cave!

Jenolan Caves House
Jenolan Caves
(02) 6359 3911 or 1300 76 33 11;
www.jenolancaves.org.au
BUDGET TO MID-RANGE

Stay on the site of the Jenolan Caves (*see* p. 26) to fully appreciate the lovely bushland setting. Accommodation options range from historic guesthouse rooms with shared bathrooms to self-contained cottages.

Megalong Ranch Guesthouse
Megalong Rd, Megalong Valley
(02) 4787 8188; www.megalong.cc
BUDGET TO MID-RANGE

Camp in the beautiful Megalong grounds with access to an amenities block with hot showers. Alternatively, stay on the ranch in a large family-sized room with a double-bed, bunk beds and ensuite, and make use of the guest lounge and kitchenette. See Megalong Australian Heritage Centre (p. 28) for information on what to see and do here.

Old Leura Dairy
Cnr Kings Rd and Eastview Ave, Leura
(02) 4782 0700;
www.oldleuradairy. com.au
MID-RANGE TO HIGH COST

You can choose from the Milking Shed and Moo Manor at this historic dairy. Kids will enjoy features such as claw foot baths, hayloft bedrooms and sloping ceilings in the self-contained cottages with garden surrounds.

Places to eat

Mount Annan Gardens Restaurant
Mount Annan Dr, Mount Annan
(02) 4647 1363;
www.rbgsyd.nsw.gov.au/annan

Set in the heart of the picturesque Mount Annan Botanic Garden, this restaurant was judged Best Family Restaurant in Australia in October 2008 by the Restaurant and Catering Association of Australia. It offers relaxed outdoor dining overlooking the gardens.

Skyway
Cnr Violet St and Cliff Dr, Katoomba
(02) 4780 0200 or 1300 SKYWAY;
www.scenicworld.com.au

For a special lunchtime experience, try the buffet at the revolving restaurant at Scenic World. For every paying adult, one child under 13 eats free of charge.

BROKEN HILL & SURROUNDS

Broken Hill is located 1170 kilometres north-west of Sydney and has its own regional airport

Suits driving holidays; best in cooler months (Apr–Oct)

WARNING This is a remote area and requires special preparation if you intend to travel without guides; beyond the town, petrol, food and other supplies are limited.

HIGHLIGHTS

Daydream Historic Mine **p. 34**

Living Desert Flora and Fauna Sanctuary **p. 35**

School of the Air **p. 31**

Silverton ghost town **p. 37**

In town

School of the Air
Lane St, Broken Hill
(08) 8087 3565; www.schoolair-p.schools.nsw.edu.au
Tourist sessions 8.30–9.30am during school term

BUDGET

Obtain tickets from the Broken Hill Visitor Information Centre (corner of Blende and Bromide streets) so that your kids can participate in a real School of the Air class. They'll have fun being in a broadcasting studio and this visit will open their eyes to the totally different lifestyle of outback kids. You'll see them grasping to understand what it would be like to live somewhere so remote that they can't even travel to school. Can they imagine taking all their lessons via computer in a room in their own homes, with only brothers and sisters for companions? It will be an experience that lingers and keeps them thinking.

INSIDER TIPS

- Visitor times are weekdays 8.30–9.30am, but you need to arrive by 8.15am.

- Tourists usually watch classes without participating, but if you come from another country you might be invited to introduce yourselves.

DON'T MISS

- School assembly! Time your visit for a Friday to participate in a whole school assembly where everyone joins in the national anthem, the school song and singing 'Happy Birthday' to students celebrating a birthday that week.

FABULOUS FACTS

In the early 1900s, students in remote areas could study through correspondence schools, with lessons and answers being sent back and forth by post, a very slow and frustrating process. School of the Air began in the 1950s with the radio network of the Royal Flying Doctor Service being used to make two-way broadcasts. For the first time, correspondence students could speak to their teachers. In 2003, satellite classes began, and now students can see and speak to their teachers, as well as watching lessons on their computer screens.

Kid Quest
Work out what you'd miss the most if you couldn't go to school.

Albert Kersten GeoCentre
Cnr Crystal and Bromide sts, Broken Hill
(08) 8087 6538; www.collections
australia.net/org/213/about
BUDGET
Minerals and gems – including a 42-kilogram silver nugget – are displayed in this fun, interactive and educational exhibit. Learn about the science of crystals and the history of our planet. The minerals displayed were all found at Broken Hill.

Big Picture
Silver City Mint and Art Centre
66 Chloride St, Broken Hill
(08) 8088 6166; silvercitymint.com.au
Check opening times
BUDGET

Billed as the 'world's largest acrylic painting on canvas by a single artist', this amazingly realistic and detailed depiction of the outback is 100 metres long and 12 metres high. You stand on a viewing platform to see it.

Pro Hart Gallery
108 Wyman St, Broken Hill
(08) 8087 2441; www.prohart.com.au
Open daily, afternoons only on Sun
BUDGET

Show your kids the Pro Hart Du Pont carpet advertisement on YouTube before you go. Pro Hart, one of Australia's most celebrated artists, was born in Broken Hill, and even worked in the mines. Kids enjoy the humour and occasional 'paint ball' technique of his artwork.

Royal Flying Doctor Base Museum
Broken Hill Airport, Broken Hill
(08) 8080 3733; www.flyingdoctor.org.
au/about-us/visitor-centres/vc-se
Open daily, closes mid-afternoon on
weekends and public holidays
BUDGET

A tour of this working Royal Flying Doctor Service (RFDS) base is a unique experience. The Broken Hill base provides aero-medical services from New South Wales into Queensland and South Australia, covering an area larger than England and Wales combined. The attached museum has interactive displays for kids and reveals the remarkable and inspiring history of the RFDS. Entry fees go towards the purchase of new aircraft and medical equipment.

Sulphide Street Railway, Mineral, Hospital and Migrant Museum
Blende St, Broken Hill
(08) 8088 4660;
www.visitbrokenhill.com.au/accom_
result1/railway-mineral-train-museum
Closes mid-afternoon
BUDGET

This diverse and interesting museum complex covers many themes relating to the town's history. It includes old trains that kids can board and explore, a mineral collection, and separate hospital and migrant museums.

White's Mineral Art and Mining Museum
1 Allendale St, Broken Hill
(08) 8087 2878

BUDGET

Enter a dark cavern for a candlelit tour of artwork made with real minerals, and hear an ex-miner's tales about mining. You can also see models that explain mining technology, and a doll and teddy bear collection.

In the area

Daydream Historic Mine
13 km off Silverton Rd, Apollyon Valley
(08) 8088 5682; www.visitbrokenhill.com.au/accom_result1/historic-daydream-mine
Check opening times

MID-RANGE

It's a scenic drive along the Silverton road to the mine. Your experience here starts with the fun of dressing up in miners' helmets, complete with lamps and battery belts. On entering the disused mine, your kids will be competing to find the first glimpse of silver. But as the guide leads you through eerie, tight tunnels of rock, you will all start to think more about the terrible life of the miners than the treasure. It's sobering to learn that boys as young as eight worked here in the 1880s. Among the tools still lying around are the boxes these small boys had to fill with ore.

INSIDER TIPS

- The underground tours are not for the claustrophobic – but you can also do above-ground tours (lower cost).

- There are no EFTPOS or credit card facilities available at the mine, but you can pre-purchase tickets from Broken Hill Visitors Information Centre (corner of Blende and Bromide streets).

- During the underground tour, the guide may ask you to turn off your lamps so you can experience the pitch dark suffered by the miners if their candles went out.

- Wear sturdy, rubber-soled shoes for your tour.

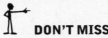

DON'T MISS

- The delicious Cornish cream teas available on site (the original miners were Cornish).

FABULOUS FACTS

Mining was an extremely dangerous and unhealthy job. As you stand in the narrow darkness breathing the smell of earth, try to picture children being sent into freshly blasted tunnels, coughing and half blinded by dust, to heave up shattered rocks with their bare hands. Their first fear was mine collapse. Look at the huge tree trunks propping up the rocks and earth of the tunnels. If one of these props started to groan, the miners scrambled for their lives. And then there was the problem of dust in their lungs and eyes. Child miners often went blind, and by the age of 13 they were coughing up blood.

Kid Quest

There is still unmined silver in the ground, so keep your eyes peeled!

Living Desert Flora and Fauna Sanctuary

Off Nine Mile Rd, Broken Hill
Broken Hill Visitor Information Centre (08) 8080 3560;
www.visitnsw.com/town/Broken_Hill/The_Living_Desert_Sanctuary/info.aspx

BUDGET

Gaze out at the vast expanse of russet-coloured earth dotted with stones and spindly silver plants, then follow the 2-kilometre cultural trail. As you trek through wooded gullies and rocky outcrops, you pass more archetypal images of the Australian outback: a reconstruction of an Aboriginal camp, a disused mine, a scarlet display of Sturt desert pea wildflowers, glowing yellow wattles, red kangaroos hopping past, and maybe a wedge-tailed eagle soaring above. Look for signage explaining the different flora and fauna you come across.

INSIDER TIPS

- Living Desert has a picnic area with gas barbecues and toilets.

- Call in to Broken Hill Visitor Information Centre, corner of Blende and Bromide streets, before visiting to obtain information, pick up a brochure on the Flora and Fauna Sanctuary and a key for the sculpture garden (*see* DON'T MISS *below*).

- In some seasons the flies are very persistent so you might want nets to put over your faces.

- Carry plenty of water in warm weather.

- The desert can be extremely cold during winter and in the evenings, so bring jackets.

DON'T MISS

- The extraordinary outdoor sculpture garden, accessible by key from the visitor information centre. Make sure you look out over the desert from the top of the hill – the vista is so vast, you'll be able to see the curvature of the earth.

FABULOUS FACTS

The electric fence around the sanctuary is designed to keep out feral animals such as rabbits and foxes. In the 19th century, European settlers released rabbits and foxes into the Australian bush to provide themselves with hunting opportunities. Without natural predators to control them, these introduced species became pests. Feral animals are now a major problem, destroying native animal habitat, spreading disease and competing with native animals for food and shelter.

Kid Quest

Take some artistic photos with interesting angles.
Get a photo of a huge sandstone sculpture standing
up against the vast blue sky.

Silverton ghost town

Silverton Visitor Information Centre, 2 Layard St, Silverton
(08) 8088 7566; www.silverton.org.au

VARIOUS PRICES

Your kids will be thrilled when you tell them you are all going to visit a ghost town. This quintessential outback town – a pub and a few dusty brown historic buildings surrounded by desert – will not disappoint. Some of the disused buildings have been turned into museums so you can see what life was like when Silverton was a thriving mining town. Visit the old gaol

Old cars outside gallery, Silverton

and lock-up, then step inside the stone-built school and let your kids imagine being students here in the 1880s.

INSIDER TIPS

■ If you think Silverton looks familiar, it probably is, as it has featured in various films, television shows and countless commercials (particularly for cars). The pub has a display of movie memorabilia.

■ For a special way to experience the area, take a camel safari with Silverton Camel Farm and imagine you are early pioneers exploring the outback; (08) 8088 5316. Rides, suitable for all ages, range from 15 minutes up to three-day treks.

DON'T MISS

■ The quintessential outback view – continue just 4 kilometres beyond Silverton to a lookout point that offers an uninterrupted view made famous by films such as *Mad Max II* (1981) and *The Adventures of Priscilla, Queen of the Desert* (1993).

FABULOUS FACTS

With the success of silver mining at Silverton (Silver Town), prospectors searched further afield, opening bigger and better mines in the area. A syndicate of seven started up The Broken Hill Proprietary Company Limited (later BHP Billiton), which would become Australia's biggest company, earning billions of dollars. As people abandoned Silverton to chase the bigger mines at Broken Hill, they actually took the buildings with them, transporting them with teams of donkeys, camels and bullocks.

Kid Quest

In the old Silverton gaol, look for the embalming bath where corpses were stored until the coroner arrived from Sydney.

Kinchega National Park

About 100 km south-east of Broken Hill
(08) 8080 3200; www.environment.nsw.
gov.au/NationalParks/parkHome.
aspx?id=N0017
BUDGET

Picnic or camp (*see* ACCOMMODATION *on facing page*) among glorious red sand dunes under a vast cobalt-blue sky. See Aboriginal hand paintings and try birdwatching (don't forget the emus) or kangaroo spotting. Fresh water (rain and bore water) are available at the historic woolshed. Regular tours and billy tea are organised by the national parks office. Nearby Menindee Lakes, a system of 12 man-made lakes, offers fishing and other water-based activities.

Mutawintji National Park

130 km north-east of Broken Hill
www.environment.nsw.gov.au
FREE

This magnificent wildlife area features hidden gorges, waterholes and caves. The park is home to kangaroos, goannas and emus, and the only known colony of endangered yellow-footed rock wallabies in New South Wales. The park is a culturally and historically significant Aboriginal area, where you can see rock carvings, ochre animal paintings and handprints dating back 30 000 years, and remnants from ancient fire places and stone tool making. Tours available through Mutawintji Eco-Tours; www. mutawintjiecotours.com.au

Accommodation

Emaroo Cottages
Various locations in Broken Hill
(08) 8595 7217;
www.emaroocottages.com.au
MID-RANGE
These self-contained, individual four-star cottages offer facilities kids will enjoy such as Xbox and free broadband, their own DVD player, soft toys and a secure backyard. The cottages are also pet-friendly.

Kinchega National Park
(08) 8080 3200;
www.nationalparks.nsw.gov.au
BUDGET
Choose between a basic campsite along the banks of the Darling River, or a bunk bed (BYO linen) in the old shearers' quarters.

Book ahead for shearers' accommodation with hot showers, toilets, a communal kitchen, dining area and gas barbecue. See facing page for information on what to see and do here.

Penrose Park Camping Site
Silverton
(08) 8088 5307;
www.visitnsw.com/town/Silverton/
Penrose_Park_Camping_Site/info.aspx
BUDGET
This is a lovely environment with tame animals and a playground for the kids. Powered caravan and camping sites are available. See Silverton ghost town (p. 37) for information on what to see and do here.

Places to eat

Barrier Social Democratic Club
218 Argent St, Broken Hill
(08) 8087 1711; www.democlub.com.au
The dining room has a kids' menu, and the play equipment will keep little wrigglers entertained.

Bells Milk Bar and Museum
160 Patton St, Broken Hill
(08) 8087 5380;
www.bellsmilkbar.com.au

Travel back in time to the 1950s! Nostalgic decor, milkshakes, sodas and spiders are on the menu at this kid-friendly venue.

Broken Hill Musicians Club
276 Crystal St, Broken Hill
(08) 8088 1777;
www.musiciansclub.com.au
This casual bistro offers an all-you-can-eat buffet and a menu for kids.

BYRON BAY & SURROUNDS

Byron Bay is located 160 kilometres south of Brisbane; there are airports at Ballina (30 kilometres south) and Coolangatta (70 kilometres north)

Beaches are best in warmer months (Nov–Apr), but there are plenty of year-round activities

HIGHLIGHTS

Macadamia Castle   *p. 43*

Tropical Fruit World   *p. 44*

Around town

Masterpiece drawn at Byron Bay Art Studio, Byron Bay

Byron Bay Art Studio
Jonson St, Byron Bay
0404 093 919;
www.byronbayartstudio.com
Bookings essential

HIGH COST

Think you can't draw? Learn to paint a portrait here in just three hours! The combined child and adult session is a unique family activity. Without any previous art experience, you can create portraits that are good enough to frame. Class times are usually scheduled for the morning.

Byron Bay Kids World

Shed 5, 17 Brigantine St, Byron Bay
Industrial Estate, Byron Bay
(02) 6685 7299;
www.byronbaykidsworld.com.au
Closed Mon except during school holidays
BUDGET

This indoor kids' play centre is aimed at babies and children to the age of 11 years. It offers climbing structures, safari rides, an adventure castle and a cafe for the adults. Make sure you bring socks.

Cape Byron and Lighthouse

Cape Byron Headland Reserve, Byron Bay
Lighthouse tours (02) 6685 5955;
www.nationalparks.nsw.gov.au
BUDGET

When you stand on Cape Byron you are as far east as you can get on the Australian mainland – a good spot to watch for turtles, dolphins and humpback whales out at sea. If you don't have binoculars, hire a pair from the Cape Byron shop, or make use of the coin-operated telescopes. You can also look for goannas, wallabies and soaring eagles by following one of the marked tracks into the rainforest of Cape Byron Headland Reserve. Guided tours of the lighthouse are available two days a week.

Circus Arts

Byron Entertainment Centre
17 Centennial Circuit, Arts and Industry
Estate, Byron Bay
(02) 6685 6566; www.circusarts.com.au
CLASSES AT VARIOUS TIMES AND PRICES

Ever wanted to join a Have a go at swinging trapeze (adults and k learn together), or le skills such as juggling acrobatics. Classes cater for babies to adults.

Kayak with dolphins

Cape Byron Kayaks: (02) 6680 9555;
www.capebyronkayaks.com
Go Sea Kayak: 0416 222 344;
www.goseakayakbyronbay.com.au
HIGH COST

The Cape Byron Marine Park offers wonderful opportunities to kayak among wild dolphins, turtles or even whales (in season). Both operators listed above offer kayaking tours that cater for children aged 5 years and over.

Snorkel with turtles

9 Marvell St, Byron Bay
(02) 6685 8333 or 1800 243 483;
www.byronbaydivecentre.com.au
HIGH COST

Swim in the bay in this marine sanctuary among turtles, manta rays and hundreds of different fish. All equipment is provided and classes cater for children

_ years and over. Start with
_sson in a pool then take a
_ive-minute boat ride to Julian
Rock. Diving lessons are available
for teenagers and adults.

A Spot of Paint Ceramic and Art Studio

9/18 Centennial Circuit, Byron Bay
0410 343 646; www.aspotofpaint.com
VARIOUS PRICES

The studio offers half- or full-day
holiday classes for children aged
6 to 14 years. It gives kids a
chance to spend a few hours
being creative in ceramic
painting, pottery, illustration,
painting, textile art, batik, tie-dye,
wire sculpture, window painting
or plaster casting.

Through A Glass Onion studio

Cavanbah Arcade (opposite the Beach
Hotel bottle shop), Byron Bay
0410 116 347;
www.throughaglassonion.com.au
FREE; CLASSES HIGH COST

The Glass Onion studio makes
jewellery out of glass. You can
watch the bead-making most
nights 6pm–9pm. For children
aged 12 and above, enquire about
glass bead–making classes (extra
cost, but a great family activity).
The classes are held at 4/102
Centennial Circuit, Byron Bay.

Whale-watching cruise

9 Marvell St, Byron Bay
(02) 6685 8333 or 1800 243 483;
www.byronbaywhalewatching.com.au
June–Nov only
Bookings essential
HIGH COST

Humpback whales pass Cape
Byron from June to July on their
annual pilgrimage north to
warmer waters and then come
past again heading south from
September to October. Vessels are
equipped with hydrophones so
you can hear the whales 'singing'.

Whale-watching, Byron Bay

In the area

Macadamia Castle
1699 Pacific Hwy, Knockrow
(02) 6687 8432; www.macadamiacastle.com.au

MID-RANGE

Will your kids be nervous or eager as they reach out to pat a large snake? They will probably be surprised to find that it does not feel cold or slippery, but quite warm. Macadamia Castle offers a range of educational animal encounters, from patting (and even holding!) a carpet python, to peeking inside a mouse house and finding out what secret activities mice get up to.

INSIDER TIPS

■ Check the website for the daily schedule of keeper talks. The tawny frogmouth is one of the more unusual animals you'll have a chance to see up close during a keeper's feed and talk.

■ There are lots of other fun activities such as the flying fox, minigolf, train rides and a playground with multistorey tree house.

■ You can see various Australian animals, some in enclosures and others, such as water dragons, just 'visiting' and running free.

■ Cafe Macca offers interesting food with a macadamia nut theme.

DON'T MISS

■ Rabbit patting – cuddle a rabbit at one of two sessions daily.

■ The chance to feed free-ranging ducks, chickens and turkeys; seed can be purchased on entry.

■ Face painting – available most Sundays and daily during the school holidays.

FABULOUS FACTS

Tawny frogmouths spend their daytime perched on gum tree branches, often low down, but you will rarely spot them in normal circumstances because they look exactly like the broken stumps of tree branches.

They are disguised by streaky, mottled plumage and the way they tilt their heads. However, if you listen at night you might hear their *ooom-ooom-ooom* call. See if you can spot the tawny frogmouth in the photo on the Australian Museum website: australianmuseum.net.au/image/Tawny-Frogmouth-during-day

Kid Quest
Are carpet pythons dangerous?
See pp. 640–4 for the answer

Tropical Fruit World, Duranbah

Tropical Fruit World
Duranbah Rd, Duranbah
(02) 6677 7222; www.tropicalfruitworld.com.au
MID-RANGE

Imagine being in a wonderful, scented environment surrounded by trees growing all sorts of unusual, exotic fruits with storybook names such as chewing gum fruit, ice-cream bean, chocolate pudding fruit and red dragon fruit! There's also plenty of bush tucker to discover.

If your kids are not usually adventurous with their food, this may be the spark that inspires them to try something new. They might even get a chance to pick their own! As well as tastings, they'll enjoy the tractor, train and boat rides, and the chance to interact with animals and play on 'Treasure Island'.

INSIDER TIPS

▦ The tour takes about two-and-a-half hours. You will do everything as part of a tour group, so you can't travel at your own pace. The only variation is an opportunity to stay longer on Treasure Island and join up with a different returning group. There may be delays and queues at various points on the tour, so bring activities to keep little ones occupied.

▦ The fruit tasting includes an informative talk. Check the website to find out which fruits will be in season when you visit. You can try chutneys, jams, spreads, salad dressings and preserves.

- Animal interactions include kangaroo, duck and fish feeding, and meeting farm animals. Watch out for a range of native animals including koalas, water dragons, carpet snakes, turtles, wild bush turkeys or kingfishers.

- Of course, there's a cafe on site where you can taste more fruity delights.

DON'T MISS

- The hidden highlights of Treasure Island – playground, cubby houses, flying fox ride and a minigolf course. Take time to enjoy the peaceful scenic areas and walks; come prepared with a picnic.

FABULOUS FACTS

Chocolate pudding fruit really does taste like chocolate, especially if you eat it with something sweet such as ice-cream. From the outside it has a similar appearance to a green tomato, but the inside does look like chocolate pudding. It is also called black sapote. It is low in fat and high in vitamin C. At Tropical Fruit World the chocolate pudding fruit should be ripe from August to January.

Kid Quest
Which is your favourite fruit?

Amaze-n-Place
149 Wardell Rd, Alstonville
(02) 6628 7518;
www.amaze-n-place.com.au
MID-RANGE
Have fun wending your way through the huge maze, then climb to the top of the tower. Pick up a Seekers Card before you start and see what you can find in the maze. There's also a cafe with puzzles to play with while you eat.

Ballina Pool and Waterslide
River St, Ballina
(02) 6686 3771
BUDGET
This municipal complex has a giant waterslide (extra cost) as well as a toddler pool, learn-to-swim pool and 50-metre solar-heated Olympic pool.

Belongil Beach, Byron Bay

Beaches

FREE

The most kid-friendly swimming beach close to Byron Bay is Little Wategos. At Brunswick Heads, there's a small, safe beach for children and families north of the breakwater, over the bridge from town. At Ballina, Shelly Beach and Flat Rock rockpools are perfect for toddlers, with a waterside cafe and wading pool built into the rocks at Shelly Beach. At Lennox Head, there's rockpool fun at the reef just off the beach at the south end of Seven Mile Beach, accessible at low tide, and kids can swim in the tea-tree lake at the north end of the village.

Byron Bay Wildlife Tours

0429 770 686;
www.byronbaywildlifetours.com

HIGH COST

On this five-hour tour you're guaranteed to see lots of native Australian land and marine animals in their natural environment.

Chillingham Bush Tucker

1292 Numinbah Rd, Chillingham
(02) 6679 1022;
www.chillinghambushtucker.com.au

FREE

Take a self-guided tour around the Chillingham Bush Tucker garden: 20 different local bush tucker species and exotic fruits are all labelled.

Crystal Castle

81 Monet Dr, Mullumbimby
(02) 6684 3111;
www.crystalcastle.com.au

MID-RANGE

Be amazed by crystals collected from all over the world, wander through tranquil gardens under the gaze of mystical statues, and relax in a cafe while the children play in the 'Fireheart' Crystal Dragon Playground.

Crystal Creek Miniatures

Cnr Numinbah and Upper Crystal Creek rds, Murwillumbah
(02) 6679 1532; www.minianimals.net
Entry by tour only; bookings essential

MID-RANGE

See and pat miniature donkeys, horses and cattle.

Eltham Valley Pantry

713 Boatharbour Rd, Eltham
(02) 6629 1418;
www.elthamvalley.com.au
Closed Mon

MID-RANGE

Pecan nuts and coffee are grown organically, then harvested and processed on the farm. Join one of the fun, interactive tours; check website for times. There is a cafe on site.

Kool Katz Learn to Surf School
Various locations south of Byron Bay
(02) 6684 3933; www.koolkatzsurf.com
Bookings essential
HIGH COST

The emphasis is on fun at this kid-focussed surf school. Equipment is provided and lessons are suitable for children aged 6 years and over. Classes are conducted in waist-deep water with small waves.

Lismore Visitor Centre Rainforest Experience
Cnr Molesworth St and Ballina Rd, Lismore
(02) 6626 0100 or 1300 369 795
BY DONATION

The centre has an educational and indoor rainforest display where kids can find out about endangered species and see stuffed examples of rainforest animals. Nearby Heritage Park has an adventure playground (suitable for littlies) with a miniature train ride, barbecues, picnic tables and toilets.

Nightcap National Park
Terania Creek Rd, Terania Creek
(02) 6627 0200;
www.environment.nsw.gov.au
FREE

Experience sheer cliffs, spectacular waterfalls and lush green gullies. Park in the Terania Creek Picnic Area and take the easy walk through bangalow palms to the base of Protestors Falls (45 minutes, 1.4 kilometres return). This area was the scene of major anti-logging protests in 1979. The falls are home to the endangered Fleay's barred frog, so swimming is forbidden, but there are barbecues, toilets, tables and shelters. Rocky Creek Dam just south of the park has forest walks with interpretive signs, picnic spots and a playground. Warning: Nightcap National Park has the highest annual rainfall in the state!

Tie Dye Fun!
Byron Bay Craft Market (1st Sun of month); The Channon Craft Market (2nd Sun of month); Bangalow Market (4th Sun of month)
www.tiedye.com.au
MID-RANGE

Fancy a rainbow-coloured pair of socks, or a multi-coloured T-shirt? Bring a white, natural fibre item along (or the dyers will provide a T-shirt or singlet for you) and have a go at tie-dyeing with non-toxic, sun-activated dyes!

Special event

Lismore Lantern Parade
June
(02) 6622 6333; www.lanternparade.com
This spectacular parade of lanterns, bands, street theatre, carnival dancers, illuminated puppets and pyrotechnics is the highlight of an extended art, craft and regional food festival. Make your own lantern at an afternoon workshop and join in the winter solstice parade.

Accommodation

Besakih
Unit 10, 5–9 Somerset St, Byron Bay
(02) 6684 1726;
www.stayz.com.au/13465
MID-RANGE
This two-bedroom, Asian-style apartment has a large private tropical garden. It is in a quiet location, in easy walking distance to both shops and the beach

The BlueGreen House
Secret location, 12 min from Byron Bay;
details will be emailed on booking
www.takeabreak.com.au/The-BlueGreen-House.htm
HIGH COST
This luxurious, family-friendly, two- or three-bedroom holiday house is located, on a 2-hectare property, with a lake, gazebo and heated pool. Kids can feed chickens, collect eggs, hand-feed alpacas or ride behind a tractor.

Cape Byron State Conservation Area Cottages
Cape Byron Headland Reserve, Byron Bay
(02) 6685 6552;
www.environment.nsw.gov.au
MID-RANGE TO HIGH COST
There is a range of accommodation here in the picturesque surrounds of the conservation area, just five minutes by car from the centre of Byron Bay. The cottages range from heritage lighthouse keepers' houses, with period furniture and modern appliances, to stunning modern holiday homes.

First Sun Caravan Park
Lawson St, Byron Bay
(02) 6685 6544; www.bshp.com.au
BUDGET TO MID-RANGE
There's a choice of two-bedroom, self-contained cabins or waterfront caravan sites and campsites. The park is within easy walking distance of shops, restaurants, cafes and beaches.

Places to eat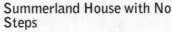

Chameleon

3/109 Jonson St, Byron Bay
(02) 6680 7798
This global food cafe serves healthy, fresh food. The pizzas are a favourite with the kids.

Harvest Cafe

18 Old Pacific Hwy, Newrybar
(02) 6687 2644; harvestcafe.com.au
Fancy an elegant dinner in an award-winning restaurant? This picturesque historic cottage in the hinterland welcomes kids and provides highchairs and a toy box for littlies.

Summerland House with No Steps

253 Wardell Rd, Lynwood
(02) 6628 0610;
www.summerlandhouse.com.au
This macadamia and avocado farm provides employment and training opportunities for people with disabilities. Enjoy the on-site cafe while your kids have fun in the waterspray park and shady playground. Everyone can have a go at the giant chess set.

CENTRAL COAST

The region's main holiday town, The Entrance, is located 100 kilometres north of Sydney

Day trip or holiday destination

Beaches are best in warmer months (Dec–Mar), but there are plenty of year-round activities

HIGHLIGHTS

Australian Reptile Park   *p. 54*

TreeTop Adventure Park   *p. 56*

Tuggerah Lake   *p. 50*

On the coast

Tuggerah Lake
www.centralcoastaustralia.com.au/AreaInfo/towns_TheEntrance.asp

FREE; VARIOUS PRICES FOR ACTIVITIES

This large, shallow coastal lagoon is the place for an old-fashioned family holiday by the water. Picture the whole family riding along the water's edge on bikes, tossing in lines to catch fish, wandering down the long, wooden jetty licking ice-creams, or putt-putting around in a hire-boat. On the lake shore in Memorial Park, you can relax with a picnic, fly a kite, kick a ball or ride the historic carousel; best of all, at 3.30pm daily you can see wild pelicans fly in for a free feed on the ocean side of the park. In school holiday time and weekends, there's a carnival atmosphere in Memorial Park with rides, face painting and shows.

INSIDER TIPS

- Boats can be hired from the Long Jetty Catamaran and Boat Hire company; www.longjettyboathire.com. Take your pick of a two-person catamaran (ideal sailing boat for novices), aluminium runabout (a little fishing boat with an outboard motor), single, double or triple kayak, or four-seater pedal boat (for a good leg workout!). Lifejackets are provided in all sizes from toddler up.

- Bikes can be hired from Tour De Long Jetty Cycle Hire; 0411 258 899. They have a range of classic 50s-style upright bikes, geared bikes, kids' bikes, and adult bikes with baby seats.

- Make sure you get a fishing licence before you fish.

DON'T MISS

- The toddler play area in Vera's Water Garden, Memorial Park – the littlies love the coloured fountains and paddling ponds.

- Playing a game of chess with a giant outdoor chess board in Memorial Park.

- The craft markets – on Sundays.

FABULOUS FACTS

Australian pelicans have the biggest beaks of any bird in the world. They use these pouched beaks like nets to trap fish, then swallow the fish whole. Pelican feeding at The Entrance began as an accident when staff from a fish and chip shop threw scraps outside. It has become not just a tourist attraction, but a way of keeping an eye on the pelicans to see if they have any problems, such as fishing hooks or lines tangled in their gullets or wings.

Kid Quest

What sort of sound do pelicans make?
See pp. 640–4 for the answer

Aquafun
Heazlett Park via Ficus Ave, Avoca Beach
0413 808 394; www.aquafun.net.au
Open Sept–Apr, school holidays and
weekends
MID-RANGE
Hire a pedal boat, kayak or surf ski to explore Avoca Lake. Look out for jumping fish, pelicans, herons, cormorants and frogs.

Bouddi National Park
20 km south of Gosford
Central Coast office (02) 4320 4200;
www.environment.nsw.gov.au
BUDGET
Visit small, beautiful beaches surrounded by forests and cliffs. Take a bushwalk, keeping your eyes peeled for echidnas, swamp wallabies and white-breasted sea eagles, and see if you can find any of the Aboriginal rock engravings of fish and whales.

Central Coast Steam Model Co-Op Ltd
Lot 73A, Showground Rd, Narara
(02) 4388 2416; www.narara.cjb.net
Only open 1st Sat of month, 11am–4pm
BUDGET
Take a ride on the model steam trains. Fully enclosed shoes must be worn.

Central Coast Surf School
Avoca, Terrigal and Umina
0417 673 277;
www.centralcoastsurfschool.com.au
Seasonal operation; check website
HIGH COST
Join in a two-day school holiday course or book a private or group lesson. Soft surfboards, wetsuits and sunscreen are provided.

Erina Fair
620 Terrigal Dr, Erina
(02) 4367 7655; www.erinafair.com.au
Open till late
FREE ENTRY; VARIOUS PRICES FOR ACTIVITIES
This is the largest shopping and entertainment centre on the Central Coast. Erina Fair has its own ice skating rink, cinemas, playground and public library, as well as several department stores and over 300 specialty stores.

Gosford–Edogawa Commemorative Garden
36 Webb St, East Gosford
(02) 4325 0056;
www.gosfordregionalgallery.com
FREE
Situated in the Gosford Regional Gallery and Arts Centre complex,

this large, traditional Japanese garden has meandering pathways, a teahouse, stone lanterns and a pond filled with koi (Japanese fish).

Henry Kendall Cottage
27 Henry Kendall St, West Gosford
(02) 4325 2270;
www.henrykendallcottage.org.au
Check opening times
BUDGET

A favourite exhibit for kids at this historic house and museum is the outdoor double dunny. The cottage was once occupied by the famous poet Henry Kendall, and his typewriter and old school books are on display. You might like to read and discuss his poem *The Last of his Tribe*.

Kidz HQ
2C Amy Close, North Wyong
(02) 4355 4455; www.kidzhq.com.au
MID-RANGE

This is an indoor play centre with lots of bounce and excitement. Older kids can have fun shooting foam balls from cannons while toddlers can stay safe in their own dedicated zone.

Lollipops Playland
315 The Entrance Rd, The Entrance
www.theentrance.lollipopsplayland.
com.au
Open daily and open till late Fri and Sat
BUDGET

This indoor play centre has slides, a ball pit, jumping castle and

toddlers' area with ride-on cars. Meals are available from diggers@the entrance (*see* PLACES TO EAT p. 60).

Norah Head Lighthouse
40 Bush St, Norah Head
(02) 4343 4444 or 1300 132 975;
www.norahheadlighthouse.com.au
Entry by tour only; weekends and daily in school holidays, 10am
Suitable for ages 5+
MID-RANGE

The tour guide will talk about the duties of a lighthouse keeper, tell stories of shipwrecks and give a lesson on how to signal with flags. Climb the 96 stairs and imagine what it would be like to be a lighthouse keeper. For a real lighthouse experience, stay here overnight (*see* ACCOMMODATION p. 59).

Terrigal

www.terrigal.org

FREE

The beach is lovely here, and there are lots of short walks around the headlands and through the bush.

Toowoon Bay Beach

FREE

This is a particularly safe family beach. You can snorkel in the calm waters protected from the surf by nearby breakwalls.

Hinterland

Australian Reptile Park

Pacific Hwy, Somersby
(02) 4340 1022; www.reptilepark.com.au

MID-RANGE

This is a zoo with all the buzz and fun of a theme park. It starts from the moment you arrive and see the giant frill-necked lizard crouched over the gate. A rap-dancing 'spider' will invite you into Spider World, where everything is larger than life, seen from the viewpoint of a small spider. Your kids will scream with delight at the sight of giant 3-metre-high animated spiders, not to mention the real bird-eating spiders, red-backs and deadly tarantulas! They are sure to dive eagerly through the mouth of a 20-metre-long crocodile into the Lost World of Reptiles, where weird, live reptiles are watched over by the glowing eyes of a giant Egyptian crocodile god.

Australian Reptile Park, Somersby

INSIDER TIPS

■ There are entertaining and educational shows about the different animals throughout the day. If you've ever wanted to get up close to a giant python or a 160-kilogram Galapagos tortoise, this is your chance!

■ Besides the reptiles and spiders, the zoo has exotic birds and various Australian native animals. You can cuddle up with a wombat, feed a kangaroo and have your photo taken with a koala.

■ As well as animal exhibits, there's an adventure playground.

■ There are picnic areas and free barbecue facilities if you want to bring your own food, or you can eat at the Hard Croc Cafe.

DON'T MISS

■ The world's only funnel-web spider 'milking' show. This is not just for entertainment — the venom milked from the spiders is used to make antivenom and save lives.

■ The other entertaining and educational shows running throughout the day.

■ The giant python and the 160-kilogram Galapagos tortoise, both huge favourites with the kids.

FABULOUS FACTS

Sadly, in the year 2000, much of the Australian Reptile Park went up in flames, and most of the reptiles and spiders perished. One of the only survivors was an alligator snapping turtle who crawled through the hot embers and out of the collapsing building. Over the next few weeks there was a frantic effort to source new animals and reopen the zoo in temporary buildings. Some of the most urgently needed replacements were funnel-web spiders because antivenom supplies were needed in hospitals. Local residents hunted for male funnel-web spiders and brought them in so the program could start again.

Kid Quest
See if you can find Incey Wincey Spider being washed down the drain.

TreeTop Adventure Park, Wyong Creek

TreeTop Adventure Park

1 Red Hill Rd, Wyong Creek
(02) 4025 1008;
www.treetopadventurepark.com.au
Open daily, entries after 2pm must be booked in advance

HIGH COST

Kids always enjoy tree houses and tree climbing, but imagine having the freedom to swing and scramble from treetop to treetop like a monkey! This adventure park in the beautiful Ourimbah State Forest has giant rope spiderwebs, flying foxes, Tarzan ropes, tunnels, tightropes and swinging bridges, all suspended in the trees. There are sure to be ripples of nerves and excitement as the kids (and you!) don your safety helmets.

Following a safety induction course you'll be off, scrambling up into the trees. There are different levels of difficulty depending on age, confidence and ability, but everyone is attached to cables, so children as young as 3 years of age can join in.

INSIDER TIPS

- Children aged from 3 to 10 years are attached to a continuous belay safety system which they don't disconnect throughout the climb.

- Children aged from 10 to 15 years (and at least 1.4 metres tall) can participate in more difficult courses which are higher off the ground, but they must be accompanied by an adult (not just watching them from below). One adult may accompany up to four children. These courses involve use of two carabineers (metal clips used by cavers and rock climbers) which can be released. You will practise disconnecting them on your safety induction course first.

- Allow a minimum of one-and-a-half hours for the easier course and two hours for the more advanced version.

- The park operates in wet weather but closes if there is lightning or strong winds.

- It is worth booking to avoid disappointment, but you might have to phone a few times before someone answers.

- You'll need comfortable clothes, with your waist covered, and closed shoes. Body-piercings will need to be removed or taped over, and if you have long hair, you'll need to bring something for tying it back.

- This attraction is next door to Amazement (*see below*).

DON'T MISS

- The trees! Make sure, while you are having fun climbing and flying around, you take time to admire the forest around you.

- The terrific mountain bike track in Ourimbah State Forest – bring your own bikes.

FABULOUS FACTS

You are probably puzzled that someone has been allowed to build an adventure park in the middle of a state forest, but TreeTop Adventure Park was built under partnership with Forests NSW. The structures are specially designed not to harm the trees. The platforms were built without drilling into the trunks or branches, and all the structures allow room for the trees to grow without restrictions.

Kid Quest

If you're under 10 years of age, see if you can do your course blindfolded, or going backwards! Those who are over 10 years of age can take on the Green Course – watch out for signs giving you information about the forest.

Amazement
170 Yarramalong Rd, Wyong Creek
(02) 4353 9900; www.amazement.com.au
Open daily, last entry at 2pm

MID-RANGE

As the name suggests, this is the place to come if the kids love mazes. Other attractions include the farm animals, electric toy farm machines that the littlies can actually drive, and the Games Courtyard with sandpit and trampoline. Young detectives can have a go at solving the Farm Trail Quiz.

Australia Walkabout Wildlife Park

Cnr Peats Ridge and Darkinjung rds, Calga
(02) 4375 1100;
www.walkaboutpark.com.au

MID-RANGE

This park provides a wonderful opportunity to walk among free-ranging Australian animals including kangaroos, emus and wallabies. There are ancient Aboriginal rock art sites on the grounds and you can take a tour to learn about the Aboriginal heritage and the use of plants for bush tucker and traditional medicine. You can also stay overnight (*see* ACCOMMODATION *on facing page*).

Glenworth Valley Outdoor Adventures

69 Cooks Rd, Peats Ridge
(02) 4375 1222; www.glenworth.com.au

VARIOUS PRICES

Try mountain-biking, quad-biking (minimum age 12 years),

horseriding, abseiling or kayaking in over 1000 hectares of unspoilt wilderness. You can also camp here.

Koolang Astronomical Observatory

RMB 266B George Downs Dr, Bucketty
(02) 4998 8216; users.hunterlink.net.
au/~demcm/home_0_overview.htm
Open Fri and Sat, 8.30–10.30pm
Bookings essential

MID-RANGE

This centre is set up especially for public access and education. There's a huge telescope and a space science display about Mars, Jupiter and the early days of manned space flight.

Springfield Trail Rides

RMB 1511, Yarramalong
(02) 4356 1148;
www.springfieldtrails.com.au
Bookings essential

VARIOUS PRICES

These escorted horse rides traverse Watagan State Forest.

En route from Sydney

See Cruise with the Riverboat Postman (p. 16) and Ku-ring-gai Chase National Park (p. 17).

Accommodation

Australia Walkabout Wildlife Park
Cnr Peats Ridge and Darkinjung rds, Calga
(02) 4375 1100;
www.walkaboutpark.com.au

HIGH COST

Wild Sleep-out is a very special experience. Spacious new tents, meals and hot showers are provided and the tariff includes full-day access to the park. Your tents are pitched right in the wildlife park where the animals roam freely. Rangers will lead you on exclusive behind-the-scenes encounters, including a night stroll. See p. 58 for more information about the park.

Norah Head Holiday Park
Victoria St, Norah Head
(02) 4396 3935;
www.norahheadhp.com.au

BUDGET

This park is ideal for a water-based holiday, with a pool on site, and safe beaches on your doorstep.

Norah Head Lighthouse
40 Bush St, Norah Head
(02) 4343 4444 or 1300 132 975;
www.norahheadlighthouse.com.au

MID-RANGE TO HIGH COST

For something different, stay in the original lighthouse keepers' quarters! There are two historic cottages, each with three bedrooms, outstanding views and an enclosed garden for kids to play in. Linen hire is extra or BYO. There is a minimum stay of seven days in peak time. For more about the lighthouse see p. 53.

Oak Apartments
89 The Entrance Rd, The Entrance
(02) 4334 8000 or 1800 682 006;
www.oakshotelsresorts.com

MID-RANGE

These apartments are located on the beachfront and boast a heated pool. Accommodation includes studios and one- or two-bedroom apartments with cooking and laundry facilities.

Toowoon Bay Holiday Park
Koongara St, Toowoon Bay
(02) 4332 2834;
www.toowoonbayhp.com.au
BUDGET

Enjoy an absolute beachfront location on Toowoon Bay Beach (*see* p. 54). Choose a self-contained cabin (some have spas and air-conditioning) or a campsite with options of powered or ensuite facilities.

Waldorf Apartment Hotel
18 Coral St, The Entrance
(02) 4334 8800 or 1300 030 020;
www.the-entrance-waldorf.com.au
HIGH COST

This apartment hotel with swimming pool has a range of air-conditioned accommodation options including four-star studios and self-contained apartments with up to three rooms.

Places to eat

Various clubs offer large casual dining areas, or you can buy fish and chips from The Snapper Spot or Bluebells in Terrigal and eat them on the beach.

diggers@the entrance
315 The Entrance Rd, The Entrance
www.diggersattheentrance.com.au
Kids can romp in Lollipops Playland (*see* p. 53) while you eat. Have a light cafe meal and keep an eye on the kids yourself, or take advantage of the Drop 'n Dine service and go upstairs for a leisurely meal in one of the restaurants while the kids are supervised by someone else.

The Greens Bowling Club
Cnr Park Rd and Warrigal St,
The Entrance
(02) 4332 5955;
www.thegreenstheentrance.com.au
The 'all you can eat' Star Buffet

Family Restaurant offers a range of different cuisines and special kids' prices.

Mingara Recreation Club
Mingara Dr, Tumbi Umbi
(02) 4349 7799; www.mingara.com.au
There are several choices of cuisine at the club and relaxed family-friendly eating areas. The Terrace has an attached, enclosed playground so you can relax with your meal while the kids let off steam. Alternatively, take advantage of the childminding service in The Playhouse with its adventure play equipment, art and craft activities, and video games.

COFFS HARBOUR & SURROUNDS

Coffs Harbour is located 540 kilometres north of Sydney and has its own regional airport

Beaches are best in warmer months (Dec–Mar), but there are plenty of year-round activities

HIGHLIGHTS

Dorrigo National Park   *p. 66*

Muttonbird Island Nature Reserve   *p. 61*

Pet Porpoise Pool   *p. 63*

Around town

Muttonbird Island Nature Reserve
Coffs Harbour
Coffs Harbour National Park Office (02) 6652 0900; www.environment.nsw.gov.au
FREE

The sun dips towards the horizon, and you peer into the greying sky. Below your feet there are tiny rustlings from twig- and grass-lined burrows. Listen for the lonely *kooka-rooka-rah* of adult shearwaters sitting on eggs and the squeaks of newly hatched chicks waiting expectantly for food. Suddenly, your kids point excitedly upwards to darker shapes soaring against the sky – the adult birds are returning after a long day foraging, bringing home food for their mates or chicks. The birds almost skim your heads as they fly in to a wild cacophony of greeting before disappearing into their burrows.

INSIDER TIPS

- The island is accessed from the eastern end of the northern breakwall in Coffs Harbour. The walkway is 500 metres long and a return walk takes about 30 minutes. It is important not to step off the paved walkway as the ground is undermined by the birds' burrows and could easily cave in and kill or injure the birds (and you!).

- Wedge-tailed shearwaters are migratory birds. They can only be seen on the island from September to May. They come here to breed, so the activities you see will vary from courtship, to sitting on eggs, to feeding chicks (from late January), and finally to the chicks learning to fly.

- Interpretive signs begin at the start of the walkway and explain the views of the adjacent coast as well as the life cycle and habits of wedge-tailed shearwaters.

- If you plan to see the evening return of the birds to feed mates or chicks, start your visit in daylight so you can see the shallow burrows, the views, and the interpretive signs. If you plan to wait until evening, bring snacks and activities to keep the littlies occupied.

- Apart from the wedge-tailed shearwaters, you might see other seabirds that visit and breed on the island, such as sooty shearwaters, short-tailed shearwaters, lesser frigatebirds, storm petrels, crested terns, sooty oystercatchers and silver gulls.

- Bring jackets for protection from sea winds and cooler evening temperatures.

DON'T MISS

- The opportunity to join a guided tour run by the national park – it's worth phoning ahead to check times. Tours are often provided by Aboriginal guides, who explain the cultural significance of the site. According to Dreamtime legend, the moon fell into the sea here and a huge moon-man guardian kept the birds on the island for people to collect as food.

- The 360-degree view of the ocean, beaches, mountains and city from the highest point on the island. Make sure you pause here to take a breather and look around.

- Humpbacked whales passing from June to September – there's a lookout platform at the eastern end of the walkway.

FABULOUS FACTS

By mid-April, wedge-tailed shearwater chicks are so fat they can barely squeeze out of their burrows; they have actually grown bigger than their parents! The chicks need this fat to survive when their parents head north and leave them behind. The little ones have to manage without meals until they have learnt to fly. For two to three weeks they spend time out of their burrows, exercising their wings. When they can skim over the water and dive in to catch their meals of krill, squid and fish, they are ready to leave. The young birds begin their migratory flight of thousands of kilometres to South-East Asia, without any older birds to lead the way.

Kid Quest

Why is the island called Muttonbird Island?

See pp. 640–4 for the answer

Pet Porpoise Pool

Orlando St, Coffs Harbour
(02) 6659 1900;
www.dolphinmarinemagic.com.au

MID-RANGE

The Marine Magic Presentations are fun – seals riding skateboards and dolphins playing rugby – but the really unique moments are the close encounters on offer. Imagine your kids' faces when they feel a sloppy kiss from a seal or dolphin. For a magical experience, pay an extra fee and they can join the seals

Pet Porpoise Pool, Coffs Harbour

or dolphins in the water for a chance to cuddle and feed these friendly creatures and maybe even have a ride! If your kids weren't in love with dolphins before they arrived, they will be by the time they leave.

INSIDER TIPS

- There are at least two Marine Magic Presentations a day; the morning show is usually less crowded.

- Children must be 8 years old or over to swim with the seals. Sessions are limited to three people.

- To swim with dolphins, you can choose either Junior Encounter (for kids only, 6–11 years of age, must be under 160cm tall, limited to groups of four), or Family Encounter (two adults and two children aged 6–15 years).

- You are not allowed in the seal or dolphin pools if you have any open cuts or infections, and if you have beads in your hair you will need to bring a swimming cap to cover your hair.

- Apart from dolphins and seals, this venue has little penguins, which you can feed, kangaroos, emus, cockatoos and a reef tank with fish, turtles and Port Jackson sharks.

- There are picnic areas if you want to bring your own food, or you can eat at the Creekside Cafe.

DON'T MISS

- Being kissed by a seal or dolphin. Arrive 30 minutes early for the Marine Magic Presentation and you'll get your chance, then hang around after the show and you might get to pat the stars or play ball with them.

- The opportunity to swim with seals or dolphins – so book ahead!

FABULOUS FACTS

Dolphins are cetaceans, a special type of mammal. Like other mammals, they are warm-blooded, give birth to live young, provide milk for their nourishment, and breathe air. However, unlike land mammals, cetaceans spend their lives in water. All the dolphins at Pet Porpoise Pool were either found injured or were born there. When injured dolphins are brought to pool, staff try to heal them and return them to the wild unless they are unable to be fully rehabilitated.

Kid Quest

How do dolphins breathe?

See pp. 640–4 for the answer

Big Banana, Coffs Harbour

Big Banana

351 Pacific Hwy, Coffs Harbour
(02) 6652 4355; www.bigbanana.com

MID-RANGE

This Coffs Harbour icon has inflatable water slides, toboggan rides, an ice-skating rink, trike rides and a puppet shop. The World of Bananas is a high-tech audiovisual presentation, followed by a short tour of a working banana plantation.

Botanic Garden

Hardacre St, Coffs Harbour
(02) 6648 4188; www.ncrbg.com.au

FREE

Kids can test the human sundial, explore the turf maze and follow the nature trail. Don't miss the carnivorous plants and the sensory garden.

Clog Barn

215 Pacific Hwy, Coffs Harbour
(02) 6652 4633; www.clogbarn.com.au

BUDGET

Watch wooden Dutch clogs being carved (three times daily) and see a miniature Dutch village with working windmills and a train.

Kegel 9 Pin Bowling

6/380 Pacific Hwy, Coffs Harbour
(02) 6652 2068;
www.kegel9pinbowling.com.au
Open till late

MID-RANGE

This all-weather activity is similar to 10-pin bowling, but the balls are smaller and lighter, and no special shoes are needed.

Zip Circus School

All classes held at Novotel Coffs Harbour Pacific Bay Resort, Coffs Harbour
(02) 6656 0768; www.zipcircus.com.au
Open Wed–Sun; bookings essential

HIGH COST

This is a school with a difference! Children 3 years of age and over can take flying trapeze lessons or try out the bungee trampoline.

In the area

Dorrigo National Park

Dorrigo Rainforest Centre, Dome Rd, Dorrigo
(02) 6657 2309; www.environment.nsw.gov.au
FREE

The walkways at Dorrigo National Park provide a unique and breathtaking experience of a World Heritage area. Start by taking the Wonga Track from The Glade Picnic Area. Under tall, lush trees you'll venture into the heart of the rainforest where your kids can slip behind a waterfall into a rock cavern and look out through a veil of cascading water. Back at the picnic area, take the raised boardwalk which winds up into the trees, and you'll find yourselves perched among the flowers and seedpods and nesting birds. Lastly, for the highest view of all, go to the Dorrigo Rainforest Centre and take the Skywalk, a stunning boardwalk which soars 70 metres above the rainforest floor.

INSIDER TIPS

■ Before you visit, read a book on dinosaurs with your children. When you wander together through Dorrigo's ancient, primeval setting, you'll be able to imagine dinosaurs just out of sight behind the dense rainforest foliage.

■ The Glade Picnic Area is one kilometre by road from the Dorrigo Rainforest Centre. It has a large shelter and electric barbecues.

■ The walk on Wonga Track to the waterfall, Crystal Shower Falls, is 3.5 kilometres if you head back once you reach the waterfall, but longer if you keep going.

■ The boardwalks are short and easy, but if you plan to walk for any distance into the rainforest, make sure you have essentials such as food, water and suitable clothes for bushwalking. Stick to the marked tracks and walkways, and let someone know your plans before you set out.

- Be wary of stinging trees with their large, bright green leaves.
- In damp weather you might pick up a few leeches. Ask the staff at the Dorrigo Rainforest Centre how to deal with these.
- If you want to bring a picnic, The Glade has a large shelter and electric barbecues.

DON'T MISS

- Dorrigo Rainforest Centre – start your visit here. The interactive display reveals how the rainforest evolved and you can find out about some of the animals you might spot. Make sure you pick up other advice, such as safety warnings and walking maps. There's a cafe and toilet here too.

FABULOUS FACTS

Many millions of years ago, Australia was part of a larger continent called Gondwana which was down in the Antarctic Circle. When Australia broke away, and moved to a warmer part of the globe, the cool-adapted Gondwanan rainforests were reduced to a narrow strip along south-eastern Australia. In Dorrigo National Park there are still primitive plant families that have direct links with the birth and spread of flowering plants over 100 million years ago.

Kid Quest

Watch out for animals. You might see brush turkeys, swamp wallabies, red-necked wallabies, red-legged pademelons, long-nosed potoroos, or even a spotted-tail quoll.

Beaches

FREE

There are several lovely beaches in the area. Jetty Beach, inside the harbour and protected from rough tides, is popular with families, and kids love jumping off the jetty. Sawtell Beach is a patrolled beach with rockpools to explore.

Boambee Beach, Sawtell

Anywhere along the coast there can be blue bottle jellyfish (also known as Portuguese man-of-wars) in the water, so watch out for warning signs.

Bellingen Bat Island
Bellingen
www.bellingen.com/flyingfoxes
FREE

Thousands of flying foxes hang upside-down in the trees in this island in the centre of the small town of Bellingen. During the day you'll see them fanning their wings to keep cool, grooming, and tending young (from October to April). At dusk they fly away to feed. As protection from stinging nettles, mosquitoes and leeches, wear long sleeves, pants and closed shoes, and put on a hat to shield you from droppings!

Butterfly House
5 Strouds Rd, Bonville
(02) 6653 4766;
www.butterflyhouse.com.au
Open daily except Mon during school term
MID-RANGE

Enter a magical indoor rainforest alive with hundreds of fluttering butterflies – some of them might even land on you. You can learn about the butterfly life cycle and have a go at the outdoor maze.

Carobana
125 James Small Dr, Korora
(02) 6653 6051 or 1800 700 118;
www.carobana.com.au
Closed Sun
FREE

Visit this factory in a lovely rainforest setting to see where carob and honeycomb products are manufactured. There are free tastings and on Monday to Thursday mornings you are likely to see production in progress.

Honey Place
Pacific Hwy, Urunga
(02) 6655 6160; www.honeyplace.com.au
FREE

Watch the bees in their glass hive and compare the taste of different honeys. You will also find dolls, teddies and dollhouse furniture for sale here.

Nambucca Heads
Nambucca Heads
www.coffscoast.com.au
FREE

For something completely different, check out the graffitied Vee Wall Breakwater at the Nambucca River entrance. Visitors are encouraged to leave their mark on the boulders!

Raleigh Raceway
Valery Rd, The Pines, Raleigh
(02) 6655 4017;
www.raleighraceway.com.au
Phone for opening times
MID-RANGE

Drive a go-kart on a challenging circuit that climbs up and down hills, catch a ride on the Big Foot Tractor through bush and water courses, play on water slides, have a game of putt-putt golf, or paddle in the wading pool.

Valley of The Mist

Cnr Congarinni Rd North and Talarm Rd, Congarinni, near Nambucca
(02) 6568 3268;
www.valleyofthemist.com.au
Bookings essential

VARIOUS PRICES

Take a walking tour around a bush tucker farm set in pristine wetlands or tour the wetlands in a canoe. All tours include an opportunity to taste the jams, marinades and sauces made on site.

Woolgoolga Guru Nanak Sikh Temple

River St, Woolgoolga
(02) 6654 0059;
www.visitnsw.com/town/Woolgoolga.aspx
Open weekends

FREE

Take your shoes off and have a look inside this impressive exotic building. If you like Indian food, there are plenty of authentic options in town.

Accommodation

Boambee Bay Resort

8 Barber Close, Toormina
1800 028 907;
www.boambeebay.com

MID-RANGE

This affordable family resort located in the quieter Sawtell area offers one- or two-bedroom apartments. On-site activities include minigolf, kids' games room, playground and a large adventure pool (heated in winter).

Darlington Beach Holiday Park
104–134 Eggins Dr, Arrawarra
(02) 6640 7444;
www.darlingtonbeach.com.au
BUDGET TO MID-RANGE

This is a holiday experience, not just a place to stay, with organised kids' activities at most times. Adjacent to a pristine beach, only 20 minutes, drive from Coffs Harbour, the park offers a host of facilities including playground, swimming pools, waterslides, giant jumping pillow and BMX track. The villas and campsites are set in lush, sprawling grounds full of wildlife.

Emerald Beach BIG4 Holiday Park
Fisherman's Dr, Emerald Beach
(02) 6656 1521 or 1800 681 521;
ebhp.com.au
BUDGET TO MID-RANGE

This park boasts a year-round heated pool, giant jumping pillow, kids' games room, go-karts and facilities for tennis, volleyball and basketball. Choose from villas, cabins and campsites.

Novotel Pacific Bay Coffs Harbour
Cnr Pacific Hwy and Bay Dr, Coffs Harbour
(02) 6659 7000;
www.pacificbayresort.com.au
MID-RANGE

This hotel boasts a kids' club and activities, including Zip Circus School (*see* p. 65). Family rooms have kitchen and laundry facilities.

Places to eat

The Fishermen's Co-operative
69 Marina Dr, Coffs Harbour
(02) 6652 2811
Sit at an outdoor table and enjoy your freshly caught fish (and chips) while you watch the boats come in with their latest catch. From here, you can take a walk to Muttonbird Island Nature Reserve (*see* p. 61).

Greenhouse Tavern
Cnr Pacific Hwy & Bray St, Coffs Harbour
(02) 6651 5488; www.greenhousetavern. com.au
Relax in this family-friendly environment with indoor and outdoor playgrounds, computer games and even a kids' cinema centre. The extensive, reasonably priced menu has options for under-6s as well as under-12s.

PORT MACQUARIE & SURROUNDS

Port Macquarie is located 400 kilometres north of Sydney and has its own regional airport

Beaches are best in warmer months (Dec–Mar), but there are plenty of year-round activities

HIGHLIGHTS

Billabong Koala and Wildlife Park   *p. 71*

Sea Acres Rainforest Centre   *p. 72*

Timbertown   *p. 76*

Around town

Billabong Koala and Wildlife Park
61 Billabong Dr, Port Macquarie
(02) 6585 1060;
www.billabongkoala.com.au

MID-RANGE

The ranger lifts the koala off its perch. One by one, you reach out and stroke its back. The grey fur feels warm and downy. The park offers a range of other special encounters: you'll chat to a cockatoo, meet wombats, cassowaries, quolls, crocodiles, lizards and snakes, as well as exotic animals such as cute little black-handed spider monkeys. In the kangaroo enclosure, the kangaroos will come right up to you, nuzzling for food.

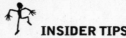

INSIDER TIPS

■ You can purchase food for feeding the kangaroos.

■ You might want to bring a picnic. There are barbecue facilities and lovely gardens with billabongs covered in water lilies and stocked with koi (Japanese fish).

■ There is also a cafe on site.

DON'T MISS

■ Presentations, feeding and keeper talks – check times when you're planning your visit. Koala patting only takes place during the koala presentations, and the black-handed spider monkey feeding time is lots of fun. On weekends and school holidays there are also reptile presentations.

FABULOUS FACTS

The rainforest depends on cassowaries to survive. These large birds eat the rainforest fruit and the seeds are excreted still intact to form new plants in the large piles of dung. Unfortunately, Australia's southern cassowaries are endangered. There are little more than 1000 left in the wild and they are only found in a couple of regions in north-eastern Australia. Most of their habitat has been destroyed by humans and many are killed by cars. They are the third-largest birds in the world (after the emu and ostrich). They can't fly, but they can swim.

Kid Quest
Which is larger, the male or the female cassowary?
See pp. 640–4 for the answer

Sea Acres Rainforest Centre
Pacific Dr, Port Macquarie
(02) 6582 3355; www.environment.nsw.gov.au

BUDGET

Imagine being able to walk along a boardwalk that leads up into a rainforest canopy, past tree ferns towering 7 metres high, and huge trees draped in flowering vines, with your kids shouting excitedly

'There's another one! There's another one!' as they spot the koalas (or the stag and elkhorn ferns) perched in the forks of the branches. The 1.3-kilometre loop passes through Sea Acres Nature Reserve, an important corridor for the Port Macquarie koala colony.

INSIDER TIPS

- The boardwalk is accessed from the Sea Acres Rainforest Centre and there is a fee to use it; the loop takes about 30 minutes to complete. Guided rainforest tours are included in the entry fee to the boardwalk, or you can take the walk on your own and read the entertaining and informative signs along the walk.

- At the visitor centre you can also buy tickets for the electronic Rainforest Exhibition and watch a film in the theatre.

- There's the Sea Acres Rainforest Cafe in the centre (*see* PLACES TO EAT, p. 80).

DON'T MISS

- Specialised Aboriginal bush tucker tours, offered on the third Saturday of each month; bookings essential.

- Shelley Beach, which is adjacent to the reserve. Keep a lookout for huge goannas.

FABULOUS FACTS

The Aboriginal Birpai people are no longer permitted to gather food in this area because it is now a reserve, but in the past this was an abundant source of food. Here, where the forest meets the sea, the Birpai hunted brush turkeys, possums and flying foxes; they used stones to create rockpool traps where they could spear fish, ate the red berries of the walking stick palm, sweetened their meals with honey from the native bee hives, and used the native ginger to flavour their food.

Kid Quest
How many koalas can you spot in the trees?

Beaches

FREE

Many of Port Macquarie's beaches are surf beaches, but the southern part of Town Beach, situated at the mouth of the Hastings River, is safe and sheltered for swimming. The section of Lighthouse Beach south of Watonga Rocks is pleasant and secluded and this is where you can go on a Camel Safari (*see below*). Other popular family beaches include the beach on the shore of Lake Cathie, Shelly Beach with its natural tidal lagoon, and Flynns Beach which has a shady picnic area.

Camel Safari

Southern end of Lighthouse Beach, Port Macquarie
0437 672 080;
www.portmacquariecamels.com.au
Sun–Fri, closes early afternoon

HIGH COST

In addition to the camel ride (which is an interesting experience in itself), you'll be introduced to the animals and find out about their behaviour and their history in Australia. Camels were imported to Australia in the 19th century and were very valuable to early explorers and settlers.

Hydro Golf and Putt-Putt

Boundary St, Port Macquarie
(02) 6583 3200; www.hydrogolf.com.au

MID-RANGE

This is one of Port Macquarie's most popular family tourist attractions. The 27-hole putt-putt course has water traps, sand bunkers and creative holes for a challenging, fun game.

Kayak tours

Port Sea Kayak, cnr Hollingsworth and Buller sts, Port Macquarie
0409 776 566; www.portkayak.com.au
Check tour times

HIGH COST

Glide through the mangroves in your kayak and spot wildlife along the way, or have fun shooting the rapids.

Koala Hospital

Lord St and Roto Pl, Port Macquarie
(02) 6584 1522;
www.koalahospital.org.au

BY DONATION

About 200 koalas are brought to the hospital every year and you can visit them in their recovery yard. They spend most of the day sleeping so the best time to visit is when they are fed at 3–3.30pm daily. At that time a carer will

also give you information about the patients. You can help support the hospital by donating through 'Adopt A Wild Koala'.

Mid North Coast Maritime Museum
William St, Port Macquarie
(02) 6583 1866
www.visitnsw.com/town/Port_Macquarie/Mid_North_Coast_Maritime_Museum/info.aspx
Closed weekends
BUDGET
Kids will enjoy the antique relics from actual shipwrecks and the scale models of ships. You start in William Street in the two pilots' cottages from 1896, then go down to the wharf to see the historic MV *Wentworth*.

Pick your own strawberries
Ricardoes Tomatoes
221 Blackmans Point Rd, Port Macquarie
(02) 6585 0663; www.ricardoes.com
FREE (PAY FOR STRAWBERRIES YOU PICK)
As well as picking your own strawberries, you can take a free guided farm tour (weekdays at 11am) to see how the hydroponic tomatoes and strawberries are grown.

Port City Wave Bowl
159 Hastings River Drive, Port Macquarie
(02) 6583 2238;
www.portcitybowl.com.au
Open till late
MID-RANGE
This bowling venue is ideal for families – try Bumper Bowling with brightly coloured lightweight balls for kids.

Port Macquarie Astronomical Association
Rotary Park, Port Macquarie
0403 683 394; www.pmobs.org.au
Open Sun and Wed nights, phone for presentation time
BUDGET
There are not many observatories as easy to access as this one, right in centre of town. The one-hour presentation (just the right length for kids) begins indoors with a tour of the night sky using spectacular images of astronomical objects. It concludes outside with the opportunity to view the night sky through the observatory's telescope.

Roto House
Macquarie Nature Reserve,
Port Macquarie
(02) 6584 2180; www.hastings.nsw.gov.au/www/html/969-roto-house.asp
Open Mon–Sat; closes 1pm on Sat
BY DONATION
This historic house is surrounded by the tranquil Macquarie Nature Reserve, ideal for picnics. It's near the Koala Hospital (*see facing page*).

St Thomas' Church
Hay St, Port Macquarie
(02) 6584 1033
Check open hours
FREE
Port Macquarie district was built by convicts and this church from

the 1820s gives a real insight into a fascinating past. You can see the high sides around some of the pews, designed to separate the convict worshippers from the free families. The convicts were marched into church each week under guards who carried fixed bayonets. Kids will have fun looking for the fingerprints and other marks left on the handmade bricks by the convicts who laid them. Lime for the mortar was made by burning oyster shells from Limeburners Creek. The square nails and spikes were forged by female convicts.

Whale-watching cruise

Dolphin and Whale Watch Centre floating ticket office, 1 Short Street Wharf, Port Macquarie 1300 555 890; www.cruiseadventures.com.au Seasonal operation; bookings essential
MID-RANGE TO HIGH COST

With only 12 passengers to a boat, everyone gets a good view on these cruises. Humpback whales can be sighted from May to the end of November, and dolphins can be seen all year round.

In the area

Ride on a stage coach at Timbertown, Wauchope

Timbertown

2325 Oxley Hwy, Wauchope (02) 6586 1940; www.timbertown.com.au
MID-RANGE

When your kids enter Timbertown, they will step into a bygone era when the streets resonated with the sounds of harnesses clinking, whips cracking and horses whinnying, and the air was filled with the smell of sawn wood. In this recreated village they'll find stables, wood-craftsmen and blacksmiths at work, a lolly shop and a working steam sawmill.

INSIDER TIPS

- Timbertown is set amongst 87 acres of natural blackbutt forest. You can take a forest tour on a wagon drawn by Clydesdale horses.

- There is a kids' playground with cubby houses, including a cubby in a sawn-off tree trunk.

- When you want a break from historic sights, there are farm animals to visit and pat.

- A large number of retailers sell artwork, jewellery and crafts in the Timbertown grounds.

- At the time of writing this book, Timbertown has been taken over by new management and there may be changes.

DON'T MISS

- The bullock demonstrations where you can see how the bullockies harnessed and controlled the teams of massive beasts as they manoeuvred the long, unwieldy drays loaded with logs.

- The miniature train ride through a farmyard.

- Joining in an olden-days class in the 1880s schoolhouse – you can have a go at writing with a slate or dip pen.

FABULOUS FACTS

Before European settlers arrived in this area and cut down the trees for timber, the land was covered in forest. This forest supplied most of the things the local Aboriginal people needed. They hunted animals that lived in the forest for food. They made canoes by gathering up the ends of sheets of bark, and stood up to propel themselves along with poles. They made huts from branches arched over to form a dome. A cradle for a new baby was made by hollowing out a branch and lining it with soft layers of tea tree bark.

Bellrowan Valley Horse Riding

*Crows Rd, Beechwood via Wauchope
(02) 6587 5227;
www.bellrowanvalley.com.au
Bookings essential*

HIGH COST

One- or two-hour trail rides are
available for any level of rider.
Trails are through beautiful
scenery and include morning or
afternoon tea.

Ellenborough Falls

*Bulga Plateau, Elands
(02) 6592 5444 or 1800 801 522*

FREE

At Ellenborough Falls water
plunges 200 vertical metres into
a magnificent gorge. You can see
the waterfall from the viewing
platform near the carpark or
follow a timber walkway to the
base of the falls.

En route from Sydney

Kayaking in Myall Lakes National Park

Myall Lakes National Park

*(02) 6591 0300;
www.environment.nsw.gov.au*

BUDGET

This significant wetland is
popular with waterbirds and
humans alike. Play on the
beaches or hire a boat and
explore the lakes in one of the
most visited parks in New South
Wales. On Stony Creek Road (off
the Pacific Highway, just north of
Bulahdelah) you will find The
Grandis, a flooded gum that is
an incredible 76 metres high,
reputedly the tallest tree in
the state.

Accommodation

Flynns Beach Resort
68 Pacific Dr, Port Macquarie
1800 833 338;
www.flynnsbeachresort.com.au

BUDGET

This sub-tropical hideaway is just three minutes walk from Flynns Beach. Kids will love the gardens and natural creek where they'll find koalas, ducks, turtles, eastern water dragons and chatty cockatoos. The resort offers spacious, two-bedroom, self-contained apartments. Facilities include picnic and barbecue areas, two swimming pools with shallow toddler sections, a full-size tennis court and kids' activity area.

Ki-ea Beachside Apartments
67 William St, Port Macquarie
(02) 6584 6466;
www.ki-ea.com.au

MID-RANGE

This could be your perfect location, halfway between town and beach. The self-contained apartments with up to four bedrooms are modern and spacious. Facilities include a stunning roof deck, barbecue and heated pool, and kids receive small free gifts such as activity books on arrival.

Kookaburra Cottage Farmstay
564 Marsh Rd, Bobs Farm, Port Stephens
(02) 4982 6379;
www.nswfarmstay.com.au

BUDGET TO MID-RANGE

If you are driving to Port Macquarie from Sydney, you might want to stop here overnight, arriving in the afternoon so the kids can have fun with the animal feeding. There are chickens, calves, a donkey, goats, alpacas, sheep and ducks. Accommodation is in self-contained cottages or cabins.

Port Pacific Resort
14 Clarence St, Port Macquarie
(02) 6583 8099;
www.portpacific.com.au

MID-RANGE

Located in the central business district, these self-contained, serviced apartments have up to three rooms and are close to all amenities. The resort itself has a compact tennis court, heated swimming pool and kids' wading pool, playground, table tennis and pool tables, video games, library and collection of board-games.

Places to eat

Bay Street Brasserie
1 Bay St, Port Macquarie
(02) 6580 2300; portmacquarie.
panthers.com.au
Open for lunch and dinner every day, this venue has a kids' menu and even offers child-minding. Eat lunch outdoors and watch for the blue-tongue lizards lounging in the sun.

Hire a barbecue boat
Jordan's Boating Centre and Holiday Park, McInherney Close, Port Macquarie
(02) 6583 1005; www.jordans.com.au
For something fun and different, hire a barbecue boat and sail while you cook!

Jumbos Playland
17 Merrigal Rd, Port Macquarie
(02) 6581 0909;
www.jumbosplayland.com.au
Have breakfast or lunch in the cafe and let the kids burn off energy in the large indoor play centre which includes Tiny Town, ride-in cars, a huge bouncing slide and a three-storey climbing maze.

Sea Acres Rainforest Cafe
Pacific Dr, Port Macquarie
(02) 6582 3355;
www.environment.nsw.gov.au
Have a relaxed lunch among the bangalow palms in the Sea Acres Rainforest Reserve, accompanied by birds, goannas and brush turkeys.

SSS BBQ Barns Steakhouse
74 Clarence St, Port Macquarie
(02) 6583 2239; www.sssbbq.com.au
This family-friendly venue is decorated like a saloon from an old cowboys' movie.

SOUTHERN HIGHLANDS & SOUTH COAST

The region begins about 85 kilometres south of Sydney

Suits driving holidays from Sydney

Beaches are best in warmer months (Dec–Mar), but there are plenty of year-round activities

HIGHLIGHTS

Booderee National Park   ***p. 81***

Coomee Nulunga Cultural Tours   ***p. 83***

Illawarra Fly Treetop Walk   ***p. 88***

On the coast

Booderee National Park
Jervis Bay Rd, Jervis Bay
(02) 4443 0977; www.booderee.gov.au

BUDGET

Standing on the ruins of the Cape St George Lighthouse with the waves rolling in below, you experience an eerie sense of the past – of the many ships wrecked here and the sad stories of lives lost (*see* FABULOUS FACTS p. 82). Suddenly a spout of vapour shoots out of the sea and the mood changes. 'Look! Whales!' You all peer at the water, shrieking with excitement every time you see another blow or glimpse that famous view of a tail raised out of the water.

INSIDER TIPS

■ Stop at the visitor centre at the entrance and find out about all the things you can see and do in addition to whale-watching.

- Green Patch is great for birdwatching. Look for crimson rosellas, kookaburras, king parrots and wood ducks. You can also ride bikes here.

- If you are quiet on the walking trails, you might see wallabies, grey kangaroos echidnas and lizards.

- Murrays Beach rock platform is a good base for snorkelling.

- Booderee has campsites so you can stay overnight.

- Watch out for spiders, snakes and ticks.

DON'T MISS

- The chance to see humpback and southern right whales heading north (June–July) or south (September–November). Looking out from the lighthouse you might see some of the following whale antics: a blow (a 2–3 metre vapour cloud), a breach (the whale rearing out of the water), a pectoral fin slap (flippers slapping the water), a fluke-up dive (the tail lifting so you see the flukes underneath) or a tail slap.

- Booderee Botanic Gardens inside the park, where you can find out about local Aboriginal use of plants for bush tucker or medicine. Check the closing times so you don't get locked in!

FABULOUS FACTS

When the Cape St George Lighthouse began operating in 1860 it was actually the cause of numerous shipwrecks – it was in the wrong place and ships could not see its light! This was also an unlucky place for the lightkeepers' families. Several of their children died from illnesses, one of them was killed falling off a cliff and another was accidentally shot. After 38 years, the lighthouse was blown up and replaced by another in a different location.

Kid Quest

Who is buried in the grave in the Green Patch camping area?

See pp. 640–4 for the answer

Coomee Nulunga Cultural Tours

Ulladulla

(02) 4455 5883

Tours by request (minimum of four people)

MID-RANGE

Your kids will be fascinated as an Aboriginal guide leads you through the bush and shares the knowledge of the Murramarang people.

He will tell local Dreamtime stories and explain how some of the surrounding plants can be eaten or used for medicine. When you arrive on the beach, the past will come to life as you see a huge shell midden,

Coomee Nulunga Cultural Tours, Ulladulla

and realise this was created over thousands of years by people living and eating here and tossing their scraps onto the same pile. Your guide will show you hunting tools, including boomerangs and authentic ancient axe heads and spear points.

INSIDER TIPS

- The tour takes up to two hours.

- Explore more Aboriginal cultural and historic areas on your own by visiting the Murramarang Aboriginal Area (*see* p. 86).

DON'T MISS

- The gallery you are given the chance to visit on the tour. It's an opportunity to see local arts and crafts, and the small museum has indigenous artefacts from around the world.

FABULOUS FACTS

The first Aboriginal people sighted by Captain James Cook on his famous voyage to Australia in 1770 were the Murramarang people. In the 1820s, Europeans came to settle in the area and gradually destroyed many traditional sacred sites and food sources. However, Aboriginal cultural practices survived, and still continue today.

Australia's Industry World Port Kembla

BlueScope Steel, Northgate Entrance,
Springhill Rd, Coniston
(02) 4275 7023; www.aiw.org.au
Entry by tour only; two days a week
Bookings essential
Minimum age 10 years
MID-RANGE

Public tours of the Port Kembla Steelworks are a real eye-opener. You'll see molten iron being tapped from the blast furnaces and watch the fiery inferno transform molten iron into steel. All visitors must wear long pants and flat-heeled, fully enclosed shoes. Safety equipment is provided.

Batemans Bay

FREE

The bay has various lovely, clean beaches, some with shallow waters suitable for small kids. If you're here around noon, visit Pelican Point, a rocky outcrop on the banks of the Clyde River, opposite Rafters Restaurant, and you'll see wild pelicans coming in for a free feed. At Pebbly Beach in Murramarang National Park, just north of Batemans Bay, you share the beach with kangaroos!

Birdland Animal Park

55 Beach Rd, Batemans Bay
(02) 4472 5364;

www.birdlandanimalpark.com.au
MID-RANGE

It's not often that you get the chance to cuddle a wombat, but at Birdland Animal Park you can get up close and pat not only wombats, but koalas and snakes as well, if you fancy the idea! There are 50 different Australian animal species to meet and there is also a deer who thinks he's a kangaroo.

Bombo Beach and Headland

Just north of the Kiama township,
eastern side of Princes Hwy
FREE

The spectacular rock formations here, created by basalt quarrying in the 1880s and 1900s, could be mistaken for a lunar landscape. Watch for whales from the headland between May and September. Warning: the water here is only for accomplished surfers and is not suitable for children.

Dolphin, whale and seal cruises

www.dolphincruises.com.au
MID-RANGE TO HIGH COST

In the right season, Jervis Bay offers some of the best whale-watching experiences in Australia, and all year round you can see dolphins or seals. There are various cruise options.

Fleet Air Museum

489A Albatross Rd, Nowra
(02) 4424 1920; www.navy.gov.au/Fleet_
Air_Arm_Museum

BUDGET

This terrific display of heritage and modern aircraft covers the history of the air arm of the Australian Navy from World War I to the present.

Fossils at Black Head

End of Stafford St, Gerroa

FREE

Park in the carpark and follow the track to the rock platform below. *Take care*! The waves can be dangerous. There are lots of tree fossils in the rock, and if you look carefully, you'll find fossils of small sea creatures as well. Breaking or removing rocks is forbidden.

Futureworld

Northcliffe Dr, Warrawong
(02) 4274 2939; www.futureworld.org.au
Closed Fri to Sun

MID-RANGE

While kids have fun playing with the interactive activities and displays, they'll learn about renewable energy, greenhouse gas reduction and water conservation.

Historical Aircraft Restoration Society

Illawarra Regional Airport, cnr Airport
Rd and Boomerang Ave, Albion Park Rail
(02) 4257 4333; www.hars.org.au

MID-RANGE

In this interesting corner of the airport, historic aircraft are restored to flying condition. There is a museum of historic aircraft and the kids will have fun clambering on board some classic old planes.

Jamberoo Action Park

Jamberoo Rd, Jamberoo (near Kiama)
(02) 4236 0114; www.jamberoo.net
Seasonal operation; check opening times

HIGH COST

This theme park has water slides, bob-sled, a chair lift, child-size racing cars and minigolf.

Jervis Bay

FREE

The beaches of this magnificent bay are supposed to have the whitest sands in world. The clear blue waters are a marine park where you can snorkel, learn to surf, or cruise with the dolphins and whales (*see facing page*).

Kayaking

VARIOUS LOCATIONS

There are several beautiful locations for kayaking or canoeing, such as Jervis Bay or the Kangaroo Valley River.

Various companies offer hire and tours, including Kangaroo Valley Tourist Park which caters for children aged 5 and over; www.canoeandkayakhirekangaroovalley.com.au

Kiama Blowhole, Kiama

Kiama Blowhole
Blowhole Point Rd, Kiama
Kiama Visitor Centre (02) 4232 3322;
www.kiama.com.au/pages/blowhole
FREE

Just a short distance from the town centre, you can see a spectacular jet of water shoot up from the Kiama Blowhole when the weather is right – usually when there is a south to south-easterly breeze.

Lady Denman Heritage Complex
Cnr Dent St and Woollamia Rd, Huskisson
(02) 4441 5675;
www.ladydenman.asn.au
BUDGET

There's something here for everyone. After taking a look at the historic *Lady Denman* ferry, you can browse the shipping and Aboriginal culture exhibits in the museum, peer into a pond to spot the fish, stroll along a mangrove boardwalk looking for crabs, and see how a boat is constructed in the boatshed.

Lands Edge Surf School
Beaches near Gerroa and Shellharbour
(02) 4234 3278; www.landsedge.com.au
Bookings essential
HIGH COST

Surf lessons are run on weekends and during school holidays. There are classes that are suitable for children 6 years of age and over.

Murramarang Aboriginal Area
40 km north of Batemans Bay, via Murramarang Rd, off the Princes Hwy at Termeil
(02) 4887 7270;
www.environment.nsw.gov.au
FREE

The Murramarang Aboriginal Area has a 1.5-kilometre/two-hour self-guided loop walking track. Park at the Sandmine carpark, just north of the Racecourse Beach Caravan Park and south of Bawley Point. Follow the sand track east towards the coast for about 800 metres to the beginning of the Murramarang Aboriginal Area walking track. The highlight of the walk is the huge midden on the beach and there is signage explaining its significance.

Nowra Wildlife Park
23 Rockhill Rd, North Nowra
(02) 4421 3949;
www.nowrawildlifepark.com.au
MID-RANGE
See over 100 species of native Australian animals, birds and reptiles in beautiful native bushland on the banks of the Shoalhaven River. There are animal shows throughout the day, including dingo and crocodile feeding, and opportunities to pat koalas or feed kangaroos. Campsites are also available (*see* ACCOMMODATION p. 93).

Timezone Funland
Floor 1, Rowens Arcade, 93 Princes Hwy, Ulladulla
(02) 4454 3220; www.funland.com.au
Open till late Fri, Sat and school holidays
PAY AS YOU PLAY
Three floors of fun for all ages, including little kiddie rides, air hockey and high-tech video games. Try your shooting skills in the laser skirmish zone, or have a go at racing, skiing or bowling on the high-tech simulators.

Valhalla Horse Riding
Falls Rd, Falls Creek
(02) 4447 8320;
www.valhallahorseriding.com.au
Bookings essential
HIGH COST
Have a gentle pony ride on a lead, or take a ride into the bush where you might see native Australian animals and birds. You can also have a go at archery or canoeing.

Wollongong Science Centre and Planetarium, NSW
University of Wollongong, Northfields Ave, Wollongong
(02) 4286 5000; sciencecentre.uow.edu.au
MID-RANGE
There's never a dull moment at this interactive science centre: journey through a virtual coal mine, dig for fossils, tremble at the sight of roaring dinosaurs, or get immersed in a spectacular planetarium show filmed in full-dome. While in Wollongong, have a peek at the trompe l'oeil painting on the rear of the town hall.

Special event

South Coast Children's Festival
Sept/Oct
www.ics.org.au/sccf
For three days Wollongong offers live entertainment, with roving performers, and art and music workshops. The festival's theme is 'inspiring children's creativity' and past activities have included making musical instruments out of rubbish and working with dinosaur puppets. It's aimed at babies and children up to 12 years of age.

Southern Highlands_

Illawarra Fly Treetop Walk, Robertson

Illawarra Fly Treetop Walk

182 Knights Hill Rd, Robertson
(02) 4885 1010 or 1300 362 881;
www.illawarrafly.com

MID-RANGE

A little hand clutches yours as you climb the walkway together up into the treetops. There are gaps in the grill under your feet and you can see right through to the forest floor, a terrifying 25 metres below. The walkway sways slightly and you glance sideways. The child walking next to you is wearing a scared, but exhilarated, expression. From the viewing platform you can see right over the valley to Lake Illawarra and the South Pacific Ocean. But your companion tugs your hand. Knights Tower beckons, 45 metres high, with a staircase winding all the way to the top...

INSIDER TIPS

- The Illawarra Fly Treetop Walk is 1500 metres long and takes 45 minutes to an hour to complete. You travel from ground level up through the trees right to the top of the forest canopy so you experience all levels of a warm temperate rainforest.

- The walkway is open in all weathers. Dampness and mist add an element of mystery to the experience.

- The best time to see animals is early or late in the day; sunrise guided walks are available.

- Wear suitable shoes for walking on a grid.

- There is a cafe on site.

- If your kids enjoy unusual train trips, you can arrive on the heritage Cockatoo Run from Sydney or Wollongong (high cost); 1300 653 801; www.3801limited.com.au

DON'T MISS

- The interpretive signs along the walk – find out more about the view and the surrounding flora and fauna.

- The birds hiding in the trees. You'll hear them, but can you spot them? Stand still and watch for a tiny coloured flash from a crimson rosella. You might also see yellow-tailed black cockatoos, kookaburras, white-naped honeyeaters or eastern yellow robins.

FABULOUS FACTS

The epiphytes (small ferns, orchids, mosses and lichens) you see growing on the trees do not harm the plants they grow on. In fact, they can grow on rocks as well as on plants. Epiphytes obtain nutrients from organic debris, such as dead leaves. They can even get nutrients from the air! On the tree trunks you will also see vines and creepers climbing up towards the sun.

Kid Quest
Can you spot the wombat burrow?

All Aboard Braemar Model Railway
68–72 Old Hume Hwy, Braemar
(02) 4871 2966; www.highlandsnsw.com.
au/allaboard
BUDGET
Young (and old!) train buffs will be transfixed by these detailed miniature worlds with working trains. For those who can't resist, you can purchase your own model trains sets here as well.

Berrima Court House Museum
Wilshire and Arglye sts, Berrima
(02) 4877 1505; www.berrimacourthouse.
org.au
BUDGET

This courthouse saw trials of murderers, bushrangers and cattle thieves from the 1840s to the 1870s. In World War I it housed German prisoners of war. Get a feeling of the building's history from the lifelike models and audiovisual display.

Berrima District Museum
Market St, Berrima
(02) 4877 1130; www.berrimadistrict
historicalsociety.org.au
Open weekends, public and school
holidays
BUDGET
This small country museum has changing displays of items related

to the history of Berrima, including clothes, furniture, photos, and items made by German prisoners of war in World War I.

Fitzroy Falls, Morton National Park

Nowra Rd, Fitzroy Falls
(02) 4887 7270; www.highlandsnsw.com.
au/nature/fitzroy_falls.html

FREE

The cascading waters of the Fitzroy Falls are breathtaking. Take a 100-metre boardwalk along a creek, through restored native bushland, to a lookout at the top of the falls.

Harper's Mansion

9 Wilkinson St, Berrima
(02) 4877 2310;
www.harpersmansion.com
Open weekends and public holidays;
check opening times

BUDGET

This furnished historic Georgian country house is set in large, picturesque grounds complete with a garden maze.

The International Cricket Hall of Fame

St Jude St, Bowral
(02) 4862 1247;
www.internationalcrickethall.com

MID-RANGE

This hall of fame encompasses aspects of cricket from all around the world. Learn about the game, the history and the greatest players through interactive touch-screens. The Bradman Museum of

Cricket is incorporated into the site, and die-hard cricket fans will want to stop here for a dose of cricketing memorabilia.

Kangaroo Valley Pioneer Museum Park

2029 Moss Vale Rd, Kangaroo Valley
(02) 4465 1306;
www.kangaroovalleymuseum.com
Check opening times

BUDGET

This museum has a variety of structures on display, including a typical 19th-century farmhouse, a dairy, a forge and a double-seater outside toilet, but a highlight for kids is crossing a deep gorge on a 72-metre-long suspension bridge that sways underfoot.

Minnamurra Rainforest Centre,

Budderoo National Park, Minnamurra Falls Rd (Tourist Drive 9), via Jamberoo
(02) 4236 0469;
www.environment.nsw.gov.au

BUDGET

Choose from a network of paved tracks and elevated boardwalks that lead you into a rainforest where creeks trickle, birds call, waterfalls tumble and thick strangler figs wrap around the trees.

Mogo Zoo
222 Tomakin Rd, Mogo
(02) 4474 4930; www.mogozoo.com.au
MID-RANGE

This wonderful privately owned zoo prides itself on breeding endangered animals. See over 200 animals representing more than 42 rare and exotic species, including snow leopards and pygmy marmosets. There are keeper talks and sessions during the day, and intimate animal encounters are available for those who are 12 years old and over (extra cost).

Neeny's Playhouse
Unit 1, 227 Old Hume Hwy, Mittagong
(02) 4871 3750
Closed Mon

BUDGET

Looking for a wet weather venue for your under-12s? This indoor play centre has a mini climbing wall and jumping castle. There is a separate toddler area and a cafe.

Original Gold Rush Colony
Cnr Annett La and James St, Mogo
(02) 4474 2123;
www.goldrushcolony.com.au
MID-RANGE

At this recreation of an old gold-rush town, you can pan for gold, explore a mine tunnel, visit a diggers' camp, watch craftspeople at work, or just picnic by the lake. There are four informative guided tours daily.

Wombeyan Caves
Wombeyan Caves Rd, Wombeyan Karst
Conservation Reserve
(02) 4843 5976;
www.thesouthernhighlands.com.au
SOME CAVES ARE FREE ENTRY

There are several spectacular limestone caves in this reserve, and they can be viewed by both guided and self-guided tours. Access is by a rather scary, winding dirt road. There are bushwalks and picnic areas in the surrounding reserve, and a gorge where you can swim in summer.

Stalactite formations at Wombeyan Caves, Wombeyan Karst Conservation Reserve

Places to eat

In addition to the following, try one of the many local clubs for reasonably priced, casual dining.

Shellharbour Fish and Chips
5 Addison St, Shellharbour
(02) 4296 5640
For an alfresco meal in summer, buy some takeaway and eat by the water.

Trevi Fountain
221 Kinghorne St, Nowra
(02) 4423 0285
This Italian restaurant offers plenty of kids' favourites. Expect big serves and lots of variety.

Accommodation

Booderee National Park
Jervis Bay Rd, Jervis Bay
(02) 4443 0977; www.booderee.gov.au
BUDGET
Green Patch camping area has unpowered tent and caravan sites with toilets and hot showers. *See* ON THE COAST for information on the national park.

Cedars Cottages Farm Stay
Bunkers Hill Rd, Kangaroo Valley
(02) 4465 1147; www.cedarscottages.com
HIGH COST
This working farm offers plenty to see and do. Kids can collect eggs and help with the draught horses. You can also follow bush tracks to spot echidnas, lyrebirds, wallabies, parrots, platypus, kookaburras, wombats, kangaroos and wedge-tail eagles. Families can stay in Misty Glen cottage (accommodates four) or The Homestead (accommodates eight).

Green Patch
Vincentia (near Jervis Bay)
www.stayz.com.au/49157
BUDGET DEALS FOR ONE-WEEK STAYS
Not to be confused with the Green Patch camping ground at Booderee National Park (*see* p. 81), this three-bedroom, two-bathroom holiday home accommodates up to eight people and is walking distance to the beach. The large yard is fenced and has a child-size table and chairs and toddler wading pool. Inside, you'll find a portacot, play pen, baby monitor, highchair, bath seat, baby bouncer, change table and even a microwave steriliser, as well as toys and an Xbox for

older kids. There is even a collection of beach gear for your use! There is a minimum stay of two nights.

Nan Tien Temple

Berkeley Rd, Berkeley (near Wollongong)
(02) 4272 0600; www.nantien.org.au

MID-RANGE

Stay a night in the grounds of Nan Tien, the largest Buddhist temple in the Southern Hemisphere. Pilgrim Lodge overlooks a lotus pond, the Temple, and peaceful gardens. There are family rooms available. While there, you can take part in a guided tour of the Temple and experience the drum and bell ceremony.

Novotel Wollongong Hotel Northbeach

2–14 Cliff Rd, North Wollongong
(02) 4224 3111;
www.novotelnorthbeach.com.au

MID-RANGE TO HIGH COST

The hotel rooms are spacious here. If your kids will share a double bed, you can fit a family of four in one room. Otherwise, ask for a half-price family deal on a second room. Kids' club activities are offered over the summer holidays. There is a pool on site and the beach is just over the road.

Nowra Wildlife Park

23 Rockhill Rd, North Nowra
(02) 4421 3949; www.nowrawildlifepark.
com.au/camping.html

BUDGET

Looking for a slightly different experience? Camp in the wildlife park and wake up to the early-morning sounds of animals (*see* ON THE COAST). Facilities include toilet blocks with hot showers, and an on-site cafe for a break from cooking. There is a river on site.

Parma Farm

Parma Rd, Falls Creek
(02) 4447 8098;
www.parmaescapes.com.au

BUDGET

Good central location for touring the area. Choose from a variety of self-contained historic cottages in a farm setting. Kids can ride bikes on the farm roads, paddle a canoe, catch yabbies and collect eggs from the hens.

En route from Sydney

Sri Venkateswara Temple

Temple Rd, Helensburgh
(02) 4294 9233; www.svtsydney.org
Phone for opening times

FREE

This is a huge, magnificent Hindu temple. If you are lucky, you might catch one of the beautiful festivals.

Sydney Tramway Museum

Princes Hwy, Sutherland
(02) 9542 3646;
www.sydneytramwaymuseum.com.au
Open Wed till mid-afternoon, Sun and public holidays

MID-RANGE

Trams operated in Sydney from 1861 to 1961. In the museum you can see some of these old Sydney trams – there's even a prison tram used for transport between Long Bay Gaol and Darlinghurst Court House.

Sydney Tramway Museum, Sutherland

WESTERN PLAINS

Dubbo is located 400 kilometres north-west of Sydney via Bathurst, Orange and Parkes; accessible by air and rail

Suits short stays or driving holidays from Sydney

Hot in summer (Dec–Feb), but can be cold, foggy and wet in winter

HIGHLIGHTS

Old Dubbo Gaol **p. 95**

Wellington Caves **p. 96**

Western Plains Zoo **p. 98**

Around Dubbo

Old Dubbo Gaol
90 Macquarie St, Dubbo
(02) 6801 4460; www.olddubbogaol.com.au

MID-RANGE

How would your kids like to meet a ghost? Old Dubbo Gaol's animatronic displays, with their full-size models of prisoners, guards and the ghost of a hanged man, bring the terrible living conditions of the 19th-century gaol to life. You'll see a prisoner trying to escape over the wall, the hangman's scaffold and noose, and lots of authentic and rare gaol artefacts. You can even go inside the solitary confinement cell, close the door, and see what it was like being locked up in the pitch dark!

Old Dubbo Gaol, Dubbo

INSIDER TIPS

■ Pick up a kids' Super Sleuth activity pack on the way in.

■ The tours of the prison are self guided, but there is plenty of information around to help you gain an insight into the penal system of the 1800s.

■ Arrive 15 minutes early for the theatrical displays (*see* DON'T MISS *below*) to make sure you get seats.

DON'T MISS

■ The live theatrical performances which make you feel as if you have gone back in time and joined the unhappy criminals in gaol! Phone ahead or check the website to find out days and times for these shows.

■ The family twilight tours, which are two hours of spooky fun. These are very popular so phone ahead to book.

FABULOUS FACTS

There were eight men hanged at Old Dubbo Gaol. One of the most notorious, Jacky Underwood, lived as an outlaw for several months in early 1900, rampaging and murdering several people before he was eventually captured. Underwood was involved in the Breelong Massacre, which famous Australian author Thomas Keneally used as the basis for his novel *The Chant of Jimmy Blacksmith*.

Kid Quest

How did 'Nosey Bob the Hangman' lose his nose?
See pp. 640–4 for the answer

Wellington Caves

Caves Rd, Wellington
(02) 6845 1733 or 1800 621 614; www.visitwellington.com.au
Entry by tour only

MID-RANGE

Join a tour of Gaden Cave and enter a natural fairyland filled with sparkling calcite crystals. On a tour of Cathedral Cave, you'll be in awe of the giant limestone formation that towers above like a three-storey building. Before the Phosphate Mine tour your guide hands out hard hats and the kids pull them on, giggling at the way everyone looks. It's time to descend into the darkness of the restored historic mine, to marvel at the tunnels that humans have carved deep into the earth, and to wonder what it was like to work down here day after day.

INSIDER TIPS

- Each tour takes about one hour.

- The caves are quite airy, with fresh air circulating from the entrances. Bring jackets as it might be cooler inside the caves.

- You will need to climb more than a hundred steps in and out to reach the caves, whereas the Phosphate Mine is reached without steps.

- Snacks are available in the Wellington Caves kiosk.

DON'T MISS

- The secrets hidden in the Phosphate Mine. Peer carefully among the pick marks and drill holes left in the walls by the miners. Can you see anything that looks like a bone? If you do, it might be the remains of a Diprotodon or giant wombat, the largest known marsupial that ever lived (*see* FABULOUS FACTS *below*).

FABULOUS FACTS

Diprotodons were still roaming Australia when the Aboriginal people arrived, but they became extinct about 20 000 years ago. They were hairy, and a similar shape to the modern wombat, but hundreds of times the size, being about 3.8 metres long, 1.7 metres high and weighing 2800 kilograms! They probably fed on shrubs and consumed about 100 kilograms of food a day. Australia had other megafauna including some that looked like kangaroos and koalas.

Kid Quest
While you're in the caves and the mine, keep your eyes peeled for threatened bent-wing bats.

Western Plains Zoo, Dubbo

Western Plains Zoo
Obley Rd, Dubbo
(02) 6881 1400;
www.taronga.org.au/western-plains-zoo.aspx
HIGH COST

Imagine your kids' faces as a giraffe leans towards them, long tongue lolling, and eats right out of their hands. At this wonderfully interactive zoo you can feed giraffes, shake paws with kangaroos, pat a huge Galapagos tortoise and rub the tummy of a wombat. There are no cages, only natural unobtrusive barriers, such as water or deep ravines. The zoo covers a vast area, and as you look at elephants, rhinoceroses, and tigers roaming almost freely, and watch monkeys swinging from island to island on the lake, you feel as if you are on an African safari not inside a zoo.

INSIDER TIPS

■ Ticket price includes two days' entry, so don't rush your visit. Watch out for special offers for free kids' entrance to the zoo, sometimes available on the website or around the town of Dubbo.

■ The zoo is so vast you will want to drive your car around, or hire a bike or electric buggy (available near the information centre). On a very hot day, an air-conditioned car might be the most comfortable option; otherwise the other modes of transport are lots of fun. On busy days the buggies 'sell out' early. Remember to bring bottles of water if you are riding bikes.

■ The animals are more alert in the morning. Later in the day, especially in hot weather, many of them laze around, seeking shade under trees or at the back of their enclosures, and might be hard to see.

■ If kids want a break from the animals, there's a fun playground as well.

■ Bring your own picnic if you don't want to pay the high kiosk prices.

DON'T MISS

■ Keeper talks and feeding times – check the website to plan your visit around these. Kids especially enjoy seeing the otters and the apes feed. Note: there is a small extra cost for the giraffe feeding.

FABULOUS FACTS

Western Plains Zoo is participating in the National Recovery Plan for malleefowl. These ground-nesting birds are very vulnerable to predators and habitat loss. They are also incredibly hard working. The male malleefowl spends 10 months constructing a huge earthen nest, then in September he digs a special chamber in it for the female to lay her eggs. Every few days she goes inside and lays an egg until she has laid as many as 35 eggs! Instead of either bird sitting on the eggs to keep them warm, the male keeps the earth nest at a constant 35 degrees Celsius for seven weeks. The chicks hatch inside the mound and immediately have to start working hard to dig their way out!

Kid Quest
What colour is a giraffe's tongue?
See pp. 640–4 for the answer

Dubbo Observatory
17L Camp Rd, Dubbo
(02) 6885 3022; us.sydney.com/town/
Dubbo/Dubbo_Observatory/info.aspx
Open evenings only; seasonal
opening times
MID-RANGE

The one-and-a-half-hour tour begins with an audiovisual display, and then you go outside to use the high-tech telescopes. From this location, the sky is spectacular. You should see the Milky Way, planets, including Jupiter and its moons, and maybe some shooting stars.

Dundullimal Homestead
23L Obley Rd, Dubbo
(02) 6884 9984;
www.nsw.nationaltrust.org.au
Open Tues–Thurs
BUDGET

This restored 1840s building is possibly the oldest slab house still in existence in Australia. The property also includes stables, outhouses, extensive gardens and farm animals.

Elston Park
Cnr Gipps and Cobra sts, Dubbo
(02) 6801 4000

FREE

Enjoy a bit of water play here with a water cannon and tipping buckets.

Traintasia
13L Yarrandale Rd, Dubbo
(02) 6884 9944
Open Mon–Sat; open Sun during school holidays

BUDGET

This interactive, extremely detailed model railway display is adjacent to a hobby shop.

Western Plains Riding Centre
Merrilea Rd, Dubbo
(02) 6884 3155
Bookings essential

HIGH COST

Take a trail ride on a gentle horse.

Around Bathurst

Australian Fossil and Mineral Museum
224 Howick St, Bathurst
(02) 6331 5511;
www.somervillecollection.com.au
Open daily, closes mid afternoon on Sun

BUDGET

Dinosaur lovers will want to explore this terrific collection that includes fossilised dinosaur eggs and the only complete tyrannosaurus rex skeleton in

Australia. There is also a sparkling array of crystals and gems from around the world.

Mount Panorama
Pit Complex, Pit Straight,
Mount Panorama, Bathurst
(02) 6333 6158;
www.mount-panorama.com

FREE

This is fun for petrol heads as Mount Panorama is a public road, and you can drive around at 60 kilometres per hour while imagining you are driving in the Bathurst 1000.

Around Orange

Lake Canobolas Reserve
2 km off Cargo Rd, Orange
1800 069 466; www.visitorange.com.au

FREE

Follow the walking track round the lake to look for echidnas, grey kangaroos, wallabies, wombats, koalas and native birds. And for contrast, there's also a restored old pumphouse for those with an interest in machinery. The reserve has picnic and barbecue facilities, and water activities, including paddle boats in summer.

Ophir Reserve
Ophir Rd, Orange
(02) 6393 8226 or 1800 069 466;
www.orange.nsw.gov.au

FREE

The Australian Gold Rush started here! The first payable gold in Australia was discovered at Ophir in 1851. Hire a pan from the Orange Visitor Information Centre, corner of Byng and Peisley streets, and try your luck panning for gold in the creek, or just bushwalk along one of the walking trails.

Orange Adventure Park
Yellow Box Way, Orange
1800 069 466;
*www.visitnsw.com/town/Orange/Orange_*
Adventure_Playground/info.aspx

FREE

Playground equipment here includes a farm tractor, tree house, rocket, swings, tunnels and a climbing wall.

Borenore Caves Reserve
On the Orange–Forbes Rd,
17 km from Orange
www.orange-nsw.com/borenorecaves.
html

FREE

Have a picnic and then explore the caves. You don't need a guide for these caves, but you will need a torch and sturdy shoes. There are also walking tracks through the reserve.

Around Parkes

Eugowra Bushranger Trail
Start at Eugowra Rocks, Eugowra,
30 km south-east of Parkes
(02) 6392 3200; www.eugowra.aus.net/
thingstoseeanddo.htm
FREE

Escort Rock, now a pleasant picnic spot, was the scene of Australia's largest armed gold robbery when Frank Gardiner, Ben Hall and other bushrangers held up a gold escort in 1862. Look for the plaque, and you might even find a few old bullets. From here, you can take a driving route described on the website above, which takes you to several other historic sites related to bushrangers. The kids can have fun running around pretending to be bushrangers.

Parkes Observatory
473 Telescope Rd, Parkes
(02) 6861 1777; outreach.atnf.csiro.au/
visiting/parkes
FREE; EXTRA COST FOR SHOWS

The observatory's giant telescope helped relay telemetry and television pictures of the first moon landing and featured in the movie *The Dish*. The visitors centre has displays and interactive exhibits about its famous telescope. There are fees for watching the astronomy-related shows in the two theatres, but entry to the visitors centre is free. Interesting note: the town of Parkes is named after Sir Henry Parkes, who is often called the Father of Australia's Federation. His face appears on the $5 note.

Macusani Alpacas
10 km south of Parkes on the Newell Hwy,
Tichborne
(02) 6863 1133;
www.alpacacountryshop.com.au
Check opening times
FREE

The owners of this little alpaca business are happy to take the kids out to pat an alpaca and show them how the wool is spun.

Parkes Observatory, Parkes

Accommodation

BIG4 Dubbo Parklands
154 Whylandra St, Dubbo
(02) 6884 8633 or 1800 033 072;
www.big4dubboparklands.com.au
BUDGET TO MID-RANGE
This BIG4 park is very conveniently located right on the cycling and walking track around Dubbo and a 10-minute ride from the Western Plains Zoo. Cabins, caravan sites and campsites are available and facilities include a recreation room with large-screen TV. There are plenty of kids' activities on offer, with a shaded heated pool, a kids' playground, jumbo jumping pillow and a BMX track.

Country Apartments
230 Brisbane St, Dubbo
(02) 6885 1141; www.
countryapartments.com.au
MID-RANGE
These self-contained, air-conditioned apartments are spacious and homely. They are in a quiet garden setting with a pool.

Dairy Park Farm Stay Bed and Breakfast
Mandurama
(02) 6367 5264; www.dairypark.com.au
MID-RANGE
Stay in a self-contained cabin on a farm in the picturesque rolling hills of the central tablelands. Help with farm activities including feeding hens, collecting eggs, and mustering sheep and cattle. You can also ride horses, or play tennis.

Wellington Caves Caravan Park
Caves Rd, Wellington
(02) 6845 2970;
www.visitwellington.com.au
BUDGET
The park offers self-contained units, caravan sites and campsites. Facilities include a swimming pool, barbecue areas and a kiosk. For information on Wellington Caves see p. 96.

Western Plains Zoo
Taronga Western Plains Zoo Obley Rd, Dubbo
www.taronga.org.au/western-plains-zoo/ plan-your-visit/overnight-stay.aspx
Zoofari Lodge (02) 6881 1488; Roar and Snore (02) 6881 1405
HIGH COST
At Zoofari Lodge, you sleep in an African-style canvas-covered lodge right beside the roaming giraffes, elands, zebras and buffalo. The tariff includes zoo entry for two days, meals, bike hire, discount vouchers and behind-the-scenes tours where you can feed some of the animals. There is a restaurant and saltwater swimming pool. With the more informal Roar and Snore option, an empty tent is

provided and you bring your own sleeping bags. The tariff includes behind-the-scenes tours, meals and zoo entry for one day. This option is available Saturday nights and extra nights during the school holidays. Note that children must be 5 years old to participate in Roar and Snore. For more information on the zoo, see p. 98.

Yarrabin
Beaconsfield Rd, O'Connell
(02) 6337 5712; www.yarrabin.com
HIGH COST

Yarrabin provides comfortable homestead accommodation with ensuite bathrooms, use of homestead lounge, games room and pool. Meals are provided and there are plenty of activities to enjoy on this 1000-hectare property. Visitors can swim, ride horses, see kangaroos, fossick for gold and help look after the farm animals.

Places to eat

Kidzoo
Shop 1, 195 Cobra St, Dubbo
(02) 6885 5522
Kids can play in the giant indoor playground on the climbing equipment, slippery dip, and rock climbing wall (separate baby play area) while you have a relaxed lunch in the cafeteria.

Macquarie Inn's Bistro
Cnr Wheelers La and Birch Ave, Dubbo
(02) 6884 1955;
www.macquarieinn.com.au
There is a relaxed family atmosphere here and a children's play area so you can enjoy your meal while the kids let off steam. The bistro is open for breakfast, lunch and dinner. You'll find great steaks and a special kids' menu.

Robin Hood Hotel
30 Burrendong Way, Orange
(02) 6363 1999
This casual bistro has a kids' menu, and you can eat outdoors while the younger members have fun in the shaded playground.

Windmills on Welcome
33 Welcome St, Parkes
(02) 6863 5255
This is a modern, family-friendly restaurant with a play area and a kids' menu.

Another Holiday Idea for New South Wales

Ski in the Snowy Mountains

New South Wales has four wonderful ski resorts, each with its individual character. Perisher Resort is family friendly with designated toboggan and snow-play areas, and you can try snowtubing as well as skiing. Selwyn Snowfields is also family friendly, but with no accommodation on the snow you need to stay at a nearby town and get up the mountain with your own transport. Thredbo has the steepest slopes and caters for the more serious skiers. Charlotte Pass is the highest and quietest resort. It is snowbound, and you have the unique and fun experience of travelling there by an oversnow transport vehicle.

Find out more at www.snowymountains.com.au

Skiing at Perisher Resort, Snowy Mountains

AUSTRALIAN CAPITAL TERRITORY

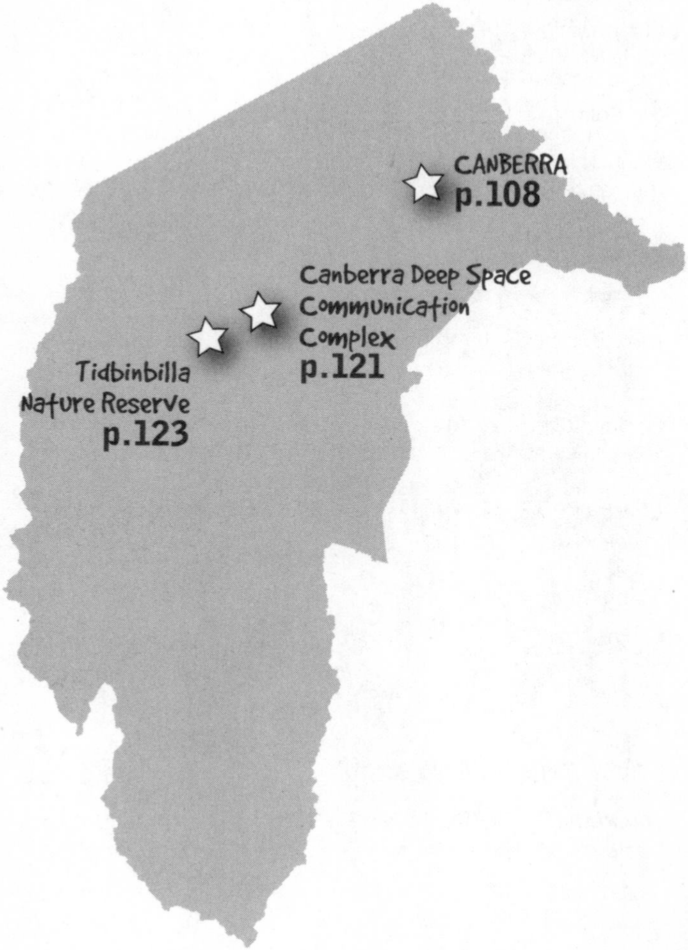

CANBERRA
p.108

Canberra Deep Space
Communication
Complex
p.121

Tidbinbilla
Nature Reserve
p.123

FAVOURITES _____

Australian Institute of Sport – a chance to come face-to-face with sporting stars **p. 108**

Australian War Memorial – immerse yourselves in the soldiering life through realistic displays **p. 110**

Big Splash Water Park – just lots of fun! **p. 119**

Canberra Deep Space Communication Complex – spaceships, moon rocks and messages to Mars **p. 121**

Cockington Green Gardens – be entranced by a world of miniatures **p. 119**

Lake Burley Griffin Boat Hire – hire paddleboats and race to the Captain Cook Memorial Jet **p. 116**

National Dinosaur Museum – for the millions of kids who are fascinated by dinosaurs **p. 119**

Questacon – discover the science in fun and the fun in science **p. 114**

Tidbinbilla Nature Reserve – giant moths, endangered wallabies and corroboree frogs **p. 123**

TOP EVENTS

MAR/APR Enjoy the week-long spectacle of Canberra Balloon Fiesta p. 120

SEPT–OCT Activities for the whole family at the month-long Floriade flower festival p. 121

CANBERRA

Around the lake_____

Australian Institute of Sport, Bruce

Australian Institute of Sport
Leverrier St, Bruce
(02) 6214 1010; www.ausport.gov.au/ais
Entry by tour only; 10am, 11.30am,
1pm and 2.30pm daily

MID-RANGE

Your kids will be awed and inspired to walk the halls of Australia's elite sports academy, but the highlight of the tour will be the chance to have a go at some of the sports themselves. Picture your budding little soccer stars kicking virtual balls towards goal — will they get it past the on-screen goalkeeper who reacts to the direction and strength of their kicks? They can also experience the challenges faced by wheelchair athletes by trying to shoot a basketball through a normal-height hoop while sitting in a wheelchair.

INSIDER TIPS

- The one-and-a-half-hour tour will be conducted by an athlete who is training at the institute.
- Your best chance to see the stars actually training will be during a 10am or 2.30pm tour.
- You don't need to book for tours, but during school holidays it is best to arrive about 15 minutes before they start.
- The tour includes 30 minutes at Sportex, where you can all have a go at different sports and browse the display of sporting memorabilia.
- You will also visit the gymnastics hall and the high-tech pool which has facilities to monitor swimmers and provide them with feedback.
- There is a cafe on site.

DON'T MISS

- A swim in the pool where Australia's best swimmers train. You never know who you might meet there! The pool is open to the public for limited hours. If you'd like to have a swim, check when it will be open so you can time your visit to fit in.

FABULOUS FACTS

The only way to enter the Australian Institute of Sport is to be a fabulous athlete and be offered a scholarship. Nobody can pay their way in. The training consists not only of coaching by the top coaches, but also the use of state-of-the-art facilities and help from massage therapists, dieticians, sport psychologists and sport scientists.

Kid Quest
Keep your eyes peeled for a famous athlete.

Australian War Memorial
Treloar Cres, Campbell
(02) 6243 4211; www.awm.gov.au

FREE

Your kids will have fun dressing up in army uniforms, playing with the controls on an Iroquois helicopter and trying out a toilet seat in a submarine, but they will also start to understand the harsher realities of war. In the recreated World War I trench, a special-effects video covers their feet in virtual frostbite and the G for George exhibit immerses them in a night-time flying operation from 1943, complete with searchlights and the terrifying roar of approaching German fighters.

Australian War Memorial, Campbell

INSIDER TIPS

- Allow at least two hours for your visit.

- Exhibits are less crowded on weekends or during school holidays.

- Before your visit, find any information you can about relatives or friends who represented Australia in wars so your family can research them when you come. A volunteer will help you look up the research centre records.

- There are two cafes on site.

DON'T MISS

- The Discovery Zone, where kids can dress up in uniforms and try out the activities described above.

- The ceremonial commemoration to the fallen, every day at 5pm. This moving ceremony consists of a dirge played on bagpipes or the last post played on a bugle.

- Anzac Hall, to experience four immersive audiovisuals, including G for George and a midget Japanese submarine (*see* FABULOUS FACTS *on facing page*).

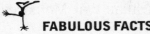

FABULOUS FACTS

Many people do not realise that Sydney came under attack during World War II. On the night of 31 May 1942, three midget Japanese submarines slipped into Sydney Harbour. One submarine was caught in an anti-torpedo net, the two crew members destroying themselves and their vessel with demolition charges. Another fired a torpedo under HMAS *Kuttabul*, killing 21 sailors before escaping. The third was spotted and sunk by the Royal Australian Navy.

Kid Quest

Place a poppy (available for purchase) on the roll of honour which lists the names of all Australia's war dead.

CSIRO Discovery

Black Mountain Laboratories
Clunies Ross St, Acton
(02) 6246 4646; www.csiro.au/places/CSIRO-Discovery.html
Open 9am–5pm Mon–Fri, 11am–3pm Sun

BUDGET

Take your kids on a scientific adventure! On entering OptusLab their eyes will pop open when they see the equipment at their disposal: test tubes filled with coloured liquids, and droppers, microscopes and slides. The liquids in the tubes are only simple substances found in your own kitchen, but this activity, like all the others at CSIRO Discovery, aims to promote the excitement of experimentation and teach a few scientific principals.

INSIDER TIPS

- Check the website for science experiments you can do at home.

- There is a cafe on site, but it is closed on Sundays.

DON'T MISS

- The two floors of working laboratories with big viewing windows; watch real CSIRO scientists at work.

- The fun and informative 3-D movies. Continuously screening through the day, they cover topics such as polymer glues, omega-3 fish oil and sense of smell.

- The Little Live Animals exhibit. See and touch turtles, stick insects, tropical fish, yabbies and mice.

- The interactive CD-ROM games area. Build your own bay or manage a rainforest.

Inspecting an insect at CSIRO Discovery, Acton

FABULOUS FACTS

CSIRO stands for Commonwealth Scientific and Industrial Research Organisation. The scientists here work on a huge diversity of projects, making discoveries and solving problems for industry, society and the environment. CSIRO scientists have discovered endangered handfish that use their fins for 'walking' instead of swimming, worked on technologies for saving lives during bushfires, and even produced cookbooks for healthy eating.

Kid Quest
What is the most important project you think the CSIRO should be working on?

National Museum of Australia
Lawson Cres, Acton Peninsula
(02) 6208 5000; www.nma.gov.au

FREE

Kids love the KSpace gallery where they get the chance to design houses and vehicles of the future. With fierce concentration, they use the touch screens to select shapes, colours and alternative energy sources. In the 3-D theatre they don special glasses and see their own designs come to life in an animated sequence, complete with sound track.

INSIDER TIPS

- Pick up or download a family trail brochure that will take you all on a quest through the museum.

- You can buy food from the cafe and restaurant or bring your own to eat in the hall; highchairs are available.

- There is a small time-out space in the Australian Journeys gallery – kids can read and play near the *Little Red Riding Hood* wall hanging.

- Another way to rest your feet is to watch a screening in the revolving cinema, CIRCA.

- The museum shop sells *Making Tracks*, a collection of children's fictional books, each based on an object in the museum collection.

 DON'T MISS

- The First Australians gallery where kids can audition to be radio announcers for the Goolarri interactive radio studio, or learn Aboriginal dancing by following projected images and using an interactive, pressure-sensitive floor.

- The Batman Land Deed (*see* FABULOUS FACTS *below*) in the Landmarks gallery.

- The Wiggles T-shirts and *Play School* flower clock in the Eternity gallery.

- Mobile touch trolleys throughout the museum.

- The PS *Enterprise*, moored outside on Lake Burley Griffin.

 FABULOUS FACTS

One of the most important objects in the museum is the Batman Land Deed, the first document to acknowledge that Aboriginal people owned land in Australia before Europeans. It was drawn up between pioneer John Batman and the Aboriginal people of the Port Phillip Bay area in Victoria. Museum curators invented a special display case to protect this document from the deteriorating effects of heat, light and oxygen. The case is filled with argon gas, which is heavier than oxygen and pushes any oxygen to the top where it can be extracted.

Kid Quest

The cradle in the Australian Journeys gallery was never meant to be used by a baby. What was it for?

See pp. 640–4 for the answer

Questacon

King Edward Tce, Parkes

(02) 6270 2800 or 1800 020 603; www.questacon.edu.au

MID-RANGE

Questacon appeals to children's instinct to take up a challenge, to inquire and experiment, but while they are having fun, they learn about scientific principals, such as gravity and relative motion. Your kids will want to have a game of Curve Ball in the spinning chairs – it's hard to predict where the ball (and their hands) will go next. And the 6-metre-high Free Fall exhibit is irresistible for young daredevils.

INSIDER TIPS

▓ You'll find the Curve Ball and Free Fall activities in the SideShow exhibition (though displays are frequently updated, so these may have changed).

▓ You can buy a '3 in Fun' ticket for reduced entry to Questacon, Cockington Green Gardens (*see* p. 119) and the Australian Institute of Sport (*see* p. 108).

▓ During very busy periods, time restrictions apply for entry to the Mini Q gallery (*see* DON'T MISS *below*).

▓ Mini Q has children's toilets.

▓ There is a cafe on site.

DON'T MISS

▓ Mini Q, if you have a child under six. Activities here involve exploring spaces, balancing, role-playing, and experimenting with flowing water.

▓ The live educational shows throughout the day (included in your entry fee). On Stage are fun, interactive performances for all ages: Puppet Shows are for the littlies and Science Talks are for those with a deeper interest.

FABULOUS FACTS

One of the scariest interactive exhibits in the museum is Guillotine in SideShow. During the French Revolution, thousands of people really had their heads chopped off by guillotine. Now you can find out how they felt! Questacon gives you a chance to find out about all sorts of scientific phenomena, including your own fear responses...

Kid Quest
Are you brave enough to stick your neck under the guillotine?

Australian National Botanic Gardens
Clunies Ross St, Black Mountain
(02) 6250 9540; www.anbg.gov.au
Open daily, including evenings in summer
FREE
Follow the Aboriginal shield signs to find out about the use of plants for food and medicine, or use the kids' activity brochure from the visitor centre and go on an adventure trail. The shady lawns are ideal for picnics.

Balloon Aloft
Meet at Park Hyatt,
Commonwealth Ave, Yarralumla
(02) 6285 1540;
www.canberraballoons.com.au
Depart half an hour before sunrise,
weather dependent
Minimum age 6
HIGH COST
You travel to the lift-off point, watch as the hot-air balloon is set up, then sail away on your scenic adventure over Canberra...

Black Mountain Tower
Black Mountain Dr, Acton
1800 806 718;
www.blackmountaintower.com.au

Open 9am–10pm daily, including
Christmas Day and Good Friday
BUDGET
Take a lift up this 195-metre communications tower to viewing galleries (indoor and outdoor) with 360-degree views of Canberra and surrounds; binoculars are provided. You can enjoy a meal with a view from the cafe or revolving restaurant.

Canberra Model Yacht Club
Off Bowen Dr, Bowen Park, Barton
(02) 6241 3070; www.cmyc.org.au
Every Sunday morning, weather permitting
FREE
Come and watch model boats racing on Lake Burley Griffin.

Canberra Museum and Gallery
Cnr London Circuit and Civic Sq,
Canberra City
(02) 6207 3968;
www.museumsandgalleries.act.gov.au
Open daily, closed weekend mornings
FREE
There are always fun art and craft activities happening here for littlies, and there's a quiet reading corner with picture books. Phone ahead or check the website for details.

Calthorpe's House, Red Hill

Calthorpe's House
24 Mugga Way, Red Hill
(02) 6295 1945;
www.museumsandgalleries.act.gov.au
Sat and Sun afternoons

BUDGET

This is a time capsule of family life in Canberra's early days. You can see children's toys and climb inside a World War II shelter in the backyard.

Embassy drive
Includes area around Empire Circuit, Forrest, and Forster Cres, Yarralumla
www.visitcanberra.com.au
(select 'Things to do and see')

FREE

Nearly 80 embassies and high commissions are located in Canberra. It's fun to drive around this precinct and see how many you can identify. Watch for the longhouse-style building from Papua New Guinea, the Cape Dutch-style structure from South Africa and traditional pagoda-style roofs on the Chinese Embassy.

Lake Burley Griffin Bike Hire
Barrine Dr, Acton
(02) 6257 1188; www.mrspokes.com.au
Seasonal operation

MID-RANGE

Hire a family-pack of bikes, complete with helmets, locks and maps and set off to explore the tracks around the lake. You can also try a pedal car!

Lake Burley Griffin Boat Hire
Acton Ferry Terminal,
Barrine Dr, Acton
(02) 6249 6861; www.actboathire.com
Daily Sept–May, open morning to late evening weekends, public and school holidays

VARIOUS PRICES

Choose from paddle boats, kayaks or two- and three-person canoes. You can paddle up to the Captain Cook Memorial Jet, which operates from 11am until 4pm.

Paddle boats on Lake Burley Griffin

Merry-go-round, Canberra

Manuka Pool
Manuka Circuit, Barton
(02) 6295 1349;
www.manukapool.com.au
Open mid-Oct – end Mar
BUDGET
Summer visitors will find welcome respite in the 30-metre outdoor pool and shaded toddler pool. The centre also features a pirate ship playground and large grassed area to play on.

Merry-go-round
Petrie Plaza, Canberra City
0412 482 676
BUDGET
Give the kids a ride on this classic 1914 carousel with its original organ, twisted brass poles and hand-carved wooden horses and elephants.

Museum of Australian Democracy
Old Parliament House,
King George Tce, Parkes
(02) 6270 8222; www.moadoph.gov.au
BUDGET
This historic building now houses a museum filled with interactive displays. Kids can dress up in costumes and stand against backdrops to become part of important events in the history of democracy. Guided and self-guided tours are available.

National Capital Exhibition
Regatta Point,
Commonwealth Park, Parkes
(02) 6257 1068;
www.nationalcapital.gov.au
FREE
Start your visit to Canberra with these interactive displays, models and audiovisual presentations that tell the story of the making of the national capital.

National Carillon
Aspen Island, Parkes
(02) 6257 1068
www.nationcapital.gov.au
FREE
The tall, white sculpture on an island in the middle of Lake Burley Griffin houses an enormous clavier, or series of bells. You can hear these chiming the hour or listen to complete concerts (check website for times). Have a picnic in Commonwealth Park while you listen.

National Zoo and Aquarium, Yarralumla

National Zoo and Aquarium
Lady Denman Dr,
Scrivener Dam, Yarralumla
(02) 6287 8400;
www.nationalzoo.com.au
MID-RANGE

The zoo houses mammals and reptiles from around the world, and the aquarium has sharks, colourful reef fish and some unusual aquatic creatures. Don't miss the keeper talks and daily activities. If you'd like to go behind the scenes to meet and feed some of the animals, you can do a Family Tour (high cost, limited hours) or Zoo Venture (high cost, minimum age 10).

Parliament House
Capital Hill
(02) 6277 5399; www.aph.gov.au
FREE

See the centre of Australian government with its iconic 81-metre flagpole. On sitting days (check the website for dates) attend the lively question time at 2pm (free, but it's a good idea to book ahead) and you should spot a few famous faces. Don't miss: walking on the grass lawn on *top* of the building, seeing one of the only original copies of the Magna Carta, and standing before Tom Roberts' famous painting of the opening of the first Federal Parliament of Australia. Guided tours explain the interesting symbolism of the building.

Royal Australian Mint
Denison St, Deakin
1300 652 020; www.ramint.gov.au
FREE

You can look down on the 'money factory' through huge viewing windows and see coins being made with the help of Titan, one of the world's strongest robots. There is also a rare and historic coin collection to marvel at and a display that gives insight into the designs on Australian coins. Best of all, kids can use a machine to make their own coin. Note: while you are here, pop down the road to Beale Crescent for a look at some stunning embassy buildings.

Vintage train ride
Depart Canberra Railway Station,
Kingston
(02) 6284 2790; www.arhsact.org.au
Check website for timetable
VARIOUS PRICES

Take a ride on a century-old diesel train. Various trips are offered, including a journey through scenic countryside to Bungendore (one hour each way), with a stop for an hour to run around before returning. Train buffs can also visit Canberra Railway Museum at Geijera Place in Kingston (open Sunday afternoons).

Further afield

Australian Reptile Centre
O'Hanlon Pl, Gold Creek Village, Nicholls
(02) 6253 8533;
www.canberrareptilesanctuary.org.au
MID-RANGE
See a range of Australian and exotic snakes, lizards, crocodiles and frogs. For an extra cost, you can feed or cuddle them!

Big Splash Water Park
1 Catchpole St, Macquarie
(02) 6251 1144;
www.bigsplashwaterpark.com.au
Summer only
MID-RANGE
There's no shortage of water-based fun here with six heated pools, nine water slides, a children's play area and kiosk.

Cockington Green Gardens
11 Gold Creek Rd, Gold Creek Village,
Nicholls
(02) 6230 2273 or 1800 627273;
www.cockingtongreen.com.au
MID-RANGE

Kids (and adults) are entranced by the little replicas of villages from around the world nestled in landscaped gardens. Miniature steam train rides are available.

National Dinosaur Museum
Barton Hwy, Gold Creek Village, Nicholls
(02) 6230 2655 or 1800 356 000;
www.nationaldinosaurmuseum.com.au
Closed Fri
MID-RANGE
Most kids are fascinated by dinosaurs and this is a wonderful chance to see some impressive full-size skeletons. Exhibits are set up to take visitors on a

journey from Earth's beginnings to the present.

Walk-In Aviary
Federation Sqr, O'Hanlon Pl,
Gold Creek Village, Nicholls
(02) 6230 2044;
www.canberrawalkinaviary.com.au
Seasonal times

MID-RANGE

Not only can you walk amongst hundreds of finches and parrots in this huge aviary, but you are given pieces of apple so you can tempt them down to feed out of your hands.

Special events

Balloons taking off, Canberra Balloon Fiesta

Canberra Balloon Fiesta
One week in Mar/Apr
www.events.act.gov.au
Young photographers and adventurers will be inspired by the spectacle of dozens of hot-air balloons drifting over the city and reflecting on the lake. Novelty balloons to feature in the past have included a pair of dancing honey bees, Vincent Van Gogh's head and a Scottish bagpiper.

Taking a photo of the floral display, Floriade

Floriade
Four weeks during Sept–Oct
www.floriadeaustralia.com
One of the highlights of this annual flower festival is a huge, living artwork created with plantings of thousands of flowers. There are activities for the whole family.

Day trips

Canberra Deep Space Communication Complex
Tourist Route 5, 421 Discovery Dr, Tidbinbilla
(02) 6201 7838; www.cdscc.nasa.gov
35 km/ 40 min south-west
FREE

One of the towering antenna dishes here is the height of a 22-storey skyscraper. It is awe-inspiring to realise these huge structures are 'talking' to the solar system. There are only three deep space communication facilities around the world: this one, another in California's Mojave Desert and one near Madrid in Spain. Inside the visitor centre, the first thing the kids demand to see is the moon rock. It's hard to believe that this small, insignificant-looking stone really came from the moon. All around, exciting evidence of space exploration calls out to be inspected: space suits, astronaut food, engines from the rockets that took men to the moon...

INSIDER TIPS

- There are lovely grounds around the complex, with picnic areas and play equipment.

- If you want to take the weight off your feet for a while, you can watch one of the documentary films.

- There is a cafe on site.

- Tidbinbilla Nature Reserve (*see facing page*) is very close by.

DON'T MISS

- The switch that enabled people all over the world to see the first men walk on the moon (*see* FABULOUS FACTS *below*).

- The retired antenna equipment outside; it's astounding to see how big each part of the giant antennas had to be.

- The full-scale replicas of the twin robot rovers sent to Mars to collect data.

FABULOUS FACTS

Although the first spaceship to land on the moon was American, the images received in the United States were upside down because the switch on their antennas was incorrectly installed. To make sure millions of people all over the world did not have to stand on their heads to watch the landing, the images of the first men walking on the moon were broadcast from tracking stations in Australia where the switch was the right way up!

Kid Quest

Most people know that the first two people to walk on the moon were Neil Armstrong and Buzz Aldrin. Who was the third person to walk on the moon?

See pp. 640–4 for the answer

Tidbinbilla Nature Reserve

Tidbinbilla Rd, Tidbinbilla
(02) 6205 1233; www.tams.act.gov.au
35 km/45 min south-west

BUDGET

A kangaroo bounds into view and your kids point excitedly at the joey's foot poking out of her pouch. You are walking through a stand of grass trees with dark, stumpy trunks and a fountain of long strands sprouting from the top. In the distance is the high calling note of a lyrebird. A moment later, a huge emu comes stalking towards you, a string of endearing stripy chicks trotting behind. You watch till they are out of sight, then the kids start running up the path. They can see an enticing heap of rocks they want to climb.

INSIDER TIPS

- The walk described above leads to Gibraltar Rocks. The full walk takes two-and-a-half hours, but a shorter loop will take you to the grass trees (*Xanthorrhoea*) and a chance to see animals. You can download walking maps from the website.

- Check the website for timetables for interesting guided walks and talks which are run on weekends in the reserve.

- Early morning or evening is the best time to see kangaroos and emus moving around. These are also the times to spot elusive platypus in the ponds; keep very quiet and watch for tell-tale bubbles in the water.

- If you visit in winter, you won't have to worry about snakes or flies, but remember to wear plenty of layers of warm, waterproof clothing.

- During spring you can see swans with cygnets and male emus looking after their chicks.

- If you come in November or December, keep an eye out for huge bogong moths.

- Drinking water is available at the Sheedys and Flints picnic areas. There is no cafe in the reserve and no bins, so bring food to eat and a rubbish bag to take home.

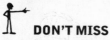

DON'T MISS

■ Endangered northern corroboree frogs in the visitor centre. These spectacular yellow and black frogs are about the size of a fingernail and are being bred successfully at Tidbinbilla.

■ The Nature Discovery Playground near the visitor centre – but leave this until the end as the kids might not want to move on! There are flying foxes, spider webs, water pumps, graded slippery dips, bouncing kangaroos, and barbeques.

■ The sanctuary where you can walk amongst free-ranging Australian wildlife, including endangered brush-tailed rock wallabies, koalas, echidnas, platypus, reptiles and birds.

■ The rock shelter at Hanging Rock – Aboriginal people used this shelter for 20 000 years.

FABULOUS FACTS

Wallabies always have a second fertilised egg (called a quiescent blastocyst) ready to develop as soon as the joey in their pouch is ready to leave. The rangers at Tidbinbilla are making use of this fact to speed up the breeding of endangered brush-tailed rock wallabies. The rangers remove joeys from their mums and give them to tamar wallabies to rear, setting off the development of the second fertilised eggs.

Kid Quest

Grass trees live for about 600 years, but they grow at the slow rate of only 1–2 centimetres a year. Look for a grass tree and try to guess how old it is by its height.

Corin Forest Mountain Recreation

On Tourist Drive 5, Corin Dam Rd, Smokers Gap
(02) 6235 7333; www.corin.com.au
27 km/35 min south-west
Check opening times

VARIOUS PRICES

Take a breathtaking bobsled ride on a stainless steel track down a mountainside; you can ride 800 meters or 1.2 kilometres! Children 8 years of age and over can ride on their own and littlies can share with an adult. There are also bushwalking tracks, a water slide and a flying fox.

Lanyon Homestead

Tharwa Dr, Tharwa
(02) 6235 5677;
www.museumsandgalleries.act.gov.au
30 km/40 min south
Check opening hours

BUDGET

This mid-19th-century homestead is set in rambling gardens that are ideal for running around in. Kids adore the little parlour with toys and craft activities set out as if the family has just walked out and they are fascinated by the 'toilet' facilities in the bedroom. Don't miss the convict barn with its display about the lives of convicts who worked in and around the homestead. Tidbinbilla Nature Reserve (*see* p. 123) is very close by.

Murrumbidgee River Corridor

13 2281; www.tams.act.gov.au
Various locations

FREE

There is no coastline in the Australian Capital Territory, but along the Murrumbidgee River you can find sandy beaches and swimming spots. One of the easiest to access is Casuarina Sands, off Cotter Road, 25 kilometres/30 minutes west of Canberra.

Namadgi National Park

Namadgi Visitor Centre, Naas Rd
(2 km past Tharwa)
(02) 6207 2900; www.australianalps.
environment.gov.au/parks/namadgi.html
35 km/45 min south

FREE

Located at the northern end of the Australian Alps, this vast park offers scenic picnic spots, nature walks, Aboriginal rock drawings, and snow play in winter. It is also home to the tracking station which helped in the first moon landing. Call in to the visitor centre to pick up information, crawl in the 'wombat tunnel' and see interpretive displays about the flora, fauna and early settlers of the area. Camping is available here (*see* ACCOMMODATION p. 126).

Accommodation

Canberra City YHA

7 Akuna St, Canberra
(02) 6248 9155;
www.yha.com.au/hostels/nsw/canberra/
canberra-city

BUDGET

For cheap family accommodation right in the centre of town, try out the fun and vibe of a youth hostel. The family rooms have a double bed, two bunk beds and a private bathroom.

Manuka Park Serviced Apartments

1 Oxley St, Manuka
(02) 6239 0000 or 1800 688 227;
www.manukapark.com.au

MID-RANGE

Conveniently located near shops and eateries, these apartments have a swimming pool and garden setting. The two-bedroom versions offer a queen bed, two single beds and a kitchen and laundry. Cot, highchair and baby bath are available if required.

Namadgi National Park

Book at Namadgi Visitor Centre, Naas Rd
(2 km past Tharwa)
(02) 6207 2900;
www.australianalps.environment.gov.
au/parks/namadgi.html

BUDGET

How about spending a few nights camping in the wilderness? Namadgi National Park has a variety of camping areas. From Honeysuckle Campground you can walk to the site of the tracking station. A three-night limit applies at all Namadgi campgrounds. For more information on what to see and do in the park see p. 125.

Waldorf Apartment Hotel Canberra

2 Akuna Street, Canberra
(02) 6229 1234 or 1800 188 388;
www.waldorfcanberra.com.au

HIGH END

Right in the heart of the city, this apartment hotel has an indoor heated pool, half-size tennis court and table tennis table. The apartments are fitted with kitchens and laundry facilities.

Places to eat

Canberra Southern Cross Club
92–96 Corinna St, Woden
(02) 6283 7200; www.cscc.com.au
This club has a fine dining
restaurant but also welcomes
kids. There is a soft play area for
littlies and computer games for
the older ones.

Hellenic Club of Canberra
Matilda Street, Woden
(02) 6281 0899;
www.hellenicclub.com.au
Enjoy a relaxed meal in the
bistro with a kids' menu and an
'all you can eat' salad, soup and
pasta option, then let the kids
burn off a bit of energy in the
play area.

Woolley Street, Dickson
If you are after an Asian meal,
there are lots of options here.

VICTORIA

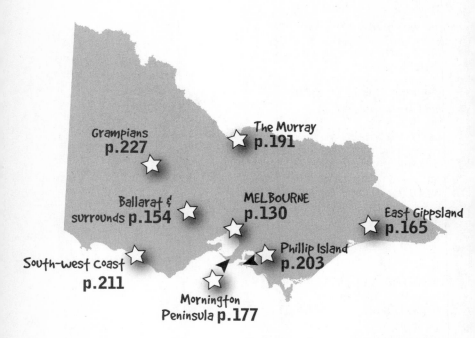

Grampians
p.227

The Murray
p.191

Ballarat &
surrounds p.154

MELBOURNE
p.130

East Gippsland
p.165

South-west coast
p.211

Phillip Island
p.203

Mornington
Peninsula p.177

FAVOURITES

Flagstaff Hill Maritime Village – enter the world of shipwrecks, climb a lighthouse and watch a spectacular sound and light show *p. 218*

Fort Nepean – an underground fort with real old guns and a fascinating history *p. 179*

Gippsland Lakes Cruise – see how many waterbirds you can spot *p. 171*

Great Otway National Park – treetop walks, tiny glow worms, waterfalls and a lighthouse *p. 211*

Melbourne Museum – meet live spiders, almost-live dinosaurs, and a stuffed racehorse *p. 133*

National Sports Museum – a special treat for sports-mad kids *p. 135*

Penguin Parade – see Victoria's famous little penguins *p. 203*

Sovereign Hill – catch gold fever in this recreation of a 19th-century gold rush town *p. 156*

Swan Hill Pioneer Settlement – churn butter, ride a paddlesteamer, and dance to a pianola *p. 195*

TOP EVENTS

EARLY MAR Melbourne's famous Moomba Parade and three days of free fun p. 148

JULY More than a week of indoor activities at Warrnambool's massive Fun4Kids Festival p. 223

EARLY OCT Step into the past at the Port of Echuca Heritage Steam Festival p. 194

MELBOURNE

HIGHLIGHTS

In town

Cook's Cottage at Fitzroy Gardens, Melbourne

Fitzroy Gardens
Cnr Wellington Pde and Clarendon St, Melbourne
(03) 9419 4118; www.fitzroygardens.com
FREE; BUDGET ENTRY FOR COOK'S COTTAGE

In the middle of the park is the incongruous sight of a tiny 18th-century English cottage. This child-scaled house was once occupied by the family of Captain James Cook, a famous figure in Australian history (*see* FABULOUS FACTS *on facing page*), and was moved here from England, brick by brick. It is furnished as if the family still lives here, and recorded voices make you feel as if you are overhearing their conversations.

INSIDER TIPS

■ At Cook's Cottage you can have fun taking photos with your heads stuck through the cut-outs in a picture of an 18th-century family. The house is nestled in an authentic English cottage garden. Information charts explain how herbs and plants were used for food or medicine.

■ During summer, there are free performances in Fitzroy Gardens.

■ If you visit the gardens around dusk, you'll see possums starting to move around the trees in search of food. These native mammals have adapted well to an urban environment and, although they can be a pest in suburban backyards, they are protected.

■ There's a cafe located near the Fairy Tree and Model Tudor Village (see DON'T MISS *below*).

DON'T MISS

■ The grand avenues of old English elm trees. Aged elm trees are rarely seen now in other parts of the world where they have been decimated by Dutch Elm Disease.

■ The Fairy Tree in the middle of the gardens. If you look carefully at this old tree stump you'll see all sorts of fairies and goblins carved into it.

■ The model Tudor Village, just near the Fairy Tree. It was sent as a gift from the citizens of Lambeth, England, in gratitude for food parcels from Australia during World War II.

■ The large conservatory (accessible at no extra cost) with its spectacular floral displays.

■ The old horse trough, just over the road in the Treasury Gardens. It was used in the days of horse-and-cart traffic.

FABULOUS FACTS

In the 18th century, people in England did not know what lands existed in the Southern Hemisphere. Captain James Cook set out from England in 1769 to explore the Pacific in his little wooden sailing ship, the *Endeavour*. In 1770, he discovered the eastern side of Australia. Nearly twenty years later, the English parliament sent convicts to this southern land to start a new colony.

Melbourne Aquarium

Cnr King and Flinders sts, Melbourne
(03) 9923 5925; www.melbourneaquarium.com.au

MID-RANGE

The Antarctic exhibit here is a favourite with all kids. The large king and gentoo penguins waddle right up to the glass and kids crouch down, thrilled to be nose-to-beak with these endearing creatures. They laugh and point at the clumsy gait of the penguins as they clamber around on snow, then watch in awe at the effortless way the same animals glide through water. Other highlights for kids: having giant stingrays swim right overhead, and the excitement of seeing divers in the water with sharks.

INSIDER TIPS

▨ The layout of the aquarium is rather confusing, with exhibits spread out on several levels connected by ramps, lifts and escalators. Luckily, there are plenty of helpful staff members.

▨ The cafe offers reasonably priced kids' meals.

▨ On weekdays there is a constant stream of school groups between 10am and 3pm, but there seems to be room for everyone, and you can listen in on some of the guides' commentaries.

▨ As you go down the ramps to enter the Sharks Alive exhibit, little people might be disconcerted by the huge jaws on display and some of the film footage of sharks being projected on the wall.

▨ There is the option of a glass-bottomed boat ride in the tank filled with sharks and stingrays (extra cost). This includes a behind-the-scenes tour and the chance to talk to the divers. The minimum age is 4 years; book at the front desk or phone ahead.

▨ A fun way to reach the aquarium is by the City Circle Tram, a vintage tram that offers a free ride with commentary around the city; 1800 800 166; www.metlinkmelbourne.com.au/route/view/1112

DON'T MISS

- Keeper talks and feed times throughout the day; check the website for details. One of the favourites for kids is 'Talk to a Diver', when a diver answers questions inside a tank full of sharks.

- The Rock Pool exhibit, a real hit with the littlies. There is a special Touch and Feel presentation here once a day, but hands-on opportunities such as patting a live starfish, touching a shark egg or squeezing a sponge are available all the time. And don't miss the amazingly camouflaged flounders!

- Little kid-size tunnels under some of the tanks. Kids like crawling inside and finding their own special viewing domes in the middle of the tanks.

FABULOUS FACTS

King penguins have the longest breeding cycle of any bird. It takes the parent birds 14–16 months to raise a single chick. The fluffy, brown chicks look nothing like their parents. King penguins are the second largest penguins in the world (emperor penguins are the largest).

Kid Quest

Find out how the keepers give the penguins their vitamin tablets.

See pp. 640–4 for the answer

Melbourne Museum

Carlton Gardens, Nicholson St, Carlton
(03) 8341 7777 or 1300 130 152; www.museumvictoria.com.au/melbournemuseum

BUDGET; EXTRA COST FOR SOME TEMPORARY EXHIBITIONS

Watch your children as they press the button to light up a window … and come face to face with a huge, live tarantula, just on the other side of the glass! Adults might shudder, but kids run in delight to the next window, looking for an even larger and scarier creepy-crawly. They wriggle excitedly into the child-size tunnel in the ant house so they can bob up right in the middle of the ant colony and see what all the busy little ants are up to. Melbourne Museum is filled with unique exhibits such as Bugs Alive! that are guaranteed to keep your kids entranced.

INSIDER TIPS

- If you want to take some weight off your feet for a while, watch a screening in the IMAX Theatre. Book tickets in advance to make sure you don't miss out.

- Browse the museum website – you'll find kids' activities and heaps of interesting information.

- The museum cafe has high chairs and offers a special lunch box for kids, but the queues can be very long, so you might want to bring a few snacks of your own. The cafe closes at 4.30pm.

- There are several play areas in the museum, including an outdoor playground next to the ground floor cafe.

DON'T MISS

- The Forest Gallery, with a real temperate Victorian forest, live birds and reptiles. In winter, it closes at 4.30pm so the birds can roost in peace.

- The Touch Trolleys – kids love getting their hands on real objects.

- The Discovery Centre, where museum staff can answer questions about science, Australian history or Indigenous culture. This is a must for kids who are always asking questions!

- The dinosaur exhibition – a perennial favourite.

- The special Children's Gallery, with educational activities aimed at 3–8 year olds (though older kids enjoy it too).

- Phar Lap, Australia's most famous race horse, who died in suspicious circumstances in the 1930s.

- The Bunjilaka Aboriginal Cultural Centre, for an insight into Victoria's Koorie history and culture.

- The Melbourne Story exhibition, which brings Melbourne's history to life and highlights the things that make it unique. Kids have fun running in and out of historic workers' cottages and peering into the shared backyard dunny (toilet).

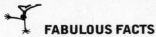

FABULOUS FACTS

Some of the tarantulas in the Bugs Alive! exhibit were confiscated from people trying to smuggle them into Australia. The museum holds them in quarantine before they are put on display. Quarantine is a maximum security area. There is not the tiniest crack anywhere, and all surfaces are painted white and lit 24 hours a day. Only a few people are allowed to enter, and they have to go through a series of sealed doors. No tarantulas or their parasites can escape.

Kid Quest
What is an ant kiss?
See pp. 640–4 for the answer

National Sports Museum
Gate 3, Olympic Stand, Melbourne Cricket Ground,
Jolimont St, Jolimont
(03) 9657 8879; www.nsm.org.au

MID-RANGE

Your kids are sure to be impressed by the size of a real footballer's huge boots, especially when they get the chance to slide their own small feet inside! Watch them determinedly pit their skills against some of the sporting greats – testing their goal kicking talents against Australian Football League (AFL) players and trying to run out Adam Gilchrist on a

National Sports Museum, Jolimont

virtual cricket pitch. This museum, located in the Melbourne Cricket Ground (MCG), touches on nearly all sports played in Australia. It is far from a 'look but don't touch' experience, with lots of opportunities for participating in sporting activities. There is also a wealth of world-famous sporting icons to ogle and virtual reality spaces for interacting with sporting stars!

INSIDER TIPS

- Allow plenty of time – there is a lot to see and do here!
- Weekdays can be less crowded than weekends.

- You can pick up a self-guided audio tour.

- In the Game On area, apart from cricket and football, everyone can have a go at archery, netball, soccer, and cycling, or try out being a newspaper reporter on the sports-desk.

- For the same ticket, the National Sports Museum gives you access to the Melbourne Cricket Club (MCC) Museum, except on MCG event days. For a timetable of event days, see www.thatsmelbourne.com.au.

- You can reach the MCG on the free Melbourne City Tourist Shuttle Bus (Stop 3); www.thatsmelbourne.com.au. Note: Stop 3 is not operational on MCG event days.

- There is a cafe on site.

- For really keen sports fans, take a tour of the MCG as well (*see* p. 139). You can purchase a combination ticket for the MCG tour and National Sports Museum.

DON'T MISS

- The Cricket Found Me exhibit. See a virtual Shane Warne, one of the most famous cricketers of recent times, open his locker, pick up his cricket bat and move around the room as he chats to you.

- The Off the Bench exhibit, where you'll come face-to-face with a virtual James Hird (AFL legend).

- Historic icons from the world of sport, such as Ian Thorpe's full-body swimsuit, the first Brownlow medal, Cathy Freeman's swift suit from the Sydney 2000 Olympics, and a collection of baggy green caps from Australian cricket history.

- The Olympic exhibit with memorabilia from the 1956 Games, which took place right here in the MCG.

FABULOUS FACTS

A highlight of the year for Victorian sporting fans is the AFL Grand, Final, which has traditionally been played here, at the MCG. The AFL code is commonly referred to as Aussie Rules and was started in the 1850s as a way of keeping cricketers fit over winter. Nowadays, the oval shape of the football is an Australian icon, but in the early years, players used either round or oval balls.

Kid Quest

Have a go at a sport you have never tried before.

ANZ Banking Museum

Lower ground floor of the 'Gothic Bank',
380 Collins St, Melbourne
(03) 9273 4369; www.anz.com/about-us/
our-company/profile/facts/banking-
museum
Open weekdays (excluding public
holidays) 10am–3pm
FREE

Interactive exhibits cover the early Indigenous economy, 19th-century banking and banking in the future. When you enter, collect an ATM Game Card for the chance to win a moneybox.

Artplay

Birrarung Marr, Melbourne
(03) 9664 7900;
www.melbourne.vic.gov.au/artplay
MID-RANGE

This venue is a combination of indoor and outdoor play areas, exhibition and performance spaces. It offers creative weekend and holiday workshops for children aged 5–12 years.

Atrium, Crown Entertainment Complex

8 Whiteman St, Southbank
(03) 9292 8888;
www.crowncasino.com.au/crown-atrium
Open morning till night
FREE

The huge, black marble atrium has sound and light displays running every day. Music pours from invisible sources, water jumps and trickles in time with the beat, and coloured lights play on the sparkling crystal ceiling. The most spectacular shows are in the evening, and during special events, such as Christmas or Chinese New Year, animated characters are incorporated.

Aussie Rules Footy Match

Various locations, including the
Melbourne Cricket Ground
(03) 9643 1999; www.afl.com.au
Seasonal
VARIOUS PRICES

Victorians are fanatical about Aussie Rules (Australian Football League code), which started in this state. Join the locals for an action-packed game and experience the emotion of being part of thousands of people urging on their teams. Scream along with the rest of them! Visit the website and select 'Premiership' and 'Fixtures' to find out the latest schedule.

Australian Centre for the Moving Image

Federation Sqr, cnr Swanston and
Flinders sts, Melbourne
FREE; EXTRA COST FOR MOST SCREENINGS AND SOME TEMPORARY EXHIBITIONS

Exhibits at Australian Centre for the Moving Image (ACMI) range from rare early film footage to the latest in digital lifestyle. Kids have fun with the interactive exhibits, including huge video games projected onto the floor.

Birrarung Marr Playground
Behind Federation Sqr, Melbourne
(03) 9658 9658;
www.melbourne.vic.gov.au/parks
FREE
This colourful playground has a network of boardwalks and rope structures to clamber on, a climbing wall, hammocks, sandpits, swings and slides. The Federation Bells chime most days in the nearby Middle Terrace at 8–9am, 12.30–1.30pm and 5–6pm. You can compose and publish your own composition for the bells at www.federationbells.com.au.

Capital City Trail
The 30 km sealed, car-free bike path that loops around Melbourne
www.bv.com.au/bikes-&-riding/43792
FREE; EXTRA COST FOR BIKE HIRE
Hire a bike at Federation Square (*see* RENTABIKE p. 140) and set off on an adventure. You can access

Eureka Skydeck 88, Southbank

the Melbourne Cricket Ground, Melbourne Zoo, Melbourne Aquarium, Como Historic House and Garden, Collingwood Children's Farm and Yarra Bend Park. Make sure you check the map and trail notes on the website before you set off; maps also available from Bicycle Victoria, (03) 8636 8888.

Chinese Museum
22 Cohen Pl, Melbourne
(03) 9662 2888;
www.chinesemuseum.com.au
BUDGET
Find out about Chinese life in Australia since the 19th century. See dioramas of life on the goldfields, magnificent opera costumes and Chinese lions and dragons used in parades. The Millennium Dragon is the largest in the world and needs six people just to carry its head.

Eureka Skydeck 88
Riverside Quay, Southbank
(03) 9693 8888;
www.eurekaskydeck.com.au
MID-RANGE
Take a lift that travels upwards at more than 9 metres per second. Step out on the 88th floor to an amazing 360-degree view of Melbourne. Kids will have fun with the telescopes, and there are signs to help you identify the sights. If you are game enough, pay extra and enter The Edge, a cube made of clear glass (floor and all!) that juts out 3 metres into space.

Federation Square

Cnr Swanston and Flinders sts,
Melbourne
(03) 9655 1900;
www.federationsquare.com.au

FREE

'Fed Square', as this space is affectionately known, houses the NGV Kids Corner (*see* p. 140) and ACMI (*see* p. 137), and is the centre for a wonderful program of activities and festivals. Make sure you check out what is happening here while you are in Melbourne. It adjoins the Birrarung Marr Playground and Artplay (*see* pp. 137 and 138).

Fire Services Museum of Victoria

39 Gisborne St, East Melbourne
(03) 9662 2907
Phone to check opening times

BUDGET

Australia's largest collection of fire brigade memorabilia includes vintage fire engines, pumps, uniforms and models.

Hardrock rock climbing

501 Swanston St, Melbourne
(03) 9631 5300; www.hardrock.com.au
Afternoons and evenings
Minimum age 10 years

MID-RANGE

Kids will have fun gearing up in harnesses and shoes and learning how to do real rock climbing (indoors).

Koorie Heritage Trust Cultural Centre

295 King St, Melbourne
(03) 8622 2600;
www.koorieheritagetrust.com

BY DONATION

Koories are Aboriginal people from Victoria and southern New South Wales. Their history and Creation stories are told here though interactive displays. The shop sells children's books with an Aboriginal theme and genuine Indigenous art and craftwork, including toys.

Melbourne Cricket Ground Tour

Gate 3, Melbourne Cricket Ground,
Yarra Park, Jolimont
(03) 9657 8888; www.mcg.org.au
Depart regularly on non-event days,
10am–3pm

MID-RANGE

For sporting fans it is a unique thrill to tour behind the scenes of the iconic Melbourne Cricket Ground (MCG or 'The G'), where many historic cricket matches, AFL (Australian Football League) Grand Finals, and other important sporting and cultural events have taken place.

NGV Kids Corner

The Ian Potter Centre: NGV Australia,
Federation Sqr, cnr Flinders and
Russell sts
(03) 8620 2222;
www.ngv.vic.gov.au/ngvkids
Closed Mon
FREE

In this wonderful space, kids can interact with creative installations and activities specially designed to encourage their appreciation of art. Older kids will want to explore other parts of the Ian Potter Centre as well; the Indigenous collection is likely to interest most ages. If you'd like to visit the international collection at NGV International (180 St Kilda Road, closed Tuesdays), check out the downloadable family trails at www.ngv.vic.gov.au/ngvkids/activities.html.

Old Melbourne Gaol and Justice Experience

377 Russell St, Melbourne
(03) 8663 7228;
www.oldmelbournegaol.com.au
Open daily, live performances Sat afternoons
More suitable for teenagers
MID-RANGE

If you think your kids will cope with this spooky environment of gaol cells, gallows and death masks, you can do a self-guided tour, or watch a Saturday live performance about famous bushranger Ned Kelly. In school holidays, check if children's tours are being offered, with tales of child criminals and other amazing prison stories. Other guided tours and experiences are not recommended for children.

Polyglot Theatre

Various locations and prices
(03) 9827 9667;
www.polyglottheatre.com
Performances for children aged 5–12 years. Check the website or phone ahead to find out about shows and locations.

Rentabike

Federation Wharf (below Federation Sqr)
Cnr Swanston and Flinders sts,
Melbourne
0417 339 203; www.rentabike.net.au
MID-RANGE TO HIGH COST

Hire a bike (kids' sizes, baby seats and tag-alongs available) and take a ride around Docklands, or set off for a day along the Capital City Trail (*see* p. 138). Rentabike also runs entertaining bike tours around Melbourne for children aged 12 years and over, or enquire about personalised family tours catering for younger riders.

State Library of Victoria

328 Swanston St, Melbourne
(03) 8664 7000; www.slv.vic.gov.au
Open till late Mon–Thurs, closed public holidays
FREE

For a bit of quiet time, visit the library's Experimedia where you'll find Play Pod, a space for families with young children to cuddle on bean bags and share stories and activities. You can read, or watch a digitally manipulated version of yourselves on a special computer screen. For older kids, there are free computer games and iMacs for creating music, animations and videos. Make sure you climb the grand staircase to the main reading room and take a look at the massive sky-lit dome.

Victoria Police Museum
637 Flinders St, Melbourne
(03) 9247 5214
Closed on weekends and public holidays
FREE
Kids will be interested to see historic armour from the Kelly Gang (notorious Victorian bushrangers). Other items on display include remains of the car blown up in the Russell Street Police Headquarters bombing and the latest in crime scene investigation technologies.

Williamstown Ferry
Travels between the city and Williamstown
(03) 9517 9444;
www.williamstownferries.com.au
Seasonal departure times and locations
MID-RANGE
Williamstown is a picturesque and historic seaport. There are stops en route at Crown Entertainment Complex, Melbourne Aquarium, *Polly Woodside* and Scienceworks. If you hire a bike you can take it with you on the ferry. Pay attention to return times, but if you miss the last ferry back, you can return to Melbourne by train.

Docklands

Icehouse
105 Pearl River Rd, Docklands
1300 756 699;
www.icehouse.com.au
MID-RANGE
Give the whole family a really 'cool' time! Hire a pair of skates and let off steam zooming around (or wobbling around) on the ice. Check beforehand for General Skate session times or special activities. Nearby is Wonderland Fun Park (*see* p. 142).

Kayak the Yarra
Departs Shed 4, Docklands
0424 397 498;
www.kayakmelbourne.com.au
Minimum age 12 years
HIGH COST
Paddle the Yarra River on an urban kayaking tour around the Docklands area.

Typical scene along the Yarra River, Melbourne

interactive exhibits about Polly's life story and what it was like to sail on her, but the best part is going on board and imagining sailing away on adventures.

Polly Woodside
South Wharf Precinct, Clarendon St, South Melbourne
National Trust Office (03) 9656 9800;
www.pollywoodside.com.au
MID-RANGE
Polly Woodside is a three-masted iron barque built in 1885. The interpretive centre has fun,

Wonderland Fun Park
120 Pearl River Rd, Harbour Town, Docklands
(03) 9602 1311;
www.wonderlandfunpark.com.au
Open weekends, public and school holidays
FREE ENTRY; PAY FOR RIDES
Take your pick from a range of carnival rides including dodgem cars, giant slide, grand carousel, teacup ride and bungee trampoline. Icehouse is located nearby (*see* p. 141).

Suburbs

Melbourne Zoo
Elliott Ave, Parkville
(03) 9285 9300; www.zoo.org.au
MID-RANGE
Standing in the huge, humid Butterfly House your kids will be entranced by the sight of coloured butterflies drifting all around them. You whisper to them to keep still and hold out their arms. And then it happens, a butterfly alights on an outstretched hand. The zoo tries to create enclosures as close to natural habitats as possible. Walking along the Elephant Trail you have the distinct feeling that you've landed in Thailand, and a visit to the seal enclosure feels like a trip to the coast.

INSIDER TIPS

- Allow a full day if you want to look at all of the exhibits.

- Ask about complimentary guided tours run by Friends of the Zoos volunteers.

- The website has lots of interesting information about the various animals, as well as a map of the zoo and information about a range of animal encounters available at extra cost; tickets can be purchased online.

- If your kids are keen for close encounters, the Animal Photo Experiences are available for an extra fee. Book ahead on (03) 9285 9458 or call into the Zoo Photos office from 10am. You can have a photo with a giant tortoise (11.00am), meerkats (11.30am, minimum age 5 years, maximum four people) or kangaroos (2.00pm). Wear flat, enclosed shoes and avoid wearing strong perfume or bright colours, which could disturb the animals.

- If you want time out from animals, the zoo also has a lovely playground and a carousel.

- There are food outlets on site, but the prices are high. You might want to bring a picnic and eat in the rotunda.

- The zoo holds outdoor twilight concerts during the summer months.

- Car parking is available (small charge) or you can take a tram or train to the door.

- Melbourne Zoo is one of three zoos run by Zoos Victoria. The main native animal exhibits are located at Healesville and there is a safari-style zoo at Werribee (see p. 150).

DON'T MISS

- Meet-the-keeper talks and feed times throughout the day. Check the website for the timetable and for announcements about additional talks.

- The entertaining monkeys and meerkats – always favourites with kids.

- A walk through the kangaroo enclosures, where free-roaming kangaroos often hop up to you, close enough to pat.
  Look for joeys poking out of their mothers' pouches.

FABULOUS FACTS

The elephants' Asian village enclosure is unusual because it shows not just animals, but a human side to the story. When people encroach on forests where wild animals live, it can bring difficulty and danger to the humans as well the animals. In Asia, herds of wild elephants sometimes invade plantations to feed on fruit growing on the trees, causing thousands of dollars of damage. Conservationists need to find solutions that will protect the elephants without disadvantaging people.

Kid Quest
What is your favourite animal at the zoo?

Nitty Gritty Super City at Scienceworks, Spotswood

Scienceworks
2 Booker St, Spotswood
(03) 9392 4800;
www.museumvictoria.com.au/scienceworks
BUDGET

At Scienceworks little folk get the chance to do some of the fascinating activities usually reserved for adults. What will fulfil your own kids' dreams? Will they rush onto the 'building site' and climb on the digger to press buttons and make the digger's arms work? Will they slip gleefully behind a counter in a 'cafe' to take orders and prepare a meal? Will they choose to be TV presenters and record their own weather reports? Whatever they choose, everything they explore in this feast of interactive exhibits will introduce them to scientific principles.

INSIDER TIPS

- The activities described above are in Nitty Gritty Super City, designed for children aged 3–8 years. There are plenty of other wonderful exhibits for older kids.

- Try to allow a whole day for exploring this museum.

- A fun way to reach the museum is by the Williamstown Ferry (*see* p. 141).

- The Planetarium (extra cost) has tilting seats and you view a film about the universe, climate change or the solar system screened on the dome. Afterwards, a presenter explains what to look for in the night sky at the end of that day. Further details and bookings for this 30-minute presentation are available online.

- In the Lightning Room (extra cost), a presenter explains and demonstrates lightning with a two-million-volt simulated lightning flash; another chance to rest your feet for around 30 minutes. To avoid disappointment, book online.

- Guided tours of the Pumping Station (*see* FABULOUS FACTS *below*) are free, but you need to book on arrival.

- There is a cafe on site, but it closes an hour before the museum does on weekdays.

DON'T MISS

- The Sportsworks exhibit, where kids can test their athletic skills against real sporting stars and explore how their bodies work.

- The science 'buskers' (weekends only). Check on arrival what time the buskers will be teaching science-in-the-kitchen tricks, such as how to make slime out of cornflour.

- The Muck Bunker Stormwater Experience (in the Pumping Station). This interactive exhibit demonstrates how rubbish, such as cigarette butts and dog poop, end up in the waterways.

FABULOUS FACTS

Scienceworks is built on the grounds of an old sewage treatment plant. The Pumping Station is now classified as an important industrial heritage site. It no longer treats sewage, but if you take a guided tour you can see one of the giant pumps in action, and you can peer down at the contents of a sewer!

Kid Quest

What things live inside your bathroom drain?
(Hint: look in the House Secrets exhibit.)

See pp. 640–4 for the answer

Collingwood Children's Farm

End of St Heliers St, Abbotsford
(03) 9417 5806 ; www.farm.org.au

BUDGET

Enjoy a breath of fresh air in this lovely bushland location just 5 kilometres from the city. See (and help) the cows being milked twice daily, pat the animals and help with farm activities such as looking for eggs and bottle-feeding lambs (in springtime).

Diamond Valley Railway

Eltham Lower Park, Main Rd, Eltham
(03) 9439 1493; www.dvr.com.au
Limited hours, most Sun

BUDGET

Kids adore riding around on a miniature train through mini tunnels, railway crossings and stations. The park, in a bushland setting, has an adventure playground, picnic sites and barbecues.

Living Legends

Oaklands Rd, Greenvale
(03) 9307 1165;
www.livinglegends.org.au
22 km from the city centre, just north of Melbourne Airport

Limited opening hours

BUDGET

Ever wondered what happens to champion racehorses when they grow too old to be useful? In the picturesque grounds of Woodlands Historic Park you can meet some retired champions. You can also visit a historic homestead, enjoy the parklands and hug the massive river red gums.

Luna Park

18 Lower Esplanade, St Kilda
(03) 9525 5033; www.lunapark.com.au
Seasonal opening times

FREE ENTRY; PAY FOR RIDES

This century-old amusement park with its large, toothy face looming over the entrance is a Melbourne icon. Try traditional old-fashioned rides such as the carousel, Ferris wheel and rollercoaster, or give the real thrill-seekers a go on the more modern rides. St Kilda Beach is just over the road.

Luna Park, St Kilda

Pony rides, Catani Gardens
Jacka Blvd, St Kilda West
Sun, public holidays and most Sat
BUDGET
Pony rides are available in these attractive, formal gardens beside St Kilda Beach.

Rippon Lea
192 Hotham St, Elsternwick
(03) 9523 6095;
www.ripponleaestate.com.au
Check opening hours and tour times
BUDGET ENTRY TO GARDEN; HOUSE EXTRA COST
Rippon Lea is a magnificent historic home (access by guided tour only), but its magical garden with lake, ducks and bridge is usually the highlight for kids. For a gold coin donation you can pick up a children's trail brochure and go on an activity hunt around the garden.

Royal Botanic Gardens
Birdwood Ave, South Yarra
(03) 9252 2300;
www.rbg.vic.gov.au
Ian Potter Children's Garden closed most of winter and reserved for school groups Mon–Tues
FREE
Kids will love the lakes, ducks, swans and expansive lawns to roll on, but there's lots more to do here. Check the website or phone ahead to find out what's on, from Aboriginal Heritage Walks to craft days at the Plant Craft Cottage. Don't miss the special Ian Potter Children's Garden near the main Observatory entrance where kids can explore, paddle, hide, dig and climb (bring a spare set of clothes).

Yarra Bend Park
Entrances at various locations
13 1963; www.parkweb.vic.gov.au
Varied operating times for activities
FREE ENTRY; VARIED PRICES FOR ACTIVITIES
Yarra Bend Park is one of the last original stands of bushland in inner Melbourne. At the bottom of the website page you can download a brochure with a map and list of activities. Kids will enjoy looking for flying foxes from the viewing platform at Bellbird Picnic Area or hiring a boat from Studley Park Boathouse (03) 9853 1972; www.studleyparkboathouse.com.au

Special events

Moomba
Early Mar
www.moombafestival.com.au
The Moomba program varies from year to year, with a mixture of old favourites and a few surprises. Three days of free family fun include the famous Moomba Parade.

Chinese New Year
Date varies
Little Bourke Street and surrounds
www.chinesenewyear.com.au
Melbourne's huge Chinese community puts on a colourful and noisy show to celebrate the top event in the Chinese calendar. The Chinatown setting dates back to the 1850s and makes this one of the most atmospheric Chinese New Year events in Australia.

Royal Melbourne Show
Sept
www.royalshow.com.au
This fun, 10-day event includes dog judging, woodchopping, craft and cake decorating displays, carnival rides and lots of opportunities to see animals. And there are the showbags!

Moomba festival parade, Melbourne

Day trips

Dandenong Ranges National Park

(03) 9758 7522 or 1800 645 505
www.parkweb.vic.gov.au
45 km/1 hr east

FREE

This magnificent forest area has walking trails and lovely picnic spots in the midst of tall gums and lush tree ferns. Download a nature walk guide from the website. You will probably see colourful crimson rosellas, but you will need to look harder to see superb lyrebirds – large brownish-grey birds with long tails – scratching around in the undergrowth. Puffing Billy Steam Railway is nearby (see p. 150).

Fairy Park

2388 Ballan Rd, Anakie
(03) 5284 1262; www.fairypark.com
90 km/1 hr 15 min west

MID-RANGE

Over 20 scenes from fairytales 'come to life' when you push a button. There are also model trains and a Camelot playground where kids can explore secret passages, tunnel mazes, towers and dark dungeons.

Ford Discovery Centre

Cnr Gheringhap and Brougham sts, Geelong
(03) 5227 8700;
www.forddiscovery.com.au

75 km/1 hr south-west
Closed Tues

BUDGET

Kids love wheels and they'll see plenty of them in this display of Ford vehicles from around the world. Exhibits explain production processes and kids can even help 'build' a car using a control panel. Ford Discovery Centre is en route to Fairy Park (*see above*).

Healesville Sanctuary

Badger Creek Rd, Healesville
(03) 5957 2800;
www.zoo.org.au/HealesvilleSanctuary
90 km/2 hr north-east
Open every day including Christmas Day

MID-RANGE

The sanctuary houses 200 species of Australian animals in a natural bushland setting with large, walk-through exhibits. Don't miss the free-flight birds of prey displays, and check the timetable for keeper talks and feeding times. Behind-the-scenes animal encounters are available for extra cost.

Puffing Billy Steam Railway

Departs from Belgrave Station, Belgrave
(03) 9757 0700; www.puffingbilly.com.au
40 km/1 hr east
Operates daily; check website for times

HIGH COST

This 100-year-old steam train wends its way through the scenic Dandenong Ranges from Belgrave to Gembrook. Don't miss the opportunity to hop off midway at Emerald Lake Park for a picnic or swim. Note: only prams that fit under seats can be accommodated.

RAAF Museum Point Cook

Point Cook Rd, RAAF Base Williams, Point Cook
(03) 9256 1040;
www.airforce.gov.au/RAAFMuseum
30 km/35 min south-west
Closes mid-afternoon on weekdays and closed Mon

FREE

This museum houses an interesting historical display of aircraft and Royal Australian Air Force artefacts dating back to World War I. At 1pm on Tuesday, Thursday and Sunday you can even see one of the heritage aircraft being flown, and this may include an aerobatic display. Visitors aged 16 years and over need to bring photo ID to obtain entry to the RAAF base where the museum is housed.

Tank Ride

Werribee area
(02) 8324 9999 or 1300 791 793;
www.adrenalin.com.au
35 km/30 min south-west
One day per month; check website

HIGH COST

Hop aboard a World War II Centurian Tank and find out what it was like to be a soldier inside this 52-tonne monster, then go on an exciting 20-minute ride over hills and through holes and puddles!

Werribee Open Range Zoo

K Rd, Werribee
(03) 9731 9600; www.zoo.org.au
WerribeeOpenRangeZoo
35 km/30 min south-west
Extended weekend hours in summer
Last tour departs 3.40pm daily

MID-RANGE

Take an African safari ride to see lions, rhinos, giraffes, zebras, monkeys, cheetahs and hippos. Phone ahead or check the website for special animal encounters; some cost extra and most need to be booked in advance. For pre-schoolers, there

Werribee Open Range Zoo, Werribee

are short Junior Safaris with puppets and music on Tuesdays, and on weekdays from 10am to 2pm the African Safari Hut has an interactive musical dance show. You can also stay the night as part of the Zoo Roar'n Snore (*see* ACCOMMODATION p. 152).

Yarra Valley Railway
Departs from the old Healesville station, Healesville–Kinglake Rd, Healesville
(03) 5962 2490;
www.yarravalleyrailway.org.au
70 km/1 hr 15 min north-east
CHECK OPERATING HOURS

Fancy a fun, half-hour, clackety-clack ride on open trolley cars, including a trip through a tunnel?

Enquire about steam train rides as well, and don't miss the playground over the road from the station.

See also Mornington Peninsula (p. 177), Phillip Island (p. 203)

Accommodation

Darling Towers South Yarra
Head Office, 32 Darling St, South Yarra
(03) 9525 4028 or 1300 858 607;
www.darlingtowers.com
BUDGET TO MID-RANGE

A range of two- and three-bedroom, self-contained apartments are available in this up-market inner suburb close to public transport, shops and eateries.

Habitat HQ
333 St Kilda Rd, St Kilda
(03) 9537 3777 or 1800 202 500;
www.thehabitathq.com.au
BUDGET

Located in a fun beachside suburb close to Luna Park,

transport and eateries, this four-star backpacker accommodation has a private motel floor with ensuite bathrooms for families. Rooms have a double bed and two bunk beds, and you can use the communal kitchen and lounge downstairs.

Quay West Suites
26 Southgate Ave, Southbank
(03) 9693 6000 or 13 1515;
www.mirvachotels.com
HIGH COST

Splurge on a fabulously located luxury apartment with three bedrooms and two bathrooms in this five-star, all-suite hotel with an indoor heated pool.

Quest on Bourke
155 Bourke St, Melbourne
(03) 9631 0400;
www.questonbourke.com
MID-RANGE
A two-bedroom, standard apartment in this great city location has a kitchen, laundry, living room, spa bathroom and DVD player.

Zoo Roar'n Snore
Melbourne Zoo, Elliott Ave, Parkville
1300 ZOOS VIC or (03) 9285 9300;
*www.zoo.org.au/Melbourne/Roar_n_*
Snore
Selected nights from Sept–May
Minimum age 5 years
HIGH COST, INCLUDES MEALS AND ADMISSION TO ZOO

Fancy a night with the animals? Sleep in a safari tent in a historic elephant enclosure! Tent, mattresses and meals are provided; bring sleeping bags and pillows. Explore the zoo in the dark when the nocturnal creatures are stirring, and in the morning there are opportunities for special behind-the-scenes encounters.

Places to eat

Colonial Tramcar Restaurant
Departs Tramstop 125, Normanby Rd, South Melbourne
(03) 9696 4000;
www.tramrestaurant.com.au
Suitable for ages 8+
It is a unique Melbourne experience to have an elegant meal on a moving tram. Choose between a lunchtime meal (with a better view of the passing streets) or the early dinner service. The meal is a set menu but you can pre-book a simplified version for kids at a slightly reduced price. Some staff make a special effort for kids, such as singing or teaching them origami. Arrive no later than 15 minutes prior to departure.

mr. wolf
9–15 Inkerman St, St Kilda
(02) 9534 0255; www. mrwolf.com.au
This trendy, kid-friendly eatery in beachside St Kilda provides colouring pictures and crayons. The dining room opens at 5pm and the Italian menu has special 'bambini' options for the kids.

The Slow Coach Horse Drawn Dining Carriage

260 Chum Creek Rd, Healesville
(03) 5962 2511; www.slowcoach.com.au

If you are visiting Healesville, you might like to try the unique experience of having breakfast, lunch or dinner in an 1890s omnibus drawn by three magnificent Clydesdales, surrounded by antique furnishings and travelling through the scenic Yarra Valley. A kids' menu is available.

Southgate Riverside Food Court

3 Southgate Ave, Southbank
(03) 9686 1000;
www.southgate-melbourne.com.au

Bright, casual and right on the riverside promenade, the food court has a range of takeaway food, so everyone can choose what they want and sit down together at the tables and seats provided.

Victoria Street Vietnamese restaurants

Victoria St, Richmond

Close to the city, this interesting strip of authentic Vietnamese (and other Asian) restaurants offers tasty, fast, casual and low-cost dining.

BALLARAT & SURROUNDS

Ballarat is located 115 kilometres north-west of Melbourne; accessible by train
Year-round day trip or holiday destination

HIGHLIGHTS

Blood on the Southern Cross   *p. 154*

Sovereign Hill   *p. 156*

Around town

Blood on the Southern Cross, Ballarat

Blood on the Southern Cross

Bradshaw St, Ballarat
(03) 5337 1199; www.sovereignhill.com.au/sound-light-show

HIGH COST

You are standing in the dark, under the night sky. Your children huddle close, shivering with cold and excitement. In front of you, there's a burst of noise. Buildings roar into flame. There are voices shouting in fury, and the rat-a-tat of gun fire... This is a re-enactment of the battle between gold miners and Government forces that took place in Ballarat in 1854. As the sound and lighting effects explode among the tents and buildings of a recreated gold town, you can imagine how it must have felt to be part of the battle.

INSIDER TIPS

- The show doesn't start until after sunset, which means a 9.15pm start from December to January. The earliest commencement times are 6.45pm, from April to September. You can check all times on the website.

- The performance runs for about one-and-a-half hours and you move around the grounds of Sovereign Hill during the show, boarding motorised carriages at some points. The show is also available in German, Japanese, Chinese and French; phone (03) 5337 1199 for details.

- At the beginning there is a short movie explaining the Eureka rebellion.

- Warn your kids that this is a sound and light show without actors. There is a voice-over narration, but it is necessary to imagine the people in the scenes.

- Most of the action takes place at a distance, like watching from the back of a football stadium. One of the highlights is when a burning runaway wagon careers towards the audience, then explodes in a ball of fire.

- Dinner is available on site.

- You can purchase combined tickets for the show with dinner, accommodation, and/or a visit to Sovereign Hill.

- This is a night-time activity in the open air, so dress appropriately.

- Before you visit, you might want to read a book about the Eureka rebellion with your kids, for example *The Night We Made the Flag: A Eureka Story* by Carole Wilkinson and Sebastian Ciaffaglione.

DON'T MISS

- The chance to stay overnight at Sovereign Hill Lodge (*see* ACCOMMODATION, p. 163). It's a short walk back to your room at the end of the show and you'll have no trouble filling two days at Sovereign Hill (*see* p. 156).

⚡ FABULOUS FACTS

Blood on the Southern Cross is a re-enactment of an event known as the Eureka Stockade. In late 1854, in the gold town of Ballarat, a miner was murdered and the Eureka Hotel's proprietor, the prime suspect, was not charged. Thousands of protesting miners stormed the hotel and burned it. The miners formed a society demanding better rights. They built themselves a wooden stockade. At sunrise on 3 December, government troops attacked. The diggers lost the battle, but a few months later fairer laws were introduced, including the right to vote. Many claim the Eureka Stockade was the beginning of democracy in Australia.

Kid Quest
The men in the Eureka Stockade created a flag. What did it look like? If you made a flag for your family, what would it look like?
See pp. 640–4 for the answer

Panning for gold at Sovereign Hill, Ballarat

Sovereign Hill
Bradshaw St, Ballarat
(03) 5337 1100; www.sovereignhill.com.au
HIGH COST

With the promise of real gold to be found, your kids will grab gold panning dishes and get stuck into the mud. As they shake eagerly, watching for microscopic specks of gold, they will understand the fever which brought people flocking here from all over the world in the 1850s. Surrounded by the sounds and sights of the recreated goldfields – tents of miners, the clatter of horses and carts, and people wandering around in 19th-century dress – they will feel as if they have gone back in time.

INSIDER TIPS

■ Allow a full day for this attraction – and even then you won't see everything!

■ There are various food outlets, but they can get very crowded and sometimes sell out early. You can pre-order, or you might want to bring your own picnic.

■ Sovereign Hill is spread over a large area so there is lots of walking involved and you'll spend most of your time outdoors. If you visit in winter, wear warm jackets and old shoes – it gets very muddy underfoot, just as it did in the real goldfields.

■ You can purchase tickets online. There are sometimes long queues at the entrance, but these generally move quickly.

■ There are a few activities not covered by the entry ticket, such as carriage rides and the guided mine tour.

■ You can reach Sovereign Hill by V/line train on the Goldrush Special. It takes you from Melbourne's Southern Cross Station to Ballarat Station, where you are met by a courtesy coach. For more information see www.vline.com.au (select 'Discover Victoria').

■ Troopers march around and sometimes fire their muskets (the sound might scare littlies).

■ The guided mine tour (extra cost) is led by a character in costume who pretends that you are new workers about to start.

DON'T MISS

■ The free underground Red Hill mine tour, which is self-guided with audiovisual activation.

■ The melting and pouring of a large ingot of gold at the Gold Smelting Works.

■ The chance to take home a horseshoe memento from the blacksmith with your names stamped into it (extra cost).

■ Having a family portrait taken at the photography studio – with everyone dressed in period costume. Phone ahead to book an appointment (extra cost).

- The school house. If you are lucky, it will be filled with children in 1850s dress having a class. Your kids will be intrigued by the different lessons – students reciting the 17 times table – and a strict teacher wielding a cane.
- The performances in the Victoria Theatre (no extra cost).
- Other favourites such as bowling, seeing how to make wooden carriage wheels, and confectionary making, all included with entry cost.
- The Gold Museum across the road (*see facing page*), entry included with Sovereign Hill admission.

FABULOUS FACTS

The discovery of gold in Ballarat and surrounding districts in 1851 heralded a boom time for the state of Victoria. The population doubled in a year. Canvas villages and solid towns sprang up all over the countryside, and Melbourne was transformed in one decade from a muddy frontier town to a city of grand buildings.

Kid Quest
Have a go at panning for gold and see what you find!

Ballarat Bird World
408 Eddy Ave, Mt Helen
(03) 5341 3843;
www.ballaratbirdworld.com.au

MID-RANGE

Follow a 1-kilometre walkway through bushland to see over 200 colourful native and exotic parrots and cockatoos in their enclosures. Kids like the large free-flight aviary where they can walk among the birds.

Ballarat Botanic Gardens
Wendouree Pde, Ballarat
(03) 5320 5135

FREE

Ballarat's historic gardens include grand old trees, marble sculptures, elegant rotundas and an intriguing conservatory made of zigzag glass roofs. There is a fabulous adventure playground adjacent to Lake Wendouree in the middle of the park. The Prime Ministers Avenue provides an introduction to Australian political history.

Ballarat Vintage Tramway and Tramway Museum

South Gardens Reserve, Botanical Gardens, Ballarat
(03) 5341 1580; www.btm.org.au
Trams run weekends, public and school holidays, 12.30–5pm
BUDGET
Take a rattling ride on one of the Tramway Museum's collection of vintage trams. You travel along 1.6 kilometres of track around the suburbs of Ballarat.

Ballarat Wildlife and Reptile Park

Cnr York and Fussell sts, Ballarat East
(03) 5333 5933;
www.wildlifepark.com.au
MID-RANGE

Ballarat Wildlife and Reptile Park, Ballarat East

This is a chance for close encounters with Australian animals: you can feed kangaroos, have your photo taken with a koala and, on weekends and holidays, there are interactive shows with crocodiles, snakes and spotted-tail quolls.

Eerie Tours of Ballarat

Depart from Ballarat's Old Cemetery Gates
1300 856 668;
www.eerietours.com.au
Seasonal times
Bookings essential
Suitable for ages 6+
Mid-range
If your kids are keen on ghosts and ghoulies you can do a one-and-a-half-hour walking tour of Ballarat's haunted sites. Be warned, though, the content of the tour may be disturbing for children (or adults!) of any age.

Gold Museum

Bradshaw St, Ballarat
(03) 5337 1107;
www.sovereignhill.com.au
PRICE INCLUDED IN SOVEREIGN HILL ENTRY
This is where you can see some real gold nuggets found in the area. The museum display includes a video by local Aboriginal people about the impact of the Gold Rush on their lives.

Her Majesty's Theatre

17 Lydiard St, Ballarat
(03) 5333 5800; www.hermaj.com
Check the website in advance to see what's on — it's a real experience to see a performance in this gorgeous historic theatre.

Her Majesty's Theatre, Ballarat

Horse Monument

Sturt St, Ballarat
Ballarat Visitor Information
Centre 1800 446 633
FREE
This statue of a horse, dedicated to the hundreds of thousands of horses killed in World War I, is part of a statue walk. You can pick up a brochure or an audio tour on the walk from the visitor information centre at the Art Gallery, 40 Lydiard Street North, and while you're there make sure you see the original Eureka flag.

Kirrit Barreet Aboriginal Art and Cultural Centre

407 Main Rd, Ballarat
(03) 5332 2755;
www.aboriginalballarat.com.au
Open weekdays
FREE
See displays of traditional artefacts of the Aboriginal people, particularly the local Wathaurong clans — you can touch and feel some of the exhibits, including a possum skin cloak.

In the area

Bendigo Pottery
146 Midland Hwy, Bendigo
(03) 5448 4404;
www.bendigopottery.com.au

BUDGET

For a fun, messy time, there's a clay play area for kids, and you can also have wheel-throwing lessons (bookings recommended). An interpretive museum has dioramas on the production processes and working conditions of pottery makers here since 1858.

Big Tree
Cnr Fryers and Ballarat sts, Guildford
(signposted off the hwy)

FREE

For kids who like to see giant things, this magnificent ancient red gum is supposed to be the largest of its kind in Victoria. It is 26 metres high and has a circumference of 12.8 metres.

Castlemaine Diggings National Heritage Park
Covers a 7500 ha area to the south and east of Castlemaine
www.parkweb.vic.gov.au

FREE

See the remains of house sites, puddling machines and gullies where people hunted for gold in the 1850s. A map and brochure of walking and driving trails can be downloaded from the website. Have a go at panning for gold in Forest Creek where so many diggers found their fortunes.

Central Deborah Gold Mine
76 Violet St, Bendigo
(03) 5443 8322;
www.central-deborah.com

MID-RANGE

Put on hard hats and miners' lamps before descending 61 metres underground into a real gold mine. If your kids are 8 years of age or over, you can take them on the Adventure Tour which includes climbing ladders and working mine drills to search for gold.

Castlemaine Diggings National Heritage Park

Chocolate Mill

5451 Midland Hwy, Mount Franklin
(03) 5476 4208; www.chocmill.com.au
Open Tues–Sun,
demonstrations twice daily

FREE VIEWING

Watch a presentation on chocolate making and taste yummy handmade chocolates and hot chocolate drinks. The chocolatier is located inside an interesting straw-bale building.

Discovery Science and Technology Centre

7 Railway Pl, Bendigo
(03) 5444 4400; www.discovery.asn.au

MID-RANGE

Ever wondered how to use a pair of thongs to play a tune? Well, find out here, along with all the other fun, hands-on, quirky science activities for kids.

Golden Dragon Museum

5 Bridge St, Bendigo
(03) 5441 5044;
www.goldendragonmuseum.org

BUDGET

Indoors you can see the oldest Imperial (five-clawed) Chinese

Golden Dragon Museum, Bendigo

Dragon in the world, and his replacement, the longest Imperial Chinese Dragon in the world. Outdoors you can wander through a beautiful, authentic Chinese garden.

Gum San Chinese Heritage Centre

31–33 Lambert St, Ararat
(03) 5352 1078; www.gumsan.com.au

MID-RANGE

Through real relics, life-like sculptured characters and state-of-the-art presentations, you can immerse yourselves in the life of Chinese immigrants during Ararat's gold rush. You can also learn a bit of calligraphy and Chinese language.

Tangled Maze

2301 Midland Hwy, Springmount
(03) 5345 2847;
www.tangledmaze.com.au

MID-RANGE

Lose yourselves in the garden maze with its 2-metre-high walls made of thousands of flowering creepers, and choose from minigolf, bocce, quoits, giant chess, and noughts and crosses.

Tuki Trout Farm

Stony Rises, Smeaton
(03) 5345 6233; www.tuki.com.au

MID-RANGE

Choose between well-stocked ponds – where even little fisherfolk are guaranteed to catch a fish – and more challenging ponds for the more experienced.

You can have your catch cooked in the restaurant, or cleaned and packaged ready for you to take away.

Victorian Goldfields Railway

Trains run between Maldon and Castlemaine
(03) 5470 6658; www.vgr.com.au
Wed and Sun
Check timetable

MID-RANGE

Take a ride on a heritage steam train through the goldfields district. For a small extra charge you can organise to ride in the engine cab!

Victorian Goldfields Railway passing by Muckleford

Accommodation

Bedsconnect

Ballarat area
www.bedsconnect.com.au

BUDGET TO MID-RANGE

This service offers various B&B or self-contained accommodation options that you can check out and book online. Choices include a cottage with books and toys for kids, and a modern townhouse in the middle of a forest.

BIG4 Holiday Parks

Ballarat area
www.ballarat.vic.big4.com.au

BUDGET TO MID-RANGE

There are three different BIG4 Holiday Parks in the Ballarat area: Goldfields, Welcome Stranger and Windmill. All offer a choice of camping sites or two- or three-bedroom cabins and have a variety of facilities including pools, jumping pillows, minigolf, playgrounds, ball games, recreation rooms with free computer games, kids' programs and holiday movies.

Sovereign Hill Lodge

Magpie St, Ballarat
(03) 5337 1159;
www.sovereignhill.com.au

MID-RANGE

You can stay in a motel-style family room on the grounds of Sovereign Hill (*see* p. 156). Packages are available that include some meals and entry to Sovereign Hill.

Places to eat

Ballarat Leagues Club
52 Humffray St, Ballarat
(03) 5331 5830;
www.ballaratleaguesclub.com.au
While you dine, keep an eye on
your kids enjoying Kids Korner,
with its Xbox computer games,
TV, movies, books and board
games. When they are ready to
eat, they can choose from an
imaginative and varied kids'
menu.

Da Uday
7 Wainwright St, Ballarat
(03) 5331 6655; www.dauday.com
No more arguments about what
to eat – Da Uday has three
different cuisines. This child-
friendly restaurant has Italian,
Indian and Thai menus and a
special kids' selection.

Robin Hood Family Bistro
33 Peel St (Nth), Ballarat
(03) 5331 3433;
www.robinhoodfamilybistro.com.au
There is an indoor children's
playground and a kids' menu
here. Prices are generally
reasonable and you can opt for a
smorgasbord dinner.

EAST GIPPSLAND

The region starts near Bairnsdale, 280 kilometres east of Melbourne and encompasses Lakes Entrance and the Wilderness Coast

Best suited to driving holidays, although Bairnsdale is accessible by train

Year-round holiday destination

HIGHLIGHTS

Bataluk Cultural Trail   *p. 165*

Buchan Caves   *p. 169*

Gippsland Lakes cruises   *p. 171*

Around Bairnsdale

Bataluk Cultural Trail
Various sites throughout East Gippsland
www.maffra.net.au/bataluk/sites.htm

Quietly, in single file, you wend your way down into a deep, rocky gorge. It opens out and you find yourselves in a rainforest gully. Mossy trees are entwined with vines and a creek trickles at your feet before vanishing into a gaping cavern known as the Den of Nargun. In a soft voice, you relate the myth of the Nargun (*see* FABULOUS FACTS p. 167). You picture the Aboriginal women and children sitting around their campfires telling the same tale. This is just one stop on the cultural trail that takes you into the world of the Koorie people.

INSIDER TIPS

■ The signposted Bataluk Cultural Trail extends from Sale in the east, through Stratford, Mitchell River National Park, Bairnsdale, Metung, Lake Tyers, Buchan and Orbost to Cape Conran in the west.

■ You can find more details about this driving trail on the website, and you should be able to pick up brochures at local visitor centres.

■ The trail follows the trading routes created by the traditional owners of the land before white settlement.

■ At Knob Reserve (western end of Stratford) you can find deeply grooved stones by the river where Koorie people used to sharpen axe heads, and at the wetlands near Sale, interpretive signs around Lake Guthridge give information about the plants, birds and raw materials that could be gathered here.

■ The Den of Nargun is located in the Mitchell River National Park (*see* p. 169). There is a carpark and picnic ground with barbecues and toilets at the southern end of the park.

■ Sometimes the mouth of the cave is screened by mist or a waterfall.

■ The walk to the cave takes approximately 15 minutes each way.

■ Natural stepping stones lead into the den, but the local Aboriginal community prefer you not to enter, as this is still a significant cultural site. You are especially asked not to touch any fragile stalactites forming inside.

DON'T MISS

■ The signposted turn-off to Burnt Bridge Reserve from the Princes Highway between Lakes Entrance and Nowa Nowa. This borders Lake Tyers Aboriginal Reserve, the site of the first successful Aboriginal Land Rights claim in Australia's history.

■ Salmon Rock at Cape Conran, east of Marlo. From the platform at Salmon Rock you can view an Aboriginal shell midden that could be 10 000 years old. Koorie people must have gathered here for generations to feast, celebrate and perform ceremonies.

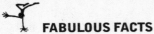

FABULOUS FACTS

According to legend, the Nargun is a large, half-stone, half-human female creature who lives in the cave. She abducts children who wander off on their own, and if you try to throw stones or spears at her, they will just bounce off. Women used to warn their children about the Nargun to make sure they stayed close to camp and did not enter the sacred cave.

Bairnsdale Archery, Mini Golf and Games Park
459 Princes Hwy, Bairnsdale East
(03) 5156 8655;
www.bairnsdalefunpark.com.au
PAY PER ACTIVITY OR BUY A PACKAGE

This games park has more than minigolf on offer. Archery is the big drawcard and there's bungee trampolining, a jumping castle, a batting cage, spaceball, a solar heated pool complete with waterfall, and a merry-go-round. There are also free activities, picnic facilities and a cafe.

Bancroft Bay pelican feeding
The Metung Hotel, Kurnai Ave, Metung
(03) 5156 2206;
www.metunghotel.com.au
FREE

Watch the pelicans being fed at noon every day outside the Metung Hotel.

Riding along the East Gippsland Rail Trail

East Gippsland Rail Trail
www.eastgippslandrailtrail.com
FREE

Go on a cycling (or walking) adventure along the path of the old railway line from Bairnsdale to Orbost. Travel through forests and over fantastic old rail bridges (no steep climbs). Watch for emus, wallabies, kangaroos, eagles, goannas and other wildlife. The trail extends 100 kilometres in total, but you can undertake small sections if you choose. There is accommodation along the way as well as options for camping. Bike hire and trail maps are available Monday–Saturday from Riviera Cycles, 193 Main Street, Bairnsdale; (03) 5152 1886; www.rivieracycles.com.au

Gippsland Vehicle Collection
1A Sale Rd, Maffra
(03) 5147 3223;
www.gippslandvehiclecollection.org.au
Open Fri–Mon
BUDGET
This ever-changing display of road vehicles includes classic and modern cars, motorbikes, horse-drawn carriages, trucks and related memorabilia.

Howitt Park Adventure Playground
Princes Hwy, East Bairnsdale
FREE
Kids will release some energy on the super slide, 40-metre flying fox and other play equipment

including swings, sandpits, bridges, and see-saws. It is also a stop on the Bataluk Cultural Trail (*see* p. 165). When the golden wattles came into bloom, Aboriginal people came here to harvest fat eels in the river. Women wove baskets from reeds and filled them with mussels, fruit and roots. Look for a scarred tree where the men peeled away the bark to make a canoe.

Krowathunkooloong Keeping Place
37–53 Dalmahoy St, Bairnsdale
(03) 5152 1891
Closed weekends
BUDGET
Learn about the cultural heritage of East Gippsland's Indigenous people through videos and check out the display of artefacts such as shields, boomerangs, bark canoes and baskets.

Metung
FREE
Wander along the boardwalk, play on the safe family beach on the shores of Lake King, and keep an eye out for dolphins. Look for the Legend Rock, part of the Bataluk Cultural Trail (*see* p. 165), which stands in the sea opposite the Metung Yacht Club. According to legend, a group of hunters were turned into stone for disobeying tribal law. The other stones were destroyed for roadworks in the 1960s.

Mitchell River National Park
25 km north-west of Bairnsdale
www.parkweb.vic.gov.au
FREE

The rugged gorges and lovely rockpools of the Mitchell River are a short (but steep) walk from the main carpark. It's a spectacular setting for a picnic and a bit of exploring. Kids will be intrigued by the giant kanooka trees which grow out of the water in a tangle of vines and ferns. See if you can spot any satin bowerbirds – or their bowers – in the park. The Den of Nargun that forms part of the Bataluk Cultural Trail (see FABULOUS FACTS p. 167) is also located here.

Raymond Island
In the Gippsland Lakes
www.raymondisland.net
BUDGET

Accessible from Paynesville by a 3-minute car ferry ride, the island is one of the best places in the world to see koalas. It is inhabited, and there are eateries and accommodation.

Around Lakes Entrance

Buchan Caves
Buchan–Bruthen Rd, Buchan
(03) 5162 1900; www.parkweb.vic.gov.au
MID-RANGE

Before you even arrive, your kids will be intrigued by the name 'Fairy Cave'. When you venture down underground and they see the glistening stalactites and stalagmites, they will not be disappointed. As your guide relates the story of the cave's discovery, you will know your kids are imagining what it was like to be Frank Moon, that first adventurer back in 1907, who lowered himself by rope 15 metres down a dark hole into the unknown, and how it would feel to come across this amazing sight for the first time.

Buchan Caves, Buchan

INSIDER TIPS

- This is a stop on the Bataluk Cultural Trail (*see* p. 165).

- Buchan Caves can only be accessed by guided tours that run several times daily; check the website for times.

- There are usually two caves open to the public: Fairy Cave and Royal Cave, both of which have lighting and walkways. Royal Cave is known for its calcite-rimmed pools.

- The surrounding reserve has campsites, a picnic ground, playground, toilets, kiosk and visitor centre.

- If you dare, you can take a dip in an icy pool fed by natural spring water from the depths of the caves.

- The caves are a constant 17 degrees Celsius, so dress appropriately.

- For the record, stalactites are the ones hanging down from the roof and stalagmites are the ones growing up from the floor. They are both created by a build up of droplets of rain water seeping through cracks and dissolving some of the limestone.

- Luxury camping is available at Wilderness Retreats (*see* ACCOMMODATION, p. 175).

DON'T MISS

- Kangaroos grazing on the grassy slopes of the reserve, especially in the early morning and at dusk.

FABULOUS FACTS

Electricians who recently replaced the ageing, dangerous lighting in the caves found the job an interesting challenge. Not only did they have to carry their equipment 1.5 kilometres underground but, after working in the dark environment for five months, they had to be tested for Vitamin D deficiency. And what's more, they discovered if they tried to call out to workmates around a corner, their voices didn't carry.

> ### Kid Quest
> *Aboriginal people inhabited caves in the Buchan region more than 18 000 years ago. Design a cave you would like to live in.*

Gippsland Lakes cruises

Gippsland Lakes Coastal Park
1800 637 060; www.parkweb.vic.gov.au

VARIOUS COSTS

You're on a real research expedition, chugging along the water in a small cruiser. Everyone is supplied with binoculars and a booklet with coloured photos of birds to identify and count. There's a squeal of glee as a line of seabirds comes into sight, perched on a rock wall. Your kids eagerly riffle though their booklets and start to count. In this cruise packed full of excitement and educational opportunities, they identify more than a dozen birds, learn how to tell the difference between gastropod and bivalve shells, spot seahorses and help in a research project to find out the best salinity levels to sustain seahorses.

INSIDER TIPS

- Gippsland Lakes is the largest expanse of inland waterways in the Southern Hemisphere. It is made up of Lake Wellington, McLennans Strait, Lake Victoria and Lake King, and joins the waters of Bass Strait through a man made entrance at Lakes Entrance.

- The research expeditions are on the *Lakes Explorer*, (03) 5155 5027 or 0458 511 438; www.lakes-explorer.com.au. They depart Wednesday–Sunday and last about two hours, including island stops. You can take home the bird identification booklets as souvenirs. The minimum age is 4 years.

- Other, less interactive, cruises are offered on the *Stormbird:* www.lakesentrance.com/cruises/peels-stormbird-cruise.html

- You can hire your own boat to explore the lakes from Bulls Cruisers, 54 Slip Road, Paynesville, (03) 5156 1200; www.bullscruisers.com.au. All the way round you will find islands, villages, parks and marinas where you can pull up your boat and explore. You can fish in the lakes and keep an eye out for dolphins and pelicans.

- The lakes are bordered by The Lakes National Park and Gippsland Lakes Coastal Park, where you can camp or go for walks. You can download information brochures from the Parks Victoria website.

- There are safe swimming sites along the sheltered shores of Bunga Arm.

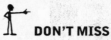

DON'T MISS

- The iron hull of the sailing ship *Trinculo*, wrecked here in 1879, still visible in the sand west of Delray Beach.

- Rotamah Island, home to many native waterbirds and wildlife. Kids have fun watching from bird hides.

- Raymond Island (*see* p. 169).

FABULOUS FACTS

The Gippsland Lakes have the largest concentration of migratory waders in East Gippsland. If you don't do the research cruise, bring a bird identification book and see how many birds you can spot. One of the endangered birds you might see is the little tern which migrates to Rigby Island and Ninety Mile Beach in September to breed. If you walk on the beach during October, be careful not to step on their well-camouflaged eggs and nests. The eggs are light brownish grey, with brown and purple splotches, and the nests are just shallow scrapes in the shell grit.

Kid Quest
The way to tell black-faced cormorants from little pied cormorants is by their black 'trousers' (black-feathered legs). How many of each bird can you spot?

Lake Tyers Forest Park
20 kilometres north-east of Lakes Entrance via Princes Hwy; access from Burnt Bridge Rd or Tyers House Rd (both unsealed) Lakes and Wilderness Tourism Centre (03) 5155 1966; www.parkweb.vic.gov.au
FREE
Take a picnic and go for a bushwalk – Marsdenia Rainforest Walk is a short, easy loop – and see how many birds you can spot. You can also fish in the lakes.

Lakes Entrance
The narrow arms of the lakes around Lakes Entrance are ideal for paddling around in a pedal-boat, aqua bike or catamaran available for hire from Lakes Paddle Boats, (03) 5155 2753; www.lakes-entrance.com/paddleboats

Lunch near the Surf Life Saving Club, Lakes Entrance

National Dollhouse Gallery and Cafe Puppenhaus
24 School Rd, Swan Reach
(03) 5156 4436 or 1300 791 099;
www.nationaldollhousegallery.com.au
Closed Aug and Mon, Tues and public
holidays

MID-RANGE

Gaze in wonder at the array of tiny houses and shops, both modern and antique, containing the most amazingly detailed miniature furnishings. There is a dollhouse shop and cafe on site.

Ninety Mile Beach
www.parkweb.vic.gov.au

FREE

An endless expanse of unspoilt golden sands, lapping waves, dolphins ... and hardly a soul in sight! The fine sand harbours more animals per square metre than most other marine habitats in the world, so look for tiny creatures scurrying and burrowing. Warning: this is a potentially hazardous (and often windy) ocean beach; while small sections are patrolled during peak seasons, do not come here in search of calm waters.

Surf Shack Surf School
507 Espl, Lakes Entrance
(03) 5155 4933; www.surfshack.com.au
Bookings essential
Minimum age 8 years
Weather dependent and minimum three
people

HIGH COST

Lessons include board, wetsuit, sunscreen and instructions in surf safety.

Wyungara Nature Sanctuary
Veldens Rd, Lakes Entrance
(03) 5156 5863;
www.lakesentrance.com/activities/
wyungara-nature-sanctuary.html
Bookings essential
Seasonal times

MID-RANGE

On a two-and-a-half hour spotlight tour you will see nocturnal animals such as gliders, possums, koalas, wallabies, wombats, bats and owls living wild in a natural a bush environment.

See also Bataluk Cultural Trail (p. 165)

Wilderness Coast

Croajingolong National Park

Lighthouse tours (03) 5158 4268;
www.parkweb.vic.gov.au

FREE

This wild and beautiful park sprawls along 1000 kilometres of coast, offering opportunities for camping, fishing, surfing, boating and wildlife-watching. You can visit a lighthouse at Point Hicks, the first part of Australia sighted by Captain James Cook in 1770. Daily tours of the lighthouse are available.

Paddlesteamer *Curlip*

Departs from Marlo
(03) 5154 1699;
www.paddlesteamercurlip.com.au
Ring to check cruise times

MID-RANGE

Go back 100 years and take a cruise up and down the Snowy River on a replica paddlesteamer, the PS *Curlip*. Marlo is a scenic area where the Snowy River joins the sea.

See also Bataluk Cultural Trail (p. 165)

Accommodation

BIG4 Whiters Holiday Village

Cnr Whiters and Roadknight sts, Lakes Entrance
(03) 5155 1343; www.whiters.com.au

BUDGET TO MID-RANGE

Choose a campsite or self-contained cabin in this park,

only a short walk to the centre of town. The cabins have a double bed and two single beds or a bunk; some have private gardens. Facilities included three solar-heated pools, a tennis court, playground, barbecues and a TV/video lounge.

Bulls Cuisers

54 Slip Rd, Paynesville
(03) 5156 1200;
www.bullscruisers.com.au

HIGH COST

Experience the vast inland lake system on your own cruiser! Imagine being able to pull up whenever you like to hop on shore and explore. Some boats are more suitable for kids than others, so ask for the most appropriate vessel.

Eastern Beach Caravan Park
42 Eastern Beach Rd, Lakes Entrance
(03) 5155 1581;
www.easternbeach.com.au
BUDGET TO MID-RANGE
This park is walking distance to the surf beach and nature reserve. It offers a playground, jumping pillow and organised holiday activities on site. Choose a campsite or self-contained, two-bedroom cabin with air-conditioning and TV.

Fountain Court Apartments
Lake St, Lakes Entrance
(03) 5155 1949;
www.lakes-entrance.com/fountain
BUDGET
These self-contained, family-friendly apartments are located in the heart of Lakes Entrance. It features games room, half-size tennis court, pool and garden for the kids.

Lakes Apartments
35 Church St, Lakes Entrance
(03) 5155 6100;
www.thelakesapartments.com.au
MID-RANGE
Enjoy the comforts of a modern, self-contained, two- or three-bedroom apartment in the heart of town. Relax in the large pool or head for the recreation room.

Wilderness Retreats
Located at Cape Conran Coastal Park
and Buchan Caves Reserve
Book through Parks Victoria
(03) 8627 4700 or 13 1963;
www.parkweb.vic.gov.au/
wildernessretreats
MID-RANGE
This is luxury camping in permanent, elevated tents with large wooden sundecks. Enjoy a real bed on this 'camping' trip: there is a queen-size bed and two pull-out single beds; linen is supplied! You'll also have a fridge and cooking utensils on hand. There are communal bathrooms with hot showers and a communal barbecue.

Places to eat_____

Lakes Entrance Bowls Club
Cnr Rowe and Bulmers sts,
Lakes Entrance
(03) 5155 3578; www.lakesbowls.com.au
Kids can have fun in the
playroom while you enjoy a
relaxed meal. There are
Australian, Asian and kids' menus
on offer, and if you buy one kid's
meal you get one free.

The Lakes Sports and Community Club
38 Church St, Lakes Entrance
(03) 5155 3500
There is an outdoor playground
and indoor play equipment here.
Meals are traditional Australian
bistro-style, with a kids' menu.

MORNINGTON PENINSULA

*The region starts 70 kilometres south of Melbourne; driving
holiday or day trip*

*Beaches are best in warmer months (Dec–Mar), but there are
plenty of year-round activities*

HIGHLIGHTS

On the coast

Cape Schanck Lighthouse

420 Cape Schanck Rd, Cape Schanck
1300 885 259; www.parkweb.vic.gov.au
Free park entry; charges for lighthouse tours

Snug in your beds in a little historic
cottage, you listen to the wind howling
and waves crashing outside. The
adjacent lighthouse sends out its
warning beacon to ships, just as it has
for 150 years. In the morning, the sun
sparkles. Heady with excitement and
sea air, your kids scurry along the
boardwalk to the tip of Cape
Schanck. After splashing in the
rockpools, searching for starfish
and sea slugs, it's time to climb the
lighthouse for dramatic views of
the rugged coastline below.

Cape Schanck Lighthouse, Cape Schanck

INSIDER TIPS

- Accommodation at Cape Schanck is available in the assistant keepers' cottages (*see* ACCOMMODATION p. 189).

- You can take a self-guided tour of the lighthouse, or guided tours are available on request.

- The boardwalk is accessed by a short track from the lighthouse kiosk. Warning: waves can wash over the rocks.

- You can download a brochure with a map of walking tracks and facilities from the Parks Victoria website; keep to the tracks to avoid damaging fragile coastal vegetation.

- The lighthouse has a kiosk and toilets.

- Find out more about the history and construction of the lighthouse at www.lighthouse.net.au

DON'T MISS

- The lighthouse museum with displays about the history of different lighting techniques used in lighthouses. The Cape Schanck Lighthouse still has some original mechanisms.

- Fingal Picnic Area, 2 kilometres north of the cape. It has electric barbecues, toilets, tables, a games area and walking tracks (steep in places) leading to spectacular views of basalt cliffs and Fingal Beach (exposed at low tide).

- Magnificent coastal scenic views from the Bushrangers Bay track (from the eastern carpark); the full return walk takes about two hours, but you could do an abbreviated version if necessary.

FABULOUS FACTS

Despite many shipping disasters along the northern coast of Bass Strait in the early 1800s, government bureaucrats were reluctant to finance the building of lighthouses, claiming the shipwrecks were due to poor judgement on the part of ships' captains. Eventually, lighthouses were built, and Cape Schanck started operating in 1859. Nowadays, Global Positioning Systems (GPS) are reducing the need for many traditional lighthouses.

Kid Quest

How many steps are there to the top of the lighthouse?

See pp. 640–4 for the answer

Fort Nepean

Point Nepean National Park
End of Point Nepean Rd, Portsea
(03) 5984 6000; www.parkweb.vic.gov.au

FREE ENTRY; EXTRA COST FOR THE TRANSPORTER SERVICE

Leave behind the beautiful coastal scenery, birds and wallabies, and descend into a murky world of guns and warfare. Your kids will be thrilled to enter the underground tunnels, chambers and gun emplacements of a real fort. All around them, audiovisual displays bring the past back to life. The voices of people who served here tell tales of defending the Victorian coast from the 1880s to the 1940s. In the depths of a dark tunnel, there is an ominous rattling noise – a recording of the sound a 'disappearing gun' made when it was drawn down into a pit, to be kept secret from invaders' eyes until it was time to load and fire again.

INSIDER TIPS

■ Until 1988, Point Nepean was a prohibited area reserved for defence and quarantine purposes. Now a national park, you can visit the fort and other interesting sites. Download maps and information from the website, or pick up a brochure from the visitor centre.

■ A transporter service operates from the visitor centre, stopping at key sites around the national park. It is best to book ahead to make sure you get seats.

■ Alternatively, you can ride a bike to each site. Bikes are available for hire from the visitor centre. However, there are hills to negotiate and the route is shared with other vehicles.

■ There are steep ramps and steps inside the fort complex.

■ Walking tracks depart from each of the sites, and podcasts for each walk are available on the website.

■ Weather conditions can change rapidly at Point Nepean so bring a range of clothes – from weatherproof jackets to sunscreen and hats.

- Obey all warning signs. Make sure your kids stick to paths and do not climb on any fortifications. There could still be unexploded shells from artillery practice in the area, and cliff edges can be unstable. Swimming is forbidden around Point Nepean as the water is too dangerous.

- There is no food available in the national park except from vending machines, so bring your own.

- Toilets can be found at various locations.

DON'T MISS

- Views of the notorious 'Rip' and Cheviot Beach from the lookout on Cheviot Hill. The 'Rip' is the rough sea between Point Nepean and Point Lonsdale, one of the world's most hazardous harbour entrances. It was from Cheviot Beach that former Prime Minister of Australia, Harold Holt, disappeared in December 1967. He went for a swim and was never seen again; his body has never been found.

- The Quarantine Station (*see* FABULOUS FACTS *below*).

- Swamp wallabies, echidnas and sea eagles, commonly seen throughout the park.

FABULOUS FACTS

- In November 1852, a ship called the *Ticonderoga* was heading towards Australia with 300 sick passengers on board. It was stopped at Port Nepean and the passengers were off-loaded and housed in old lime-burners cottages. This was the beginning of the Port Nepean Quarantine Station. If you visit the site today, you can still see the old quarantine buildings, and displays reveal what it was like to live in quarantine. Guided walks of the station are available on weekends, public and school holidays; (03) 5984 9222; www.nepeanhistoricalsociety.asn.au/quarantine.html

---

Kid Quest

Shots were fired from Fort Nepean in both World War I and World War II. Who were they fired at?

See pp. 640–4 for the answer

French Island

Peninsula Visitor Information Centre 1800 804 009; www.parkweb.vic.gov.au

Imagine the excitement of boarding a small ferry, knowing you are crossing the water to a secluded island. On the other side, the kids leap onto Tankerton Jetty. You are now in another, almost forgotten world. There are hardly any cars and there is no mains electricity, piped water or sealed roads. There is just one store and it also serves as the post office. Only about 70 people live here, and the tiny school has less than ten pupils. But there are thousands of koalas, and lots of other wildlife and adventures to discover.

INSIDER TIPS

- It's a good idea to bring your own drinking water to the island. Water supplied at campsites must be boiled or purified.

- The northern two-thirds of the island is a national park. In spring, the national park is a blaze of colour from the hundreds of different indigenous plant species that grow here, including over 100 orchid species.

- The northern shore of the island is a marine park, which means that killing or taking fish or other marine creatures is forbidden.

- The only way to access the island is by a 30-minute passenger ferry ride from Stony Point, 30 kilometres north-east of Flinders (or from Cowes on Phillip Island). Contact Inter Island Ferries, (03) 9585 5730 or www.interislandferries.com.au.

- Hire a mountain bike (children's sizes available) from French Island General Store and Bike Hire, Tankerton Road; (03) 5980 1209. The roads are all gravel and sand but they are not hilly. You can book ahead and have bikes waiting at the jetty.

- If you want to stay overnight, there are farm stays, B&Bs and campsites.

- There are public toilets at the Fairhaven campsite on the western foreshore

- Open fires are banned at all times because the vegetation of the island is highly combustible, but portable gas stoves are permitted.

- Organic lunches and dinners are available at McLeod Eco Farm, McLeod Road; (03) 5980 1224.
- For organised tours of the island, contact French Island Eco Tours, www.frenchislandecotours.com.au, or French Island Tours, www.frenchislandtours.com.au.

DON'T MISS

- The historic Bayview Chicory Kiln in Bayview Road. You can have afternoon tea, pat farm animals and browse historical displays
- The koalas (see FABULOUS FACTS). There is also a large population of long-nosed potoroos, but these are nocturnal so you are less likely to see them.
- Birds feeding in the mudflats and mangroves of the marine park at low tide. You'll see them in summer when they migrate from the Northern Hemisphere, some from as far away as Alaska and Siberia.

FABULOUS FACTS

Koalas were introduced to the island from the mainland just across the water over 100 years ago. French Island now contains the largest population of disease-free koalas in Victoria. Koalas breed here so successfully that park rangers are kept busy planting manna gum trees to keep them supplied with food, and many are transferred to reserves in other parts of Victoria.

Kid Quest

What language is spoken on French Island?

See pp. 640–4 for the answer

Ace-Hi Ranch

810 Boneo Rd, Cape Schanck
(03) 5988 6262; www.ace-hi.com.au
Open Sat, Sun, public and school
holidays

VARIOUS PRICES

This Western-style park offers bush and beach horseriding (minimum age 7 years), pony rides for littlies, and a free-range wildlife park with emus, parrots, cockatoos, peacocks, kangaroos, wallabies, deer and dingoes.

Bay beaches

FREE

A curve of lovely, safe, swimming beaches stretches from Safety Beach to Rye on the Port Phillip Bay side of the peninsula. Near Rye's main beach there's also a playground and walking tracks. Capel Sounds Bay Beach, between Rosebud and Rye, is particularly good for small children with warm, shallow water and clean sand. On the Western Port side of the peninsula, the waters of Shoreham and Somers are ideal for families.

Coolart Wetlands and Homestead

Via Lord Somers Rd, Somers
(03) 5931 4000

BUDGET

Coolart is a historic mansion in a wonderful garden setting where you can find birds, lizards and other animals. In winter and spring you'll see hundreds of

Australian white ibis and other waterbirds congregating on the lagoon. The visitor centre has farm and beachcombing activity sheets for kids.

Dolphin and seal cruises

Sorrento and Portsea
Twice daily, seasonal times

HIGH COST

Cruises in Port Philip Bay not only take you to view dolphins and seals, but also offer the magical opportunity of getting in the water and swimming with these playful and endearing creatures. Cruises from Sorrento:
- Moonraker Dolphin Swims
  (03) 5984 4211;
  www.moonrakercharters.
  com.au
- Polperro
  (03) 5988 8437;
  www.polperro.com.au

Cruises from Portsea:
- Bay Play
  (03) 5984 0888;
  www.bayplay.com.au/dolphin-swims.html

Flinders Blowhole
Blowhole Track, off Boneo Rd opposite
Razorback Rd, Flinders
www.discovermorningtonpeninsula.
com.au
FREE

The walk towards the ocean and blowhole is via a well-made track, but when you reach the rocks, take great care. Large swells and waves can be dangerous here. On the right you will find Little Bird Rock (look for seabirds), and then Elephant Rock, with the blowhole at the end.

Frankston Boat Hire
510N Nepean Hwy, Frankston
(03) 9783 2032;
www.aussiefishing.com.au
SEASONAL

Motorboats, kayaks, canoes and paddle boats are available for hire. Cruise Port Phillip Bay or canoe the Kananook Creek. Fishing rods can also be hired.

Mushroom Reef Marine Park
Access from Cook St, Flinders
www.parkweb.vic.gov.au
FREE

These are some of the best rockpools you will ever explore. Check the website to find out about some of the sea life you can expect to see. Go straight to www.parkweb.vic.gov.au/education/marinekit/section8.htm to download a kids' marine park activity pack.

Octopuses Garden
Under the pier, Rye
www.visitmorningtonpeninsula.org
FREE

This easy, self-guided 200-metre marine trail is designed for novice snorkellers. Follow the pier pylons and the bright interpretative signs will direct you where to look. Find octopuses on the sandy floor, sponges on the pylons, and fish or seahorses darting amongst the seaweeds.

Portsea Back Beach
London Bridge Rd, Portsea
FREE

This is not a safe swimming beach, but this ocean beach is worth a visit to see the sculptural London Bridge rock arch.

Queenscliff Maritime Museum
Weeroona Pde, Queenscliff
(03) 5258 3440;
www.maritimequeenscliffe.org.au
Open daily
(afternoons only on the weekend)
Ferry information (03) 5258 3244;
www.searoad.com.au
BUDGET

Take a 40-minute ride on a car ferry from Sorrento to historic Queenscliff; keep an eye out for the dolphins that sometimes follow the boat. The Queenscliff Maritime Museum collection includes a big heavy brass diving helmet that kids can try on, a lifeboat, rocket launching equipment used for lifesaving, shipwreck artefacts and ships' models. In Queenscliff you can also visit the Marine Discovery Centre where kids can get their hands into an educational aquarium filled with marine life from Port Phillip Bay; (03) 5258 3344 (limited opening hours).

Sand Sculpting Australia
Frankston Waterfront
Frankston Visitor Information
1300 322 842; www.visitfrankston.com
Late-Dec – Apr

MID-RANGE

No simple bucket-shaped sand castles here! Come and admire sand dragons and other amazing sand creations, join in workshops run by professional sand sculptors and enjoy the roving entertainment. While you're in Frankston, challenge the kids to decode the secret message on the 22 poles along the pier.

Sand Sculpting Australia, Frankston

Snorkel with sea dragons
Meet at Bayplay,
3755 Point Nepean Rd, Portsea
(03) 5984 0888;
www.bayplay.com.au/snorkelling.html
Twice daily, Oct–Apr
Minimum age 7 years

HIGH COST

Portsea Pier is one of the few places where you can be sure to find weedy seadragons. You are also likely to spot cuttlefish and crabs here.

Sorrento Ocean Beach
Sorrento

FREE

There's plenty of soft sand to play on and, when the tide is out, the rockpools are brimming with marine life. Some of the rockpools are large enough to snorkel in and a swimming hole to the right of the carpark has a rock platform for diving. Facilities include barbecues, picnic facilities and a kiosk.

Surf schools
Various locations

HIGH COST

Kids want to have a go at riding the waves? Lessons are available (all equipment supplied) from:
- Bayplay
  (03) 5984 0888; www.bayplay.com.au/surfing.html
- Mornington Peninsula Surf School (03) 9787 6494; greenroomsurf.com.au

Around the peninsula

Inside the maze at Ashcombe Maze and Water Gardens, Shoreham

Ashcombe Maze and Water Gardens
15 Shoreham Rd, Shoreham
(03) 5989 8387;
www.ashcombemaze.com.au
MID-RANGE

Ashcombe has a beautiful scented rose maze, tall hedge mazes and several themed gardens to explore. Kids will also enjoy the water features, Fairy Walk (where fairies live amongst masses of bluebells) and the challenge of the Great Gnome Hunt.

Boneo Maze and Wetlands Centre
695 Limestone Rd, Fingal
(03) 5988 6385;
www.boneomaze.com.au
MID-RANGE

Have fun exploring hedge mazes or playing a garden game of chess, draughts or snakes and ladders. Peek through the bird hide, and take a walk along the boardwalks to look for endangered blue bills, freckled ducks and swamp skinks.

Briars Park and Homestead
450 Nepean Hwy, Mount Martha
(03) 5974 3686
BUDGET

The historic 1840s homestead has an unexpected display of Napoleonic memorabilia, as well as historic farm machinery. The park is a wildlife reserve where you can spy on wetland visitors from bird hides and spot kangaroos, wallabies and koalas.

Enchanted Maze Garden
55 Purves Rd, Arthurs Seat
(03) 5981 8449;
www.enchantedmaze.com.au
MID-RANGE

There are lots of fun garden mazes to keep you wandering and guessing for hours, including the Children's Maze with Dinosaur Garden and the giant interactive snakes and ladders game. There's also a cafe here and an amazing lolly shop with a miniature train chuffing around the ceiling.

Gordon Studio Glassblower

Cnr 290 Red Hill and Dunns Creek rds, Red Hill
(03) 5989 7073;
www.gordonstudio.com.au
Check demonstration times

FREE VIEWING

Watch glassblowers shape molten glass with tools, add colour and blow in air to create beautiful artworks that can be purchased on site.

Main Ridge Dairy

295 Main Creek Rd, Main Ridge
(03) 5989 6622;
www.mainridgedairy.com.au
Tours to see goat milking available most Sat afternoons; bookings essential

BUDGET

This farmhouse cheese factory and goat dairy produces handmade cheeses that are available for tasting and purchase. Visit during August or September to see new little kids (the real sort!).

Moonlit Sanctuary Wildlife Conservation Park

550 Tyabb–Tooradin Rd, Pearcedale
(03) 5978 7935;
www.moonlit-sanctuary.com
Bookings essential for evening tours

MID-RANGE

This is one of the best places in Victoria to interact with Australian animals. You get the opportunity to feed and cuddle the animals and have your photo taken. School holiday programs offer special treats and there

are evening tours to meet nocturnal animals.

Mornington Tourist Railway

Moorooduc Station Two Bays Rd, Moorooduc
(03) 5975 3322 or 1300 767 274;
www.morningtonrailway.org.au
Usually runs the 1st, 2nd and 3rd Sun each month

Take a ride on a heritage train between Moorooduc and Mornington. The return trip takes about 45 minutes.

Peninsula Hot Springs

Springs La, Rye
(03) 5950 8777;
www.peninsulahotsprings.com
Early morning to late evening

MID-RANGE

As well as indulgent spa treatments for adults, there is a public bath area where children can try out the natural hot mineral springs if accompanied by an adult.

Radio Controlled Car Racing

Somerville Rise Primary School
Cnr Blackscamp and Graff rds,
Somerville
0421 990 679; www.mprccc.org
1st and 3rd Sun each month

FREE ENTRY FOR SPECTATORS

For something a bit different, come and watch little radio-controlled racing cars battle it out on their own racetrack! If you want to join in, there are hire cars available; bookings recommended.

Rain Hayne and Shine Farmyard

490 Stumpy Gully Rd, Balnarring
(03) 5983 1691; www.rhsfarm.com.au

MID-RANGE

Enjoy a real, old-fashioned family day out on a farm, with baby animals to bottle feed and cuddle, pony and goat-cart rides, and lots of other friendly animals (including a few Australian native animals) to pat and feed.

Sunny Ridge Farm Berry Picking

Cnr Shands and Mornington–Flinders rds,
Main Ridge
(03) 5989 4500; www.sunnyridge.com.au
Berry picking Nov–May

FREE ENTRY; PAY FOR STRAWBERRIES YOU PICK

Kids love the chance to pick their own strawberries, raspberries or cherries. They'll also love the cafe (check opening hours) with its ice-creams made from real fruit and the Belgian Chocolate Fondue Berries (in season).

Victorian Climbing Centre

12 Hartnett Dr, Seaford
(03) 9782 4222;
www.victorianclimbingcentre.com.au

VARIABLE OPENING HOURS AND PRICES

Looking for a rainy day activity that will burn up some energy? This venue offers indoor rock climbing suitable for all ages and levels of experience.

Sunny Ridge Farm Berry Picking, Main Ridge

Accommodation

Cape Schanck Lighthouse
420 Cape Schanck Rd,
Cape Schanck
(03) 9567 7900 or
1300 885 259;
www.austpacinns.com.au

MID-RANGE

Try a night in a historic assistant lighthouse keeper's cottage in Cape Schanck Lighthouse Reserve. It's quite an experience to spend time in this isolated location surrounded by coastal views. Cottages have kitchenettes and separate living areas. View photos on the interactive map on the website. For information on what to see and do at Cape Schanck Lighthouse Reserve see p. 177.

Hazelglen Beach House
57 Foam St, Rosebud
0400 522 258 or 0409 86 2121;
www.hazelglen.com.au

MID-RANGE

This family-friendly holiday house is a home away from home, with books, magazines, DVDs, games, puzzles and even baby toys. The house will sleep up to eight and it's only 10 minutes walk to shops and a safe swimming beach.

McLeod Eco Farm and Historic Prison
McLeod Rd, French Island
(03) 5980 1224;
www.mcleodecofarm.com
Rooms not interconnecting so not suitable for very small children

MID-RANGE

How about a night in prison? A former prison on French Island has been turned into an organic farm and tourist accommodation. You can stay in the officers' quarters, now a guesthouse, where adults have a double room and kids sleep in their own room in bunks. Bathrooms are private but not ensuite. Farm activities include feeding animals and looking for eggs. Water is limited and electricity relies on generators. For information on what to see and do on French Island see p. 181.

Mornington Gardens Holiday Village
98 Bungower Rd, Mornington
(03) 5975 7373;
www.morningtoncaravanpark.com.au

BUDGET

This peaceful, roomy caravan park has plenty of shade and a family-friendly atmosphere. Choose a cabin, ensuite site, or campsite. Facilities include a laundry, recreation room, camp kitchen and playground.

Places to eat

The Baths

3278 Point Nepean Rd, Sorrento
(03) 5984 1500; www.thebaths.com.au
Situated right on the waterfront, you can watch for bottlenose dolphins and feed pelicans while you dine. There's also a kids' menu.

Pelican Pantry

2 Marine Pde, Hastings
1300 850 297
Open for breakfast and lunch
This training cafe adjoins the Pelican Park Recreation Centre so you can enjoy a swim in the indoor heated pool before you eat. Outdoor seating overlooks the Hastings Foreshore – and lots of real pelicans. Buy a bag of fish scraps from Fishermans Wharf and give the birds a feed too.

THE MURRAY

The region covers a 600-kilometre stretch along the Murray River, from Wodonga (330 kilometres north-east of Melbourne) to Mildura (550 kilometres north-west of Melbourne)

Best suited to driving holidays, although various locations are accessible by train and Mildura has a local airport

Year-round destination, but Mildura can be very hot in the height of summer (Jan–Feb)

HIGHLIGHTS

Army Museum Bandiana **p. 197**

Port of Echuca **p. 191**

Swan Hill Pioneer Settlement **p. 195**

Around Echuca

Port of Echuca
52 Murray Espl, Echuca
(03) 5482 4248;
www.portofechuca.org.au
VARIOUS PRICES

The kids bounce impatiently on the wharf, watching a paddlesteamer churn down the river towards them. Steam drifts upwards and a sharp toot pierces the air. The paddlesteamer is arriving! An eager scramble over the gangplank, and the kids can get a close-up view of the chugging steam engines and the engineers feeding in the wood. But the best is yet to come. The skipper announces that all children on board can have a turn at steering. Your kids proudly take the wheel and return with certificates proving that they are now first mates!

INSIDER TIPS

■ A hundred years ago, paddlesteamers travelled to the Port of Echuca from as far away as Queensland to bring cargoes of wool, which were then transported to Melbourne by train. The historic buildings and vessels have been restored, and you can wander the port among people in costume, imagining you have travelled back in time.

■ Paddlesteamer cruises run four or five times a day.

■ The best time to come is the weekend, when you'll see extra steam engines in operation on the wharf.

■ Save money with a combined ticket for the port, a paddlesteamer cruise, the National Holden Motor Museum (*see* p. 194) and other attractions in Echuca.

■ Dress in sensible clothes and shoes for spending several hours outdoors.

DON'T MISS

■ The hour-long guided walk, offered once daily in the late morning.

■ The underground bar at the Star Hotel. It was built for illegal drinking and has a tunnel escape route in case of a police raid. This is included in the guided tour, but is also accessible with general entry.

■ The moored PS *Adelaide*, the oldest operational wooden-hulled paddlesteamer in the world.

FABULOUS FACTS

A miniseries called *All the Rivers Run* was filmed here in the 1980s. It starred Australian actors Sigrid Thornton and John Waters (who hosted the ABC kids' show *Play School* for many years). Try to view *All the Rivers Run* before you come (there are clips on YouTube), or teenagers might read the book by Nancy Cato on which it was based. You can peek at behind-the-scenes information on the filming at www.portofechuca.org.au.

Kid Quest

See if you can find the tin row boat that John Waters
used in the filming of All the Rivers Run.
See pp. 640–4 for the answer

Billabong Ranch

2831 Tehan Rd, Echuca
(03) 5483 5322; www.justhorses.com.au
VARIOUS PRICES

Take a horse trail ride (children can be led) along the banks of the Murray through magnificent red gum forests, or spend time in the fun park with activities such as pedal boats, minigolf, archery, an animal nursery, outdoor tenpin bowling and beach volleyball.

Cactus Country

4986 Murray Valley Hwy, Strathmerton
(100 km north-east of Echuca)
(03) 5874 5271; www.cactuscountry.
com.au
BUDGET

Take a self-guided tour of this strange, science fiction landscape with its thousands of spectacular desert plants from around the world. Find out how the plants have adapted to their harsh desert environments – and how you could survive if you were lost in a desert!

Canoe along the Goulburn River

River Country Adventours,
43 Edis St, Kyabram
(03) 5852 2736;
www.adventours.com.au/canoes.htm
HIGH COST

Canoeing along the Goulburn River, Kyabram

Take a 3-day canoe adventure on the Goulburn River. Spend your days looking for wildlife, fishing and swimming. At night, you can camp, or stay in organised accommodation.

Echuca–Moama Adventure Playground

Perricoota Rd, rear of Moama Sports
Club, Echuca–Moama
www.melbourneplaygrounds.com.au
FREE

Apart from the usual swings and slides, the vast, enticing wooden castle structure keeps kids happy for ages with lots of physical and imaginative play. The playground is enclosed and has barbecue and picnic facilities.

Kyabram Fauna Park

Lake Rd, Kyabram
(03) 5852 2883;
www.kyabramfaunapark.com.au
MID-RANGE

This not-for-profit park has one of Victoria's largest collections of Australian animals. See free-ranging wallabies, kangaroos and emus, and explore the large walk-through aviary. There are many other animals housed in spacious enclosures. You can also visit a restored and furnished historic settler's cottage.

National Holden Motor Museum
7 Warren St, Echuca
(03) 5480 2033;
www.holdenmuseum.com.au
BUDGET

This display of Holden cars, including rare prototypes and historic film footage, is one for petrol-head kids – and also a nostalgic trip for the adults.

Oz Maze Mini Golf
Anstruther St, Echuca
(03) 5480 2220; www.ozmaze.com.au
Check opening hours
MID-RANGE

This fun, challenging and educational wooden maze is in the shape of Australia, and as you wend your way through, you learn titbits about Australia. There is also a minigolf course.

Special event

Port of Echuca Heritage Steam Festival
Early Oct
(03) 5482 4248;
www.steamfestival.com.au
Indulge in the fun and excitement of a bygone era with a weekend of old-time games and activities. See working steam engines on the wharf, and watch the world's largest collection of paddlesteamers chug down the river.

PS Emmylou, *Port of Echuca Heritage Steam Festival, Echuca*

Around Mildura

Mildura Ballooning
Various departure points near Mildura
(03) 5024 6848;
www.milduraballooning.com.au
Daily, subject to weather
Children need to be tall enough to see
over the side of the basket
HIGH COST

After an early-morning drive to your departure point, watch as your hot-air balloon is inflated. It is an amazing experience to float gently above the ground in a basket! The price includes breakfast on your return.

Orange World
Silver City Hwy, Buronga,
New South Wales
(03) 5023 5197;
www.orangeworldmildura.com.au
Open daily, but mornings only during Feb
MID-RANGE

Take an entertaining and informative tour around a working citrus orchard, riding in a covered tractor train. Taste the fruit, see pickers at work (seasonal) and watch a mini processing display.

Perry Sand Hills
Old Renmark Rd, Wentworth,
New South Wales
FREE

Have fun playing in these remarkable red desert sand dunes. Keep an eye out for ancient mega fauna bones. You can see replicas of these giant beasts at the Pioneer Museum, Beverley Street, Wentworth; (03) 5027 3160.

Snakes N Ladders All Ages Playground
Seventeenth St, Cabarita
(03) 5025 3575
MID-RANGE

This unusual playground features a 50-metre slide, minigolf and a display of wooden old-fashioned 'dunnies' (outdoor toilets). There are barbecues on site.

Around Swan Hill

Swan Hill Pioneer Settlement
Monash Dr, Swan Hill
(03) 5036 2410 or 1800 981 911;
www.pioneersettlement.com.au
VARIOUS PRICES

Your kids peer into the old butter churn and cry out with amazement.

The cream is really changing into butter! A few more turns, and it's ready. They squeeze it though muslin and carefully shape it with a wooden butter pat and proudly spread it onto warm damper. Finally, they take a huge bite and rush to the next olden-day activity – riding on a horse and buggy, making ropes, using the old printing press, or dancing to a pianola...

INSIDER TIPS

- Tickets are valid for two days and you can buy combination packages that include various extra options.

- Pick up an activity pamphlet for the kids and go on a discovery trail around the settlement.

- There is a tearoom on site as well as a lolly shop and bakery.

- The buildings are not replicas – they are authentic pioneer structures from the 1830s to 1930s.

DON'T MISS

- The evening sound and light show (extra cost) in an open-topped car. Each building you pass lights up and tells its story.

- The photography parlour. Dress in old-fashioned costumes (small extra charge) and photos will be taken on your own camera. Pose indoors or outside among the wonderful, authentic activities.

- A ride up the river on the 1896 paddlesteamer *Pyap* (extra cost). Departures are once daily on weekdays, twice daily on weekends, public and school holidays.

- Free vintage car rides and horse-and-buggy rides.

- Listening to the pianola in the music shop.

- The blacksmith – make your own nail.

- The printing shop – print your own 'Wanted' poster.

- Heritage Island across the river, where you can do a self-guided walk and find out about bush tucker and Indigenous use of plants for healing.

FABULOUS FACTS

The gigantic 'Queen of the Murray', the paddlesteamer *Gem*, was not always as big as she is now. In 1882, just six years after she was built, she was sawn in half, by hand, and bullocks were used to drag the two halves apart so that an extra section could be added in the middle!

Kid Quest

What kind of bullet do you not shoot from a gun?
Hint: look behind the Towaninnie Homestead.
See pp. 640–4 for the answer

Lake Boga Flying Boat Museum

Willakool Dr, Lake Boga
(03) 5037 2850
Check opening times

BUDGET

After the Japanese attacked Darwin and Broome in 1942 and destroyed 16 flying boats, a remote inland safe haven for flying boats was set up at Lake Boga. The historic underground Communications Bunker is now a museum and you can see a Catalina flying boat there.

Yarrawonga–Wodonga

Army Museum Bandiana

Gaza Ridge Barracks, off Murray Valley Hwy, Wodonga
(02) 6055 2525;
www.defence.gov.au/army/AWMA_MUS

BUDGET

A security guard halts your car as you approach the gate. This is a real army barracks with strict security. The guard demands to see photo ID for all adults in the car. You are given permission to enter and stern instructions not to venture beyond the museum area. Inside, this huge military museum includes vehicles, uniforms and artillery from the Boer War to the present, many displayed in lifelike dioramas.

INSIDER TIPS

- Visitors are permitted to use the free electric barbecues in the Memorial Gardens opposite the museum.

- You can use the displays in the museum as starting points for various discussions, such as changing perceptions of war over time.

- Make sure that all people aged 18 years and over bring photo ID with them.

DON'T MISS

- The LARC (Lighter Amphibious Resupply Cargo) – a vehicle that can float on water as well as drive on land.

- The 1943 jeep, complete with backdrop, helmets and machine gun, where kids can pose for photos.

- The theatrette with DVD presentations, including one about nurses.

- The prisoners of war display, which gives a view of another side of war.

FABULOUS FACTS

Australian Army vehicles are not only used for war. The LARC has travelled and worked in Antarctica to help resupply the Australian scientific research base on Macquarie Island. As you look at this small vehicle, imagine the soldiers struggling to man it through huge seas, through ice and snow, to help carry goods to the team working on the island.

Kid Quest

The LARC is painted to look like an animal. Which animal?

See pp. 640–4 for the answer

Bike hire
Yarrawonga
Outdoors,
81 Belmore St, Yarrawonga
(03) 5744 3522;
www.yarrawongaoutdoors.com.au
VARIOUS PRICES
Hire a family pack, complete with helmets and ride together along the riverbank. Child seats are available.

Chiltern Athenaeum Museum
57 Conness St, Chiltern,
(03) 5726 1280;
www.chilternathenaeum.com.au
BUDGET
This historical Australiana display includes landscapes painted on gum leaves, and an old schoolroom with real knuckle-bone jacks, wooden pencil cases with secret compartments, and, of course, a 'strap'!

Dow's Pharmacy Museum
Conness St, Chiltern
Chiltern Visitor Information Centre
(03) 5726 1611; www.nattrust.com.au
Open daily, but closes mid-afternoon
BUDGET

This shop, now a National Trust property, operated for over 100 years from 1859. Compare the original old-fashioned shop fittings and equipment with those found in a modern pharmacy.

Kars Reef Goldmine
Depart from Visitor Information Centre,
27 High St, Yackandandah
(02) 6027 1988
Entry by guided tour only
Open daily in school holidays,
otherwise weekends only
In this historic 19th-century mine you can see all the tools lying where the last miners left them and gold still in the earth waiting to be mined! There are three tours a day; check times.

Kayaking
Yarrawonga Outdoors,
81 Belmore St, Yarrawonga
(03) 5744 3522;
www.yarrawongaoutdoors.com.au
Bookings essential
HIGH COST
Try the Freedom Self-guided Tour and Hire option. The staff will drop you off at the river with your family kayak. You can paddle, swim, and pull up at the beaches alongside for a picnic, all with the assurance you will be picked up at the end. Guided tours are also available.

En route from Melbourne

Avenel Maze

Upton Rd, Avenel
(03) 5796 2667;
www.avenelmaze.com.au
Seasonal opening times

MID-RANGE

Find your way through five different mazes and have a game of minigolf. One of the mazes is based on the theme of Ned Kelly, a notorious Australian bushranger who operated in this area.

Ned Kelly statue, Glenrowan

Ned Kelly's Last Stand

Glenrowan Tourist Centre Theme Park,
41 Gladstone St, Glenrowan
(03) 5766 2367 or 1300-NEDKELLY;
www.glenrowantouristcentre.com.au
Shows operate on the half hour

MID-RANGE

The bushranger Ned Kelly was finally captured in Glenrowan, dressed in his famous home-made suit of armour. In this interactive production, you'll be taken hostage and witness the final gunfight. Another attraction at Glenrowan is Kate's Cottage at 35 Gladstone Street, which has a replica of the Kelly home and a Kelly memorabilia museum.

RAAC Memorial and Army Tank Museum

Hopkins Barracks, Puckapunyal
(03) 5735 7285;
www.armytankmuseum.com.au
Check opening hours

BUDGET

You can see 70 armoured fighting vehicles from all over the world, and the Technology Hall displays armour and armament technology, with hands-on exhibits that demonstrate how engines work. Bring photo ID to obtain entry as this is a functioning military base.

SPC Ardmona KidsTown
Midland Hwy, Shepparton
(03) 5831 4213; www.kidstown.org.au
BY DONATION

Australia's biggest adventure playground is the ideal place to break your journey. Your kids won't know where to start! Older kids will enjoy the mazes, flying fox, tree house complex and giant slide, while toddlers and babies have their own area with mini-slide, sandpit and rocking dinosaur. Miniature train rides operate on weekends, public and school holidays (extra cost). There is a cafe on site but hours are limited.

Accommodation

BIG4 Swan Hill
186 Murray Valley Hwy, Swan Hill
(03) 5032 4372 or 1800 990 389;
www.big4swanhill.com.au
BUDGET TO MID-RANGE

Accommodation options range from campsites to four-star, self-contained two- or three- bedroom cabins (some have corner spa baths). Facilities include a jumping pillow, games room, bike hire, landscaped gardens, a swimming pool, and a toddler playground and pool. A Kids' Club is offered during holiday periods.

Calder Caravan Park
Calder Hwy (15th St), Mildura
(03) 5023 1310 or 1800 231 310;
www.caldercp.com.au
BUDGET

Enjoy the convenience of basing yourself in the centre of Mildura. There is a choice of air-conditioned Budget or Superior cabins (with dishwashers), caravan or camping sites. You'll have access to an indoor kids' entertainment area, outdoor playground, swimming pool and toddler pool.

Mildura Holiday Houseboats
Etiwanda Ave, Mildura
(03) 5024 6222 or 1800 800 842;
www.mildurahouseboats.com.au
MID-RANGE

What better way to stay in this region than sleeping in a boat on the river? Mildura Holiday Houseboats are air-conditioned and have child safety rails, sun canopies and swim decks. Cook in the kitchen (complete with dishwasher) or use the barbecue on deck. Facilities include TVs, DVD players and washing machines. Linen is included.

Rich River Caravan and Tourist Park

Crescent St, Echuca
(03) 5482 3658; www.richriver.net

BUDGET

Relax in this tranquil setting convenient to the river and the town of Echuca. There is a choice of cabins or caravan sites. Facilities include a large outdoor pool, shaded toddler pool, playground and air-conditioned games room.

Yarrawonga Holiday Park

Cnr Piper St and Burley Rd, Yarrawonga
(03) 5744 3420;
www.yarrawongaholidaypark.com.au

BUDGET TO MID-RANGE

This shady park has a river and beach frontage as well as a jumping pillow, playground and football oval. Choose from a variety of two-bedroom, self-contained cabins with air-conditioning, or a site for a tent or caravan.

Places to eat

Carriages Restaurant

423 Campbell St, Swan Hill
(03) 5032 2017

Kids enjoy this novelty restaurant where you can have lunch or dinner on a train platform or in one of the (stationary) carriages. A kids' menu is available.

Echuca-Moama RSL and Citizens Club

Merool La, Moama
(03) 5482 6677; www.rslmoama.com.au

Select from a range of family-friendly dining options including outdoor seating and kids' menus. Kids can play in the outdoor playground or free indoor Play Station Centre as long as they are supervised.

PHILLIP ISLAND

Phillip Island is located 140 kilometres south-east of Melbourne; day trip or holiday destination

Beaches are best in warmer months (Dec–Mar), but there are plenty of year-round activities

HIGHLIGHTS

· Penguin Parade **p. 203**

Phillip Island Grand Prix Circuit **p. 205**

Rhyll Trout and Bush Tucker Farm **p. 206**

Around the island

Penguin Parade
Phillip Island Nature Park
1019 Ventnor Rd, Ventnor
(03) 5951 2800; www.penguins.org.au

VARIOUS PRICES

The Penguin Parade is one of Australia's most popular tourist attractions – and rightly so. It is a magical experience to sit on a beach with darkness closing in around you, surrounded by excited whispers of a crowd, and peer out to sea, watching for small, wild creatures to appear. Suddenly, there they are, bobbing on the waves. As the little penguins cross the beach and waddle towards their burrows, you can walk beside them along a boardwalk, almost close enough to touch.

INSIDER TIPS

■ This is a night activity involving huge crowds and lots of waiting outdoors, usually in the cold. However, the penguins are worth the effort!

■ Pre-purchase your tickets by phone or online.

■ If possible, opt for the more expensive Penguins Plus option which gives you entry to a special viewing platform.

■ Penguin arrival time varies considerably depending on the season. Winter means an earlier night, but summer is not such a chilly wait!

■ If sitting on sand and waiting for an hour sounds impossible for your family, consider turning up late and just watching from the boardwalk as the penguins head for their burrows.

■ When you purchase a ticket to the Penguin Parade, you might want to buy the Three Parks Pass which gives you savings on entry to the Koala Conservation Centre and Churchill Island as well (see p. 207).

■ Bring binoculars, warm jackets, scarves, hats and gloves, and insect repellent, just in case, as you'll be sitting outdoors at dusk.

■ Bring plenty of activities, food and drink to keep the little ones occupied because you will have to sit and wait in one spot for up to an hour before the penguins appear.

DON'T MISS

■ The visitor centre interpretive displays. Allow time to look around before you view the penguins.

■ Consider adding on the educational eco-tour which commences about one-and-a-half hours before penguin viewing; tickets available where you purchase your viewing tickets.

■ Don't forget to fit in dinner as well! There are lots of eating options in Cowes, and a limited range of fast food in the visitor centre.

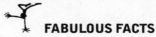

FABULOUS FACTS

Penguins have evolved into swimming birds instead of flying birds. Their wings have become flippers and they can zoom along underwater, angling their flippers to propel themselves forward. Furthermore, while other birds have light-weight, often hollow, bones to help them fly, penguins' bones are denser and heavier to help them dive. Australia's little penguins, the smallest penguins in the world, weigh a whole kilogram. This is three times as much as a magpie, though magpies are 10 centimetres taller!

Kid Quest

The dark feathers on Australia's little penguins are not actually black. When you go to the Penguin Parade, try to find out what colour they really are.
See pp. 640–4 for the answer

Phillip Island Grand Prix Circuit

Back Beach Rd, Phillip Island
(03) 5952 9400; www.phillipislandcircuit.com.au
Entry by guided tour only

MID-RANGE

The 45-minute guided tour of the grand prix circuit is a unique opportunity to see what happens behind the scenes of a motor race. Your little (and big) petrol-heads' eyes will light up with excitement when they breathe in the fumes of pit lane, see all the equipment laid out, and imagine themselves part of the frenzy. They even get a chance to stand on the winners' podium. The adrenaline rush continues with the chance to speed around a replica circuit on a go-kart, race cars on the giant slot-car track, or pick their dream cars and bikes in the History of Motorsport display.

INSIDER TIPS

- Guided tours are conducted twice a day but are not available when the circuit is in use. Make sure you book ahead.

- Go-kart drivers must be 10 years old (and 148 centimetres tall) to drive solo, but younger siblings (minimum age 5 years) can take a ride with mum or dad. Participants must wear closed-toe shoes and have covered shoulders.

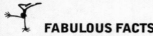

FABULOUS FACTS

Australian motor sports were born on Phillip Island. The very first
Australian Grand Prix was held there in 1928. The circuit was a rough
dirt track – cars hurtled up and down over hills, the drivers barely able
to see through clouds of dust. In the History of Motorsport display,
you can see an Austin 7 that raced in that event. Nowadays, the Grand
Prix Circuit is a smooth, purpose-built track used for racing both cars
and motorbikes. The early track still exists and is signposted off
Ventnor Beach Road.

Kid Quest
*Listen for a strange voice calling out to you. Can you spot
Robbo, the 80-year-old cockatoo, who lives on the grounds
and likes to have a chat?*

Rhyll Trout and Bush Tucker Farm
36 Rhyll–Newhaven Rd, Rhyll
(03) 5956 9255; www.rhylltroutandbushtucker.com.au

MID-RANGE

There is nothing quite like standing with a line in the water and feeling
that first bite. Listen to the squeals as your little fisherfolk
triumphantly reel in their catch. The chances are extremely good as
both indoor and outdoor pools teem with trout. And don't worry, if you
don't fancy pulling the squirming fish off the hook, there are staff on
hand to do it for you. Watch the pride on your little ones' faces as they
take their catch to the restaurant chef.

INSIDER TIPS

- This can be a reasonably priced, fun, educational and tasty way to
  spend a few hours. Take care to check the price list carefully,
  though. Apart from entry fees, you pay for the fish you catch and
  for services such as cleaning, and cooking.

- You don't need your own equipment. Rods are available for hire at
  low cost, while buckets, bait and fishing lessons are free.

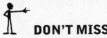

DON'T MISS

- The Bush Tucker Trail. While you wait for your fish to be cooked, get the kids to lead you down the trail. With the aid of a map and signs, they can spot all the bush foods used by local Indigenous people.

FABULOUS FACTS

The fish in these pools are rainbow trout. Originally from North America, they were introduced to Australia for sport fishing in 1894. Local anglers have been rejoicing ever since, but the native fish are probably not so enthusiastic. Rainbow trout can grow to over a metre long and weigh over 20 kilograms, and it is thought they may be the reason why some smaller native fish are now endangered.

Kid Quest

If you catch a big one, you might be in the running to win the Rhyll Fishing Competition for the year (everyone gets free entry).

A Maze 'N Things

1805 Phillip Island Rd, Cowes
(03) 5952 2283;
www.amazenthings.com.au

MID-RANGE

For many children this is the highlight of their trip to Phillip Island. There's a challenging maze, large-size minigolf course, Puzzle Island, optical illusion room and Puzzle Cafe.

Churchill Island

Off the coast of Newhaven
(03) 5956 7214; www.penguins.org.au

MID-RANGE

There's something inherently adventurous about being on a tiny island. On Churchill Island you'll discover an old homestead, farm animals and activities, waterbirds, mangroves and mudflats.

Koala Conservation Centre

Phillip Island Nature Park,
Phillip Island Tourist Rd
(03) 5951 2800; www.penguins.org.au

MID-RANGE

A raised boardwalk among the trees makes it easy to spot koalas at this popular destination.

National Vietnam Veterans Museum

25 Veterans Dr (formerly Churchill Rd South), Newhaven
(03) 5956 6400;
www.vietnamvetsmuseum.org
BUDGET

This little-known museum tells of Australia's involvement in the Vietnam War. See the audiovisual display, weapons, tanks, aircraft, uniforms, models and dioramas.

The Nobbies

Phillip Island Tourist Route, Phillip Island
(03) 5951 2820; www.penguins.org.au
FREE

At The Nobbies there is a fur seal information centre with underwater cameras for viewing seals out on the rocks, coastal boardwalks among seabirds and their nests, a blowhole, and a cafe with an indoor 'Just for Pups' kids' play area.

Pelican feeding

San Remo pier
www.srfco.com.au/pelicans
FREE

At noon every day, wild pelicans drop in for a feed of fish provided by the fishermen's cooperative.

Phillip Island Chocolate Factory

930 Phillip Island Rd, Newhaven
(03) 5956 6600;
www.phillipislandchocolatefactory.
com.au
MID-RANGE

There are free tastings at this chocoholic's heaven. Invent and make your own chocolate bar, play with a model chocolate village complete with working train, and discover how chocolate is manufactured.

Phillip Island Wildlife Park

2115 Phillip Island Rd, Cowes
(03) 5952 2038;
www.piwildlifepark.com.au
MID-RANGE

Dozens of Australian reptiles, birds and mammals can be found here. Pat and hand feed the free-roaming wallabies and kangaroos, and follow the raised boardwalk to see the koalas.

Seal-watching cruise

Departs from Cowes
1300 763 739;
www.wildlifecoastcruises.com.au
Various operating hours
HIGH COST

This two-hour cruise with commentary will take you within metres of Australia's largest wild fur seal colony. There are children's activities on board.

Silverleaves Beach

Silverleaves
FREE

Just east of Cowes, this idyllic, child-friendly beach has long stretches of clean sand and shallow water.

Surf School
225 Smiths Beach Rd, Smiths Beach
(03) 5952 3443;
www.islandsurfboards.com.au
HIGH COST

Learn how to surf at this year-round school which caters for all ages. All equipment (including wetsuits) is provided.

Seal-watching cruise, Phillip Island

En route from Melbourne

Australian Garden, Cranbourne
1000 Ballarto Rd, Cranbourne
(03) 5990 2200;
www.rbg.vic.gov.au/rbg_cranbourne
Closed on days of extreme fire danger
BUDGET; FREE ENTRY TO BUSHLAND

The Australian Garden is adjacent to over 300 hectares of bushland made up of heathlands, wetlands and woodlands, with walking trails, bike paths and picnic spots. Within the Australian Garden you'll find Desert Discovery Camp, where kids can dig in sand and discover fossils, and a wonderful play space with a 'Hortasaurus' to clamber on. Check the website for details of tours and kids' activities.

Maru Koala and Animal Park
1650 Bass Hwy, Grantville
(03) 5678 8548;
www.marukoalapark.com.au
Open daily including late Christmas afternoon
MID-RANGE

This is one of the few places where you can hand-feed native animals and have your photo taken with a koala. You can also try your hand at minigolf in a pirate ship.

Warrook Station Farm
4150 South Gippsland Hwy, Monomeith
(03) 5997 1321; www.warrook.com.au
MID-RANGE

Stop at the heritage homestead for a billy tea and damper. There are farm activities and baby animal petting pens.

Accommodation

There is a standard range of accommodation on the island, including numerous caravan parks, but holiday house rental is often the best value and it's worth contacting the local real estate agents for up-to-date listings.

Cowes Caravan Park
164 Church St, Cowes
(03) 5952 2211
BUDGET

This clean and well-maintained park is right on the beach and has a playground. If you're hoping to take the family dog, this park allows dogs on leashes.

Silverwater Resort
17 Potters Hill Rd, San Remo
(03) 5671 9399;
www.silverwaterresort.com.au
MID-RANGE

The location is out of town so you have to drive to beaches, shops and restaurants, but these are luxurious, self-contained apartments in an attractive garden setting. The resort offers a tennis court, games room, playground, billiards, table tennis and both indoor and outdoor swimming pools.

Places to eat

Bedrocks Family Restaurant
2185 Phillip Island Rd, Cowes
(03) 5952 6968;
www.woodbynecottages.com/restaurant.html

This Flintstones-themed restaurant has child-friendly food and an indoor playground.

Panhandle Tex Mex Family Cantina
145 Thompson Ave, Cowes
(03) 5952 2741

This restaurant is family friendly and you can eat your Mexican meals surrounded by the fun of Mexican-themed decor.

SOUTH-WEST COAST

The region starts at Torquay (100 kilometres south-west of Melbourne) and takes in the Great Ocean Road and Warrnambool

Best suited to driving holidays; some destinations are accessible by a train/coach combination

Beaches are best in warmer months (Dec–Mar), but there are plenty of year-round activities

HIGHLIGHTS

Great Ocean Road

Great Otway National Park

Apollo Bay Visitor Information Centre (03) 5237 6529; www.parkweb.vic.gov.au

Under the lush, arching canopy of myrtle beech, blackwood and giant tree ferns a river trickles alongside the walking track. Your kids scamper ahead, pretending to spot dinosaurs in this primeval rainforest. There are real creatures hiding in Melba Gully and night is the time to see them ... Returning later by torchlight you reach the depths of the forest and pause to turn off your torch. All around you thousands of tiny pinpricks of light spring up as if by magic – these are the lights of glow worms.

INSIDER TIPS

■ You begin your walk into Melba Gully from a picnic area with grassy open spaces, tables, gas barbecue and toilets. Camping is not allowed here, but you can camp in other parts of the national park.

■ To reach the picnic area, turn off the Great Ocean Road 3 kilometres west of Lavers Hill and travel a further 2 kilometres. Madsen's Track is a 1-kilometre/30-minute walk into the gully.

■ The glow worms live in the soil banks and overhanging ledges along the track. There are guide rails beside the best viewing areas, but you won't see the glow worms unless it is absolutely pitch dark around you. Switch off your torches, keep quiet and wait.

■ At night, you might also see owls, gliders, possums and bats. If you spot any rare, endangered spotted tail quolls, take note of the time, date and location and report your sighting to Parks Victoria on 13 1963.

■ Great Otway National Park covers a vast area and there are lots of other things to see and do. Check out the website before you go.

■ This is a rainforest, so take rain jackets when you go for a walk. The dampness brings out beautiful colours in the scenery.

■ Canoe tours of the forest (high cost, minimum age 5 years) are available through Otway Eco Tours; (03) 5236 6345; platypustours.net.au

■ Otway Eco Tours also offer mountain bike hire or guided bike tours (minimum age 8 years).

DON'T MISS

■ The Cape Otway Lightstation Reserve (*see* p. 225).

■ The Otway Fly Treetop Walk (*see* p. 216).

■ Erskine and Triplet falls (*see* p. 214 and 217).

FABULOUS FACTS

Glow worms are not really worms. They are the larvae of the fungus gnat, a fly-like insect. The purpose of the light (which shines from their abdomens) is to attract their dinner. As well as glowing, they produce silken threads with sticky droplets. Other insects are attracted to the light, get stuck on the threads, and the glow worms reel them in and eat them.

Kid Quest

See if you can find a rare Otways black-snail, found only in the Great Otway National Park. It has a long body, shiny black shell and eats worms, spearing them with long, curved teeth and sucking them in alive.

Argo Buggy Adventure Tour

Depart from Kookaburra Cottages,
5750 Great Ocean Rd, Apollo Bay
(03) 5237 6341
Bookings essential
Minimum age 5 years

HIGH COST

Ride in an 8x8 all-terrain vehicle through a water-filled dam, into a rainforest and up a hill to a spectacular lookout.

Bass Strait Shell Museum

12 Noel St, Apollo Bay
(03) 5237 6395
Check opening hours

BUDGET

Your little beachcombers will find plenty of inspiration in this display of unusual sea shells, coral, and preserved sea life specimens.

Blazing Saddles horse trail rides

115 Bimbadeen Dr, Aireys Inlet
(03) 5289 7322;
www.blazingsaddlestrailrides.com

VARIOUS PRICES

Explore scenic beaches and bushland on a guided horseride and keep your eyes open for kangaroos, koalas and echidnas along the way. Book ahead to avoid disappointment. Littlies too small to ride a horse can have a pony ride or play in the playground.

Cape Otway Lightstation Reserve

Otway Lighthouse Rd via Great Ocean
Rd, Cape Otway
(03) 5237 9240; www.lightstation.com

MID-RANGE

Climb to the top of the oldest surviving lighthouse in mainland Australia. The lighthouse has operated continuously since 1848 and has a fascinating history of which maritime navigation is only a part. Visit the Telegraph Station and see the secret World War II Radar Bunker. If you visit between May and October, remember to keep an eye out for whales. The website is packed with useful material, including a kids' activity pack to download. Accommodation is also available (*see* p. 225) and there is a cafe in the Assistant Lighthouse Keeper's Cottage.

Cudgee Creek Wildlife Park
22 Trotters La, Cudgee
(03) 5567 6260
Seasonal opening times
MID-RANGE

This wildlife park has an interesting collection of animals including deer, wallabies, kangaroos, emus, monkeys, crocodiles and birds (walk-through aviary). There are picnic and barbecue facilities.

Eco-Logic Tours
Various locations near Aireys Inlet
(03) 5263 1133; www.ecologic.net.au
School holidays only
VARIOUS PRICES

Eco-logic offers a range of guided tours and activities including rockpool rambles, spotlight walks, spooky lighthouse tours and environmental working bees.

Erskine Falls
Great Otway National Park
Access at the end of Erskine Falls Rd, 10 km north-east of Lorne
FREE

This is one of the highest waterfalls in the Otways. You can see it from a viewing point above, or take a steep walking track to the base of the falls.

Hopkins Falls
Hopkins Falls Rd, Wangoom
FREE

This pretty picnic spot is well worth a visit after heavy rain when the waterfalls are at their most impressive. If you visit in spring, you might witness the spectacle of baby eels migrating up the falls.

Jirrahlinga Koala and Wildlife Sanctuary
Taits Rd, Barwon Heads
(03) 5254 2484
MID-RANGE

Sick and injured animals are cared for at this koala sanctuary, but you can visit and meet koalas, kangaroos, lizards and other Australian animals.

Koalas at Grey River
Grey River Rd, near Kennett River
FREE

Come to Grey River for guaranteed koala sightings in the wild! Take the Grey River Road from Kennett River village and after about half a kilometre start looking out for koalas in the trees. The best time to see them is late afternoon when they are more likely to be moving about.

Koorie Cultural Walk
Point Addis
Turn off the Great Ocean Rd 7 km north-east of Anglesea, continue 3 km to the carpark
FREE

Stretch your legs on this 1-kilometre loop through the nature reserve. Interpretive signs offer an insight into Aboriginal life here over thousands of years.

Enjoy the wonderful clifftop views and see how many different birds you can spot along the way.

Loch Ard Gorge
Loch Ard Gorge carpark,
Port Campbell National Park
www.parkweb.vic.gov.au
FREE

This spectacular rocky part of the coastline is where the ship the *Loch Ard* was wrecked in 1878 (*see* FLAGSTAFF HILL MARITIME VILLAGE p. 218). An easy 1.4-kilometre, one-hour walk retraces the steps of the two survivors who were cast ashore here and takes you to the Loch Ard cemetery where victims of the wreck were buried. Loch Ard Gorge is near Twelve Apostles (*see* p. 217).

Lorne
Consider basing yourself in one of Victoria's favourite family holiday destinations, with plenty of eateries, accommodation options, a long, protected sandy beach and several areas of natural beauty nearby.

Marriners Falls
Barham River Rd, Apollo Bay
FREE

This lovely scenic spot has an abundance of large tree ferns. An easy, marked track leads from the carpark to the waterfalls. Kids love hopping on large stepping stones in the creeks. Warning: the track can flood after rain.

Loch Ard Gorge, Port Campbell National Park

Otway Fly Treetop Walk

360 Phillips Track, Beech Forest
(03) 5235 9200 or 1800 300 477;
www.otwayfly.com

MID-RANGE

How would you like to walk in a forest canopy 25 metres above ground? The bridges bounce slightly and are an open grid so you can see under as well as around you – not for those who are scared of heights! If you're game, you can climb a spiral staircase to an even higher viewing platform. You can also enquire about abseiling off the fly; bookings essential.

Otway Fly Treetop Walk, Beech Forest

Shipwreck Trail

110 km of coastline from
Moonlight Head to Port Fairy
FREE

Signs along the Great Ocean Road point to information plaques at sites where ships have been wrecked. Brochures are available at visitor centres along the route.

Surfing lesson

Westcoast Surf School, Torquay,
Anglesea and Ocean Grove
(03) 5261 2241;
www.westcoastsurfschool.com
Weekends Nov–Easter, daily in summer
school holidays
Bookings essential
Minimum age 7 years
HIGH COST

The whole family can join in a beginner lesson together, but participants need to be able to swim at least 50 metres without assistance. Wetsuits and soft malibu surfboards are supplied.

Surfworld Museum Torquay

Beach Rd, Torquay
(03) 5261 4606; www.surfworld.com.au
BUDGET

Enter the world of surfing through interactive exhibits. Find out how surfboards are made and how they have changed over time.

Tiger Moth World and Adventure Park

Torquay Airport,
325 Blackgate Rd, Torquay
(03) 5261 5100;
www.tigermothworld.com
Closed Tues–Wed during winter

MID-RANGE

Kids can play in a giant Tiger Moth theme park, canoe across the Pirates Lagoon to the Islands of Surprise, or board the *Jolly Roger*. Joy rides are available in real Tiger Moth planes (high cost), and a museum displays memorabilia of vintage open-cockpit Tiger Moths.

Torquay beaches

Free

You might want to visit the famous Bells Beach, 7 kilometres west of Torquay, site of a world-championship surfing contest every Easter, but for safer family swimming, try Torquay's sandy Front Beach.

Triplet Falls

Lavers Hill–Beech Forest Rd, 3 km from Otway Fly Treetop Walk

FREE

This is one of the most impressive waterfalls in the Great Otway National Park (see p. 211). The 2-kilometre loop walk has platforms for viewing the three cascades. There's a small picnic area near the carpark.

Twelve Apostles

Port Campbell National Park
www.parkweb.vic.gov.au

FREE

These upright limestone formations rising like ruined pillars from the sea are some of the most photographed and recognisable images of the Victorian coastline. If you visit on a summer evening, watch out for thousands of short-tailed shearwaters (muttonbirds) flying inland to their nest burrows. There is a kiosk and toilets on site. The Twelve Apostles are near Loch Ard Gorge (see p. 215).

Warrnambool–Portland

Flagstaff Hill Maritime Village

89 Merri St, Warrnambool
(03) 5559 4600 or 1800 556 111; www.flagstaffhill.com

HIGH COST FOR BOTH VILLAGE AND SHOW, ENTRY VALID FOR TWO DAYS

As you sit looking out over the darkened harbour, lights flicker and mist swirls on the water. Anticipation builds as you hear a storm approaching. Then thunder roars, lightning strikes and a huge sailing ship looms up, wallowing and foundering in the waves. Suddenly, you are swept up in a gripping re-enactment of the 1878 sinking of the *Loch Ard*. The lighting and visual effects blend so well with the real harbour, it's as if you are on board with the crew as they cry out in terror and struggle to save their sinking ship.

INSIDER TIPS

- In the daytime, Flagstaff Hill Maritime Village offers an immersive experience in an old port village created around an original 1859 lighthouse and fortifications. There are people in costume, and appropriate activities such as a blacksmith at work.

- Entry is cheaper if you just visit during the day and miss the evening Shipwrecked Sound and Laser Show.

- Most kids find the evening show fascinating and exciting, but it is an emotionally powerful re-enactment of a shipwreck and some might get distressed.

- Whether you are visiting daytime or evening, this is an outdoor experience, so dress appropriately (and if you sit in the front during the show, you might get splashed!).

- The show runs at dusk, so commencement time depends on the season. It is advisable to book ahead.

- There are two ways to reach the evening performance area: walking through the village by lantern light with a guide, or travelling by horseless carriage. There is no price difference.

- When you enter the village, make sure your kids pick up a Sea Chest Challenge Trail which takes them on a quest to search for clues and collect stamps. If you select 'Education Resources' on the website you'll find more fun activity sheets for kids.

- Kids also get a bag of food for the farm animals, which include chickens, ducks and piglets.

- There is a tearoom on site but it is has limited opening hours.

- There is also a restaurant, Pippies by the Bay (closed Mondays in winter). You can purchase a package which includes dinner at Pippies and the Sound and Laser show.

- Accommodation is available in a lighthouse keeper's lodge (*see* ACCOMMODATION p. 225).

DON'T MISS

- The intact battery and guns installed in the 1880s when the colony of Victoria feared a Russian invasion.

- The child-friendly guided tours that operate twice daily and are led by costumed volunteers.

- The interpretive centre, which shows the hardships and bravery of people who came out to Australia on sailing ships in the 19th century.

- The shipwreck display in the Great Circle Gallery. More than 180 ships have been wrecked along the 'Shipwreck Coast'. Many artefacts and stories of these tragedies are on display. Look for the treasure that was concealed in a communion goblet from the wreck of the *Schomberg*. You'll have to make up a story about why it was hidden!

- The climb to the top of the lighthouse.

- The tall ship for kids to play on.

FABULOUS FACTS

Loaded on board the *Loch Ard* was a magnificent Minton porcelain peacock, headed for the Melbourne International Exhibition of 1880. Amazingly, the packaging around this fragile artwork kept it from being smashed during the storm which sank the *Loch Ard* and it was washed ashore. It now has pride of place among the shipwreck artefacts on display and is valued at millions of dollars. The Flagstaff Hill curators recently discovered the bird's head had been broken off and invisibly glued back on.

Kid Quest
Can you detect the join where the peacock's neck has been mended?

Tower Hill State Game Reserve
Princes Hwy, 14 km west of Warrnambool
www.parkweb.vic.gov.au

FREE ENTRY; TOURS EXTRA COST

The air is filled with the scents of the Australian bush, koalas peer down from the trees and you are encircled by the rim of an extinct volcano. Your Aboriginal guide holds out a she-oak leaf for tasting. Will your kids be brave enough to take a bit? Yes! You all have a nibble and your saliva glands start to water at the sour taste. This is an Indigenous survival trick for dealing with thirst. Your kids are thrilled to be learning these secrets – and soon they are whooping with excitement as your guide teaches them how to throw a boomerang.

INSIDER TIPS

■ The Aboriginal tours are offered daily at 11am and operate from the Worn Gundidj Visitor Centre in the reserve, (03) 5565 9202 or 0428 318 876; www.worngundidj.org.au

■ Night tours can also be arranged by booking ahead; minimum numbers apply. At night time you see nocturnal animals such as sugar gliders.

■ The reserve has picnic tables, electric barbecues, and toilets.

■ If you miss the tour you can take your own walk around the reserve. The easiest track is the half-hour boardwalk. Keep your eyes open for koalas and kangaroos – they are more active in cooler, wet weather.

- The visitor centre displays information about the history of the reserve and sells local Indigenous arts and crafts.

- Emus often try to steal food in the picnic area. If they become aggressive, or the kids are frightened, an adult should hold up one hand in an emu pose. This sighting of a larger 'emu' frightens the real ones away.

- As this is a game reserve, duck shooting may be permitted in open season, usually between March and June. Check with the Department of Sustainability and Environment 13 6186; www.dse.vic.gov.au

DON'T MISS

- Ancient Aboriginal grinding stones and axes in the visitor centre. These were found in the volcanic ash, and indicate that Aboriginal people occupied this area 30 000 years ago when the volcano was active.

- The copy of Eugène von Guérard's landscape of Tower Hill painted in 1855. If you follow the road around the rim of the volcano you'll come to the lookout point where von Guérard painted the landscape.

FABULOUS FACTS

A few years after von Guérard painted his landscape of Tower Hill, European settlers stripped away the beautiful ferns and trees to create grazing land. Luckily, 100 years later, thanks to the detail in von Guérard's painting, authentic revegetation of the area was able to be undertaken. Since the 1960s, volunteers (including thousands of school children) have been replanting and reintroducing native animals.

Kid Quest
How does the modern view from von Guérard's lookout point compare with his painting of the same view 150 years ago?

Bridgewater Bay

Near Portland

FREE

At Bridgewater Bay you can find white sands, deep blue water and jagged cliffs. A short walking track leads to views of an eerie sand-petrified forest. Longer tracks lead to breathtaking lookouts, a fur seal colony and blowholes.

Kid's Country Treasure Hunt

Depart from Warrnambool Visitor Information Centre, 600 Raglan Pde (03) 5564 7837 or 1800 637 725

FREE

Kids aged 5–15 years can pick up a Kid's Country Treasure Hunt Guide. Follow the trail, answer a simple quiz, and win a lucky dip prize! You can also play in the recreational area around the visitor centre.

Lake Pertobe Adventure Playground

Pertobe Rd, Warrnambool

FREE

For many kids, this extensive playground near Lady Bay Beach is the highlight of their trip to Warrnambool. Equipment includes flying foxes, a maze, water features, suspension bridges to small islands on the lake, a fort, giant slides and real boats to paddle around the lake. There are also walking tracks, bird hides, picnic/barbecue areas and minigolf.

Logans Beach Whale Watching

Logans Beach Rd, Warrnambool

FREE

Most years, from June to October, southern right whales return to the waters near Logans Beach to give birth and raise their young. A viewing platform has been constructed, but bring binoculars. For information on recent sightings contact the visitor centre; (03) 5564 7837 or 1800 637 725.

Mahogany Ship Walking Track

Thunder Point carpark, Warrnambool, to Griffiths Island carpark, Port Fairy

FREE

During the 19th century, there were several sightings of a wrecked ship, apparently built of mahogany, half-buried in sand. Many people believe it was a 16th-century sailing ship used by Portuguese explorers. The 22-kilometre track, which can be accessed at various points, passes the spot where the ship was last seen. Maybe you can find the lost 'Mahogany Ship', and unravel the mystery.

Port Fairy

FREE

This pretty, historic fishing village is well worth exploring and would make a pleasant holiday base. Throw a line in the water, look for wildlife, especially swans, pelicans and shearwaters, watch fishing boats unload their catches, or take a walk looking for shipwrecks. Seal, fishing and whale-watching cruises are also available.

Boats at Port Fairy

DISCOVERY TRAIL, SOUTH AUSTRALIA p. 296). A highlight for kids is the chance to sit inside the gigantic skeleton of a sperm whale. Make sure you pick up the 'message in a bottle' activity quest for kids.

Portland Maritime Discovery Centre

Lee Breakwater Rd, Portland
(03) 5523 2671 or 1800 035 567;
www.maritimeworld.net

BUDGET

Exhibits include a historic lifeboat used to rescue 19 survivors from the *Admella* shipwreck in 1859 (*see* ADMELLA

Portland Powerhouse Motor and Car Museum

Cnr Percy and Glenelg St, Portland
(03) 5523 5795
Check opening hours

BUDGET

Exhibits include a fully set up workshop and a sectioned car engine that starts up at the push of a button.

Special event

Fun4Kids Festival

8–10 days of July school holidays
www.fun4kids.com.au
Warrnambool's Fun4Kids Festival is aimed at kids aged

2–12 years, but the whole family will enjoy the fun of the live performances, hands-on activities and inventive workshops – and it all takes place indoors!

En route from Melbourne

Craft activity at the National Wool Museum, Geelong

National Wool Museum

Cnr Moorabool and Brougham sts, Geelong
(03) 5227 0701; www.nwm.vic.gov.au
Open daily, afternoons only on weekends
BUDGET

The first free European settlers to Australia were lured by the chance to grow rich on the thriving wool industry. Follow the story of that industry from the 1840s to today and learn how wool travels from the sheep's back to your wardrobe.

See also Werribee Open Range Zoo (p. 150)

Accommodation

Anglesea Beachfront Family Caravan Park

35 Cameron Rd, Anglesea
(03) 5263 1583;
www.angleseafcp.com.au.

BUDGET TO MID-RANGE

This ideal family holiday location boasts both beach and river frontages, and is walking distance to shops and eateries. Choose a cabin or campsite and enjoy the playgrounds, giant jumping pillow, resort-style heated swimming pool and indoor spa complex, bike hire, and large recreational area with cricket pitch, beach volleyball court and basketball rings. Indoor entertainment is also available with a TV room, toddlers' playroom and large games room.

The Boomerangs

3815 Great Ocean Rd, Johanna
(03) 5237 4213;
www.theboomerangs.com

MID-RANGE

These self-contained cottages are shaped like boomerangs. Each cottage has two queen beds and single trundle available on request. The magnificent garden setting is a haven for birds.

Cape Otway Lightstation Reserve

Otway Lighthouse Rd via
Great Ocean Rd, Cape Otway
(03) 5237 9240; www.lightstation.com

MID-RANGE

Stay in the historic Lightkeeper's Cottage with views of the lighthouse and ocean and enjoy the special experience of wandering around this property at night. Keep an eye out for ghosts! Choose from self-catering or B&B options. There are wood fires and electric heaters in the bedrooms. There's no TV reception, but DVDs are supplied.

Fauna Australia Wildlife Retreat

5040 Colac–Lavers Hill Rd, Lavers Hill
(03) 5237 3234;
www.faunaaustralia.com.au

MID-RANGE

Try out the unique experience of sleeping in a cottage on a wildlife retreat which is not open for day visitors. As part of the experience, you have personal encounters with the animals. The retreat offers a range of cottages with varying facilities and is well located for accessing other attractions.

Gwinganna Country House

Killala Rd, Apollo Bay
0418 121 779; www.gwing.com.au

MID-RANGE

Escape the hustle and bustle of the coastal strip at this house set in a huge garden backing onto the rainforest in the hills behind Apollo Bay. There's even a separate rainforest bungalow room for real tranquillity. The house sleeps ten in three double beds and four single beds, and has a games room with billiard and tennis tables.

Lighthouse Lodge

Flagstaff Hill Maritime Village,
Merri St, Warrnambool
(03) 5559 4600 or 1800 556 111;
www.flagstaffhill.com

HIGH COST

Stay in a historic lighthouse keeper's residence and pretend to be lighthouse keepers! The lodge has a kitchen, lounge area, outdoor area and three bedrooms with ensuite facilities, large-screen TVs and DVD players; you can request single beds for the kids. Enjoy views of the lighthouse, which is still operational.

Places to eat

Apollo Bay Hotel
95 Great Ocean Rd, Apollo Bay
(03) 5237 6250;
www.apollobayhotel.com.au
This pub offers relaxed indoor and outdoor dining overlooking the beach. The cuisine is modern international and Australian, and there's a kids' menu.

Kermond's Hamburgers
151 Lava St, Warrnambool
(03) 5562 4854
This Warrnambool institution has been around for half a century. Make sure you taste an old-style Kermond's burger.

Ba Ba Lu Bar
6a Mountjoy Pde, Lorne
(03) 5289 1808; www.babalubar.com.au
This relaxed, family restaurant offers fresh, tasty Spanish-style meals for the whole family. The kids' menu includes healthy items such as steamed vegetables and free-range chicken.

Wisharts at the Wharf
29 Gipps St, Port Fairy
(03) 5568 1884; www.wisharts.com.au
Located right on the dockside, you can order fresh fish and chips, and munch while you watch the cray fleet at work.

Another Holiday Idea for Victoria

Camping in a national park

Why not forget museums, zoos and hotel rooms, and get back to nature? In the Grampians (260 kilometres west of Melbourne) you can camp among koalas and kangaroos, take easy bushwalks, and find rock art in caves where Aboriginal people used to shelter. At 'The Prom', as Wilsons Promontory (200 kilometres south-east of Melbourne) is affectionately known, you can play on pure white sand, swim safely in Tidal River, and there is so much wildlife you have to take care not to hit any animals as you drive in. But book well ahead – camping at Tidal River is so popular, there is a ballot for campsites during the peak summer period!

Find out more about camping at these and other national parks from Parks Victoria 13 1963; www.parkweb.vic.gov.au

Camping in Grampians National Park

SOUTH AUSTRALIA

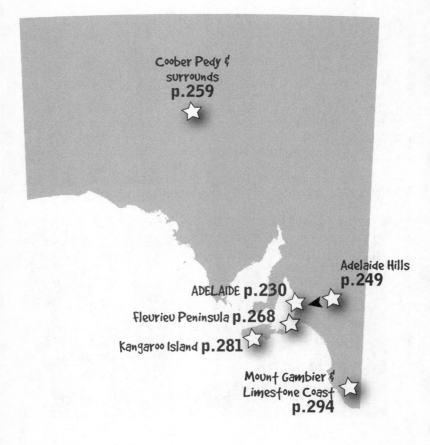

Coober Pedy &
surrounds
p.259

Adelaide Hills
p.249

ADELAIDE **p.230**

Fleurieu Peninsula **p.268**

Kangaroo Island **p.281**

Mount Gambier &
Limestone Coast
p.294

FAVOURITES

Adelaide Gaol – a fascinating insight into prison life over the years; not for the faint-hearted! *p. 230*

Admella Discovery Trail – the challenge of a quest, and the adventure of a shipwreck without the pain! *p. 296*

Flinders Chase National Park – a close-up encounter with wild seals, and scenic beauty you can clamber around on *p. 282*

Hahndorf – a European village and fairy dell *p. 249*

Naracoorte Caves National Park – venture into the lost world of giant kangaroos and koalas, extinct for 50 000 years *p. 297*

Old Timers Mine – be tantalised by the opals still there in the ground and find out how to noodle for opals yourself *p. 259*

South Australian Maritime Museum – Ahoy me hearties! Step back into a world of pirates and sailing ships *p. 241*

South Australian Whale Centre – giant whale skulls, glow-in-the-dark skeletons and X-rays of snakes *p. 271*

Warrawong Wildlife Sanctuary – pat and feed kangaroos in a wild bush setting *p. 253*

TOP EVENTS

EARLY JULY Celebrate the start of the whale-watching season at Victor Harbor's Whaletime Playtime Festival p. 275

DEC Spectacular Christmas light displays at Lobethal p. 257

ADELAIDE

In town

Adelaide Gaol
18 Gaol Rd, Thebarton
(08) 8231 4062; www.adelaidegaol.org.au
Open Sun–Fri

MID-RANGE

Kids who enjoy gruesome thrills will relish this window into prison life. Whippings and executions were carried out in this jail from 1841 to 1964. See the gallows that were employed for hangings and the cruel whipping frame with manacles that once held prisoners in position. You can imagine sleeping in the tiny, uncomfortable cells, set up just the way they were when they were occupied, complete with bucket toilets. In the interactive exhibits, try out the lock-picking devices, or put on handcuffs and manacles. If you sense the presence of ghosts as you walk around, that might be because hanged men were buried in pine coffins in the jail grounds. You can still see the graves here.

INSIDER TIPS

- Guided tours run on weekends, except on days of extreme heat; check website for times. The last tour starts one-and-a-half hours before closing.

- On weekdays you conduct your own self-guided tours with a handout.

- Ghost tours are also available; phone to check times.

- There is no cafe on site, so bring your own snacks.

DON'T MISS

- Solitary confinement cells, nicknamed 'The Fridge'. Feel a chill run down your spine as you enter these small, airless rooms with their solid, soundproof doors and fridge-like handles.

- The toilet bucket cleaning machine, used until porta-potties were introduced in the 1980s.

- The dentist's chair, which looks more like an instrument of torture!

- Open excavations in Yard Two. Archaeologists have peeled back five layers of occupation, beginning in Aboriginal times. Artefacts found in the dig are on display.

FABULOUS FACTS

More than 200 prisoners died at the jail during its 147-year history. Some were hanged, some died of self-inflicted wounds, but many died because of the unsanitary conditions. The prison's first well became polluted from the disposal of toilet waste in the grounds. Its water caused diseases such as small pox, typhus fever, impetigo, and tuberculosis (some of which were caught by prison guards as well as prisoners).

Kid Quest

Why were prisoners happy when bags of soiled nappies from Adelaide's maternity hospitals were delivered for washing in the prison laundry?
See pp. 640–4 for the answer

Adelaide Zoo

Frome Rd, Adelaide

(08) 8267 3255; www.zoossa.com.au/adelaide-zoo

MID-RANGE

Giant panda at Adelaide Zoo, Adelaide

The giant pandas are the big drawcard at Adelaide Zoo, and it's true that kids do love to watch these black and white furry balls as they laze around behind the glass. But there's so much more to see and do here! There's an amazing range of activities on offer daily. Join an Animal Encounter tour (extra cost) for a very different perspective on animals you usually only see from far away. How else would you find out that a giraffe's head, which looks quite small from a distance, is really huge, or that it has thick, black eyelashes and a long, rough tongue? Kids giggle delightedly at the feeling of this huge beast's tongue gently slurping carrots right out of their hands.

INSIDER TIPS

- When planning your visiting time, be aware that most animals are more active in the morning and several of the zoo exhibits close at 4pm.

- If you plan to see the giant pandas, check if you need to book a panda pass before you go. Note that pandas have an hour's break from public viewing from 2.45pm. Don't expect a spectacular display – pandas don't actually do very much.

- Animal Encounters need to be booked ahead by phone or online. Most encounters have a minimum age requirement of 8 years. Don't book an Animal Encounter if your child won't cope with the experience. In most encounters you feed the animals, but are not allowed to pat them. In the spider monkey encounter you have to be able to stand quietly to imitate a tree while these cheeky little creatures – who look as if they have been playing in yellow paint – climb on your head and down your arms to eat from a bowl of vegetables. Some children will be thrilled at the feel of tiny claws gripping them, but others will be frightened.

- There are more extensive behind the scenes tours available (high cost).

- The cafe is closed by 4pm (though you can still get snacks and drinks from vending machines) so you may want to bring your own food.

- The zoo has no car park and street parking has a four-hour limit in very expensive meters. However, the zoo is near the CBD and can be accessed by foot or public transport.

- If you plan to visit Monarto Zoological Park as well (*see* p. 245), purchase a Two Zoos Pass, only available at the gate.

- You can stay the night at the zoo (*see* ACCOMMODATION p. 247).

DON'T MISS

- The Children's Zoo, which offers an opportunity to feed and pat kangaroos, wallabies and some farm animals. Designated times are: 10am–12pm and 2–4pm. Limited supplies of animal food are available from the Children's Zoo gatekeeper.

- The free keeper talks throughout the day. Check the website or pick up a leaflet at the entrance.

- Free walkabout tours with volunteer guides, which depart from different points around the zoo every half hour (look for the special yellow signposts). Check the website or pick up a leaflet at the zoo entrance.

- The walk-through aviary, which has wetlands and rainforest zones. See if you can spot bowerbird bowers and the long-nosed potoroo (not a bird) who confidently wanders around and waits at the gate between the zones to be let through.

- Treasures hidden in the bamboo forest leading to the panda enclosure – look for the pretend panda embryo in a lump of amber, and statues of pandas at various ages, which kids can climb on.

- The male panda's specially chilled stone. He likes to rest on his half, but you can try out the other half outside the glass.

FABULOUS FACTS

Wang Wang and Funi are stars at Adelaide Zoo because this is the only place in Australia where you can see giant pandas. Less than 2500 giant pandas remain in the wild in the mountains of South West China. They live in bamboo forests and have to spend more than ten hours a day eating in order to meet their nutrition needs! At the zoo, they are kept separate because in the wild they live a solitary lifestyle. You can find out more about the zoo's giant pandas at www.giantpanda.org.au.

Kid Quest
Everyone knows that cockatoos can 'talk', but what other type of Australian bird is good at mimicking sounds?
See pp. 640–4 for the answer

South Australian Museum

North Tce, Adelaide
(08) 8207 7500;
www.samuseum.sa.gov.au

FREE

Stuffed animals, fossils and minerals in glass cases – this museum is itself a step back in time – but encourage the kids to look inside the

cases and discover some of the intriguing artefacts and the stories that go with them. Stand inside Sir Douglas Mawson's recreated hut from Antarctica and discover the human behind the legend of this great explorer. Down at child height in the glass cases the kids will notice a little black rag doll given to Mawson for good luck by the ballerina Anna Pavlova. In a nearby cabinet those who have read the *Swallows and Amazons* series of novels by Arthur Ransome will be thrilled to recognise the name 'Pemmican' written on a tin. Mawson took this protein mix of fat, dried fruit and meat on his sledding expeditions.

INSIDER TIPS

- While free tours are offered by the museum, they are aimed more at adults than kids.

- Before you visit, you might want to go to the website and download kids' activity trails; during school holidays these are also available from the information desk.

- The cafe, which overlooks the museum's interesting display about whales, has a kids' menu and colouring pencils and pictures for kids.

- If kids ask, the stuffed animals in the World Mammals Gallery nearly all died of natural causes, many coming from the original Adelaide Zoo.

- If your kids are interested to see more Mawson artefacts and the remains of a real giant squid, continue on to the tiny nearby Science Centre (rear of library next door, only open 10am–4pm weekdays).

DON'T MISS

- The giant squid (actually a model) that fills a whole lift shaft! Start at the top and look down on it from a glass floor, then work your way down each level looking at the huge head, eyes and tentacles.

- The largest collection of Australian Indigenous cultural objects in the world.

- The meteorites, minerals, dinosaurs and Diprotodon skull (the largest marsupial that ever lived) in the Origin Energy Fossil Gallery.

FABULOUS FACTS

Douglas Mawson led an expedition to explore Antarctica in 1911. While he was sledding across the snow and ice with two other people, Mertz and Ninnis, he heard a loud cry. Ninnis, with his sled and dogs, had fallen into a crevasse and disappeared. There was no way to rescue them. Desolately, Mawson and Mertz turned and struggled back towards base camp. Most of their provisions had been on the lost sled.

Without enough food, they had to kill and eat the remaining dogs. However, Mertz became ill and died. Mawson was the only one to make it back to camp.

Kid Quest

Look for the skeleton of a 'Chimera', a fantasy creature made by mixing bones from several different animals.

Adelaide Botanic Garden
North Tce, Adelaide
(08) 8222 9311;
www.environment.sa.gov.au/
botanicgardens
FREE
Kids love the ducks, large fish and turtles in the ponds, and have fun climbing over the buttress roots of huge trees and exploring little winding pathways. These shady gardens are dotted with an interesting combination of historic and modern buildings. In the warm, moist environment of the Bicentennial Conservatory (extra cost), kids have fun exploring the walkways that lead from the floor to the treetops.

Adelaide Festival Centre Kids Entertainment
King William Rd, Adelaide
(08) 8216 8600;
www.adelaidefestivalcentre.com.au/afc/
something-on-saturday.php
VARIOUS PRICES
From May to September the centre offers 'Something on Saturday' – a different show each Saturday afternoon for children aged 3–10 years (and their

families). For a reasonable price you can watch a performance of dance, puppetry, circus, musical theatre, kids' cabaret and much more. Before or after the show there are free Kids Corner Craft Workshops that provide an opportunity to get creative without even attending the show.

Adelaide Showground Farmers Market Kids Club
Entrance Leader St, Goodwood
www.asfm.org.au/kids_club.html
FREE
Join in the free cooking classes, gardening and other kids' activities every Sunday.

Ayers House Museum
288 North Tce, Adelaide
(08) 8223 1234;
www.ayershousemuseum.org.au
Open all day Tues–Fri,
afternoons only on weekends and
public holidays
MID-RANGE
Sir Henry Ayers, Premier of South Australia in the late 19th century, lived here with his family. View the impressive reception rooms with trompe l'oeil

paintings and the upstairs bathroom, bedrooms, and children's nursery. The kitchen and servant quarters reveal the contrast between the living conditions of servants and family.

Blackeby's Old Lolly Shop

28 James Pl (off Rundle Mall), Adelaide
(08) 8231 5166;
www.blackebysweets.com.au
FREE ENTRY

You'll all adore this quaint and enticing old-fashioned lolly shop, just like something out of a story book. The range of sweets is unbelievable.

Bradman Collection and Tours of Adelaide Oval

Adelaide Oval, North Adelaide
(08) 8300 3800; www.cricketsa.com.au
Open weekdays; oval tours 10am
FREE ENTRY; OVAL TOURS BUDGET

Sir Donald Bradman is arguably the greatest batsman in the history of cricket. The museum, located on the first level of the Sir Donald Bradman Stand, includes items of his clothing, photographs, balls, trophies and film footage. Aspiring cricketers can test their skills in the interactive displays. The tour of the historic and picturesque Adelaide Oval includes the scoreboard and players' dressing room.

Carclew Youth Arts Program

11 Jeffcott St, North Adelaide
(08) 8267 3958; www.carclew.com.au
VARIOUS PRICES

This is the place to come for terrific art and craft activities in South Australian school holidays.

Haigh's Chocolates Visitors Centre

154 Greenhill Rd, Parkside
(08) 8372 7070 or 1800 819 757;
www.haighschocolates.com.au
FREE

You can book a free 20-minute tour Monday to Saturday at 11am, 1pm or 2pm. Kids will enjoy the free chocolate tastings and peeking through the factory windows to watch the chocolates being handmade (factory is not fully operational on Saturday). Note: the commentary is fast paced and aimed more at adults than children.

Ice Arena

23 James Congdon Dr, Thebarton
(08) 8352 7977; www.icearena.com.au
MID-RANGE

Are you looking for the 'coolest' place in Adelaide? Rug up and come along for some ice-skating fun for the whole family.

Kart Mania Indoor Go-kart Racing

6–9 Deacon Ave, Richmond
(08) 8443 9755; www.kartmania.net.au
Open late morning till evening
MID-RANGE

Children aged 9 years and over (138 centimetres tall) drive on the Rookie Track and those who are 13 years and over (150 centimetres tall) use the Grand Prix Track. Alternatively, they can put on the battle gear and have a go at a laser skirmish.

Migration Museum

82 Kintore Ave, Adelaide
(08) 8207 7570;
www.history.sa.gov.au/migration
Open all day on weekdays, afternoons only on weekends and public holidays
FREE

This small museum covers the various cultural groups who have settled in South Australia since 1836. Kids enjoy looking at children's clothes and toys, and are fascinated by the rooms set up to show lifestyles of immigrants.

Parks

FREE; VARIOUS PRICES FOR ACTIVITIES

Adelaide is dotted with attractive parks. At Rymill Park, have a picnic overlooking the lake with its ducks and rowboats. In Elder Park you can hire paddle boats, listen to a band playing in the rotunda or ride a bike along the banks of the River Torrens. *Popeye* motor launch leaves from the jetty in Elder Park and cruises down the river to Torrens Weir and Adelaide Zoo (*see* p. 232).

Rundle Mall

(08) 8203 7200; www.rundlemall.com
FREE

This is the shopping heart of Adelaide, the place to find toy shops and department stores. Kids have fun climbing on the bronze pigs – Truffles, Oliver,

Bronze pig statue at Rundle Mall, Adelaide

Horatio and Augusta – and watching the buskers. Don't miss Blackeby's Old Lolly Shop in a laneway off the mall (see p. 237), and if you are there at night time, make sure you see the Rundle Lantern, a giant digital art display of moving computerised coloured lights at the corner of Pulteney Street. Check the website to see what's happening here during the South Australian school holidays.

Tandanya National Aboriginal Cultural Institute
253 Grenfell St, Adelaide
(08) 8224 3200; www.tandanya.com.au
GALLERY ENTRY FREE
The gallery showcases modern Aboriginal and Torres Strait Islander art, and the performances (Tues–Sun, 12pm, extra cost) offer a variety of cultural experiences, which might include traditional Torres Strait Islander dances, storytelling or didgeridoo playing.

Suburbs

Bay Discovery Centre
Glenelg Town Hall,
Moseley Sqr, Glenelg
(08) 8179 9508;
www.baydiscovery.com.au
BY DONATION
Official European settlement of South Australia began here, on the shore of Holdfast Bay, in 1836. Entertaining multimedia exhibitions reveal the changing face of this area over the years. Play arcade games from the 1930s or watch a film of a rollercoaster ride from the old Luna Park.

The Beachouse
Colley Tce, Glenelg
(08) 8295 1511;
www.thebeachouse.com.au
VARIOUS PRICES
Your kids will be excited as soon as they catch a glimpse of this massive indoor play centre. The Beachouse offers endless 'wet and wild' fun as well as old-fashioned fairground rides: blaster boats with shooting water cannons, dodgem cars, a play castle, 18-hole minigolf course, ferris wheel and water slides. It's advisable to buy a package rather than separate ride tokens!

Carrick Hill

46 Carrick Hill Dr, Springfield
(08) 8433 1700;
www.carrickhill.sa.gov.au
Open Wed–Sun and public holidays;
closed July

FREE ENTRY TO GARDENS AND GROUNDS;
BUDGET ENTRY TO HOUSE

Pick up a free Children's Literary Trail guide from the office and set off on a hide-and-seek adventure in the extensive gardens. Can you find the key to open The Secret Garden, or the dragon lurking around the Hobbit's house, the fairies hidden in The Magic Faraway Tree, or all the other secrets on the trail? If you're interested, you can also look inside the mansion (extra cost), built in the 1930s and decorated with antiques. Guided tours are available. Note: there may be a cost for entry to the grounds during special events.

Mangrove Trail and Interpretive Centre

Fooks Tce, St Kilda
(08) 8280 8172

BUDGET

Carrick Hill, Springfield

Meander along a 2-kilometre boardwalk through a mangrove forest. Look for tiny fish in the water and see how many of the 200 species of birds you can spot. Visit the interpretive centre to find out more about this coastal wetland.

St Kilda Adventure Playground

Fooks Tce, St Kilda

FREE

There's loads of active fun to be had exploring this playground. Features include a giant wave slide, flying foxes, tunnels, monorail and mazes. Cross a drawbridge to explore a castle or sail a ship.

St Kilda Tramway Museum

St Kilda Rd, St Kilda
(08) 8280 8188;
www.trammuseumadelaide.com.au
Limited opening hours

MID-RANGE

Kids can climb on board an intriguing collection of old horse-drawn trams, electric trams, and trolley buses. During the day, historic trams travel back and forth along the 2 kilometres of track between the museum and adventure playground (*see above*); admission to the museum covers unlimited rides.

Port Adelaide

South Australian Maritime Museum
126 Lipson St, Port Adelaide
(08) 8207 6255; www.history.sa.gov.au

BUDGET

As your kids leap across the gangplank to board the *Active II* and clasp hold of her wheel, you'll know they are caught up in an imaginary world of pirates and adventure. To the accompanying sounds of screeching seabirds, howling storms and creaking sails (all recorded), they'll scramble up and down the ladders, run their hands along the ropes and explore the hold and the cabins. With lots of kid-oriented exhibits, levers to turn and surprises to find, this museum appeals to all ages.

South Australian Maritime Museum, Port Adelaide

INSIDER TIPS

- The museum has three levels crowded with a maze of exhibits, so take your time to explore and find everything.

- The museum ticket includes entry to the 1869 lighthouse only a short walk away. Kids love climbing the spiral staircase and getting out at the top to look, but this exhibit has very limited opening hours.

DON'T MISS

- Your opportunity to 'dig' for buried treasure in the archaeological display.

- The detailed recreation of life on board emigrant ships from three different periods. In the 1840s exhibit, kids can try out hard bunk beds with smelly hessian mattresses and listen to recorded stories about people dying on the voyage out. In stark contrast, the 1950s Orient Line emigrant ship has individual cabins and washing facilities.

- The pulley exhibit where your kids will be able to lift giant weights.

FABULOUS FACTS

The *Active II* ketch inside the museum building is not really a pirate ship. It is a copy of the type of sailing ship used to carry cargo between South Australia and the rest of Australia from the late 19th century until the end of World War II. These useful little sailing ships were known as the Mosquito Fleet. Nowadays, the same work is done by land rigs and bulk cargo-handling vessels.

Kid Quest
If you were a sailor in the olden days you would eat lots of 'ships biscuit' – but before you put it in your mouth, you would bang it on the table. Why?
See pp. 640–4 for the answer

Dolphin spotting
Various locations, Port Adelaide

FREE

The Port River is a sanctuary for the Indo-Pacific bottlenose dolphin. Pick up a Dolphin Trail map from the Port Adelaide Visitor Centre, 66 Commercial Road, or download it from www.portenf.sa.gov.au, and check out six hotspots where dolphins are commonly sighted. Alternatively, there are various dolphin-watching cruises available, or you can try a kayak adventure (www. adventure-kayak.com.au).

Kids Port Walks
Visitor Information Centre, 66 Commercial Rd, Port Adelaide
(08) 8405 6560

FREE

Pick up a Kids Port Walks backpack from the visitor information centre and your kids can have fun leading the family on a guided tour of Port Adelaide

Kids Port Walk, Port Adelaide

State Heritage Area. The pack contains a compass, binoculars, photos to help identify buildings, and activity suggestions. On completion of the walk, the young guides receive a coloured map of the area and stickers. Photo ID is needed as deposit to borrow the pack, which must be returned by 4pm.

National Railway Museum Port Adelaide
Lipson St, Port Adelaide
(08) 8341 1690;
www.natrailmuseum.org.au
MID-RANGE

This amazing assemblage of rail craft is designed for serious train enthusiasts, but it includes fun, interactive exhibits for kids. There's a Tea and Sugar Train where kids can board, get their 'pay' from the banking carriage, chat with the butcher in the butcher van, and shop in the provision store. In the Relay Brake Van they can pretend to be really taking a ride, sleep in the bunks, and cook and picnic in the kitchen. There's also a model railway. Take a few safety precautions here – be sure kids don't climb on roofs, running boards or tenders, or enter areas that are chained off. Also watch out for large gaps between trains and platforms, and be prepared for high, dangerous steps into cabs. Train rides are available and are included in the entry fee.

Seahorse Farm
20 Divett St, Port Adelaide
(08) 8447 7824; www.saseahorse.com
MID-RANGE

Touch a shark egg, pat young Port Jackson sharks and watch an interesting video about seahorses. Afterwards, see who can pick the boys from the girls in the aquariums filled with the fascinating seahorses. The Seahorse Farm is next to the South Australian Maritime Museum.

Semaphore
Just east of Port Adelaide
Seasonal opening times
VARIOUS PRICES FOR ACTIVITIES

This old-fashioned seaside village has a ferris wheel, historic

Seahorse Farm, Port Adelaide

South Australian Aviation Museum, Port Adelaide

carousel, sideshows, waterslide, minigolf, and a miniature steam train (October–April).

South Australian Aviation Museum
Lipson St, Port Adelaide
(08) 8240 1230; www.saam.org.au
BUDGET
You can climb aboard a 1940s Douglas Dakota RAAF VIP plane, take the controls in the cockpit of a 6-seater Aero Commander 608, board a navy helicopter and test your coordination in a RAAF Air Crew Recruitment tester used from 1950 to 1990. However, this is largely a museum for serious aircraft enthusiasts, and you'll have to make sure your kids don't climb on fragile historic timber planes.

Day trips

Monarto Zoological Park
Princes Hwy, Monarto
(08) 8534 4100;
www.zoossa.com.au/monarto-zoo
65 km/55 min south-east

MID-RANGE

Monarto provides sanctuary and breeding programs for wildlife from Africa, Asia, South America and Australia. The animals range free in large, open habitats with low-visibility fencing. The hop-on, hop-off Zu-loop shuttle bus takes you to viewing platforms where you can see the wildlife and meet the keepers. Check the website for feeding times and keeper talks. Behind-the-scenes animal encounters (some suitable for children aged 10 years and over if accompanied by adults) are available at extra cost. If you

Monarto Zoological Park, Monarto

plan to visit Adelaide Zoo as well, purchase a Two Zoos Pass, only available at the gate. Note that there is no entry after 3pm and the zoo closes if the forecast temperature for Monarto is 40 degrees Celsius or above.

See also Adelaide Hills (p. 249), Fleurieu Peninsula (p. 268)

Accommodation

Adelaide Luxury Beach House
Henley Beach
0418 675 339; www.
adelaideluxurybeachhouse.com.au

HIGH COST

Enjoy the luxury of staying in this three-storey home on the seafront. With three televisions, two living areas, three bathrooms, spa bath, king-size four-poster bed, two queen beds, four single beds and portacot available, you shouldn't have too many arguments!

Adelaide Shores
1 Military Rd, West Beach
Adelaide Shores Caravan Park;
(08) 8355 7320 or 1800 444 567
Adelaide Shores Resort; (08) 8355 7360
or 1800 222 345;
www.adelaideshores.com.au

BUDGET TO MID-RANGE

Situated a few minutes from the centre of Adelaide, this 153-hectare beachfront reserve has a range of family accommodation, from campsites or cabins to resort-style bungalows. Facilities include heated swimming pools, a games room, kids' play equipment, bike hire (including fun 4-wheelers), and an on-site cafe. Kids can watch planes take off and land at the neighbouring Adelaide airport.

Carrington Gardens Apartments
188 Carrington St, Adelaide
(08) 8224 8888 or 1800 242 503;
www.adelaideregent.com.au
BUDGET TO MID-RANGE
These two- or three-bedroom self-contained apartments are located in the quiet south part of the city centre and feature an outdoor area with tennis court and heated pool. Make sure you request single beds in the second bedroom.

Fire Station Inn
80 Tynte St, North Adelaide
(08) 8272 1355; www.adelaideheritage.
com/unique.php
HIGH COST
For something absolutely unique, book the Fire Engine Suite in this former fire station. The kids will explode with excitement when they walk in and find a full-size, vintage fire truck right inside their bedroom, along with an original fireman's pole, a uniform to dress up in, and appropriate

decor. The large, open-plan apartment is self-contained, with a king bed and sofa bed (two roll-out beds and cot available), large spa bathroom and two toilets. It's in a great location, close to eateries and tourist attractions.

Mantra Hindmarsh Square Apartments
55–67 Hindmarsh Sqr, Adelaide
(08) 8412 3333; www.mantra.com.au
MID-RANGE
These stylish two-bedroom apartments are centrally located. They have fully equipped kitchens and living and dining areas.

Medina Grand Treasury
2 Flinders St, Adelaide
(08) 8112 0000; www.medina.com.au
HIGH COST
The Premier Grand two-bedroom apartments have the luxury and convenience of two bathrooms as well as a kitchen and laundry. The Medina Grand Treasury has a central location and boasts an indoor heated swimming pool. Note that there is no on-site parking.

Oaks Plaza Pier Glenelg
16 Holdfast Promenade, Glenelg
(08) 8350 6688 or 1300 551 111;
www.theoaksgroup.com.au/oaks-
plaza-pier
MID-RANGE
Located in a popular beachside suburb a few minutes from central Adelaide, this apartment

hotel offers a convenient alternative to city-centre accommodation. Two-bedroom apartments have a queen and double bed, and a sofa bed can be made up for an additional charge.

Travers Row Cottage
20 Travers Pl, North Adelaide
www.takeabreak.com.au/NorthAdelaide/
Adelaide/Travers-Row-Cottage.htm
MID-RANGE
This historic self-contained cottage is walking distance to shops, attractions and public transport. There are two bedrooms, one with bunk beds for the kids.

Wild night at the zoo
Adelaide Zoo, Frome Rd, Adelaide
(08) 8267 3255;
www.zoossa.com.au/adelaide-zoo
Sat nights only
HIGH COST
Sleep safari-style at the zoo in two- or three-person tents, mattresses provided. There are communal toilets, minimal showering facilities, and there is no power in tents. Accommodation includes special animal encounters (such as night walks around the zoo), zoo access the following day, and dinner and breakfast.

Places to eat

Adelaide Central Markets
Open Tues, Thurs, Fri (till late) and Sat
Wander around the fresh food stalls and eateries of Adelaide's bustling markets and you should find something to suit everyone's taste.

Chianti Classico
160 Hutt St, Adelaide
(08) 8232 7955;
www.chianticlassico.com.au
This classic Italian family trattoria boasts indoor and outdoor dining areas. It's open for breakfast, lunch and dinner every day.

Adelaide Central Markets, Adelaide

HMS *Buffalo*
Cnr Adelphi Tce and Anzac Hwy, Glenelg
(08) 8294 7000; www.thebuffalo.com.au
This replica of the sailing ship that carried the first South Australian settlers has an onboard restaurant which welcomes children. There is a kids' menu and even a themed play area. Kids can have fun touring the ship as well as playing and eating.

Chinatown
Moonta St, Adelaide
Among the pagoda roofs, red lanterns and carved lions you'll find a wide choice of fun, vibrant eateries, including an international food hall.

Just Tickled Pink
274 Unley Rd, Hyde Park
(08) 8271 6370;
www.justtickledpink.com
Afternoon high teas Wed–Sun
If your kids like things pretty, pink and elegant, they will adore this very special, old-world afternoon tea experience.

ADELAIDE HILLS

The region stretches from the eastern outskirts of Adelaide for about 30 kilometres; easily accessible by road or public transport

Year-round day-trip or holiday destination

HIGHLIGHTS

Hahndorf village **p. 249**

Hans Heysen House and Museum **p. 251**

Warrawong Wildlife Sanctuary **p. 253**

Around Hahndorf

Hahndorf village
Hahndorf Tourist Office 1800 353 323;
www.environment.sa.gov.au/heritage/shas/sha_hahndorf.html

FREE; VARIOUS PRICES FOR ACTIVITIES

This picturesque village, settled by Prussian migrants in the 19th century, is a kids' paradise (and fun for adults too). Wander down the German-style main street, lined with lovely old trees, and let yourself be tempted into every little shop. Sample the humbugs, ice-creams, wursts, cheeses, chocolate fondues and German confectionery. Spend hours looking at marionettes and cuckoo clocks, German costumes and carved wooden Christmas ornaments. Wander into a fairy dell and lose yourself in a fantasy world of talking frogs and flower fairies.

INSIDER TIPS
- Hahndorf is a good base from which to explore the Adelaide Hills. See The Manna (p. 257) for one suggestion, but there are lots of places within walking distance of the Main Street attractions.

- At many of the specialty food shops you can request free tastings of cheeses, pickles, mustard or mettwursts, an experience kids really enjoy.

DON'T MISS

- Misty Hollow, at 56 Main Street – a delightful miniature land, complete with tinkling stream, all under cover. See animated fairies, frogs and other fairytale creatures in a fantasy woodland setting. Enter through a shop filled with fantasy toys and gifts, and purchase a ticket (budget) to the world of Misty Hollow.

- The Fairy Garden (www.thefairygarden.com.au), at 55 Main Street, where you'll find an enchanting garden full of magical creatures and a wishing well. The garden is adjacent to a shop selling all sorts of fantasy delights.

- Hahndorf Puppet Shop (www.hahndorfpuppetshop.com.au), at 4/29 Main Street – ask Julie to introduce you to her rat puppet.

- An opportunity for creativity – make jewellery at Beads and Leadlight (44b Main Street).

FABULOUS FACTS

The village is named after Dirk Hahn, captain of a ship that carried a group of Prussian immigrants to South Australia in 1838. It was a terrible, dangerous sea voyage and the passengers were so grateful to the captain who brought them safely to land that they immortalised his name. You can see memorials to Hahn and those pioneering families in the Pioneer Gardens in Main Street.

Kid Quest

Be bold and challenge your taste buds by tasting some unusual mustards, pickles, cheeses and sausages!

Hans Heysen House and Museum

Heysen Rd, Hahndorf
(08) 8388 7277; www.hansheysen.com.au
Closed Mon except on public holidays
Entry to house and studio is by tour only; check times

BUDGET

Hans Heysen lived at the Cedars with his wife and children from 1912 until his death in 1968, and the house has a cosy, homely feeling as if the painter and his family still live there. Keep an eye out for the many objects and locations around the house that feature in Heysen's paintings, especially his still lifes. In the tour of the studio, the guide reveals practical secrets of how Heysen worked, which kids will be eager to try with their own artwork.

INSIDER TIPS

▓ The guide adjusts the content of the tour to suit a child audience, however if you prefer you can just explore the grounds (*see* DON'T MISS *below*).

DON'T MISS

▓ The Artist's Walk around the extensive grounds – stand on the very spots where Heysen painted some of his wonderful landscapes. Eleven viewing boxes display prints of his paintings and kids will be intrigued to compare the artwork with the living landscape.

FABULOUS FACTS

Heysen was one of the first artists to recognise and paint the individual, distinctive character of the Australian landscape and light. He was also one of the area's earliest conservationists, buying up neighbouring properties to save trees from being cut down. Instead of trees just being a background to his scenes, he painted 'portraits' of gum trees. He loved the mottled patterns on their trunks and the way the bark hung in tatters. He was awarded the Wynne Prize (the Archibald equivalent for landscape artists) nine times and his vision influenced many later Australian artists.

Kid Quest

Have a go at painting or drawing your own portrait of a gum tree.

Beerenberg Strawberry Farm

Mount Barker Rd, Hahndorf
(08) 8388 7272; www.beerenberg.com.au
Seasonal

BUDGET

Pick your own strawberries during South Australia's strawberry season, usually from October to May. On weekdays you can look through the viewing windows to see jam being cooked in big vats and then bottled.

Hahndorf Farm Barn

Lot 100 Mount Barker Rd, Hahndorf
(08) 8388 7289; www.farmbarn.com.au
MID-RANGE

Depending on the time you arrive, you might have the chance to bottle feed lambs and kids (the goat variety), help milk a cow, see sheep being shorn, cuddle rabbits, see newly hatched chicks, watch an educational show about farm animals, or go in the paddock to pat and feed the deer, ducks, peacocks, wallabies, kangaroos and emus.

Beerenberg Strawberry Farm, Hahndorf

In the hills _____

Warrawong Wildlife Sanctuary

Cnr Stock and Williams rds, Mylor
(08) 8370 9197; www.warrawong.com

FREE ENTRY 9AM–4PM

As kangaroos bound towards you from all directions, you hastily tip a
little kangaroo feed into each child's cupped hands. The next moment,
your kids are cooing in delight (or squealing in fright!) as furry noses
snuffle greedily at the food. You're surrounded by acres of bushland,
ringing with bird calls. Tiny southern brown bandicoots hop freely
around, poking their snouts under leaves to look for food, and tammar
wallabies eye you shyly. The kangaroos in the sanctuary are all orphans
whose mothers were killed by cars or shot by farmers. They go to
animal rescue centres to be raised for the first year, then come here to
spend the rest of their lives. They are all tame, as they have been raised
by humans.

INSIDER TIPS

- Visit in September for the chance to see cute baby kangaroos. This
  is when the joeys are just starting to emerge. You'll see them
  going round in circles trying to hop after mum, then crawling back
  into her pouch.

- The Bilby Cafe is on site (*see* PLACES TO EAT p. 258).

- You can stay overnight in the sanctuary (*see* ACCOMMODATION
  p. 257).

- Pick up a trail map (or print one from the website) for a self-
  guided tour through the sanctuary.

DON'T MISS

- The shows during the day (extra cost) where your kids can learn
  about the food chain, and meet spiders, frogs, lizards and snakes.

- The family feed walk every evening an hour before sunset (extra
  cost), suitable for under-8s; bookings essential. You follow a guide
  around the sanctuary as he feeds the tammar wallabies. This one-
  hour tour provides an opportunity to get closer to these shy

creatures, and as dusk approaches you also have a good chance of seeing platypus in the pools.

- The one-and-a-half-hour guided nocturnal walk after sunset every day (extra cost), suitable for kids aged 8 years and over; bookings essential. This is your chance to see nocturnal animals such as the bettong. This tour is conducted in the dark and you'll need to bring warm clothes.

FABULOUS FACTS

If you see a cormorant sitting on a branch over a pond, it just might be giving you a clue that there are platypus in the pond. When platypus poke around at the bottom of the water, they stir up tiny creatures that attract fish. Cormorants take advantage of this, and dive down to eat the fish. The way to spot a platypus is to look for a collection of bubbles in the water and wait. You might see a little head pop up, gliding on the surface as it takes in air and chatters its bill to grind up food. The best time to spot platypus is at dawn or early evening.

Kid Quest

When you reach the tall tree forest in the sanctuary, listen for rustling leaves overhead and see if you can spot any koalas.

Big Rocking Horse and the Toy Factory
Main Rd, Gumeracha
(08) 8389 1085;
www.thetoyfactory.com.au

BUDGET

As well as climbing to the top of the 18-metre-high Rocking Horse (small charge), you can visit a park where lots of tame farm animals, ducks and kangaroos will rush up to you eager for a pat and feed; food is available from the shop counter. There is also a huge toyshop, a child-friendly cafe and a picnic area. While in the area you can also visit the National Motor Museum (*see* p. 256).

Cleland Wildlife Park

Mount Lofty Summit Rd, Crafers
(08) 8339 2444;
www.clelandwildlifepark.sa.gov.au

MID-RANGE

Dozens of kangaroos and cute little potoroos roam freely around the park, and other Australian animals are housed in enclosures designed to either let you wander amongst them or get very close. Try to catch the animals at their feed times – kids particularly enjoy the dingo feeds. Don't miss the koala patting sessions (no extra cost), however koala holding (extra cost) is only for those aged 13 years and over.

Fairyland Village

21 Adelaide Lobethal Rd, Lobethal South
(08) 8389 6200;
www.fairylandvillage.com.au
Open weekends, public and school holidays

MID-RANGE

Watch for the fairytale towers and the huge sign saying 'Fairyland' as you approach the village. In a meandering walk through this bushland park, young kids have great fun discovering characters and settings from fairytales in life-size dioramas. You'll see Cinderella, Sleeping Beauty, Little Red Riding Hood, and lots of other favourites. Each display has a storyboard to read aloud.

Four Oaks Farm

Downing Rd, Littlehampton South
(08) 8388 6361;
www.fouroaksfarm.com.au

MID-RANGE

There are farm animals to pat and feed, kangaroos to meet, and ponies to ride at this picturesque farm. Kids also love to ride the merry-go-rounds, little fire engine and pony carts.

Gorge Wildlife Park

Redden Dr, Cudlee Creek
(08) 8389 2206;
www.gorgewildlifepark.com.au

MID-RANGE

Head to the Gorge Wildlife Park for a chance to get close to koalas, kangaroos, wallabies, dingoes and wombats, including several albino varieties. Feeding the animals is permitted and there are koala-handling times daily. You can also see exotic animals such as monkeys, alligators, meerkats and otters.

Melba's Chocolate and Confectionery Factory

22 Henry St, Woodside
(08) 8389 7868;
www.melbaschocolates.com.au

FREE

Have you ever seen a 'cow pat' made of chocolate? You'll be amazed by the incredible array of confectionary on show here. Between 10am and 4pm you might see some of the chocolate being manufactured on heritage machinery.

National Motor Museum

Shannon St, Birdwood
(08) 8568 4000;
www.history.sa.gov.au/motor/motor.htm
BUDGET

This is Australia's largest and most important collection of classic motorcars and motorcycles. Those not seriously dedicated to cars can still enjoy a treasure hunt trail, the toy cars, the interactive road safety exhibit, and the extensive grounds with kids' play equipment and barbecues. The Big Rocking Horse and Toy Factory (*see* p. 254) is located nearby.

Platform 1 Heritage Farm Railway

Junction Rd, Littlehampton
(08) 8391 2696; www.platform1.com.au
Closed Wed, except school holidays
MID-RANGE

Take a train ride through the historic farmyard – the driver lets the little ones hop in the cab to ring the bell, and stops so they can play inside a 300-year-old hollow tree. The train departs hourly from 11am to 4pm. Kids can have fun in the indoor play area too, pretending to drive a historic train or work an old train signal.

National Motor Museum, Birdwood

Special event

Lights of Lobethal Festival
Late Dec
www.lightsoflobethal.com.au
Lobethal lights up with two weeks of pre-Christmas festivities culminating in a lively pageant along Main Street. Events include a 'Lights on' ceremony, Christmas markets, artistic light shows on town buildings, lanterns and solar lights, nativity scenes and a display of Christmas trees decorated by local groups.

Accommodation

The Manna
25 Main Street, Hahndorf
(08) 8388 1000 or 1800 882 682;
www.themanna.com.au

MID-RANGE
Located right in the centre of Hahndorf village (*see* p. 249), you have a choice of motel-style family rooms with tea/coffee making facilities, bar fridge, toaster and microwave, or basic self-contained two- or three-bedroom units.

Mount Lofty Railway Station
2 Sturt Valley Rd, Stirling
(08) 8339 7400; www.mlrs.com.au

MID-RANGE
This old station house has been turned into two self-contained apartments. Occasional trains still chug past the door to the delight of young rail fans. Even large families can be accommodated here.

Warrawong Wildlife Sanctuary
Cnr Stock and Williams rds, Mylor
(08) 8370 9197; www.warrawong.com

MID-RANGE
If you are visiting the sanctuary (*see* p. 253), this is a fun place to stay overnight – adults can enjoy the modern conveniences of the 'eco-cabins' with raised floors, reverse-cycle air-conditioning and ensuite bathrooms, while kids will enjoy the feeling of camping inside a canvas structure with zip-up windows. The cabins are located in lovely bushland setting.

Places to eat

Bilby Cafe at Warrawong Wildlife Sanctuary

Cnr Stock and Williams rds, Mylor
(08) 8370 9197; www.warrawong.com

If you are visiting the sanctuary, this is a great place to eat. There are wooden toys, highchairs, and a kids' menu, ranging from simple vegemite sandwiches and fairy bread, to pizzas and nuggets. You'll even find kids' specials of the day. But best of all is the outlook onto animals in the sanctuary, especially in the evening when the nocturnal animals come out. Be sure to book ahead if you're relying on this for your evening meal.

Main Street, Hahndorf

A wonderful variety of family-friendly eating places up and down Main Street offer German cuisine as well as familiar favourites.

COOBER PEDY & SURROUNDS

Coober Pedy is located 840 kilometres north-west of Adelaide

Accessible by air, train or road; best times to visit are the cooler months (May–Sept)

WARNING This is a remote area and requires special preparation and precautions if you intend to travel without guides.

HIGHLIGHTS

Old Timers Mine *p. 259*

Josephine's Gallery and Kangaroo Orphanage *p. 261*

Tom's Working Opal Mine *p. 262*

Around town

Old Timers Mine
Crowders Gully, Coober Pedy
(08) 8672 5555; www.oldtimersmine.com

MID-RANGE

This is probably the best chance you'll have to see real opals still in the ground. As you don your hardhats and descend into the depths of this historic mine, you begin to feel the anticipation the first opal miners must have felt back in 1916. Your kids will point with excitement at all the glimmers of precious stones in the

Old Timers Mine, Coober Pedy

walls around you, still waiting to be dug out. As you all peer into the shadowy hand-gouged shafts, it will seem as if time has stood still. You'll see miners (life-sized models) busily at work. Travel further and you will discover a whole underground lifestyle, including real dugout homes, still furnished, and a post office.

INSIDER TIPS

◼ This tour is self-guided (and multilingual) so you can vary the pace to suit your kids. There are lots of interesting stories to read along the way, but if the kids get impatient they can run ahead and start to noodle (fossick for opals) in the pit outside. At the time of writing, the mine was preparing audio guides that you might like to try.

◼ Make sure you look up the shafts as well – you might find some surprises.

DON'T MISS

◼ The opportunity for kids to try their luck at noodling. There are real bits of opal to find!

◼ One of the interactive demonstrations of modern mining machinery that take place three times a day. Kids can actually load dirt in the blower and watch it being sucked into the big bucket.

◼ The William Hutchison exhibit – it's a story that will capture the imagination of kids (*see* FABULOUS FACTS *below*).

FABULOUS FACTS

A 14-year-old boy called William (Willie) Hutchison was the first European to find opals in Coober Pedy. Willie was the youngest member of a syndicate searching for gold in the area in 1915. When the party split up to look for water, he was left behind to mind the camp. Against orders, he wandered off looking for water himself. When the others returned and couldn't find Willie they were anxious and angry. Then the missing boy came strolling back, grinning from ear to ear. He had found not only water, but the world's largest opal-bearing region. In the museum you can read a letter Willie wrote to his mum, and view the opal he found.

Kid Quest

What is hidden under the bed in the historic dugout home?

See pp. 640–4 for the answer

Josephine's Gallery and Kangaroo Orphanage
131–133 Hutchison St, Coober Pedy
(08) 8672 5931

BY DONATION

Your kids will love the chance to pat or cuddle the babies in the Kangaroo Orphanage, and feel their soft, downy fur. They'll giggle at the sight of joeys snuggling down in artificial pouches, or sucking eagerly from bottles of milk. The baby kangaroos you see here are red kangaroos, native to dry regions like Coober Pedy. Sometimes the mother kangaroos are killed by cars, and at other times they've been shot by local Aboriginal people hunting for food (nowadays they use guns instead of spears). If hunters find a joey in a dead mother's pouch, they bring it to the orphanage.

INSIDER TIPS

- Allow at least an hour for your visit.

- The best time to visit is during the kangaroo feeding sessions at 12.30pm and 5pm daily.

- You can also go underground here and tour an abandoned opal mine (extra cost) with some opal still visible in the seams.

DON'T MISS

- The spectacular opal display – look for the opalised fossils of a tree, seashells, and even worms!

- The extensive gallery with its many examples of local Aboriginal culture. Items range from hand-painted bookmarks to bigger purchases such as didgeridoos (lessons available if you want to buy one).

FABULOUS FACTS

When kangaroos are born they look like tiny pink worms. They are blind, hairless and only a few centimetres long. Their hind legs are just stumps, but they use their forelegs to drag themselves through their mother's thick fur into her pouch. Once inside, they start to suck on a teat, and stay there drinking milk and growing for a few months. It is hard to believe these tiny creatures can grow so big – red kangaroos are the largest marsupials in the world. They can jump 3 metres high and move forward 8 metres in one leap!

Kid Quest

What happens to the kangaroos from the orphanage when they grow up?

See pp. 640–4 for the answer

Tom's Working Opal Mine

Lot 1993 Stuart Hwy, Coober Pedy
(08) 8672 3966 or 1800 196 500; www.tomsworkingopalmine.com.au

MID-RANGE

If your kids (or you) have been inspired to take up opal mining, this underground working mine is the place to find out how to prospect for opal, how to stake a claim and how opal is formed. Don a miner's helmet and switch on the headlamp for a one-and-a-half-hour underground tour. Imagine how excited your kids will be to have a go at using a real divining rod to see if they can detect any fault lines in the ground, or to ride up and down in the bosun chair (the sling that takes the real miners down into the mine), or have a lesson in how to make explosives to blast their way into the earth!

INSIDER TIPS

- Tours operate four times daily.

- Before or after the tour, you can look at a display of opals and opal jewellery.

- There is a picnic area.

DON'T MISS

■ The fun of loading up the blower which extracts dirt from underground and blows it out above ground.

FABULOUS FACTS

Opal is Australia's National Gemstone. Over 90 per cent of the world's opals are mined in Australia – and most of them are found in Coober Pedy! No two opals are exactly the same. Black opals are the rarest and most valuable. The bright specks of colour stand out spectacularly against the dark background.

Kid Quest

At the end of the tour, have a go at noodling in the dump left by the blower. You might find some opal!

Aboriginal Bush Tucker Tour

Run by Desert Cave Hotel,
Hutchison St, Coober Pedy
(08) 8672 5688;
www.desertcave.com.au

HIGH COST

Find witchetty grubs, honey ants, wild bananas and bush toffee and discover how Aboriginal people can survive in this challenging environment. Learn some Dreamtime stories.

Catacomb Church

Catacomb Rd, Coober Pedy

FREE

The altar of this dugout church has a rustic cross and furnishings made from local mulga wood and an old miner's winch.

Honey ants up close, Coober Pedy

Coober Pedy Drive-in
Hutchison St, Coober Pedy
(08) 8672 4617 or 1800 637 076
Screenings every 2nd Sat night
BUDGET

This outback open-air cinema run by the local council offers a unique entertainment experience. Seating is available if you don't have a car.

Desert Cave Hotel Interpretive Display
Hutchison St, Coober Pedy
(08) 8672 5688; www.desertcave.com.au
FREE

The Desert Cave Hotel has an underground tunnel filled with a colourful and informative display about Coober Pedy, opals and mining.

Faye's Underground Home
Old Water Tank Rd, Coober Pedy
Open Mon–Sat
BUDGET

It is hard to believe that this lovely underground home was dug out of the ground by three women using only picks and shovels. It even has an indoor pool.

Go noodling!
Various locations, Coober Pedy
FREE/BUDGET

Have a 'noodle' or fossick in the mullock heaps left by other miners and see if you can find your own small chips of opal. Try the safe, above-ground area known as 'the Jewellers Shop' at the corner of Umoona Road and Jewellers Shop Road – there are no mine shafts and it's free for the public to noodle here. On the Old Timers Mine tour you'll find another pit where you can noodle, or the Down 'n Dirty tour run by the Desert Cave Hotel (*see above*) is a noodling tour which includes a video on opal mining and visits to working mines.

St Peter and Paul's Catholic Church
Hutchison St, Coober Pedy
FREE

Dug by the community, this was the first underground church in Coober Pedy and was originally used by all denominations. There is a tower visible above ground but the main part of the church is under the earth.

Serbian Orthodox Church
Flinders St, Coober Pedy
BY DONATION

This church dug into the side of a hill features high ceilings and rock carvings. Light streams through beautiful stained glass windows on the open side.

Umoona Opal Mine and Museum
Hutchison St, Coober Pedy
(08) 8672 5288;
www.umoonaopalmine.com.au
FREE

Explore the museum of fossils found in the mines, view a documentary about opal and visit the Aboriginal Interpretive

Centre. Guided tours of mine and underground house are also available (extra cost).

In the area

You can visit the following sights on one trip, either by guided bus tour or by driving yourself. If you drive yourself, observe sensible safety procedures as this in an unsealed road in an outback location. In suitable weather it can be done in a two-wheel drive vehicle, but check with visitor information before proceeding. The loop is approximately 70 kilometres, so allow at least two hours.

The Breakaways
30 km north
FREE

Stare amazed at this weird landscape of flat-topped mesas in a patchwork of rich red ochres, golds and browns. Here and there are unexpected patches of green from specially adapted plants.

The Breakaways

Dog Fence
15 km north-east

FREE

This fence, originally built to protect sheep in the south from dingoes in the north, begins east of Surfers Paradise in Queensland and stretches 5300 kilometres, ending north of Ceduna in the Great Australian Bight. It is referred to as the longest continuous construction in the world. Kids who have seen the film *Rabbit Proof Fence* might be interested to see this one.

Moon Plain
15 km north-east

FREE

Used as a set in several movies, this vast, rocky expanse really does make you feel as if you are standing on the surface of the moon, but this area was actually a sea 120 million years ago. Part of the backbone of a 5-metre-long ichthyosaur (an ancient marine creature that looked a bit like a dolphin) has been found here.

Further afield

Mail Run
Long day tours that depart 9am Mon and Thurs; bookings essential
Depart from the Underground Bookshop
(08) 8672 5226 or 1800 069 911;
www.mailruntour.com.au

HIGH-COST

Join the real mail delivery, travelling on unsealed roads to the distant outback towns of Oodnadatta and William Creek, as well as remote cattle stations. Transport is in an air-conditioned four-wheel drive vehicle with an entertaining and informative commentary, but you travel hundreds of kilometres and it is a 12-hour day.

Accommodation

Down to Erth B &B
Lot 1795 Wedgetail Cres, Coober Pedy
(08) 8672 5762; www.downtoerth.com.au

MID-RANGE

Five minutes out of town, this spacious, self-contained apartment has its own private pool! Kids will enjoy the warm welcome and underground lifestyle; encourage them to ask for a chance to look for bits of opal in the Secret Pile.

Underground Motel

375 Catacomb Rd, Coober Pedy
(08) 8672 5324;
www.theundergroundmotel.com.au

MID-RANGE

The motel's two-bedroom suite features a double bed, four bunk beds, living and dining areas, kitchenette and large private veranda. There's also a kids' play area with a cubby.

Places to eat_____

All Coober Pedy eateries are casual and welcome families.

Tom and Mary's Taverna

Hutchison St, Coober Pedy
(08) 8672 5622
There's a range of food here with kid-appeal, including Greek-style grilled lamb and beef dishes, pasta and pizza.

FLEURIEU PENINSULA

The region starts at McClaren Vale, 40 kilometres south of Adelaide

Day trip or holiday destination; could combine with visit to Kangaroo Island

Beaches are best in warmer months (Dec–Mar), but there are plenty of year-round activities

HIGHLIGHTS

Victor Harbor

Granite Island Penguin Centre

Granite Island, Victor Harbor
(08) 8552 7555;
www.graniteisland.com.au
Check opening times
BUDGET

Although this is a rehabilitation centre for sick and injured little penguins, the ones you meet are well on the road to recovery. At feeding time the carer introduces each penguin by name. You might meet Charlie, who dives into the pool for his fish when you shout out 'One, two, three!', or hear the story of how Jeffrey became blind in one eye. Usually, little penguins can only be viewed after sunset when they come in from their daylong fishing trips, so this is a rare opportunity to see them in the daytime – great for littlies who can't stay up to see them in the evening.

INSIDER TIPS

- Access to Granite Island is via a 630-metre causeway. You can walk out, or take a ride on a horse-drawn tram (*see* p. 273). On the way, look for the stone statue of a seal and see how many live New Zealand fur seals you can spot in the water.

- If the kids are interested in exploring the island, make sure they keep to the walking trail and beware of slippery rocks and freak waves. The circular boardwalk is approximately 3 kilometres long and takes about 40 minutes.

- Granite Island features in an Aboriginal Dreamtime legend about a hero called Ngurunderi; leaflets are available from the tour office.

- There is The Reef Cafe on Granite Island (*see* PLACES TO EAT p. 280).

DON'T MISS

- The diorama with a display of stuffed little penguins – meet the tiny, realistic hologram of a talking, moving pixie.

- The touch-table with shells and sponges – ideal for littlies.

- An opportunity to dress up – kids can try on shark, stingray or penguin costumes.

FABULOUS FACTS

The way a male little penguin attracts a mate is to make an attractive burrow. He collects leaves and twigs and tries to make it comfortable. The carers at the Penguin Centre sometimes give their blind male penguins a bit of a helping hand by leaving useful material near the entrance to the burrow.

Kid Quest
Why do penguins have to eat more and put on weight before the moulting season?
See pp. 640–4 for the answer

Granite Island Penguin Tour

Granite Island, Victor Harbor
(08) 8552 7555; www.graniteisland.com.au
Seasonal times (tours depart at sunset)
Bookings essential

MID-RANGE

It's dark and cold as you set off after the ranger with his torch, everyone trying to keep quiet as they search the darkness for signs of little black and white shapes among the rocks. During the tour, you usually see the penguins come in from the sea after a day of fishing, and then you glimpse them making their way to the burrows. 'Look!' hisses the ranger, pointing to a lone penguin silhouetted on the shoreline with the sea behind him. Suddenly squawking noises come from the darkness behind you and everyone spins round. The ranger shines his torch up the cliff. There's another one somewhere up there. You can see the dark holes of the burrows, and then a flash of movement...

INSIDER TIPS

- When the penguins first come out of the sea, you might see them spreading oil from a gland near their tails with their beaks. This protects them from the cold.

- You won't get to touch any live penguins, but at the end of the tour you will be offered the chance to pat a pelt from a dead penguin to see what it feels like.

- Tours don't start till after sunset, which can be as late as 9pm in summer. When you begin the tour it is still dusk, but by the end you are walking in darkness. The tour takes about an hour and children will need to be patient and quiet throughout. Bring warm clothes as nights are usually cold.

- The horse-drawn tram (*see* p. 273) finishes at about 4pm and private cars cannot be driven onto the island so access to the tours usually means a 20-minute walk in each direction.

- If you are doing a tour that finishes late, be sure to organise food beforehand as eateries in the area generally finish serving by about 8pm. The Reef Cafe on Granite Island (*see* PLACES TO EAT p. 280) stays open until the tour departs, but on some days only snacks are available.

DON'T MISS

- The different sounds the little penguins make – a growl is a territorial sound, and a bark is calling to a friend.

- Seasonal penguin activities such as nest building or parents feeding their fluffy little chicks.

- The other island and marine life! The little penguins might steal the show, but you're also likely to see possums and water rats, seals and dolphins.

FABULOUS FACTS

First for the good news: New Zealand fur seals, which were almost extinct, are rapidly increasing in numbers in the area around Granite Island. Now for the bad news: New Zealand fur seals eat little penguins, which means that the number of penguins on Granite Island is rapidly declining.

Kid Quest
Are little penguin wings hard or soft?
See pp. 640–4 for the answer

South Australian Whale Centre
2 Railway Tce, Victor Harbor
(08) 8551 0750; www.sawhalecentre.com

BUDGET

This is only a small museum, but it is packed with exhibits in hidden nooks and crannies. Watch your kids turn into little marine scientists as they set up real X-rays of animals on a viewer and try to identify each skeleton – snakes and starfish are easy, but some creatures are more challenging – or look through magnifying glasses at bits of baleen and other marine artefacts. On a large model whale boat, kids are challenged to find and identify the oars, harpoons and more obscure parts such as the piggin (the bailer), and then push buttons to make the right parts of the model light up to check if their answers were correct.

INSIDER TIPS

- Pick up an exploration trail sheet and pencils as you enter the museum. These are fun activity sheets for kids to fill in.

- There is no cafe in this museum, but there are plenty of places to eat in the surrounding area.

DON'T MISS

- The giant skull of a southern right whale.

- The chance to dig for fossils in the sandpit.

- Kids Zone cubby house guarded by a giant squid – kids love to crawl inside and see glow-in-the-dark skeletons. Also in Kids Zone is a touch table where they can learn how to identify and recognise shells they might find on the beach.

- The Rodney Clark shark exhibit – how many of the true/false questions can the kids (or you) get right?

- The Ngarrindjeri (local Indigenous) dwelling made of whale ribs. Discover other Ngarrindjeri uses for whales beached in the area: they not only ate the meat, but also used the ear bones for drinking vessels, and rubbed the oil on their skin to keep off winter cold.

FABULOUS FACTS

A new-born southern right whale is 4–5 metres long and weighs 1 tonne, and it can double its weight in the first week! Before the coming of whale hunters in the 19th century, there were probably 100 000 southern right whales in the sea around southern Australia. There are now only about 7000. They were hunted nearly to extinction before they became protected in 1935. They were called 'southern rights' because they lived in the Southern Hemisphere and they were the 'right' ones to hunt since they swam very slowly, close to shore, and floated when they were killed.

> ## Kid Quest
> *See if you can find a fossilised lump of poo in the museum.*
> *What sea creature did it come from?*
> *See pp. 640–4 for the answer*

Horse-drawn tram, Victor Harbor

Horse-drawn tram
Victor Harbor
(08) 8551 0720;
www.horsedrawntram.com.au
Departs every 40 min (more frequently at busy times)
BUDGET

Take a ride on the only horse-drawn tramway in Australia. These two-storey heritage trams pulled by Clydesdale horses take you across the 630-metre causeway to Granite Island. Check out the kids' club on the website to download colouring pages (or you can pick up colouring pages at the tourist office). Ask the driver for your horse's 'business card', which includes a portrait, the horse's likes and dislikes, and even an email address! In the Southern Hemisphere, 1 August is the official birthday for all horses. Celebrate with a party for the Clydesdales in Victor Harbor.

Cockle Train
Departs Victor Harbor Station
Mon–Sat 1300 655 991 or
Sun (08) 8552 2782;
www.steamranger.org.au
Wed and Sun; daily during most public and school holidays
Check timetable
VARIOUS PRICES

In the early days of settlement, residents took a horse-drawn train to Goolwa to collect cockles from the beaches. You can now take a steam train along the same coastal route, enjoying spectacular views as you chug along the cliff-top track.

Dunes Mini Golf Park
The Causeway, Victor Harbor
(08) 8552 8911;
www.dunesminigolf.com.au
MID-RANGE

The 18-hole minigolf course has a fun Victor Harbor theme with icons such as a whale and lighthouse.

Greenhills Adventure Park
Waggon Rd, Victor Harbor
(08) 8552 5999 or 1300 365 599;
www.greenhills.com.au
Closed Aug
HIGH COST

You'll find enough land- and water-based activities here to keep kids amused all day: minigolf, go-karts, waterslides, flying foxes, archery, aqua bikes, canoes, a climbing wall, a maze, and moon bikes. There are four-wheel motor bikes for children as young as 5 years, and mini electric cars for pre-schoolers.

Playground
The Causeway, Victor Harbor
FREE

This playground on the seafront opposite Granite Island has lots of fun equipment, including an old steam train for kids to clamber about on. During school holidays, a fairground is set up nearby with ferris wheel, jumping castle and dodgem cars.

Ride a bike
BIKEWAY FREE, BIKE HIRE VARIOUS PRICES

The 30-kilometre Encounter Bikeway links Victor Harbor to the river port of Goolwa via Port Elliot and Middleton. Pick up a brochure from the Victor Harbor Visitor Information Centre. Bikes can be hired from Victor Harbor Cycle and Skate, 73 Victoria Street, Victor Harbor, (08) 8552 1417.

Urimbirra Wildlife Experience
Adelaide Rd, Victor Harbor
(08) 8554 6554
MID-RANGE

Picnic by a billabong under an Aboriginal canoe tree – you can see where canoes were carved out of the bark of this huge red gum. Eastern grey kangaroos hop freely around you, ducks splash in the billabong, and clouds of corellas alight in the trees. This park gives you the opportunity to feed kangaroos and meet other Australian animals. Phone ahead to find out times for koala and crocodile feeding and snake handling.

Special event

Whaletime Playtime Festival

Early July
www.whaletimeplaytimefestival.com.au
Brighten up the middle of winter
and celebrate the start of the
whale-watching season with a
weekend of kids' activities in
Victor Harbor. There are
performances all day long, as well
as marine-themed activities, face-
painting and games.

Around the peninsula

Horseshoe Bay

Beaches

FREE
Most of the beaches in the area
are surf beaches. By contrast,
Horseshoe Bay is safe and
sheltered, though it is not
patrolled. For beautiful
snorkelling spots try Rapid Bay
Jetty and Second Valley where
confident swimmers can swim out
from shore (200–300 metres) to
find leafy sea dragons.

Medlow Confectionery & FruChoc Showcase

203 Main Rd, McLaren Vale
(08) 8323 9105

FREE ENTRY
There's a video showing
confectionary being
manufactured, a viewing area to
see the chocolate-coating process,
and a showcase of original old
machinery with buttons to push
to make the parts move. If you
purchase lollies, you can have
them chocolate coated as
you watch.

Red Poles Art classes

Red Poles Gallery, McMurtrie Rd,
McLaren Vale
(08) 8323 8994;
www.redpoles.com.au/class.html
MID-RANGE
Red Poles Gallery runs fun,
creative art and craft classes for
kids in school holidays.

South Coast Surf Academy

500m along Surfers Parade, Middleton
0414 341 545; www.danosurf.com.au
HIGH COST
Learn sun awareness and get
an introduction to coastal
conservation while learning to
surf. Classes are suitable for
children and adults.

Strathalbyn National Trust Museum

1 Rankine St, Strathalbyn
(08) 8536 2656;
www.strathmuseum.org.au
Open Sat, Sun, public and school
holidays, afternoons only
BUDGET
Strathalbyn is a quaint historic
village, and the museum gives you
a peek at the way people used
to live here. You'll see rooms set
up in the style of the Victorian
era with personal belongings,
including old toys. There is also
a courtroom, police station,
medical display, farm machinery,
a blacksmith's shop and a school.

Wetland Boardwalk

Arthur Rd, Mt Compass
BY DONATION
Start at the interpretive centre
then take the 600-metre
boardwalk to look for endangered
species such as the southern emu
wren. The walk was established by
the Mount Compass Area School.

Whale-watching

For sighting updates call the
Whale Information Hotline
1900 WHALES (1900 942 537) –
calls are billed per minute – or see
www.sawhalecentre.com
FREE
Southern right whales visit the
sheltered, warm waters of
Encounter Bay to mate and give
birth. The most likely times to see
them are July and August. Whale-
watching hotspots are The Bluff,
Granite Island, Chiton Rocks and
Waitpinga Beach. Find out more
about whale behaviour at www.
tourismvictorharbor.com.au/
whales_penguins.html.

Winery tour

McLaren Vale and Fleurieu Visitor Centre
Main Rd, McLaren Vale
(08) 8323 9944; www.mclarenvale.info
FREE
If the big people in your family
don't want to miss the
opportunity of touring the
famous McLaren Vale wineries,
pop into the visitor centre and
pick up a 'Fun for Kids' brochure,
which lists playgrounds and child-
friendly wineries in the area.

The Coorong

Coorong National Park
Between Goolwa and Kingston, Meningie
(08) 8575 1200;
www.environment.sa.gov.au/parks
FREE

Colin Thiele's classic book *Storm Boy* is set in the Coorong, just south of the Fleurieu Peninsula. Read this beautiful story with your children before you visit. The main characters are a young boy, a pelican and their Aboriginal friend. The Coorong is still a lonely, wild landscape of lagoons and sand dunes, a place for finding waterbirds and learning more about Aboriginal culture. You can go for a walk, or take a cruise on the *Spirit of the Coorong*: (08) 8555 2203; coorongcruises.com.au. See Coorong Wilderness Lodge (p. 278) for accommodation in the area.

En route from Adelaide

Hallett Cove Conservation Park
Heron Way, Hallett Cove
(08) 8278 5477; www.environment.
sa.gov.au/parks/sanpr/hallettcove/
index.html
FREE

If your kids are interested in geology or seeing remnants of an ancient sea bed from the time of the dinosaurs, this is worth a visit. Signage explains the geological formations and the plants adapted to the sea environment. Kids can have fun collecting perfect round pebbles on the pathway.

Accommodation

Beachside Caravan Park
Cape Jervis Rd, Normanville
(08) 8558 2458; www.beachside.com.au
BUDGET

This beachfront caravan park has powered sites and cabins. There is a games room and a playground for the kids.

Breeze Apartments
Flinders Pde, Victor Harbor
0411 141 329;
www.unwindholidays.com.au
HIGH COST

Enjoy the sea view from your balcony in these luxury, self-contained apartments. There is a choice of two- or three-bedroom apartments, each with two bathrooms. Note: there is an extra charge for linen and cleaning on top of the room rate.

Compass Country Cabins
Lot 8 Cleland Gully Rd, Mount Compass
(08) 8556 8425;
www.compasscabins.com.au
BUDGET

Kids can ride ponies and fish for yabbies in this lovely bushland setting. The cabins are self-contained and air-conditioned.

Coorong Wilderness Lodge
Hacks Point, Meningie
(08) 8575 6001;
www.coorongwildernesslodge.com
BUDGET OR HIGH COST

The lodge is an ideal base for exploring Coorong National Park, south of Fleurieu Peninsula (*see* p. 277). Your Ngarrindjeri hosts offer activities such as kayak tours, storytelling, and bush tucker walks and tastings. They'll show you how to gather cockles and crabs, and you'll see the midden sites where Ngarrindjeri people have eaten and gathered food for hundreds of years. Accommodation is a choice of camping or luxury studio-style cabins on the waterfront.

Encounter Holiday Rentals
Various locations in Port Elliot
0418 817 394;
www.encounterholidayrentals.com
BUDGET

Enjoy a seaside holiday in one of these luxurious beach houses and apartments. Check out the very reasonable rates for one-week stays.

Narnu Farm
Monument Rd, Hindmarsh Island
(08) 8555 2002; www.narnufarm.com.au
BUDGET

Enjoy a farm-stay experience specially designed for kids. It starts with the fun of crossing over a bridge onto Hindmarsh Island. Once on the farm, kids can help with hand milking, animal feeding and care. Accommodation is in self-contained farm cottages that have plenty of open space for the kids. Book well in advance, though, as Narnu Farm is popular with school groups during term times.

Port Elliot Holiday Park
Port Elliot Rd, Port Elliot
(08) 8554 2134 or 1800 008 480;
www.portelliotholidaypark.com.au
BUDGET TO MID-RANGE
If you're looking for a beachfront location, this BIG4 park has sites for tents and caravans and also offers self-contained cabins. It features great family facilities such as playgrounds, jumping pillow, a beach volleyball court, basketball hoops and a grassed games area.

Victor Harbor Holiday Cabin Park
Bay Rd, Victor Harbor
(08) 8552 1949;
www.victorharborholiday.com.au
BUDGET
This park is conveniently located in popular Victor Harbor, a few minutes walk from both beach and shops. Facilities include a playground, games room, jumping pillow and communal TV room. Choose a campsite, caravan site or self-contained cabin.

Places to eat

Flying Fish Cafe
1 The Foreshore, Horseshoe Bay,
Port Elliot
(08) 8554 3504;
www.flyingfishcafe.com.au
This attractive little restaurant
right on the waterfront is a
tourist icon in the cute seaside
town of Port Elliot. Kids will
enjoy the famous fish and chips
served in a cone.

The Reef Cafe
Granite Island, 2 Ocean St, Victor Harbor
(08) 8552 7555;
www.graniteisland.com.au
Dinner is not available every night
If you're doing the penguin tour
in the evening, it's very
convenient to eat on the island.
The cafe serves snacks from
lunchtime until sunset, and dinner
is available on selected nights.

KANGAROO ISLAND

Kangaroo Island is located 200 kilometres south-west of Adelaide

Accessible by air with flights from Adelaide airport to Kingscote airport on the island, or by Sealink ferry from Cape Jervis

Year-round destination

HIGHLIGHTS

Flinders Chase National Park   **p. 282**

Kelly Hill Caves and Conservation Park   **p. 284**

Seal Bay   **p. 286**

Kingscote and Penneshaw

Kangaroo Island Penguin Centre

Kingscote Wharf, Kingscote
(08) 8553 3112;
www.kipenguincentre.com.au
Two tours nightly; closed most of Feb

MID-RANGE

The one-hour tour begins at the various aquariums, where you watch seahorses, giant cuttlefish, reef fish, rock lobsters and King George whiting being fed. Then it's outside for a quiet walk to look for little penguins with the aid of red torchlight. Depending on the season, you might see chicks waiting and calling out the front of the burrows, and the parents coming in from the sea to feed them. If the night is clear, the tour includes a guided talk about the southern night sky.

Pelican feeding at Kingscote Wharf

Water's edge behind the Kangaroo Island Penguin Centre, Kingscote Wharf
Daily at 5pm

BUDGET

If you wait on the north side of the wharf behind the Kangaroo Island Penguin Centre at 5pm, you'll see a flock of wild pelicans coming in to land, all eager for a treat. The 'Pelican Man' throws fish from his bucket and gives a talk about pelicans to his (human) audience.

Penneshaw Penguin Centre

Bay Tce, Penneshaw
(08) 8553 1103
One tour each evening; closed most of Feb
MID-RANGE

These intimate tours for 15–20 people offer a close-up view of the little penguins. After a brief informative talk about penguins from around the world, you set off for an hour's walk on boardwalks. The little penguins can be seen going about their seasonal activities only a metre from the boardwalk, and sometimes Tamar wallabies and possums put in an appearance too. The guide might also point out planets in the sky. Before the tour you can enjoy Penneshaw Beach, which offers safe conditions for swimming.

Around the island___

Flinders Chase National Park

Cape du Couedic Rd, Flinders Chase
(08) 8559 7235; www.environment.sa.gov.au/parks

FREE ENTRY TO VISITOR CENTRE; PARK ENTRY BUDGET

The Flinders Chase Visitor Centre has created a wonderful buried treasure adventure for kids. Budding young archaeologists can borrow dig kits (buckets and spades) and hunt through the excavation site (a sandpit). While you watch from the cafe, the excited hunters will uncover the plaster casts of megafauna bones and eagerly try to identify their finds from the display board alongside. The fun continues

Remarkable Rocks, Flinders Chase National Park

inside the centre, where they can use touch screens to hear animal noises, or feel the real skins of echidnas, wallabies and goannas.

INSIDER TIPS

■ Flinders Chase National Park is on the extreme west side of the island. It is about a two-and-a-half-hour drive between the park and the east coast where the airport and ferry terminal are located. Ask staff at the visitor centre how long it will take to drive to destinations inside the park. It is not safe to drive around after sunset because of the risk of hitting animals.

■ It is easy to spot kangaroos without going far in the park – they hop all around the visitor centre! From April to September there are also Cape Barren Geese around the visitor centre. This is their breeding season, so keep your eye out for the chicks.

■ Warning: the wind and waves can be extremely violent in the coastal areas of the park, so take care.

■ If you want to bring a picnic, there are gas barbecues at the visitor centre, or you can purchase meals at the Chase Cafe.

■ It is possible to camp overnight in the park or stay in one of the lighthouses (see ACCOMMODATION p. 292).

DON'T MISS

- Remarkable Rocks – kids enjoy the spectacular appearance of the rocks and the fun of climbing right inside these strange formations. Look for the signs explaining how the rocks were formed.

- Admirals Arch – follow the boardwalk to a viewing area where you can watch large colonies of New Zealand fur seals surfing the waves or sunbaking on the rocks. During summer, there will be cute seal pups as well.

FABULOUS FACTS

It is easy to tell male New Zealand fur seals from females because the males are so much bigger. While a female is 1.5 metres long and weighs 70 kilograms (about the same as a human adult female), the male is 2.5 metres long and weighs a whopping 185 kilograms! If any of the seals look as if they are crying, don't worry, it is just that they have no control over their tear ducts so their eyes tend to run. We are lucky that New Zealand fur seals still exist today. They were hunted almost to extinction in the 18th and 19th centuries.

> ## Kid Quest
> ### Do New Zealand fur seals have ears?
> See pp. 640–4 for the answer

Kelly Hill Caves and Conservation Park

South Coast Rd, Karatta
(08) 8559 7231; www.environment.sa.gov.au/parks
Entry by tour only; check times

VARIOUS PRICES

The Kelly Hill Caves are dry limestone caves with a stunning array of stalactites, stalagmites, straws, and the more unusual helictites – incredible formations that hook and twist in defiance of gravity. It's not often that kids get to go adventure caving. At Kelly Hill, children who are 8 years and over are given the opportunity to don hard hats, equipped with lights, and crawl down rocky tunnels into a subterranean cave system. The 40-minute Show Cave Tour is a prerequisite for the adventure caving option and is an impressive experience in itself.

INSIDER TIPS

- Wear sturdy, closed footwear and layered clothes as the temperature inside the caves may be different from outdoors..

- Adventure Caving takes place once a day, in the afternoon; bookings are essential and the minimum age is 8 years.

- The park has barbecues, picnic areas, shelters, and toilets.

- It is possible to purchase a Kangaroo Island Parks Pass. This is worthwhile if you plan to visit all of the following: Cape Borda Lightstation, Cape Willoughby Lightstation, Flinders Chase National Park, Kelly Hill Caves and Seal Bay.

DON'T MISS

- The above ground interpretive walking trails. Try to spot native wildlife, including echidnas, but watch out for holes (*see* FABULOUS FACTS *below*). If some members of the family are not keen to go underground, this is a great alternative.

FABULOUS FACTS

The Kelly Caves are named after a horse. In 1880 a stockman was riding through the hills on a horse called Kelly and suddenly they found themselves dropping down a big hole. The stockman managed to climb out and ran off to get help for his horse. When he returned, Kelly had disappeared. Some people think the stockman was looking in the wrong hole, while others claim the horse wandered off into the underground maze. Did Kelly die in the caves, or find a way out at the other end? We will never know, unless someone finds the horse's bones...

Kid Quest

See if you can find the bones of the poor lost Kelly.

Baby sea lion at Seal Bay

Seal Bay

Seal Bay Rd, Seal Bay
(08) 8559 4207; www.environment.sa.gov.au/parks
Late opening hours during the summer school holidays

VARIOUS PRICES

Imagine walking on a beach with huge Australian sea lions just a few metres away – the bulls weigh up to 300 kilograms! Luckily, the adults are usually exhausted from three days fishing in the sea so they just lie around on the sand. The juveniles will entertain you, though, flip-flopping around on their flippers, suckling from their mothers, and trying to chase the seagulls. You might see some of the sea lions surfing the waves as they come into shore, or waddling down from the dunes as they head back to sea for another fishing expedition.

INSIDER TIPS

- Seal Bay boardwalk and guided walks can only be accessed through the visitor centre.

- If possible, avoid visiting between 11am and 1pm which is the busiest time.

- Check ahead for guided tour times. Although you can do a self-guided walk on the boardwalk (extra cost), and read the interpretive signage, it is worth paying extra to take a guided tour so you can get down on the beach amongst the sea lions.

- Guided tours to Seal Bay beach run throughout the day and take about 45 minutes.

- During summer school holidays, you can participate in an extended guided Sunset Tour (extra cost) after other visitors have left; bookings are essential. Bring warm clothes because evenings at the beach can be cold, even in summer.

- Bring binoculars if you can and a pad of paper and pencils. Sea lions are an easy shape to draw and are likely to stay still long enough to be sketched.

DON'T MISS

- Seal Bay Visitor Centre – discover fascinating facts about the evolution of seals, the history of sealing, seal research, and pollution.

- All the other wildlife in the park! Sea lions command your attention, but look out for tracks or traces of other animals. You might see footprints or droppings from possums or kangaroos, or diggings from echidnas. Maybe you'll catch sight of short-beaked echidnas foraging, and heath goannas and tiger snakes sunning themselves. At dusk, look out for tammar wallabies or common brushtail possums.

- The birdlife – look skywards for a chance to glimpse osprey, white-bellied sea-eagles, wedge-tailed eagles or nankeen kestrels.

FABULOUS FACTS

The name Seal Bay is misleading, because sea lions are not true seals! Australian sea lions are found only in Australia and are one of the world's most endangered pinnipeds (carnivores with limbs adapted to an aquatic life). They are also very unusual because they give birth every 17–18 months, unlike other pinniped species which breed once a year. Australian sea lions like to rest on sand, unlike the New Zealand fur seals you can see at Admirals Arch which prefer to sun themselves in rocky areas.

Kid Quest

What type of skeleton is lying in the sand dunes?

See pp. 640–4 for the answer

Cape Borda Lightstation

Playford Hwy, Cape Borda
(08) 8559 3257; www.lighthouse.net.au
Check tour times

MID-RANGE

This lighthouse built in 1858 on the far north-west coast of Kangaroo Island is still operational, though it is now automated. Try to time your visit to witness the cannon firing which takes place every day during the 12.30pm tour. Check out the small cemetery where several children from lighthouse keepers' families were buried. Accommodation is now available in one of the old keeper's cottages (*see* p. 292).

Cape Willoughby Lightstation

Cape Willoughby Conservation Park,
Willoughby Rd, Willoughby
(08) 8553 1191; www.lighthouse.net.au
Entry by tour only; check tour times

MID-RANGE

This lighthouse, situated on the south-east tip of Kangaroo Island, is the oldest in South Australia. It is open for tours and accommodation (*see* p. 292). Children under 5 years of age are not permitted up the lighthouse stairs unless they are carried in an approved backpack.

Emu Ridge Eucalyptus and Craft Gallery

Willsons Rd, Macgillivray
(en route to Seal Bay)
(08) 8553 8228; www.emuridge.com.au
Closes early afternoon

BUDGET

Guided tours are available every half hour during peak season and self-guided tours are available at all times. Kids enjoy these sensory tours that offer opportunities to touch and smell.

Hanson Bay Wildlife Sanctuary

South Coast Rd, Karatta
(08) 8559 7344; www.hansonbay.com.au

BUDGET

This is a good place to see koalas during the day, and if you come back in the evening for a guided tour (extra cost), you'll be shown Tammar wallabies, kangaroos, echidnas, bats and possums as well. To avoid driving around the island after dark, you can stay here overnight. Interesting note: koalas are not native to Kangaroo Island, having been introduced in the 1920s.

Honey Farms

Cliffords Honey Farm,
Elsegood Rd, Macgillivray
(08) 8553 8295;
www.cliffordshoney.com.au
Island Beehive, 1 Acacia Drive, Kingscote
(08) 8553 0080;
www.island-beehive.com.au

FREE ENTRY; GUIDED TOURS BUDGET

The bees on Kangaroo Island are rare Ligurian bees imported from Italy in 1884. There are two places on the Island where you can learn about bee keeping, see how bees make honey and have fun tasting different honey products.

Island Pure Sheep Dairy and Cheese Factory

Gum Creek Rd, Cygnet River
(08) 8553 9110;
www.goodfoodkangarooisland.com/food/
islandpure.asp
Afternoons only

BUDGET

Most kids know that milk comes from cows, but here you can show them that it comes from sheep too! Kids can play with lambs, watch sheep being milked (3pm daily), look through the factory viewing windows to see the cheese being made, and even have a taste of the sheep's milk products.

Kayaking

Kangaroo Island Outdoor Action, Jetty Rd, Vivonne Bay
(08) 8559 4296;
www.kioutdooraction.com.au

HIGH COST

You can hire a double kayak that fits two adults and two kids, and the staff will help you launch the kayaks on the Harriet River, 400 metres away. Paddles and life jackets are provided.

Little Sahara

Off South Coast Rd, Vivonne Bay

SANDBOARD HIRE VARIOUS PRICES

In the middle of an area of bush is an amazing field of huge white sand dunes known as `Little Sahara'. The kids will be ecstatic to slide down the fine, white sand. Sandboards and toboggans are available for hire from Kangaroo Island Outdoor Action (*see above*) or Vivonne Bay Store; (08) 8559 4285. Warning: it might take a few days to get rid of all the traces of sand in your hair and clothes!

Sandboarding in Little Sahara, Vivonne Bay

Marron Farm

Harriet Rd, Central Kangaroo Island
(08) 8559 4128; www.andermel.com

FREE ENTRY

Marron (freshwater crayfish) were introduced to Kangaroo Island 40 years ago. At Marron Farm's holding shed you can observe marron up close at various stages of their life cycle. After that, if you fancy eating one, you can indulge at the cafe on site.

Murray Lagoon

Cape Gantheaume Conservation Park, Seagers Rd

FREE

The lagoon is home to thousands of ducks, swans and birdlife. You might catch a glimpse of platypus too. Take the Bald Hill walk (1 kilometre) or the Timber Creek walk (1.5 kilometres). Winter and spring are the best times to observe waterbirds.

Parndana Wildlife Park

Playford Hwy, Parndana
(08) 8559 6050;
www.parndanawildlifepark.com

MID-RANGE

If you haven't managed to spot many animals in the wild, this is your opportunity to see them – and get up close. The park has a walk-through aviary, and provides a chance to hand-feed kangaroos.

Paul's Place Wildlife Sanctuary

Stokes Bay Rd, Stokes Bay
(08) 8559 2232; www.paulsplace.com.au
Seasonal opening times

MID-RANGE

Paul's Place offers intimate, hands-on tours where you might cuddle a koala, bottle-feed a baby kangaroo, hand-feed lorikeets, pat a possum, ride a pony or get hugged by a snake!

Quad bike tour

Kangaroo Island Outdoor Action, Jetty Rd, Vivonne Bay
(08) 8559 4296; kioutdooraction.com.au
Tours at daytime or dusk

HIGH COST

For a bit of fast excitement, try a quad bike tour. The minimum age for riders is 12 years and the minimum age for passengers is 5 years. The dusk tour is a great opportunity for sighting wildlife.

Rare Breeds Farm

North Coast Rd, 2 km west of Stokes Bay
(08) 8559 2115;
www.rarebreedsfarm.com.au
Open Tues–Sat; call to confirm tour times
(closed all winter)

MID-RANGE

True to name, this farm boasts a collection of rare and unusual breeds of cattle, sheep, pigs, and poultry. See watusi cattle, with incredibly long horns, and the type of sheep that came out on the First Fleet.

Beaches

FREE

Stokes Bay Beach on the north coast has a natural rockpool which offers safe swimming for children; outside the rockpool, the sea is rough. The part kids will love best is access to the beach, which is through a rock tunnel. Vivonne Bay on the northern side of the island has a long, curved, sandy beach with safe swimming areas near the jetty and in the sandy-bottomed Harriet River that enters nearby.

Stokes Bay Beach

Accommodation

Some accommodation options on the island are quite remote and isolated, so find out where you will be able to purchase food and petrol!

Cape Borda Lighthouse Keeper's Cottage
Flinders Chase National Park,
Playford Hwy, Cape Borda
(08) 8559 7235 or (08) 8553 2381;
www.southaustralia.com/9006195.aspx
MID-RANGE

Stay in a heritage lighthouse keeper's cottage in the remote north west of the island and experience the lonely life of a lighthouse keeper. The stone-built cottage is self-contained with three bedrooms. See Cape Borda Lightstation (p. 288) for information on things to see and do.

Cape du Couedic Lighthouse Keepers' Cottages
Flinders Chase National Park,
Playford Hwy, Cape Borda
(08) 8559 7235 or (08) 8553 2381;
www.southaustralia.com/9006207.aspx
MID-RANGE

Accommodation is available in three cosy, restored lighthouse keepers' cottages. Each has three bedrooms and can accommodate up to six people. Enjoy the incredible Flinders Chase National Park after all the crowds have gone; these cottages are walking distance to Admirals Arch. See Cape du Couedic Lightstation for information on things to see and do.

Cape Willoughby Lighthouse Keepers' Cottages
Cape Willoughby Conservation Park
Willoughby Rd, Willoughby
(08) 8559 7235 or (08) 8553 2381;
www.southaustralia.com/9006200.aspx
MID-RANGE

There's a choice of two spacious lighthouse keepers' cottages here, each with five bedrooms, situated in the south-east of the island. See Cape Willoughby Lightstation (p. 288) for information on things to see and do.

Kangaroo Island Wilderness Retreat
1 South Coast Rd, Flinders Chase
(08) 8559 7275; www.kiwr.com
HIGH COST

This is a convenient base for exploring Flinders Chase

National Park. Choose a Lodge apartment with kitchenette and bedding for four- or five-star accommodation with interconnecting hotel-style rooms. You can purchase food from reception for hand-feeding the wallabies in the grounds.

Owen House
6 Flinders Ave, Kingscote (08) 8121 2779; www.takeabreak.com.au/Kingscote/ KangarooIsland/ Owen-House.htm
BUDGET
If you're seeking a comfortable and affordable place in a good east coast location, this two-bedroom private house boasts a large garden and well-equipped kitchen. It has a queen bed and two single beds.

Ozone Aurora Seafront Hotel Kingscote
Commercial St, Kingscote (08) 8553 2011; www.auroraresorts.com.au
HIGH COST
Experience the east coast in style in luxury two- or three-bedroom townhouses suitable for families. Each townhouse features a kitchen, two bathrooms and laundry facilities.

Places to eat

Kangaroo Island Fresh Seafoods
Caltex Fuel Complex, 26 Telegraph Rd, Kingscote (08) 8553 0177
Local fishermen deliver their catch here daily, and it is processed for sending all over Australia. If you like, you can watch the fish being filleted. Select a piece of fish from the display and have it cooked the way you want.

Restaurant Bella
54 Dauncey St, Kingscote (08) 8553 0400
Come here for great pizzas – always a hit with kids.

Vivonne Bay Store
South Coast Rd, Vivonne Bay (08) 8559 4285
Try the legendary Kangaroo Island whiting burger available here.

MOUNT GAMBIER & LIMESTONE COAST

Mount Gambier is located 450 kilometres south-east of Adelaide and has its own regional airport

Suits driving holidays

Year-round destination, but the best time to see Mount Gambier's Blue Lake is in summer

HIGHLIGHTS

Admella Discovery Trail **p. 296**

Naracoorte Caves National Park **p. 297**

Mount Gambier

Blue Lake
John Watson Dr, Mount Gambier
(08) 8724 9750 or 1800 087 187
FREE
The lake that fills the crater of Mount Gambier volcano mysteriously turns an amazing turquoise colour from November to March each year. The lake is the water source for Mount Gambier and you can take a tour of the aquifer system, www.aquifertours.com. If you walk around the Blue Lake (3.6 kilometres), look for the marker indicating where the poet Adam Lindsay Gordon (*see* DINGLEY DELL

COTTAGE p. 299) leapt off on horseback.

'The Lady Nelson' Visitor and Discovery Centre
Jubilee Hwy East, Mount Gambier
(08) 8724 9750 or 1800 087 187;
www.mountgambiertourism.com.au/
discoverycentre.htm
BUDGET
Board a full-size replica of HMS *Lady Nelson* and hear Lieutenant Grant tell his story of discovery. See the fossilized skull of an extinct short-faced kangaroo *Simosthenurus occidentalis*. Meet the ghost of Christina Smith, an

Umpherston Sinkhole, Mount Gambier

early European settler, as she steps out of a photograph and relates the story of her experiences with the Aboriginal people in the 1840s. Watch an electronic erupting volcano and find out about the geology of this area.

Tantanoola Cave
Off Princes Hwy, 29 km north-west of Mount Gambier
(08) 8734 4153
www.environment.sa.gov.au/parks/sanpr/tantanoolacaves
Entry by tour; tours operate hourly
MID-RANGE

This easily accessible cave with no stairs is one of Australia's most beautiful caves. It includes unusual helictites – incredible formations that hook and twist in defiance of gravity – and a 'magic pool' filled by water droplets which sparkle from the ceiling.

Umpherston Sinkhole
Jubilee Hwy East, Mount Gambier
(08) 8724 9750 or 1800 087 187
FREE

This stunning natural large rock depression has been planted with a magnificent garden. Visit in the evening when the kids will have fun venturing into the eerie depths of a floodlit cave, and seeing the large numbers of possums who come out to feed.

Valley Lake Wildlife Park and Boardwalk
Davison Dr, Mount Gambier
(08) 8724 9750
FREE

There is a recreational area with free barbecues and an adventure playground, and from the boat ramp you can take a walk into the Wildlife Park, or follow a boardwalk onto the lake to spot water birds and animals (you'll need to be quiet).

In the area _____

Admella Discovery Trail
Various locations
Download an Admella Discovery Trail brochure from www.admella.org.au or pick up a copy from Mount Gambier, Portland, Robe, Beachport, Millicent or Port MacDonnell visitor information centres
VARIOUS PRICES

Go on a family adventure trail and follow the real events of a historic shipwreck in which 89 people perished. In Nene Valley Conservation Park, walk the path taken by the two sailors who managed to make it to land and trek through the bush for help. Stand on the observation deck near the lighthouse in Canunda National Park to view the reef where the ship foundered 150 years ago. Imagine how it felt to be part of a crowd watching helplessly for eight long days as survivors tried to cling to the wreckage, being pounded by the waves. Visit maritime museums where you can see real artefacts washed up from the ship, and the lifeboat that managed to rescue 19 people.

INSIDER TIPS
- This is a driving trail which covers large distances, and access to many of the sites on the trail is along unsealed roads.

- If you cross the state border heading towards Melbourne, you can call in to Portland Maritime Museum and see the Portland lifeboat that was used to rescue many of the *Admella* survivors.

DON'T MISS
- The opportunity to read about the heroic rescuers and see a medal awarded to one of them at the Old Wool and Grain Store Museum (*see* p. 300).

- Artefacts from the wreck at the Old Wool and Grain Store Museum and the Millicent National Trust Museum (*see* p. 300).

- A professional, metre-long model of the *Admella* in full sail at the Port MacDonnell and District Maritime Museum (*see* p. 301).

- The memorial to those who perished on the *Admella*, at Cape Banks lighthouse near the town of Carpenter Rocks.

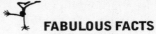

FABULOUS FACTS

In 1859, when the SS *Admella* sank, it was the first news of a shipwreck to be carried along the newly installed telegraph link between the capital cities of Australia. Because of that technology, the general public was able to hear news of a shipwreck disaster as it unfolded. For a week, newspapers published daily, harrowing updates about the rescue attempts and the state of the survivors who could be seen hanging onto the wreckage.

Kid Quest
Find out where the name Admella *came from.*
See pp. 640–4 for the answer

Naracoorte Caves National Park

Hynam Caves Rd, Naracoorte
(08) 8762 2340; www.environment.sa.gov.au/parks/sanpr/naracoortecaves
Entry to some caves by guided tour only; check times (usually operate twice a day)
Other caves open daily for self-guided tours

VARIOUS PRICES

Imagine wandering into the Australian bush and coming across strange, giant animals that are long extinct: a 5-metre striped snake strangling a wallaby in its coils, a massive-sized koala, a marsupial lion with long, sharp teeth and claws... In the Wonambi Fossil Centre you walk through a simulated forest and see dioramas of extinct animals recreated from the fossil remains found here at Naracoorte Caves National Park. Once you have seen how the live animals must have looked, tour the Victoria Fossil Cave and see their real skeletons lying in the red dusty soil where they have lain for hundreds of thousands of years.

INSIDER TIPS

■ Entry to Victoria Fossil Cave is only available through a one-hour guided tour that departs from the Victoria Fossil Cave carpark, 1.5 km south-east of the Wonambi Fossil Centre.

■ A 1.3-kilometre World Heritage walking trail leads from Wonambi Fossil Centre to Victoria Fossil Cave. Signage explains the World Heritage values of the park.

- Alexandra Cave is an easy half-hour guided tour into three beautifully decorated chambers. It departs from the front of the Wonambi Fossil Centre. This tour is ideal for families with small children.

- In the Bat Cave/Blanche Cave tour you don't go inside Bat Cave because visitors would disturb the thousands of rare bent winged bats, but you watch the bats via a camera link-up. In winter you can see bats in Blanche Cave clinging to the roof, and in summer, you can take a night tour to see bats exiting Bat Cave to feed on insects.

- Wet Cave is an easy self-guided walk, with an automated lighting system. It has two chambers. The first has a large 'window' and the natural light coming through encourages the growth of tree ferns. The second chamber is dark and mysterious and you leave from here to start your Adventure Tour (*see below*).

- Adventure Tours are only available by prior booking (minimum 4 people, minimum age 8 years). The Stick-Tomato Cave (entered from Wet Cave) is the most suitable for families, as the tunnels are larger and the squeezes into small gaps optional. Overalls, helmets and kneepads are provided, and you are taught safe caving techniques before you start.

- Bring sturdy, closed footwear and warm clothes (the cave temperature is a constant 17 degrees Celsius).

- There are barbecue and picnic facilities, a cafe and campground in the park.

DON'T MISS

- The model of an extinct giant malleefowl and its nest-mound. Kids are allowed to play on the mound!

- The tour of Victoria Fossil Cave – for the best understanding of why this is a World Heritage area. You'll see dazzling stalagmites and stalactites as well as fossils.

FABULOUS FACTS

The reason there are so many fossil bones here is that the caves acted as pitfall traps. For over 500 000 years, any unfortunate animal to wander into the area would fall inside a cave and die, and its bones eventually became fossilised. Scientists now use these fossils to try to unravel the mystery of Australia's evolutionary history.

Kid Quest

The Diprotodon australis, the largest marsupial to ever live, was once common over much of Australia, but there are very few Diprotodon bones in the caves. Why?

See pp. 640–4 for the answer

Avenue Emus

Thomas Rd, Avenue Range
(08) 8766 0085;
www.avenueemus.com.au
Phone to check opening times
BUDGET

This is a working emu farm. On the guided tour you get right in amongst 300 emus (might be a bit daunting for littlies) and learn about these unusual birds. You might feed and pat one of the quieter ones, or go on an egg hunt. Warning: some kids may get upset when they realise the connection between the animals they have just patted and the meat and other products on sale.

Beaches

FREE

Kid-friendly beaches can be found at Robe, Beachport, Kingston SE and Southend.

Coastline near Robe

Cape Jaffa Lighthouse Museum

Marine Pde, Kingston SE
www.lighthouse.net.au
Open daily school holidays
BUDGET

This lighthouse has been relocated from Margaret Brock Reef off Cape Jaffa. When in use in the 1870s, the three lighthouse keepers' families (including eleven children) had to live together on a platform 10 metres wide by 20 metres long.

Dingley Dell Cottage

Dingley Dell Conservation Park, Dingley Dell Rd, Port MacDonnell
(08) 8738 2221; www.dingleydell.net
MID-RANGE

Poet Adam Lindsay Gordon named his home Dingley Dell Cottage after a manor farm in Charles Dickens *Pickwick Papers*. Born in England, Adam Lindsay Gordon was sent to the Australian colonies in disgrace by his parents. He continued to live a dare-devil life. On the Blue Lake walk (*see* p. 294), a monument marks the place where he leapt over a fence on horseback, and landed on a narrow ledge above a 70-metre sheer drop. You can see some of his personal effects in the cottage, and go for a walk or picnic in the beautiful gardens. Adam Lindsay Gordon's poem *From the Wreck* was inspired by the shipwreck of the *Admella* (*see* ADMELLA DISCOVERY TRAIL p. 296) and the ride by Peter Black to Mount Gambier to raise the alarm.

Ewens Ponds Conservation Park
Ewens Ponds Rd, Port MacDonnell
(08) 8735 1173; www.environment.sa.
gov.au/parks/sanpr/ewenponds
FREE

You can snorkel in the ponds and look for rare Ewens pygmy perch hiding in the reeds, or freshwater crayfish. Note: all plants and animals are protected and must not be disturbed. Water temperature is chilly (10–15 degrees Celsius) so you'll need thick wetsuits.

Mary MacKillop Penola Centre
Penola
(08) 8737 2092;
www.mackilloppenola.org.au
BUDGET

This is the place where a young teacher, Mary MacKillop, helped by Father Julian Tenison Woods, founded the Sisters of St Joseph. You can see the original schoolhouse where she lived and taught. Mary MacKillop was destined to become Australia's first saint.

Millicent National Trust Museum
1 Mount Gambier Rd, Millicent
(08) 8733 3205 or (08) 8733 1192;
www.millicentmuseum.com
BUDGET

This large museum has something to interest everyone, from beautifully restored horse-drawn vehicles and machinery, to antique household items and baby clothes, oddities such as an emu egg football cup, and artefacts from the *Admella* wreck (*see* ADMELLA DISCOVERY TRAIL p. 296).

Old Wool and Grain Store Museum
Railway Tce, Beachport
(08) 8735 8013
Check opening hours
BUDGET

Find out about life in Beachport in the olden days. Displays cover domestic and Aboriginal activities, shipwrecks (including the *Admella, see* ADMELLA DISCOVERY TRAIL p. 296) and the old whaling days. You can see a whaleboat and hand harpoons, and kids will be impressed by the giant vats used to boil down whale blubber.

Piccaninnie Ponds
Piccaninnie Ponds Conservation Park
(08) 8735 1177;
www.environment.sa.gov.au/parks/
sanpr/piccaninnieponds
FREE

Take a walking trail to see the unusual sight of fresh water bubbling up on the beach. This is a good place to spot birds and shellfish.

Pool of Siloam
McCourt Rd, Beachport
(08) 8735 8029
FREE
This salt lake is supposed to be seven times saltier than the sea, which makes the water very buoyant – great for beginner swimmers! It is also supposed to possess therapeutic powers.

Port MacDonnell and District Maritime Museum
49 Meylin St, Port MacDonnell
(08) 8738 7259
Limited opening hours
BUDGET
Read tales of shipwreck disasters and see artefacts from wrecks.

There is a large collection from the *Admella* (*see* ADMELLA DISCOVERY TRAIL p. 296) and a fabulous model of the ship. Also on display is a model boat that sailed all the way from Macquarie Island in the Antarctic to a beach near Port MacDonnell, arriving intact!

Sheep's Back Wool Museum
Tourist Information Centre,
MacDonnell St, Naracoorte
(08) 8762 1399 or 1800 244 421
BUDGET
Wander round an old flour mill to see displays on the history of wool and sheep, then go outside to view the old slab woolshed, historic post office, schools museum (a favourite with the kids) and a robotic shearer.

Accommodation

Blue Lake Holiday Park
Bay Rd, Mount Gambier
(08) 8725 9856 or 1800 676 028;
www.bluelakeholidaypark.com.au
BUDGET TO MID-RANGE
This BIG4 holiday park offers wireless internet, a jumping pillow, swimming pool, tennis courts and a playground. Choose between comfortable bungalows and campsites.

Robe Long Beach Holiday Park
70–80 The Esplanade, Robe
(08) 8768 2237 or 1800 106 106;
www.big4.discoveryholidayparks.com.au
BUDGET TO MID-RANGE
Robe is a relaxing holiday destination for families and this BIG4 holiday park has a jumping pillow for kids, an indoor heated pool available year-round, and easy access to the beach. There is a choice of campsites, or one-, two- or three-bedroom units with reverse-cycle air-conditioning.

Talbot Hill Farm Bed and Breakfast

RSD 6055 Bay Rd, Mount Gambier,
(08) 8723 1670;
www.talbothillfarm.com.au or
www.takeabreak.com.au

BUDGET

This stone cottage, 4 kilometres south of town, is in the middle of a 10-hectare hobby farm, so kids can have fun with sheep, goats, alpacas and horses. It offers basic accommodation with a kitchenette, and bunk beds for the kids. Linen is supplied.

Places to eat

The Treehouse Play Cafe

25 Bay Rd, (enter via Heriot Street)
Mount Gambier
(08) 8723 2045;
www.treehouseplaycafe.com.au
Closed Tues (except school holidays),
open late Fri

Enjoy a light meal while the kids play on the indoor adventure play equipment. This venue is best suited for children under 12 years of age.

South Eastern Hotel

235 Commercial St East, Mount Gambier
(08) 8723 9090

The kids can let off steam in the play area here while you keep an eye on them through a large viewing window.

Bellum Hotel

Bay Rd, Mount Schank
(08) 8738 5269;
www.bellumhotel.com.au

The casual dining room in this country pub has interesting menus for both adults and kids. There's also an outdoor playground area, a DVD corner showing popular children's programs, and colouring-in pages with a country theme.

Another Holiday Idea for South Australia

Murray River houseboating

BUDGET TO HIGH COST

For a holiday with a difference, why not try houseboating. All you need is an unrestricted driver's license and it is much like staying in a holiday house, with the added excitement of being afloat – with life vests, buoys, and two-way radios on hand! Bring warm clothes, sunscreen, insect repellent, food and drink. Check if you need to supply your own linen. And you might want to pack a fishing rod (and bait).

If you're houseboating in the Mannum area, drop in on the Mannum Dock Museum of River History. The main feature here is the restored heritage paddlesteamer *Marion*, usually moored at the dock. Kids enjoy exploring the galley, dining room, lounges and cabins of this historic steam-driven, wood-fired paddlesteamer. See *www.psmarion.com* or phone (08) 8569 2733 for information on the occasional one-hour or three-day cruises.

Find out more at www.murrayriver.com.au/mannum/houseboats

Relaxing on the Murray River

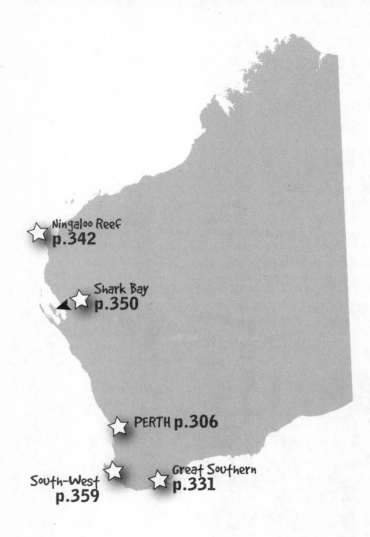

Ningaloo Reef
p.342

Shark Bay
p.350

PERTH **p.306**

South-West
p.359

Great Southern
p.331

FAVOURITES_____

Kings Park – dinosaurs, playgrounds, wishing wells and a clock made of flowers *p. 310*

Leeuwin–Naturaliste National Park – a natural wonderland above and below the ground *p. 367*

Monkey Mia dolphin interaction – feel the splash of dolphins swimming in the shallow waters around your feet *p. 350*

Ningaloo Marine Park – wade off the beach to swim with turtles on a coral reef *p. 345*

Scitech – a theme park filled with science fun *p. 306*

Valley of the Giants – take a walk up high, through the branches of giant tingle trees *p. 337*

Western Australian Maritime Museum – squeeze inside a real submarine *p. 322*

Whiteman Park – something for absolutely everyone, from kangaroos and carousels to vintage cars *p. 315*

TOP EVENTS

MAY Shark Bay Fishing Fiesta, a chance for fisherfolk of every age to test their luck and skill *p. 357*

SEPT A month of fun, springtime activities at Perth's Kings Park Festival *p. 319*

PERTH

In town

Scitech, West Perth

Scitech
City West Building, Sutherland St, West Perth
(08) 9215 0700; www.scitech.org.au
MID-RANGE

Imagine your whole family working together in an exciting race, pulling levers, pushing buttons and pumping pedals to manipulate a pile of balls up, down and around a track. Will your team be able to do it faster than another family? The Scitech team has created interactive exhibits that offer all the fun and adventure of a theme park, while at the same time teaching scientific principles. As you play the Up and Down race with balls, you will all be learning about gravity, levers, pulleys, wheels, and potential and kinetic energy.

INSIDER TIPS

- Allow at least two to three hours to participate in all the activities at Scitech.

- There is free two-hour parking in the area, but if you want to park for longer ask at the Scitech front desk for a permit.

- Scitech exhibits are changed every few months for new exciting and educational challenges, so some of the activities described here may have been replaced.

- There is a kid-friendly cafe on site.

DON'T MISS

- Discoverland, ideal for children under the age of 7 years. Kids can dress in sea-creature costumes, crawl into a bubble in the middle of an aquarium to find out about underwater life, or spy on you with a periscope to learn about mirrors and refracted light.

- The live science shows included in your entry, aimed at children aged 7 years and over. You might find out how we learn to think, or what chemistry is lurking in everyday things such as food and cars. Check performance times and topics when you arrive.

- The puppet shows for children aged 3–7 years. These interactive shows, included in your entry fee, introduce science through storytelling. Kids might meet shadow puppet dinosaurs or learn how to look after a pet. Check performance times and topics when you arrive.

- The red-and-white striped whispering dishes that let you whisper messages from one end of the floor to the other.

- Horizon – the planetarium, which offers stunning and realistic multimedia presentations about the universe on an 18-metre domed screen. The minimum age is 4 years.

FABULOUS FACTS

Scitech has hosted the Junior Western Australian Robocup for primary and secondary school students several times. In this competition, teams of students have to design and build robots that can dance to music, play a game of 2-on-2 soccer, or negotiate challenging obstacles to perform a rescue.

Kid Quest

How much power can you generate by pedalling a bicycle? Have a go here and find out whether you can turn on a light bulb or power a television.

Art Gallery of Western Australia

James Street Mall,
Perth Cultural Centre, Perth
(08) 9492 6622;
www.artgallery.wa.gov.au
Closed Tues

BY DONATION; EXTRA COST FOR SOME SPECIAL EXHIBITIONS

This is a child-friendly art gallery. Apart from interesting and varied exhibits, often accompanied by appropriate activities for kids, there is a special family space called Wonderland where kids can explore textures and colour, build a 3-D puzzle, copy poses and expressions from portraits, or just relax and read books.

Bike hire

Point Fraser Reserve (Causeway Carpark), 1–7 Riverside Dr, Perth
(08) 9221 2665;
www.aboutbikehire.com.au
VARIOUS PRICES

You can hire bicycles in all shapes and sizes – even a 'quadcycle' with four wheels and seats for two adults and one child. Explore paths along the Swan River foreshore and cross the water into Burswood Park (www.burswoodpark.wa.gov.au) where you'll find duck ponds, picnic and barbecue areas, and a playground. Inline skates are also available for hire.

Fire and Emergency Services Education and Heritage Centre

Cnr Murray and Irwin sts, Perth
(08) 9416 3402; www.fesa.wa.gov.au
Limited opening hours

FREE

Learn about the hazards that Emergency Services respond to, such as fires, flood, or tsunamis, and view vintage fire service appliances.

Museum of Performing Arts

His Majesty's Theatre, 825 Hay St, Perth
(08) 9265 0900;
www.hismajestystheatre.com.au
Open weekdays

BY DONATION

See costumes, costume designs and other theatrical memorabilia inside this gorgeous Edwardian theatre, which is still operational.

Perth Mint

310 Hay St, East Perth
(08) 9421 7223; www.perthmint.com.au
Open daily; closes 1pm on weekends and public holidays

MID-RANGE

See historic coins, a recreated gold miner's camp and real gold nuggets, including the Newmont's Normandy Nugget, the second-largest gold nugget in existence at over 25 kilograms. You can find out what your weight is worth in gold, or engrave your own coin, but the highlight for most people is watching a real gold bar melted down and poured into a mould (occurs on the hour). Guided tours are available.

Perth Wheel

Barrack Sqr, Riverside Dr, Perth
(08) 6101 1676;
www.thewheelofperth.com.au

MID-RANGE

This Ferris wheel will lift you slowly to a height of nearly 50 metres, where you'll be able to look out over the Swan River and downtown Perth.

The Place

State Library of Western Australia,
25 Francis St, Perth
(08) 9427 3111;
www.slwa.wa.gov.au/whats_on/the_place
Open daily except public holidays; also open evenings Mon–Thurs

FREE

The mezzanine level of the library is a special place for children and families. You can cuddle up on comfy cushions to share books, play with puppets and dress-ups, or look at original book illustrations.

Swan Bells

Riverside Dr, Perth
(08) 6210 0444;
www.ringmybells.com.au
Bells rung daily in the middle of the day
MID-RANGE

These historic bells from St Martin's Church in London feature in the line 'You owe me five farthings say the bells of St Martins' from the 'Oranges' and 'Lemons' nursery song. For hundreds of years they rang for the crowning of kings and for other important occasions in Britain. Climb the tower to see the bells and enjoy the view.

Western Australian Museum

James St Mall, Perth
(08) 9427 2700; www.museum.wa.gov.au
BY DONATION

This is a museum of natural science and cultural heritage. Don't miss the megamouth, one of the world's rarest sharks, and the Mundrabilla meteorite, which weighs 11.5 tonnes and is the biggest ever to hit Australia.

Suburbs

Kings Park

Kings Park Rd, West Perth
(08) 9480 3634; www.bgpa.wa.gov.au
FREE

Your kids run forward shouting with excitement at the sight of a Muttaburrasaurus dinosaur – well, a full-sized model, anyway – lying

Inspecting limestone sculptures at Kings Park, West Perth

in the sun in front of them. A moment later, one child is clambering onto its head, while another is patting its scaly back. Then they're off to explore their own little island, crossing a bridge, climbing a tower, whirling down a spiral slide, and squealing under jets of water that shoot up when they run past. Then they spot another huge replica, a Bullockornis, the largest bird ever to live on Earth, and they're off again...

INSIDER TIPS

■ The dinosaurs are located in the Synergy Parkland at the far end of Kings Park from the visitor centre. The equipment in Synergy Parkland is designed for children aged 7 years and over.

■ If you have under-7s, head for the Lotterywest Family Area near the visitor centre. The playground here is specially designed for younger ones, and has a big wooden ship, fort and drawbridge.

■ Kings Park is on a steep hill. To avoid lots of steps, enter by walking in from St Georges Terrace, or take the free Number 37 bus, which drops you inside the park.

■ Kings Park covers a vast area, and little legs are not likely to make it from one end to the other. You can travel around by car or public transport, or catch a ride on a replica vintage tram and listen to a commentary on the way; (08) 9322 2006; www. perthtram.com.au. There are bike paths, but there is no bike hire in Kings Park.

■ On the elevated section of the Lotterywest Federation Walkway (see DON'T MISS *below*), make sure you hold littlies by the hand as it is dangerous to carry them above the height of the handrail.

■ Check the website for concerts in the park during summer.

■ There are barbecues and various eateries around the park, including Stickybeaks Cafe (see PLACES TO EAT p. 329).

DON'T MISS

■ Lotterywest Federation Walkway, which takes you into the treetops.

■ The real guns used in famous wars, in Fraser Avenue Precinct. You'll find a Krupp field gun captured in the Boer War (at the memorial to Western Australian soldiers killed in South Africa), and guns from Waterloo and the Crimea (at the Queen Victoria statue).

- DNA Tower – kids love climbing the spiral stairs to the top.

- The floral clock – listen for the recorded call of a rufous whistler (bird) that sounds on the half hour.

- The wishing wells – one across the road from Fraser's Restaurant on Fraser Avenue and one near Stickybeaks Cafe in the Lotterywest Family Area.

- The Giant Boab, known as Gija Jumulu, in the Two Rivers Lookout at the end of Forrest Carpark (*see* FABULOUS FACTS *below*).

FABULOUS FACTS

The Giant Boab is about 750 years old, weighs 36 tonnes and has a massive, bulbous trunk measuring 2.5 metres in diameter. Incredibly, this tree was dug out of the ground 3200 kilometres north of Perth in the Kimberleys. It was brought here on the back of a truck, a journey that took six days. All along the way, people honked their horns and waved as it passed, and when it arrived, Perth's Indigenous Nyoongar people welcomed it with a smoking ceremony.

Kid Quest
Try the Whispering Wall at the entrance to the War Memorial Precinct in the Court of Contemplation. If you talk softly at one end of the curved wall, someone at the other end should be able to hear.

Perth Zoo
20 Labouchere Rd, South Perth
(08) 9474 0444 or (08) 9474 0333;
www.perthzoo.wa.gov.au
Open daily including Christmas Day

MID-RANGE

The Nocturnal House is dim and mysterious inside. The kids complain they can't see anything, but a moment later, their eyes have adjusted, and they are gasping and pointing. There is a scorpion glowing under ultra-violet light, and a ghost bat with pale fur and huge ears. The kids scamper from window to window, calling out proudly as they spot the secretive creatures. You peer anxiously at your watch – it's nearly time for the elephant talk, and then you'll need to rush to the primate walk-through, and then the penguin presentation ...

Perth Zoo, South Perth

INSIDER TIPS

- The zoo map costs $1 at the entrance, or you can download a free copy from the website.

- When you arrive, choose your favourite animals and keeper presentation times, and plan your visit so you don't miss out.

- The animal enclosures try to replicate the natural environment, so you may need to wait and watch in order to spot the animals among their surroundings, as you would if looking for them in the wild.

- The zoo is a short ferry ride across the river from the city, or you can even ride a bicycle there (see BIKE HIRE p. 308).

- If little (or long) legs are getting tired, you can organise your own Zebra Car Tour (small extra cost). A guide will drive you around in a zebra-painted electric vehicle for an hour.

- Close Encounters are available with a variety of animals (high extra cost). A minimum age applies, but 6-year-olds can have a little penguin encounter, and 7-year-olds can meet Australian reptiles. Encounters need to be booked well in advance.

- If you see any squirrels scampering around freely, they are Indian palm squirrels, imported by the zoo and released in 1898. They are now considered to be a pest, but they are very cute!

- There are a few food outlets around the zoo, but they may finish serving before zoo closing time. There are also barbecues and picnic areas.

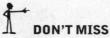

DON'T MISS

- Times for feeding and special presentations – these are listed on the website but may vary. Favourites are the elephant and reptile talks and the primate walk-through.

- The historic carousel, conveniently located near the Zoo Cafe, so adults can relax while the kids ride.

- Scene Too Believe photography just inside the zoo's main entrance (extra cost). With digital manipulation, you end up with a fun photo of your family. How would you like a photo of your bunch fending off some very hungry crocodiles?

- The free one-hour guided walking tours offered once or twice daily. Enquire at the information centre for start times and location.

- The wonderful Variety Special Playground, which has caves, tunnels, frog ponds, water-play, a periscope, musical objects and a tree house cubby.

FABULOUS FACTS

The woylie, one of the critically endangered animals in the Nocturnal House, has an unusual skill. When it needs to carry twigs and grasses for building a nest, it curls its long tail around them. You can watch a video of this on the zoo website. The woylie is a small, herbivorous animal found only in very small patches of south-west Western Australia.

Kid Quest

How many animals can you find that you have never heard of before?

Whiteman Park

Lord St, Whiteman
(08) 9209 6000;
www.whitemanpark.com.au
Open daily including Christmas Day

FREE ENTRY

VARIOUS PRICES FOR ATTRACTIONS

With animal parks, motor museums, a bouncy castle, a carousel, playgrounds, forests, cricket grounds, picnic areas, barbecues and shade shelters, there is something to please every

Marvelling at a brown falcon at Whiteman Park, Whiteman

member of the family in Whiteman Park. One child feeds a kangaroo and smiles blissfully, patting the soft fur on its head. Another squeals with excitement at the sight of vintage tractors chugging past. Then it's time to head over to the Birds of Prey Area for a flying display by eagles, falcons, kites and owls.

INSIDER TIPS

- Whiteman Park is divided into four main areas: The Village, Caversham Wildlife Park, the Children's Forest and the Mussel Pool picnic area.

- Bikes are available for hire in The Village from 11am to 3pm, weekends and public holidays.

- Watch out for vintage tram, train or bus rides operating around the park.

- There are various food outlets around the park.

DON'T MISS

- Caversham Wildlife Park (*see* p. 317).

- Motor Museum of Western Australia, located in The Village. This one is not just for rev heads! For a small entry fee, you can see historic vehicles showcased in interesting period settings such as repair workshops; (08) 9249 9457.

- Birds of Prey Flying Display (extra cost) twice daily on weekends, school and public holidays; located in Carpark 18, Mussel Pool West; 0438 388 383.

- Revolutions, a transport heritage centre, located in The Village (entry by donation). See the types of transport that have been available in Western Australia over the years, and the impact each has made; (08) 9209 6040.

- The Tractor Parade at 1.15pm on the second Sunday of every month. Failing this, you can visit the Tractor Museum (entry by donation) 10am–2pm on Wednesdays, weekends, school and public holidays; (08) 9209 3480.

- The Lolly Stop with its delectable array of lollies for sale, located in The Village. You'll find it open 11am–3pm, Wednesday–Sunday; (08) 9249 8812.

- 'Ozzi Bugs' – mini electric cars that your kids can drive themselves, with mum or dad sitting in the back seat! These are available for hire in The Village 11am–3pm, weekends, school and public holidays; (08) 9374 0080.

FABULOUS FACTS

Western Australia is famous for spectacular wildflowers. Spring is the showiest time, but in Whiteman Park there is something in flower all year – and the sound and sight of birds feeding on nectar is your best indication of where to look! Pick up a guide on the flowers from the visitor centre.

Kid Quest
Look for the giant marching ants in the Children's Forest.

Adventure World
179 Progress Dr, Bibra Lake
(08) 9417 9666;
www.adventureworld.net.au
Seasonal opening hours
HIGH COST

Come here in summer for a day of rides and water fun. Older kids can brave the Spinning Power Surge or the Tunnel of Terror, while littlies have their own rides, such as chugging round a creek in an electric-powered frog. And the whole family will enjoy the wildlife area. Once you have paid for entry, all activities are free.

Aviation Heritage Museum

Bullcreek Dr, Bullcreek
(08) 9311 4470;
www.raafawa.org.au
BUDGET

This is a wonderful opportunity to get up close to a wide variety of military and civilian aircraft from different eras.

Caversham Wildlife Park

Whiteman Park, Lord St, Whiteman
(08) 9248 1984;
www.cavershamwildlife.com.au
MID-RANGE

Enjoy a combination of Australian animal encounters and farmyard shows and activities. You can feed kangaroos, meet koalas, pat a python, bottle-feed lambs, marvel at sheepdogs or milk a cow. Entry price includes all shows, talks, animal feeding and photo opportunities. For more information on Whiteman Park see p. 315.

Claremont Museum

Mrs Herberts Park,
66 Victoria Ave, Claremont
(08) 9340 6983;
www.claremont.wa.gov.au
Limited opening hours
FREE

This historic 1860s building has had various uses over the years. Inside you can see interesting social history displays, including a carefully preserved schoolroom. The surrounding park has a playground and picnic facilities.

Cottesloe Beach

Marine Pde, Cottesloe
FREE

Play on clean, white sand, go snorkelling, eat in the cafes or picnic on the grassed areas under shady trees. The waves can get rough, so the southern end of the beach, protected by a stone groyne, is best for small children.

Great Valley Rally

Depart from Swan Valley Visitors Centre,
cnr Meadow and Swan sts, Guildford
(08) 9379 9400;
www.swanvalley.com.au
FREE

The Great Valley Rally is a clue hunt designed to be led by kids and enjoyed by the whole family. Download the clues (or pick them up from the visitor centre), then hop in your car and go on a scenic drive looking for the answers. Whiteman Park (*see* p. 315) is in this area.

Lake Monger

Lake Monger Dr, Leederville
(08) 9483 1111 or 1800 812 808;
www.westernaustralia.com

FREE

Thanks to a special breeding island, this is a great place to see black swans, the state emblem of Western Australia. If you follow the boardwalks, you'll find interpretive displays about all the birdlife around the lake.

Mettams Pool

Located in the Marmion Marine Park,
off Westcoast Dr, Trigg
www.dec.wa.gov.au

FREE

Introduce kids to snorkelling in this sheltered pool close to shore. It is less than 2 metres deep and has a great range of marine plants and animal species.

Railway Museum

136 Railway Pde, Bassendean
(08) 9279 7189;
www.railheritagewa.org.au
Open Wed and Sun afternoon

BUDGET

Rail buffs will enjoy seeing the huge steam and diesel locomotives as well as 'Freudie', the tiny 20-inch-gauge mine locomotive.

WACA Museum

Entry via Museum Gate on Hale St,
Western Australian Cricket Association,
East Perth
(08) 9265 7222;
www.waca.com.au/waca/museum.asp

Open weekdays until mid-afternoon;
closed on match days

BUDGET

See a display of memorabilia from the history of cricket in Western Australia. You can take a tour of the famous grounds of the Western Australian Cricket Association (WACA) twice daily, Monday–Thursday (extra cost).

Wanneroo Botanical Gardens

25 Drovers Pl, Wanneroo
(08) 9405 1475; www.botanicgolf.com.au
Seasonal opening hours, including some
evenings

MID-RANGE

These beautiful botanical gardens include Leapfrogs Cafe and Australia's largest minigolf course. You might take advantage of the bike hire facility and ride to Neil Hawkins Park for a picnic or barbecue among native birds and ducks, and some time in the playground.

Special event

Kings Park Festival
Sept
www.bgpa.wa.gov.au
Celebrate spring and the wonderful Western Australian wildflowers with a month of floral displays, live music, exhibitions, workshops and family activities in Kings Park.

Fremantle

Fremantle Prison
1 The Terrace, Fremantle
(08) 9336 9200; www.fremantleprison.com.au
FREE ENTRY TO GATEHOUSE AND VISITOR CENTRE;
GUIDED TOUR PRICES MID-RANGE TO HIGH COST

You peer through the door into a cell and see a tiny room furnished with nothing but a backless stool, tiny table, and hammock serving as a bed. Your kids glance at you, wide-eyed and solemn-faced, as the guide leads you into a grim, bare exercise yard surrounded by high fences. You see an execution room with the hangman's noose dangling ready, a whipping post and solitary confinement cells. But you also see amazing artwork some of the prisoners have painstakingly painted onto their walls. This is an astoundingly real and evocative glimpse into history and another side of life.

Fremantle Prison, Fremantle

INSIDER TIPS
- The only way to experience the full prison is to take a guided tour, but you can see the prison gatehouse, find out some of the history of the prison and see some artefacts of punishment in the visitor centre.

- There are several tours on offer. The one described above is the Doing Time Tour, which runs every half hour and takes about just over an hour.

- The Great Escapes Tour, which runs hourly, is another popular tour. There are discount prices if you do both tours.

- The eerie Torchlight Tour is available in the evening, but the minimum recommended age is 10 years.

- Try to go at a quiet time, such as early in the morning, as it is difficult to see the exhibits properly in large groups.

- Audio guides are available for the guided tours, if required, in Japanese, French, German, Korean and Mandarin.

DON'T MISS

- The Tunnels Tour (high cost) – a real adventure that includes paddling a replica convict punt through underground tunnels. The minimum age is 12 years.

FABULOUS FACTS

The first British colonies in Australia were built by convicts who cleared land, worked the farms and constructed buildings. Settlers in the Swan River Colony (now Perth and Fremantle) tried to manage without convicts, but failed. The first shipment of convicts was sent to Western Australia in 1850. The new arrivals lived in temporary accommodation and constructed their own prison, which opened in 1855. These are the buildings you see today.

Kid Quest
If you had to design a prison, what would it be like?

Shipwreck Galleries
Cliff St, Fremantle
(08) 9431 8444; www.museum.wa.gov.au/museums/shipwrecks
Closed Wed and some public holidays
BY DONATION

As your kids stare up at the jagged, torn timbers of the eerily lit *Batavia*, you tell the story of this wooden sailing ship, wrecked on the coast of Western Australia in 1629 (*see* FABULOUS FACTS *below*). All around you, items in the gallery bring the story to life. On display are sandstone blocks found at the scene of the shipwreck – these were being carried to Jakarta (Batavia) to form a portico for a castle. You will also see the astrolabe used in the unsuccessful navigation, and the skeleton of a stranded survivor who was attacked by mutineers.

INSIDER TIPS

■ Before visiting, you could read *Strange Objects* by Gary Crew, or *The Devil's Own* by Deborah Lisson, both teenage books based on the *Batavia* story.

■ There are cafes nearby, but none on site.

DON'T MISS

■ The video about the *Batavia* wrecking, mutiny and modern day excavation in the Dutch Wrecks Gallery.

■ The old maps recovered from various shipwrecks. See how much (or little) people knew about the world hundreds of years ago when those maps were drawn.

FABULOUS FACTS

It is often claimed that the first European to sight Australia was Captain James Cook in 1780. In fact, several European ships sighted the Western Australian coastline in the early 1600s, en route to trade for spices in the East Indies. The Dutch ship *Batavia* was making such a trip in 1629 when a line of breakers indicated the presence of a reef. According to the skipper's reckoning the ship was in the middle of the Indian Ocean, so he dismissed the sighting. When the ship hit the reef, all but 40 of the 316 people on board managed to struggle to an island 80 kilometres off the Western Australian coast, carrying silver coins, a casket of jewels and other valuable items of cargo. They thought they were saved, but a small group of mutineers murdered 125 of the men, women and children, planning to keep the loot for themselves...

Kid Quest
What happened to the mutineers?
See pp. 640–4 for the answer

Western Australian Maritime Museum

Victoria Quay, Fremantle
(08) 9431 8444; www.museum.wa.gov.au/museums/maritime
Closed Wed and some public holidays

MID-RANGE

As soon as the tour guide ushers you inside *Ovens,* an Oberon-class submarine, you start to feel claustrophobic. It is impossible to imagine living for months underwater in this confined space! But your kids clamber like monkeys up the steel ladders and through the small, round hatchways. Once the tour is over, you appreciate the light, airy spaciousness of the museum building, designed to fit the high mast and winged keel of *Australia II* (*see* FABULOUS FACTS p. 323). Exhibits reveal the stories of Western Australia's early explorers, trade routes, naval defence, and migration.

INSIDER TIPS

- It is possible to buy separate tickets for the museum and submarine tour if you don't want to see both, which makes this a budget activity.

- The submarine tour takes about one hour and leaves from the museum every half hour; bookings are essential during school holidays.

- Pregnant women and children under 5 years of age are not permitted on the submarine. Children aged 5–16 years must be accompanied by an adult.

- You need to be able to walk up and down four flights of scaffold stairs for the submarine tour. Remember to wear flat shoes. Also note that there are no toilet facilities on the submarine.

- There is a small cafe on site.

- The main shipwreck displays are in the Shipwreck Galleries (*see* p. 320).

DON'T MISS

- The magnificent *Australia II* (*see* FABULOUS FACTS on facing page).

- The Indian Ocean Gallery, where you can experience the sights, sounds and scents of a recreated 15th-century Middle Eastern marketplace with stalls of brilliant fabrics, spices, grains, gold, pearls and ivory.

- The views of a real working harbour (through the window).
- The display of pests discovered by the Quarantine Service on ships coming to Australia.

FABULOUS FACTS

When the seventh and deciding race of the 25th America's Cup began in September 1983, no country had been able to steal the winning cup from America since the prestigious race began 132 years earlier. But the Royal Perth Yacht Club's 12-metre sloop, with its controversial winged keel, was about to sail into history. To the elation of the whole of Australia, the yacht *Australia II* won the race and the America's Cup.

Kid Quest

Why does the Ovens submarine fly a pirate flag?
See pp. 640–4 for the answer

Army Museum of Western Australia

Artillery Barracks, Burt St, Fremantle
(08) 9430 2535;
www.armymuseumwa.com.au
Limited opening hours

BUDGET

The collection includes artefacts and equipment such as tanks, guns, uniforms, and even wooden legs. Exhibits are arranged in galleries from the 19th century to the present. There are full-size dioramas, including a World War I trench and an operating hut.

Fremantle Round House

10 Arthur Head, Fremantle
(08) 9336 6897 (manned on weekdays);
www.fremantleroundhouse.com.au
Open mid-morning to mid-afternoon daily

BY DONATION

This stone structure was built as a prison in 1831, and you can still be shut into stocks in the yard, if you choose! A cannon is fired at 1pm every day, just as it was in the days of sail, when ships used this signal to set their chronometers. You can book to have a turn at firing the cannon (minimum age 10 years).

Kulcha Multicultural Arts of Western Australia

www.kulcha.com.au
1st floor, 13 South Tce, Fremantle
(08) 9336 4544

VARIOUS TIMES AND PRICES

Kulcha is a space for performing and learning multicultural arts. Check the program for concerts, cultural events and workshops – your family might have the chance to take part in an African drumming class!

Spare Parts Puppet Theatre
1 Short St, Fremantle
(08) 9335 5044;
www.sppt.asn.au
Museum open weekdays
(except lunchtime)

MUSEUM FREE; PUPPET SHOWS EXTRA COST

All kids love puppets. Try to catch a show, but if you can't, check out the wonderful museum filled with thousands of puppets from around the world. There are puppet-making workshops in the holidays.

WA Circus School
Old Customs House,
8 Phillimore St, Fremantle
(08) 9335 5370;
www.circuswa.com
Minimum age 3 years

VARIOUS PRICES

If your kids have ever wanted to run away and join a circus, this is their chance! Adults participate in Tiny Tots classes, but otherwise adults' and kids' classes are separate. Phone ahead or check the website for a timetable and prices.

Hillarys _____

Aquarium of Western Australia
Hillarys Boat Harbour,
91 Southside Dr, Hillarys
(08) 9447 7500; www.aqwa.com.au

MID-RANGE

It is fitting that the state with the most extensive coastline also boasts Australia's largest aquarium. At the Aquarium of Western Australia (AQWA) you'll come nose-to-nose with 4-metre sharks, sting rays, turtles, crocodiles, deadly stonefish, unusual pineapple fish and globefish, octopus, rock lobsters, sea horses, lionfish, moon jellies, cuttlefish and living coral. Highlights are the transparent underwater tunnel and the touch pool.

Aquarium of Western Australia, Hillarys

The Great Escape

22 Southside Dr,
Hillarys Boat Harbour
(08) 9448 0800;
www.thegreatescape.com.au
Open daily, but rides are seasonal

VARIOUS PRICES

You'll find waterslides, high-rope adventures, minigolf, trampolines, rock-wall climbing and little kiddie rides... the whole family can have hours of active fun.

Naturaliste Marine Discovery Centre

39 Northside Dr, northern end
of Hillarys Boat Harbour, Hillarys
(08) 9203 0339; www.nmdc.com.au
Open weekdays till 4pm, except public
holidays

BUDGET

Learn about the creatures of Western Australia's oceans and rivers through a range of interactive exhibits, including a touch pool.

Sorrento Quay

Hillarys Boat Harbour,
28 Southside Dr, Hillarys
(08) 9246 9788;
www.sorrentoquay.com.au

FREE

This swimming beach and playground, close to shops and cafes, is a favourite family destination on a warm day. If your kids enjoy arcade games, you can pop in to Leisure Zone, Shop 32 Sorrento Quay; (08) 9243 5511.

Day trips _____

Armadale Reptile and Wildlife Centre

304–308 South Western Hwy, Wungong
(08) 9399 6927;
www.armadalereptilecentre.com.au
40 km/50 min south-east
Closed Wed except in school holidays

MID-RANGE

A main aim of the centre is to teach you how to distinguish between venomous and non-venomous snakes. Australian reptiles and other native wildlife are displayed in natural surroundings, including a walk-through finch and skink enclosure.

Calamunnda Camel Farm and Tearooms

361 Paulls Valley Rd, Paulls Valley
(08) 9293 1156; www.camelfarm.com
40 km/1 hr west
Open daily, early closing on weekdays
in school term

PRICES VARY WITH LENGTH OF RIDE

You can take a short camel ride around the farm and meet some other animals, or ride into the state forest to look for stunning wildflowers (in season), kangaroos and wallabies. While here, visit Mundaring Weir (*see* p. 327).

Cohunu Koala Park
802 Nettleton Rd, Karrakup
(08) 9526 2966; www.cohunu.com.au
50 km/1 hr south-east

MID-RANGE

You can wander among free roaming animals such as kangaroos, emus, and deer. Visitors who are 140 centimetres high or taller can cuddle a koala (extra cost); smaller children can give the koalas a pat and a feed.

Gravity Discovery Centre
1098 Military Rd, Gingin West
(08) 9575 7577;
www.gravitycentre.com.au
Closed Mon except during school holidays
80 km/1 hr 30 min north

MID-RANGE

You can have fun with science experiments, discover answers to all sorts of thorny questions about the universe, and even walk around The Solar System, a 1-kilometre path where the sun, planets and moons are shown in scale. If you have the energy, climb the 222 steps to the top of the Leaning Tower of Gingin, and drop a water-filled balloon to test the power of gravity!

Mandurah
www.visitmandurah.com
70 km/1 hr south

FREE; VARIOUS PRICES FOR ACTIVITIES

This is a lovely area for a day trip or short stay and it is easily accessible by train. Mandurah Ocean Marina has a safe, fun children's beach. You can stay on a houseboat, go fishing, catch prawns or have a go at crabbing. Take a cruise around the canals and look for dolphins.

Marapana Wildlife World
157 Paganoni Rd, Karnup
(08) 9537 1404; www.marapana.com.au
60 km/40 min south

MID-RANGE

Marapana is a petting zoo with picnic areas and a cafe. You can pat deer, alpacas and farm animals, and from 11.30am to 2.30pm, you can get up close to koalas, wombats, snakes and dingoes.

Maze Fun
1635 Neaves Rd, Bullsbrook
(08) 9571 1375; www.themaze.com.au
Closed Mon–Tues except on school holidays and most public holidays
40 km/1 hr north

MID-RANGE

Race through a variety of challenging mazes, play a game of minigolf or garden chess, walk through the kangaroo and bird enclosures, and meet the resident koalas. Cafe Iguana on site (*see* PLACES TO EAT p. 329).

Mundaring Weir

Mundaring Weir Rd, Mundaring
(08) 9295 2455;
www.goldenpipeline.com.au
40 km/1 hr west
Closed Feb; closed Mon–Tues except
for most public holidays

BUDGET

Have a picnic near the weir and visit the century-old No 1 Pump Station to learn about the engineering feat that allowed water to be pumped 600 kilometres east to the arid goldfield area. Calamunnda Camel Farm and Tearooms is located nearby (*see* p. 325).

Nearer to Nature activities

Department of Environment and
Conservation, Perth Hills Centre,
Mundaring Weir Rd, Mundaring ·
(08) 9295 2244; www.dec.wa.gov.au/n2n
40 km/1 hr west

VARIOUS TIMES AND PRICES

The Department of Environment and Conservation runs fabulous activities for families at its Perth Hills Centre and at other locations. Check the website for details.

Peel Zoo and Botanical Gardens

Sanctuary Dr, Pinjarra
(08) 9531 4322; www.peelzoo.com
90 km/1 hr 30 min south

MID-RANGE

Feed and pat several different animals, including orphaned baby kangaroos, deer, kids (the goat variety), ferrets and foxes.

This zoo has one of the largest collections of birds in Australia.

Penguin Island

(08) 9591 1333;
www.penguinisland.com.au
Island open mid-Sept – early June
50 km/45 min south
5 min ferry ride from Rockingham

VARIOUS PRICES

On this idyllic island off the coast of Rockingham (see p. 328), you can swim in warm, protected water, explore caves and beautiful sandy beaches, meet little penguins at the Discovery Centre, or take a cruise to see sea lions or dolphins.

Perth Observatory

337 Walnut Rd, Bickley
(08) 9293 8255;
www.perthobservatory.wa.gov.au
Limited operating hours; bookings
essential
30 km/1 hr east

MID-RANGE

For those keen to discover more about the universe, there are daytime activities, including using telescopes to look at sunspots, as well as night-time explorations of the stars, planets and moon.

Rockingham foreshore
Rockingham
Rockingham Visitor Centre
(08) 9592 3464
50 km/45 min south
FREE
This lovely north-facing beach is protected from the blowy effects of the 'Fremantle Doctor' and has a long stretch of safe, shallow water for swimming. It is the access point for Penguin Island (*see* p. 327).

Sandboarding
Lancelin
94 km /1 hr north
MID-RANGE
Hire a sandboard from Lancelin Surf Sports, 127 Gingin Road, Lancelin, (08) 9655 1441, www.lancelinsurfsports.com or one of the other outlets in town, and have fun on the pure white sand dunes.

Serpentine Falls
Serpentine National Park, South West Hwy, Jarrahdale
(08) 9525 2128; www.dec.wa.gov.au
80 km/1 hr 10 min south-east
BUDGET
Have a picnic in a scenic grassed area with free barbecues, and take an easy walk to the falls.

Yanchep National Park
Wanneroo Rd, Yanchep
(08) 9405 0759; www.dec.wa.gov.au
50 km/45 min north
Check times for tours and activities
BUDGET
This is not only a scenic place to enjoy a picnic and bushwalk. You can also see western grey kangaroos, stroll along a boardwalk looking for koalas, tour Crystal Cave, and participate in an Aboriginal experience. Book tours and activities to avoid disappointment. Meals are available in the tearooms and historic Yanchep Inn.

See also Another holiday idea for Western Australia (p. 373)

Places to eat

Cafe Iguana
Maze Fun, 1635 Neaves Rd, Bullsbrook
(08) 9571 1375;
www.themaze.com.au/cafe-iguana
40 km/1 hr north of Perth
This cafe is located at Maze Fun
(*see* p. 326), so you can follow up
your meal with a game of
minigolf or race through the
mazes. Breakfast with the koalas
on Sunday morning is a popular
option, but you need to
book ahead.

Cater4kids venues
Various locations
(08) 9317 7597; www.cater4kids.com.au
This free mobile entertainment
service for kids appears at
different restaurants every night
to give the whole family a fun
evening out. Kids from the age of
3 years can participate in craft
activities, puzzles, storytelling,
face-painting and electronic
games. Phone ahead or check the
website for daily locations.

Ninniku Jip
867 Albany Hwy, Victoria Park
(08) 9355 1988; www.ninniku.com.au
Right in the middle of this
restaurant is a playground with
slide, cubby house, Xbox and
PlayStation. The cuisine is a
blend of Japanese, Korean and
Western styles and the kids' menu
includes interesting items such as
honey soy chicken and fried egg
noodles with chicken and
vegetables.

Stickybeaks Cafe
37 Kings Park Rd, West Perth
(08) 9481 4990;
www.bgpa.wa.gov.au/services/eating-
places/stickybeaks-cafe
This Kings Park cafe is located
in the Lotterywest Family Area
(*see* KINGS PARK p. 310 for more
information on the setting). You
can eat on the patio or carry your
meal onto the grass and picnic
while the kids play.

Accommodation

Broadwater Resort Apartments Como

137 Melville Pde, Como
(08) 9474 4222 or 1800 644 414;
www.como.broadwaters.com.au

HIGH COST

These luxury apartments are 5 kilometres from the centre of Perth. The self-contained loft apartment has a queen bedroom with twin spa and a loft bedroom with two single beds. The resort offers a heated indoor/outdoor swimming pool, tennis court, landscaped gardens, bike hire and access to a riverside bike path.

Central Caravan Park

34 Central Ave, Ascot
(08) 9277 1704;
www.perthcentral.com.au

BUDGET

Just ten minutes from the city, this park offers camping or caravan sites, and two-bedroom cabins with kitchens and reverse-cycle air-conditioning. There is a heated swimming pool on site.

Mont Clare Boutique Apartments

190 Hay St, Perth
(08) 9224 4300;
www.montclareapartments.com

MID-RANGE

These self-contained apartments are located in the heart of Perth. Two-bedroom apartments offer one or two bathrooms. There is an outdoor heated pool, and cots and highchairs are available.

Mounts Bay Waters Apartment Hotel

112 Mounts Bay Rd,
Mounts Bay Village, Perth
(08) 9213 5333 or 1800 241 343;
www.mounts-bay.com.au

HIGH COST

These self-contained luxury apartments are located right on the edge of town near Kings Park. You can even have two bathrooms! Two swimming pools, tennis courts and bike hire are available.

GREAT SOUTHERN

*Located 400 km south-east of Perth, this region includes Albany,
Denmark and Walpole; regional airport at Albany*
Suits driving holidays
Year-round destination

HIGHLIGHTS

Valley of the Giants **p. 337**

Whale World **p. 331**

Around Albany

Whale World
End of Frenchman Bay Rd, Albany
(08) 9844 4021; www.whaleworld.org

MID-RANGE

Whale World is located in an old whaling
station and the displays are designed to
bring the past back to life as well as teach
about whales. On board the *Cheynes IV*,
your kids scramble through the cabins, the
mess, and the engine room, and exclaim in
awe at the giant harpoons waiting
menacingly in the bow. Suddenly, there is
a gun blast and a cloud of smoke wafts up
from the deck. The voices of whalers rise in
excitement. For a moment it seems as
if this old whaling ship, moored on land, is
about to set off in pursuit of a whale –
though really the voices are only
a recording.

Whale World, Albany

INSIDER TIPS

- Entry includes free access to *Cheynes IV*, all the exhibits, and a guided tour.

- Allow two to three hours for your visit.

- Tours leave on the hour and take about 30 minutes. You will view the saw once used to cut off whales' heads and the cookers where chunks of whale were thrown for processing. The historic equipment and accompanying audiotapes may be distressing for some children.

- Most of the exhibits are under cover.

- There are playgrounds in keeping with the sea theme, with barbecues and picnic areas.

- If you visit in whale season from June to October, bring a pair of binoculars.

- If you select the 'Education' link on the website, you'll find stories and activity sheets about whales.

- The Whaler's Galley cafe serves a cooked lunch as well as snacks, and looks out over spectacular scenery.

- While you are here, visit the animals at Discovery Bay's Walk on the Wild Side (*see* p. 334).

DON'T MISS

- The animated 3-D movie on the behaviour of whales.

- The Spectra Vision Cabinet where a whaler's story is told using enchanting projections of miniaturised people among real objects.

- The spectacular wildflower walk (from August to October).

- The display of skeletons of whales and other sea creatures.

FABULOUS FACTS

Whaling was a popular industry in the 19th and early-20th centuries because so much of the whale could be put to commercial use. The sperm whales hunted around here supplied ambergris for perfumes, teeth for ivory, and oil (rendered down from the rest of the whale) for cosmetics and lubricants.

Kid Quest

Look for the pygmy blue whale skeleton on display. Pygmy means small, but what size is this whale?

See pp. 640–4 for the answer

Albany Bird Park and Marron Farm

304 Two Peoples Bay Rd, Albany
(08) 9846 4239;
www.albanymarronfarm.com.au
Check opening hours

MID-RANGE

Kids can have fun cuddling guinea pigs, rabbits and chickens, and handfeeding parrots in a walk-through aviary. While here, you can have a picnic, or taste some marron at Nippers Cafe (*see* PLACES TO EAT p. 340).

Albany Dolphin and Whale Cruises

Silverstar Cruises, depart from Albany City Marina
0428 429 876; www.whales.com.au
Twice daily subject to demand and weather conditions

HIGH COST

Take a cruise on a 64-foot child-friendly catamaran for a chance to see seals, dolphins and whales (June–October). Watch an underwater video and listen for whales 'singing' through the underwater microphone. A commentary reveals highlights of Albany's maritime history as you pass Point King Lighthouse, and a rusting decommissioned whaling vessel.

Note: Albany Whale Tours also offers cruises. Ask about the family twilight cruise on Wednesdays; 0408 451 068; www.albanywhaletours.com.au

Albany Wind Farm

Sandpatch Rd, Sandpatch
www.verveenergy.com.au/mainContent/
*sustainableEnergy/OurPortfolio/Albany_*
Wind_Farm.html

FREE

For something a bit different, visit a wind farm and see twelve of the largest turbines in the Southern Hemisphere. There are boardwalks and information panels for the general public. In whale season, June to October, keep an eye out to sea for whales.

The Brig *Amity*

Albany Historical Precinct,
off Princess Royal Dr, Albany
(08) 9841 5403;
www.historicalbany.com.au/amity.htm
Check prices and times

BUDGET

The original brig *Amity* arrived in Albany in 1826, bringing the first European settlers. This full-scale replica has been made as realistic as possible, with sound effects and models of sailors and passengers. Climb aboard and imagine sailing to a new life.

Discovery Bay's Walk on the Wild Side

Adjacent to Whale World,
end of Frenchman Bay Rd, Albany
(08) 9844 4021; www.whaleworld.org

BUDGET

You can see over 25 species of rare and endangered Australian fauna, including eastern quolls, potoroos, plovers, pademelons, wombats, curlews, spotted-tailed quolls and koalas, and interact with kangaroos and wallabies in the free-range enclosures.
For something special, book a Nocturnal Tour (extra cost).

Harley Davidson Motorcycle Tours

Albany area
(08) 9842 2468; www.harleytours.ws
Minimum age 4 years

VARIOUS PRICES

Does someone in your family long to ride a Harley? A Harley trike has a back seat where three people can fit, so why not book a couple of trikes with drivers and organise a family outing? Alternatively, during the Easter and Christmas holidays, short, low-cost rides are available at Middleton Beach (*see* p. 335).

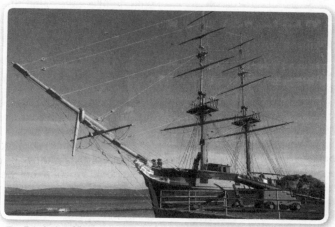

The Brig Amity, *Albany*

Middleton Beach

Middleton Beach

FREE

This is a popular beach with families. Apart from building sandcastles and swimming, you can hire bikes, kayaks or dinghies, stroll or ride along a boardwalk with views of islands and dolphins, or enjoy a meal in a nearby cafe. Bikes and sandboards are available from Albany Bicycle Hire, 223 Middleton Road, Albany; (08) 9842 2468. Other family-friendly beaches are Nanarup, Goode and Emu Point.

Old Convict Gaol

37 Duke St, Albany
(08) 9841 5403;
www.historicalbany.com.au/
convictgaol.htm

BUDGET

Kids who enjoy something spooky will appreciate this restored historic gaol with tiny 'occupied' cells (furnished with a hammock and a bucket), warders' quarters and Great Hall.

Princess Royal Fortress

Forts Rd, Mount Clarence
(08) 9841 9369;
www.forts.albany.wa.gov.au

BUDGET

This fortress was constructed during the 1890s, when Australia feared invasion, and manned until 1956. Rather than building a prominent stone structure, two concealed gun batteries were dug into the hillside. Kids love exploring the slit trenches, display of naval guns and torpedoes, and restored garrison barracks. There is a barbecue area and playground.

Torndirrup National Park

Access via Frenchman Bay Rd
www.rainbowcoast.com.au

FREE

This coastline has spectacular rock formations but it is dangerous. Do *not* ignore warnings. Several people have been swept away by unexpected waves and lost their lives.
The Blowholes are popular, but they are a long way from the carpark. Watch for rainbows in the spray at the Natural Bridge and Gap. Salmon Holes is a cove with a lovely white beach, but strong currents make the sea unsafe for kids to swim in.

Tumble Jam Indoor Play Centre and Cafe

Rear entrance, 138 Chester Pass Rd, Milpara
(08) 9842 1155; www.tumblejam.com.au
Closed Mon except for limited hours on public and school holidays

BUDGET

Kids can climb, slide, bounce and roll in this indoor play centre. Bring socks to wear on the play equipment, and book ahead in school holidays to avoid disappointment.

Two Peoples Bay Nature Reserve

Two Peoples Bay Rd, Albany
www.rainbowcoast.com.au

FREE

Keep your eyes peeled for two very rare and endangered inhabitants: the little rat kangaroos called Gilbert's potoroos (there are only about three dozen left in the wild) and the noisy scrub-bird that is true to name. Visit the interpretive centre for more information. Little Beach and Waterfall Beach are idyllic spots with white sands and sheltered water.

Western Australian Museum, Albany

Residency Rd, Albany
(08) 9841 4844;
www.museum.wa.gov.au

BY DONATION

This regional campus of the Western Australian Museum has fun, interactive displays that explore the unique biodiversity of the Great Southern and the culture of the Indigenous Minang people. Kids can try building a kaunt (a traditional shelter) and have a go at dip pens and slates in the One Teacher School building.

Around Denmark

Denmark Maze

94 Lapko Rd, Denmark
(08) 9848 2090

BY DONATION

This small maze carved into the bush provides a novel and very active way to enjoy the sights,

Pentland Alpaca Stud and Animal Farm, Denmark

sounds and smells of the landscape.

Pentland Alpaca Stud and Animal Farm

2019 Scotsdale Rd, Denmark
(08) 9840 9262;
www.pentlandalpacafarm.com.au

MID-RANGE

This is a hands-on farm and wildlife park. Try to visit at 3pm when all the baby animals are bottle-fed and your kids can cuddle orphaned joeys, newly-hatched chicks and other little creatures. Alternatively, if you come at 10am, you'll get the chance to pat and feed a koala.

Whale-watching

Viewing areas at Conspicuous Cliff,
Lowlands Beach and Ocean Beach
July–Oct

FREE

During early winter and spring, southern right whales journey from Antarctica to the protected waters of King George Sound to give birth and rear their young. You might also see humpback whales.

William Bay National Park

William Bay Rd, William Bay
www.rainbowcoast.com.au

FREE

Greens Pool is a little piece of paradise – a natural sea pool fringed by pristine white sand and sheltered by mammoth rocks. Bring a snorkel and watch the fish and stingrays swimming beside you in the turquoise water. A bit further east, you can find the Elephant Rocks, a herd of huge rounded boulders that appear to be heading out to sea. Keep an eye out for the rare blue-flowering lobelia plants in the park.

Around Walpole

Valley of the Giants

Walpole–Nornalup National Park, Valley of the Giants Rd, Nornalup
(08) 9840 8263; www.dec.wa.gov.au/content/view/355/1045

FREE; TREETOP WALK BUDGET

You feel as if you are entering the forest of a fairytale. Tingle trees tower up to the sky like real giants. Some of them even seem to have legs where the massive, gnarled trunks are hollowed out. The kids run forward, enchanted. All sorts of fairytale creatures might dwell inside these hollows. You tilt your neck back and stare at the slender steel bridges winding high above. You can see tiny figures of people moving along the famous treetop walk.

INSIDER TIPS

- The trail on the forest floor is called the Ancient Empire Walk.
- Be careful not to touch the sword grass – it is as sharp as the name suggests.
- The carpark near the visitor centre has picnic facilities and toilets.

- There is no cafe, but you can buy small snacks and coffee.

- The treetop walk was built with a minimum of equipment to avoid damaging the trees.

- If you notice an unusual scent, it is probably the smell of the karri wattle.

- The valley is accessible by sealed road, so don't follow one of the dirt tracks by mistake.

DON'T MISS

- The treetop walk. This 600-metre walk rises a height of 40 metres into the canopy of the tingle forest. It is safe for little people to walk along, but bigger people may find it daunting as you can see through the mesh floor, and it sways slightly!

- The free guided walks into the Ancient Empire. Check if any are available when you are there.

- The tiny finches and fairy wrens. From the treetop walk, stand still and look carefully among the branches of the lower storey trees. Usually, the birds are a drab colour, but in spring the males develop brightly coloured plumes. They are most active before 10am and after 4pm.

FABULOUS FACTS

This area is the only place in the world where tingle trees grow. They are a special type of eucalypt, with a shallow, spreading root system. As they age, they develop buttresses that provide support and increase their ability to absorb moisture and nutrients. They can reach a height of 75 metres, live over 400 years and achieve a base circumference of up to 20 metres.

Kid Quest
See if you can spot any runs through the sword grass that show where little night creatures travel through the forest.

Dinosaur World

*Bandit Rd, Bow Bridge (between
Denmark and Walpole)
(08) 9840 8335;
www.dinosaurworld.com.au*

MID-RANGE

This is a place for lovers of
dinosaurs and animals. See
dinosaur skeletons, including a
huge tyrannosaurus rex, and
cuddle living reptiles and birds
(handling sessions twice daily).

Giant Tingle Tree

*Hilltop Rd, Walpole–Nornalup
National Park
www.dec.wa.gov.au*

FREE

A few kilometres along this
gravel road, you will find a
carpark in the midst of a red
tingle and karri forest. From here,
an 800-metre loop walk takes
you to the Giant Tingle Tree,
which has the largest documented
girth (24 metres) of any living
eucalypt anywhere in the world.
For more information on tingle
trees, see Valley of the Giants
(p. 337).

WOW Wilderness Cruise

*Departs from Walpole Jetty Area
(08) 9840 1111 or (08) 9840 1036 (AH);
www.wowwilderness.com.au
10am daily; no tours in Aug*

HIGH COST

This is a very special tour over
land and water into the Walpole
Wilderness. Hear stories of
shipwrecked pirates, and learn
traditional Indigenous uses of
plants, such as the antiseptic
and anaesthetic properties of
the peppermint tree (which kids
enjoy smelling).

En route from Perth

Banksia Farm and Garden

Pearce Rd, Mount Barker
(08) 9851 1770;
www.banksiafarm.com.au
Seasonal opening times
BUDGET

Tours include smelling, touching and even tasting some of the remarkable variety of banksias. Kids will find out how to make gumnut whistles, banksia velvet and seed aeroplanes. Watch out for interesting banksia nuts on the ground, and be inspired by imaginative creations on display in the gallery. Before visiting, read about the big, bad banksia men in picture books by Australian author May Gibbs.

Kodja Place

143 Albany Hwy, Kojonup
(08) 9831 0500; www.kodjaplace.net.au
BUDGET

Pick up a kids' Mystery Object Trail brochure from the local visitor centre on site before you start. In the museum, unique interactive displays teach Australian history and Aboriginal culture. Outdoors, you might drink billy tea in a mia mia (a traditional dwelling) or wend your way through a rose maze and find messages that reveal three women's stories about the trials of rural life in the early 20th century.

Places to eat

Bushfood Factory and Cafe

233 Piggot Martin Rd, Youngs Siding
(between Albany and Denmark)
(08) 9845 2359; anbp.com.au
Ever wanted to taste a witchetty grub? Kangaroo meat? Crocodile? You will get the opportunity at this unique Australian bush food cafe.

Nippers Cafe

Albany Bird Park and Marron Farm
304 Two Peoples Bay Rd, Albany
(08) 9846 4239;
www.albanymarronfarm.com.au
Closed for part of winter; check opening hours
Enjoy a meal in scenic surroundings and taste the famous Western Australian marron (a type of crayfish). While you're here, take time to tour the Albany Bird Park and Marron Farm (*see* p. 333).

Venice Pizza Bar and Restaurant

179 York St, Albany
(08) 9841 3978

This is a popular, child-friendly Italian eatery with lots of kids' favourites such as spaghetti and pizza, as well as a kids' menu.

Accommodation

Cape Howe Cottages

322 Tennessee Rd South, Lowlands Beach
(08) 9845 1295; www.capehowe.com.au

MID-RANGE TO HIGH COST

If you fancy your own private spot in the wilderness without sacrificing all the comforts of home, try one of these luxury, self-contained cottages. Spend time outdoors, surrounded by wildlife, or relax indoors with TV, DVD and CD player, and a selection of games and jigsaw puzzles.

Middleton Beach Holiday Park

28 Flinders Pde, Albany
(08) 9841 3593;
www.holidayalbany.com.au

BUDGET TO MID-RANGE

Part of the BIG4 group, and located 500 metres from a beach with white sand and safe swimming, this park offers every type of family accommodation from caravan sites to two-storey chalets. There are holiday activities for kids, a playground, solar-heated pool, and entertainment centre with pool table, table tennis, and video games.

NINGALOO REEF

Ningaloo Reef is located 1200 kilometres north of Perth; regional airport at Learmonth near Exmouth

Best time to visit is in the cooler months (June–Oct); summer is a time of strong winds and extreme heat

WARNINGS Always carry water and wear sun protection. Keep in mind that fuel is only available at Exmouth and Coral Bay, and be aware that ocean conditions can change suddenly.

HIGHLIGHTS

Cape Range National Park   **p. 342**

Ningaloo Marine Park   **p. 345**

Along the coast

Cape Range National Park
Enter via Yardie Creek Rd, about 36 km from Exmouth
Exmouth Tourist Office
(08) 9949 1176
or 1800 287 328;
www.dec.wa.gov.au
BUDGET; EXTRA COST (MID-RANGE) FOR CRUISE

The kids point and exclaim in delight as a little black-footed rock wallaby peers out from a cave in the red cliff-face. With strong stripes of black and

Kayaking at Cape Range National Park

white on its face and body, it looks very different from other wallabies. You gaze around at the vertical towering walls of the gorge and marvel at the agility of the animals that live here. The cruise boat glides on. Now the guide is pointing out a grey reef heron perched among the rocks, then the bird takes off, flying with slowly flapping wings over the deep blue water of Yardie Creek.

INSIDER TIPS

- The Yardie Creek cruise, operated by the Department of Environment and Conservation, departs daily at 11am, and takes one hour. Book with the Exmouth Tourist Office.

- Cape Range National Park shares a coastline with the Ningaloo Marine Park (*see* p. 345).

- Enter the park from the north, coming down from Exmouth. The southern entry is only accessible by four-wheel drive and is frequently impassable. The road to Yardie Creek Gorge is sealed, but some of the roads to the beaches and other sites are unsealed and if you are hiring a car you will need a four-wheel or all-wheel drive vehicle. Call in to the Milyering Visitors Centre to ask about road conditions.

- If you want to have a go at real bush camping, there are campsites in the park (without power, water or shade). Entrance and camping fees apply.

- Avoid driving at night within the park because of the risk of hitting animals.

- You can paddle your own kayaks in Yardie Creek – kayaks are available for hire from Exmouth Mini Golf (*see* p. 347).

- Bring plenty of drinking water and do not attempt to walk in the hotter months (October–March).

- For a more pleasant experience, bring fly nets (available in town) to wear over your faces.

DON'T MISS

- Milyering Visitor Centre, open daily, 9am–3.45pm. You can pick up information about visiting, see displays about the wildlife in the park and watch a video.

- Yardie Creek Gorge, about 38 kilometres south of the visitor centre. As well as travelling on the creek, you can take a 500-metre, half-hour return walk around the top of the gorge. The beginning of the walk is easy but it does become steep. There is an option of a longer walk where you might spot black-footed rock wallabies.

- Sandy Bay, a lovely beach for kids, which has shallow water for playing in, and shaded picnic tables. You can fish here by just throwing in a line from the beach.

- Turquoise Bay (see Ningaloo Marine Park below).

- Mandu Mandu Gorge. Keep your eyes open for black-footed rock wallabies on this 3-kilometre, two-hour return trail that starts at the top of a ridge then drops down into the bed of the gorge. Take care where the trail crosses a steep-sided creek.

- Mangrove Bay, if anyone in the family is keen on birds. There is a shady bird hide here overlooking a shallow lagoon. The best viewing times are early morning or late afternoon, but cover yourselves well and bring insect repellent to ward off mosquitoes. There is also a fauna hide about 500 metres from the carpark.

- The wildflowers (July–October). Brochures for self-guided wildflower walks are available from Milyering Visitor Centre and Exmouth Visitor Centre.

 FABULOUS FACTS

Black-footed rock wallabies are a threatened species. They have specially textured feet for gripping rocks, and long tails to help them keep their balance. They can also climb trees with sloping trunks. It is hard to see them during the heat of the day when they tend to shelter inside cool caves. You are most likely to see these wary creatures in the early morning and evening when they emerge to feed on grasses, leaves or fruits.

Kid Quest
Try to spot a black-footed rock wallaby.

Ningaloo Marine Park

Stretches for about 300 km, from the seas around Exmouth in the north to Red Bluff in the south

Exmouth Tourist Bureau (08) 9949 1176 or 1800 287 328; www.dec.wa.gov.au

FREE

The kids gaze around in awe and delight. Soft, perfect white sand stretches left and right, while warm, turquoise blue water laps at their ankles. They could spend all day here just playing in the sand and splashing in the shallows. But something even better lies ahead. The long, dark shape of the reef is visible just a few metres away. Everyone eagerly pulls on flippers and snorkels and starts to paddle into the clear water. In moments, you are looking down on delicate branching corals, brightly striped clownfish, and colourful anemones waving their tentacles.

Green turtle in Ningaloo Marine Park

INSIDER TIPS

- The bay described above is Turquoise Bay, 60 kilometres south of Exmouth along Yardie Creek Road.

- Drift snorkelling is popular in Turquoise Bay. If you swim at the right time of day, you can enter the reef at the southern end and let the current gently carry you to a sand bar at the other end. Enter the water at the Drift carpark or walk 300 metres south from the Bay carpark. Make sure you get out of the water when you reach the sand bar, as there are strong currents beyond this point.

- An easy point near Coral Bay to access the reef is Bills Bay, via Coral Bay Road, but watch out for boat traffic in the water as this is close to a boat mooring area.

- If you want to fish, check first with the tourist office to make sure you do not fish in any of the sanctuary zones.

- Have a look at all the fun kid stuff at www.marineparks.wa.gov.au.

- There are various options for viewing the marine park, including quad bike tours, kayaks and glass-bottomed boats (see pp. 347–9).

DON'T MISS

- Snorkelling at Turquoise Bay.

- The coral spawning (March or April). About a week after the full moon, for three nights in a row, you can see millions of bright pink egg and sperm bundles float up from the coral to the surface of the water.

- The opportunity to swim with whale sharks from April to early July (*see* p. 348).

- Manta ray interaction (*see* p. 348).

FABULOUS FACTS

Ningaloo is one of the largest fringing barrier reefs in the world, the only one found on the western side of a continent, and the closest to any continental land mass. More than 500 species of fish and 220 coral species live in and around the reef. Some of the creatures found in the marine park include clownfish, lionfish, moray eels, marine turtles, whales, dolphins, dugongs, manta rays, huge cod, and sharks.

Kid Quest
How many different types of coral can you find?

Coral Bay Main Beach
Coral Bay

FREE

Coral Bay is a quiet little holiday destination with a few shops and a perfect beach. You can hire snorkel gear, boogie boards or glass-bottomed canoes on the beachfront, and paddle or swim out to the reef. At 3.30pm every day, schools of large snapper swim in to shore for a free feed. Don't miss it, but keep your feet buried in the sand so they don't nibble your toes! From October to March, you can check out a reef shark 'nursery' at Bateman Bay, a 20-minute walk north from Main Beach.

Exmouth Mini Golf
309 Murat Rd, Exmouth
(08) 9949 4644;
www.exmouthminigolf.com.au
Open daily till late

VARIOUS PRICES

Play a round of minigolf or have a bounce on the in-ground trampolines. If you're feeling more adventurous, bikes and kayaks are also available for hire here.

Glass-bottomed boat tours
Coral Bay and Exmouth
All year

HIGH COST

This is 'snorkelling' without getting wet – great for kids who don't like the sea or can't swim. You sit in comfort, viewing the corals and fish of the reef, while your guide explains what you can see. This is also a good introduction to snorkelling, so you know what to look for when you are in the water on your own. There are numerous operators, some offering semi-submersible boats and some including snorkelling opportunities. Operators include:

- Coral Bay Eco Tours
  (08) 9942 5885;
  www.coralbayecotours.com.au
- Coral Bay Adventures
  (08) 9942 5955;
  www.coralbayadventures.com
- Ningaloo Ecology Cruises
  (08) 9949 2255;
  www.ningalootreasures.com.au

Jurabi Turtle Centre
Via Yardie Creek Rd,
near Vlaming Head, Exmouth
Exmouth Visitor Centre (08) 9949 1176
or 1800 287 328;
www.ningalooturtles.org.au
Open any time

FREE

This open-air centre features displays on the three threatened species of marine turtles – green, loggerhead and hawksbill – that nest in this area. Over summer, the Department of Environment and Conservation operates evening turtle nesting tours (minimum age 8 years). Contact Exmouth Visitor Centre for dates and prices. Tours are three to four hours long.

*Manta ray in
Coral Bay*

Kayaking Tours

Depart from Exmouth or Coral Bay
Seasonal

HIGH COST

Numerous operators offer guided kayaking and snorkelling tours of the reef.

Manta ray interaction

Depart from Exmouth or Coral Bay
All year
For competent swimmers

HIGH COST

A spotter plane lets your cruise boat know where to locate the manta rays. You'll be given the opportunity to slip into the water to snorkel amongst these graceful creatures while they feed and glide around. Various operators offer tours.

Ningaloo Argo Tours

Depart from Exmouth Visitor Centre
(08) 9949 4488;
www.ningalooargotours.com.au
Tours at low tide daily

HIGH COST

Take a bumping, slipping, sliding tour in an all-terrain amphibious buggy. Along the way you'll have

a chance to see all sorts of creatures, and the ride can be as sedate or scary as you want.

Quad bike touring

Coral Bay Eco Tours, Shop 4, Peoples Shopping Village, Robinson St, Coral Bay
(08) 9942 5885;
www.coralbayecotours.com.au
All year
Minimum age 5 years

HIGH COST

How would your kids like to zoom around on a quad bike? Each adult rider can take a child passenger (the tour guide can take a child too, if needed) and the whole family can enjoy a quad bike tour together. You will explore the beaches and back tracks of Ningaloo Marine Park, and hop off for a snorkel as well.

Swim with whale sharks

Depart from Exmouth or Coral Bay
Apr–July
For competent swimmers

HIGH COST

Who is game to go for a swim with the world's largest fish? Whale sharks congregate on

Ningaloo Reef between April and July, and various tour operators run cruises to see and swim with them. These monster fish grow up to 18 metres in length, and weigh up to 21 tonnes, but they are completely harmless. With their minuscule teeth, they can only eat plankton or other tiny sea creatures.

Town Beach
Madaffari Dr, Exmouth

FREE

This easily accessible beach is safe for swimming, especially at high tide. At low tide, play on the white sand and look for treasures left by the waves. There are also grass areas for picnics.

Whale-watching
Depart from Exmouth or Coral Bay
June–Nov

HIGH COST

Various tour operators cruise Exmouth Gulf so you can see magnificent humpback whales breaching, nursing or playing with their calves. You might also catch a view of the whales through coin-operated binoculars at Vlaming Head Lighthouse lookout.

Accommodation

Exmouth Cape Holiday Park
3 Truscott Cres, Exmouth
(08) 9949 1101 or 1800 621 101;
www.apenparks.com.au

BUDGET TO MID-RANGE

Choose a campsite, caravan site or family cabin, and enjoy the facilities on offer at this park close to both shops and beach. There is a resort-style swimming pool, games room, reading room and playground.

Exmouth Escape Resort
Cnr Murat Rd and Welch St, Exmouth
(08) 9949 4800;
www.exmouthescaperesort.com.au

HIGH COST

Stay in a luxurious villa surrounded by landscaped gardens with a large in-ground pool and wading pool. Villas are self-contained with dishwashers, two bathrooms and separate bedrooms.

SHARK BAY

Shark Bay is located 900 kilometres north of Perth; regional airport at Monkey Mia

The best time to visit is in the cooler months (June–Oct); summer is a time of strong winds and extreme heat

HIGHLIGHTS

Monkey Mia dolphin interaction   *p. 350*

Ocean Park   *p. 352*

Around the bay

Monkey Mia dolphin interaction
Department of Environment and Conservation Dolphin Information Centre
(08) 9948 1366
Every morning
SMALL FEE TO ENTER MONKEY MIA RESERVE; DOLPHIN INTERACTION FREE

You stand peering out over the expanse of perfect, green sea stretching in front of you. Suddenly, the unmistakeable curve of a dolphin leaps out of the water. Everyone gasps. The kids grip your hands with excitement. The ranger starts her commentary, but no-one pays attention. All eyes are focused on those beautiful, wild creatures gliding and leaping closer and closer ... In moments, the dolphins are nosing playfully in the shallows around the ranger, only a metre away from you. As one of them lifts its head out of the water, you snap a photo of that endearing dolphin smile.

INSIDER TIPS

- Monkey Mia is accessible by sealed road.

- There is a Dolphin Information Centre on the beach with an interpretive display about dolphins and the area.

- Dolphin visiting times vary. Ring the information centre for an update on the first feed time in the morning – usually the most reliable time to see the dolphins – and be there at least 15 minutes before to ensure a good viewing position.

- During the morning, the dolphins may visit again, so stay and play on the beach.

- A few people from the watching crowd might be asked to help feed the dolphins. If you are lucky, someone in your family will be chosen. If you hang around for one of the later feeds, you have a better chance, as there are usually fewer people then.

- Don't put sunscreen on your lower legs or hands before entering the Dolphin Interaction Zone – it can wash off in the water and sting the dolphins' eyes.

- The rangers make sure nobody touches or feeds the dolphins without permission.

- Monkey Mia has public facilities, such as barbecues, toilets, drinking water and a kiosk.

- You can stay at Monkey Mia Dolphin Resort (*see* ACCOMMODATION p. 357).

 DON'T MISS

- The scene from the jetty, where you get a good, relaxed view of the dolphin interaction. Come back another morning and watch.

- The other wonderful marine creatures that live in Shark Bay Marine Park. You can take a cruise to see more of them.

- The Monkey Mia Walk Trail (Wulyibidi yaninyina) from the visitor centre. This is a 1.5-kilometre natural and cultural history discovery trail.

FABULOUS FACTS

Monkey Mia is one of the few places in the world where tourists can meet wild dolphins every single day. The dolphins who visit Monkey Mia are bottlenose dolphins. Did you know that bottlenose dolphins are actually small whales? Like other whales, they have blowholes on top of their heads for breathing. They are mammals, and even though they live in water, they have to keep coming to the surface to get air.

Kid Quest

What other large mammal (more unusual than dolphins) lives in the waters of Shark Bay?

See pp. 640–4 for the answer

Ocean Park

Shark Bay Rd,
8 km south of Denham
(08) 9948 1765;
www.oceanpark.com.au

MID-RANGE

The park guide drops a fish on a line into the lagoon and jiggles it up and down. The next moment, menacing-looking fins start cutting through the murky water towards the bridge where you are standing. Everyone squeals and points. The kids crouch down, faces pressed to the wire mesh, trying to get closer. Suddenly, two sharks are there, just beneath your feet – huge, three-metre monsters, circling round and round the fish. One of them shoots up out of the water. You stop breathing. The jaws open. You look right down the mouth of a shark, and then the jaws snap shut on the fish.

Lionfish at Ocean Park, south of Denham

INSIDER TIPS

■ All visits to Ocean Park are guided by a marine scientist who tells you interesting titbits about the exhibits, and hand-feeds them so you get a close-up look.

■ On your tour, you see rays and sharks in a shallow lagoon, sea snakes, and little loggerhead turtles.

■ Most of the turtles at the park have been found washed up on beaches, either sick or injured. As soon as they are fit and healthy again, they are released back into the wild.

■ Visitors are not allowed to touch or feed the animals.

■ Ocean Park tanks and lagoons are natural, without artificial filtration, so animals live 'in the wild'. They even eat each other!

■ The knowledgeable park guides also offer four-wheel drive tours into the Francois Peron National Park and to Steep Point, the most westerly point of mainland Australia.

DON'T MISS

■ Having a meal on the sundeck of the Ocean Park cafe with its stunning ocean views – and a chance to spot sharks, rays or other marine life cruising past, especially in summer.

FABULOUS FACTS

One of the sea creatures you see at Ocean Park, the stonefish, is the most venomous fish in the world. It really does look like a very spiky stone and it waits, camouflaged on the ocean floor, to snap up anything tasty that comes along. If it is attacked by a larger fish, or accidentally trodden on by a human, it releases venom through the spines on its back.

Kid Quest

What is the best natural cure for a stonefish sting?

See pp. 640–4 for the answer

Aboriginal eco adventures
Depart from Monkey Mia Amphitheatre
(opposite Monkey
Mia Jetty)
0429 708 847;
www.wulaguda.com.au
Three tours daily
HIGH COST

Learn the survival skills of the local Malgana people – all about bush tucker and bush medicine, and how to track animals and throw boomerangs.

Blue Lagoon Pearl farm tour
Departs from Monkey Mia beach
(08) 9948 1325; www.bluelagoon.com.au
Every morning
HIGH COST

Take a boat ride through the beautiful waters of Shark Bay Marine Park to the floating Pearl Farm where you will find out about seeding, cultivating and harvesting pearls. Tours can be purchased directly through Blue Lagoon, or included in a Monkey Mia Yacht Charters' cruise (*see below*).

Boat cruises
Monkey Mia Yacht Charters
(08) 9948 1446 or 1800 030 427;
www.monkey-mia.net
VARIOUS LOCATIONS, TIMES AND PRICES

Take a water tour to see more of the spectacular scenery and wildlife of the area. Monkey Mia Yacht Charters' cruise-boat, the *Aristocat II*, is set up for kids, with a boom net to ride in, low viewing windows, and room for prams. Other tour operators offer different options including speedboat adventures, sailing cruises, and fishing trips. Some have age restrictions. You can also hire your own boat.

Camel rides
Monkey Mia
08 9948 3136;
www.members.westnet.com.au/
sharkbaycamels
Check operating times
VARIOUS PRICES

The camel operators rescue and rehabilitate mistreated camels. You can have a short ride, and find out what it is like to be lifted up on that hump, or go for a one-hour beach safari.

Denham
You may want to base yourself here for your stay in the area. Many of the cruises operate from this little seaside village. There are shops, as well as a beach with a grassed foreshore and a playground.

Dugong tours
Tours depart Monkey Mia or Denham
Shark Bay Visitor Centre (08) 9948 1590
or 1300 135 887
All year, but fewer sightings May–Aug
HIGH COST

Over 10 000 dugongs live in Shark Bay Marine Park – more than anywhere else in the world. Despite being marine mammals, they are more closely related to elephants than to dolphins or

Dugong in Shark Bay
Marine Park

whales. They grow to 3 metres in length and can weigh over 400 kilograms. They are nicknamed 'sea cows' because they graze on seagrass instead of eating fish. Various tours take you to meet these remarkable creatures.

Eagle Bluff

Eagle Bluff Rd, 20 km south of Denham

FREE

Follow the boardwalk that projects out over the water, and peer down on whatever is swimming in the shallows below: rays, turtles, sharks or dugongs (more frequent in summer). Watch for sea eagles (ospreys), which nest on the rock island just offshore. Look at the weird blue and green ponds on the other side of the bay where the purest sea salt in the world is manufactured through evaporation.

Four-wheel-drive touring

Tours depart Monkey Mia or Denham Shark Bay Visitor Centre (08) 9948 1590 or 1300 135 887

HIGH COST

Many natural treasures of Shark Bay can only be discovered by four-wheel drive. Tour operators can take you over magnificent red sand dunes, onto deserted beaches and through dense shrub. You might see animals, learn bush survival skills, or find out traditional Aboriginal ways to obtain food and medicine in the bush. Discover for yourself why Shark Bay is listed as a World Heritage area.

Kayaks and paddle boats

Monkey Mia

VARIOUS PRICES

Hire a kayak or paddle boat, and have fun on the beautiful waters around Monkey Mia.

Little Lagoon

Lagoon Rd, 5 km north of Denham

FREE

This not-so-little lagoon, with its calm, turquoise water, shade shelters, barbecues and sandy beach, is an idyllic place to swim, picnic or fish. Look for birds, sea creatures and shells (check if there is anything living inside).

Peron Homestead

Francois Peron National Park
Open all the time

BUDGET

Follow a self-guided trail to explore the historic shearing shed, shearers' quarters and stockyards. Find out about life on a sheep station a century ago, have a picnic, and take a soak in a large hot tub fed by an artesian bore.

Quad Bike Trekking Tours

Depart from Denham (pick-up available from Monkey Mia)
(08) 9948 1081; www.sharkbaycoaches. com.au/quad-bikes.htm
Every morning

HIGH COST

Hang on tight and go on a family adventure. See spectacular scenery, kangaroos and emus while you roar up and down sand dunes and along cliff edges. Note: there are no seat belts, so kids need to be old enough to hang onto a bar across their waists.

Shark Bay Discovery Centre

Knight Tce, Denham
(08) 9948 1590; www.
sharkbayinterpretivecentre.com.au

MID-RANGE

Pick up a workbook for the kids and set off on a discovery trail through the displays of Aboriginal artefacts, historic and marine treasures.

Shell Beach

Shark Bay Rd, 45 km south of Denham

FREE

This beach is comprised of tiny white coquina shells instead of sand.

Stromatolites of Hamelin Pool

Hamelin Pool Rd, Hamelin Pool
100 km south-east of Denham

FREE

If your kids are into dinosaurs, then show them stromatolites, the first life form to appear on earth – three and a half *billion* years ago! Super-salty Hamelin Pool is one of the few places on earth where they can still be found. An educational wooden boardwalk lets you get close without doing damage. Stromatolites look like stones but they are actually living. The nearby caravan park runs a small museum and tearoom in a historic telegraph station.

Yadgalah Mini Golf, Denham

Yadgalah Mini Golf
Francis St, Denham
(08) 9948 1318
Open afternoons daily
BUDGET
If you feel like a change from sand, water and marine creatures, try a game of minigolf – it is outdoors but there are trees for shade.

Special event

Shark Bay Fishing Fiesta
May
www.ozpal.com/fiesta
This week-long fishing competition is for the whole family and fishing can be done from boats, beach or jetty. You can just watch, or participate in the Ladies, Gents or Juniors categories.

Accommodation

Denham Seaside Tourist Village
1 Stella Rowley Dr, Denham
(08) 9948 1242 or 1300 133 733;
www.sharkbayfun.com
BUDGET
This tourist village is conveniently located in Denham (*see* p. 354), right on the beach, with emus tapping at your door! There is a range of campsites and cabins available.

Monkey Mia Dolphin Resort
Monkey Mia
(08) 9948 1320 or 1800 653 611;
www.monkeymia.com.au
BUDGET TO HIGH COST
The main appeal here is the proximity to the famous dolphins. Accommodation styles range from camping to villas on the beach right next to the dolphins. Check the website map carefully when booking as some of the more pricey accommodation is close to backpacker areas and can be noisy. Don't expect fabulous TV reception, but

hopefully that is not what you have come for! Some rooms offer basic cooking facilities, and there are eateries on site. There is also a swimming pool, tennis and volleyball courts. Note: entry fees to reserve apply on top of accommodation.

Oceanside Village
117 Knight Tce, Denham
(08) 9948 3003; www.oceanside.com.au
MID-RANGE
Another option in Denham is these self-contained, air-conditioned waterfront villas, each with private veranda and outdoor furniture. There is a barbecue, games room and heated swimming pool on site.

Places to eat

Monkey Bar
Monkey Mia Dolphin Resort
(08) 9948 1320 or 1800 653 611
Enjoy relaxed family dining with views of the sea. The menu includes kids' favourites such as fish and chips, lasagne and pizza.

The Old Pearler Restaurant
71 Knight Tce, Denham
(08) 9948 1373
This unusual restaurant has walls built almost entirely of shells and decorated with maritime memorabilia. The specialty is seafood, of course, and there is a kids' menu.

SOUTH-WEST

Margaret River, in the centre of this region, is located 270 kilometres south of Perth

Year-round destination

HIGHLIGHTS

Around Augusta

Cape Leeuwin Lighthouse
Leeuwin Rd, Augusta, Leeuwin–Naturaliste National Park
(08) 9758 1920; www.lighthouse.net.au
BUDGET

Located at the most south-westerly tip of Australia, where the Southern and Indian oceans meet, this is the tallest lighthouse on the mainland, and its light beam reaches a distance of almost 50 kilometres. One of few operational towers open to public viewing, it is accessible only by guided tours, which run every 40 minutes throughout the day.

Jewel Cave
Caves Rd, 10 min north of Augusta, Leeuwin–Naturaliste National Park
(08) 9757 7411; www.margaretriver.com
Tours hourly on the half hour
MID-RANGE

The interior of this massive cave glows golden and is filled with interesting stalactite formations. The 'jewel' is a 5.4-metre-long calcite straw stalactite that is supposed to be one of the largest in the world. Your ticket also gives you free entry to CaveWorks (*see* p. 365).

Lunar Circus School
Lunar Circus site,
Vansittart Rd, Karridale

(08) 9757 2895; www.lunarcircus.com
Limited times in Jan
Minimum age 5 years

HIGH COST

For a week, the whole family can run away and join a circus! Learn acrobatics or the flying trapeze in a one-week residential camp.

Around Busselton

Busselton Underwater Observatory, Busselton

Busselton Underwater Observatory
Busselton Jetty, Queen St, Busselton
(08) 9754 0900; www.busseltonjetty.com.au
Tour only
Hourly departures

MID-RANGE

You are all going down to the bottom of the sea – safe and dry inside a tunnel. You start to descend the ramps and stairs that lead downwards. There are thick acrylic windows all around you. You can see the underside of the jetty, and the barnacles clustered on the wooden piles. A few steps further and you are below the surface of the water. You glimpse a school of silver trevally flashing past, beautiful white corals, orange sponges, a starfish... The kids' noses are pressed to the windows, and there's a loud squeal when the dark shape of a shark glides past.

INSIDER TIPS

- There is an interpretive centre at the beginning of the jetty where you pick up or purchase tickets. Watch images from the underwater camera here for a live preview of what is happening down below.

- Only 40 people can be accommodated in the underwater observatory, so bookings are essential.

Busselton Jetty, Busselton

- The observatory is located near the end of a 1.8-kilometre jetty. There is a little train that runs along it, and the fare is included in the entry to the observatory.

- If you wish to walk, be sure to wear good walking shoes and appropriate clothing. It can be cold and blowy on the jetty.

- Allow enough time to.get out to the observatory for your tour. It takes about 25 minutes to walk.

- The tunnel descends to 8 metres below sea level and there are 11 viewing windows at various levels.

- The website has a kids' section under Marine Research, and you can print out a colouring picture of sea creatures you might see at the jetty.

- Fishing is permitted off the jetty.

DON'T MISS
- The starfish, nudibranchs, sea cucumbers and small fish hidden amongst the coral and sponges.

FABULOUS FACTS
The jetty piles act as a wonderful artificial reef, and the warm currents of water flowing down this coast encourage an incredible diversity of tropical and sub-tropical marine species to thrive here. These include vividly coloured corals (which do not usually occur so far south), cuttlefish, octopus, stingrays, Port Jackson sharks and wobbegong sharks. Away from this artificial reef, the sea floor is covered with seagrass meadows that can be viewed through a special window.

Apple Fun Park

Cnr Collins and Reserve sts, Donnybrook
www.acoffeeinthepark.com/apple-fun-park-donnybrook

FREE

This claims to be the biggest free-entry fun park in Australia, and as soon as the kids see the bright-coloured play equipment, they'll be jumping out of the car. There are ride-ons, swings, towers, climbing walls, slides, rope bridges, a spacenet, flying foxes, and even an adults' gym circuit. You can picnic or have a barbecue under shady gazebos.

Busselton Archery and Family Fun Park

Bussell Hwy, Vasse (near Margaret River turn-off)
(08) 9755 4322
Check opening hours

VARIOUS PRICES

The whole family can have a go at archery and minigolf, while children aged from 5 to 15 years can ride around on little electric cars.

Busselton Beach

Busselton
www.busselton.wa.gov.au/visitors/beach/busselton

FREE

This is a great family beach. As well as lovely sand and sheltered waters, there is the Yonganup adventure playground with its large grassed area, play equipment and barbecues. You can stroll to cafes and visit Nautical Lady Entertainment World (*see facing page*), a fun park on the beachfront. If you prefer a quieter location, travel around the coast to Meelup or Eagle Bay, both beautiful, safe, swimming beaches.

Cape Naturaliste Lighthouse and Maritime Museum

1 Cape Naturaliste Rd, Leeuwin–Naturaliste National Park
(08) 9755 3955; www.geographebay.com
Tours depart every half hour

MID-RANGE

This is a relatively easy lighthouse to climb, and at the top, you can look out from a balcony. On your tour you'll be given an account of the history and functions of this working lighthouse along with some thrilling stories of ghosts past and present. Note: from here, there is easy access to the scenic Cape to Cape walking trail. Take a stroll and look for wildflowers (best viewing September–November).

Country Life Farm
1694 Caves Rd, Dunsborough
(08) 9755 3707;
www.countrylifefarm.com.au
MID-RANGE
Feed friendly farm animals and have fun on a bouncy castle, merry-go-round, boat rides and a giant slide.

Metricup Bird Park
22 Metricup Rd, Metricup, just off
Bussell Hwy
(08) 9755 7085
Check opening hours
BUDGET
While some members of the family have fun meeting friendly, hand-reared birds, others can wander amongst old farming machinery and memorabilia. You can have a picnic here.

Naturaliste Reptile Park
10 Wildwood Rd, Carbunup River
(08) 9755 1771
Closed Mon except public and school holidays
MID-RANGE
Kids who are interested in reptiles will enjoy seeing and learning about Western Australia's snakes, goannas, lizards and other scaly creatures.

Nautical Lady Entertainment World
529 Caves Rd, Busselton
(08) 9752 3473; www.nauticallady.com
Check opening times
VARIOUS PRICES FOR ACTIVITIES
Kids can have hours of fun on waterslides, trampolines, minigolf, racing cars, motorised mini jeeps and the two-storey toddler play area with mazes, slides, a ball pit, a disco room and small flying fox.

Ngilgi Cave
Yallingup Caves Rd, Yallingup
(08) 9755 2152; www.geographebay.com
Last entry to cave at 3.30pm
VARIOUS PRICES
Take a semi-guided tour to see spectacular stalactite, stalagmite, helictite and shawl formations. More adventurous tours are available for those aged 10 years and over. There are barbecue facilities, a playground and walking trails.

Wardan Aboriginal Cultural Centre

55 Injidup Spring Rd, Yallingup
(08) 9756 6566; www.wardan.com.au
Seasonal opening hours

VARIOUS PRICES

Indigenous Wardandi people have set up interactive exhibits to share their culture. You might sit inside a mia mia (traditional dwelling) or join a tour to learn traditional Aboriginal skills such as tool making or spear throwing.

Yallingup Maze

3059 Caves Rd, Yallingup
(08) 9756 6500;
www.yallingupmaze.com.au

MID-RANGE

Find your way through the wooden labyrinth and climb the five towers – the extra challenge is to climb them in numerical order! There are also parklands where you can picnic, fly a kite or kick a footy.

Yallingup Shearing Shed

Lot 115 Wildwood Rd, Yallingup
(08) 9755 2309
Show times Sat–Thurs, 11am;
no shows in Aug

MID-RANGE

Wool and sheep farming have been a vital Australian industry for over 200 years. Here you can have a taste of what it is all about. Watch sheep shearing, see sheepdogs in action, and bottle-feed lambs.

Wonky Windmill Farm and Eco Park

218 Yelverton North Rd, Yelverton
(08) 9755 7201; www.
wonkywindmillfarm.com.au

MID-RANGE

Have a picnic, meet and feed farm animals, taste preserves and olive products made on the farm, and pick mandarins and oranges from the orchard (in season).

Yallingup Maze, Yallingup

Around Margaret River

Amaze'n Margaret River
Bussell Hwy, 4 km south
of Margaret River
(08) 9758 7439;
www.amazenmargaretriver.com.au
MID-RANGE

Lose yourselves in a giant hedge maze, or have fun with outdoor games, including noughts and crosses, hopscotch, bocce, quoits, snakes and ladders, and chess. There are picnic and barbecue facilities.

Bushtucker Tours
Depart from Margaret River mouth,
Prevelly Beach
(08) 9757 9084; www.bushtuckertours.
com/canoetour/canoe.html
Depart 10am daily
HIGH COST

This is a unique Australian experience suitable for all ages and abilities. During the four hours of the tour, you will go on a caving adventure, paddle canoes, take a scenic wild food plant walk and have a gourmet bush tucker lunch.

Calgardup Cave
Caves Rd, Leeuwin–Naturaliste
National Park
(08) 9757 7422; www.dec.wa.gov.au/
content/view/2849/1440/1/1
MID-RANGE

Start by picking up torches and helmets from the ticket office, then embark on a self-guided tour. Walking on platforms raised above the cavern's watery floor you can admire the formations and reflections all around.

CaveWorks and Lake Cave
Caves Rd, 25 km south of Margaret
River, Leeuwin–Naturaliste National Park
(08) 9757 7411; www.margaretriver.com/
pages/lake-cave
CAVEWORKS ENTRY INCLUDED IN FEE FOR
LAKE OR MAMMOTH CAVES

CaveWorks is an interactive centre where kids can learn about caves through fun activities, such as a crawl-through tunnel and computer games. On the same site is Lake Cave, a fairyland of sparkling crystalline formations, reflecting in the lake. Tours depart hourly on the half hour, and include a stunning light show among the crystals.

Chilli Waters Supa Putt and Family Golf

Harmans Mill Rd, Wilyabrup
(08) 9755 6425;
www.chilliwaters.com.au
Closed Mon except for public and school holidays

MID-RANGE

Tee off amongst the gum trees with a fun game of minigolf, or try Big Ball Golf (suitable for children 5 years old and over).

Eagles Heritage Raptor Centre

341 Boodjidup Rd, Margaret River
(08) 9757 2960;
www.eaglesheritage.com.au

MID-RANGE

View the largest collection of eagles, hawks, falcons and owls in Australia, and watch twice-daily flight displays by these magnificent birds of prey.

Giants Cave

Caves Rd, Leeuwin–Naturaliste National Park
(08) 9757 7411; www.dec.wa.gov.au/content/view/2849/1440/1/2
Minimum age 6 years

MID-RANGE

A visit here is a caving adventure. You explore the huge caverns without a guide, climbing steep staircases and ladders with only torches to light your way (torches and hard hats provided). Look for the massive calcified tree roots high above you in the ceiling.

Mammoth Cave

Caves Rd, approx 20 km south of Margaret River, Leeuwin–Naturaliste National Park
(08) 9757 7411; www.margaretriver.com/pages/mammoth-cave

MID-RANGE

Enter the cave and journey back into a prehistoric world. In the gleams of light, you'll see bones and fossils from extinct animals such as Tasmanian tigers and Zygomaturas – giant wombat-like creatures. Audio headsets provide a commentary as you explore on your own.

Melting Pot Glass Studio

91 Bussell Hwy, Margaret River
(08) 9757 2252;
www.meltingpotglass.com
Check operating hours

FREE DEMONSTRATIONS

During summer, you can watch demonstrations of hot, molten glass being blown and shaped into pieces of glass art.

Ye Olde Lolly Shoppe

Shop 3 / 103 Bussell Hwy, Margaret River
(08) 9758 7555;
www.yeoldelollyshoppe.com.au

FREE

In this confectionary paradise you can buy traditional Australian favourites and lollies from all around the world.

In the area

Leeuwin–Naturaliste National Park
Stretches 120 km from Cape Leeuwin to Cape Naturaliste
www.dec.wa.gov.au

FREE PARK ENTRY

As you set off along a boardwalk through the forest, you talk about the historic Ellensbrook Homestead you are leaving behind, with its stories of struggle and love, and children who died (*see* FABULOUS FACTS p. 368). After a short distance, you come to a rocky cliff softened by green draperies of foliage. The waters of Meekadarabee Falls trickle down the rocks, and at its foot gapes the dark, mysterious entrance to a grotto. According to Aboriginal legend, this is the 'bathing place of the moon' and the spirits of two lovers, Mitanne and Nobel, dwell here.

INSIDER TIPS

- Leeuwin–Naturaliste National Park covers a huge area and includes beaches as well as forests, lighthouses, limestone caves and the homestead.

- The walk described leads from Ellensbrook Homestead and takes about 40 minutes. The Meekadarabee Falls are at their most impressive between June and November.

- Ellensbrook Homestead is open weekends and Monday public holidays (extra cost, budget). It is located at Ellen Brook Road, Margaret River, (08) 9755 5173.

- Warning: when walking among the karri trees in the Boranup Forest, be alert to sounds that may indicate falling branches (*see* DON'T MISS p. 368).

- There are various vantage points along the coast where you can look for humpback and southern right whales from September to December.

- There are a few campgrounds with basic facilities in the park.

DON'T MISS

- Cape Naturaliste Lighthouse and Maritime Museum (*see* p. 362).

- The caves! Visit at least one of the spectacular limestone caverns that honeycomb the Margaret River area (*see* pp. 365–6).

- Gnarabup beach with its beautiful white sand and clear turquoise waters, great for swimming and snorkelling.

- Boranup Karri Forest, which lies between Caves Road and the coast. The strange, grey-trunked karri trees grow up to 60 metres high.

- Boranup Forest Maze (extra cost, budget), which is on the outskirts of the park, along Caves Road, Karridale; (08) 9758 5582. This is a fun way to explore a lovely forest area.

FABULOUS FACTS

Ellensbrook Homestead was a family-run beef and dairy farm. Alfred Bussell built it in 1857 with the help of local Aboriginal people, using the surrounding trees, crushed shells and limestone. He named it after his wife, Ellen. When Ellen churned her butter, she carried it all the way to the Meekadarabee Falls to keep cool. Ellensbrook reveals the harshness of life for early European settlers. Three of the Bussells' infant children died here, and the family left in 1865.

Kid Quest

As you stand at the Meekadarabee Falls, listen for the sound of two people laughing. You are supposed to be able to hear the voices of Mitanne and Nobel.

Candies, chocolates and more
Various locations

FREE DEMONSTRATIONS

There are several outlets where you can watch (and taste!) as candies, fudges or chocolates are manufactured:

- Candy Cow, Shop 3, Botterill St, Cowaramup (08) 9755 9155
- Margaret River Chocolate Company, cnr Harmans Mill and Harmans South roads, Metricup (08) 9755 6555; www.chocolatefactory.com.au
- Margaret River Fudge Factory, 152 Bussell Highway, Margaret River (08) 9758 8881; www.fudgefactory.com.au

Horseriding
Various locations

BOOKINGS ESSENTIAL

Take lessons or enjoy a scenic bush ride:

- Margaret River Horse-Back Tours (08) 9757 3339; www.margaretriverhorse-backtours.com
- The Horse Resort (08) 9757 4444; www.thehorseresort.com.au

Yallingup Surf School, Yallingup

Surf lessons
Various locations
Seasonal

HIGH COST

There are several local surf schools that offer lessons for all ages and provide surfboards, wetsuits and accessories:

- Josh Palmateer Surf Academy (08) 9757 3850; www.mrsurf.com.au
- Margaret River Surf School (08) 9757 1111; www.margaretriversurfschool.com
- Yallingup Surf School (08) 9755 2755; www.yallingupsurfschool.com

Sometimes whales come within metres of the boat, and you might hear whale songs or see calves with their mums.

Winery tours
Various locations
Contact Margaret River Tourist Office,
100 Bussell Hwy, Margaret River
(08) 9780 5911; www.margaretriver.com/
pages/kids-stuff

FREE; GUIDED TOURS HIGH COST

If the adults in the group don't want to miss out on touring some of the wineries and breweries in this famous wine-making region, contact the Margaret River Tourist Office, or check their website to find out which wineries have playgrounds or pet animals. Alternatively, Taste the South runs a family-friendly wine-tasting tour; 0438 210 373; www.tastethesouth.com.au.

Whale-watching with Naturaliste Charters
Depart from Augusta June–Sept
Depart from Dunsborough Sept–Dec
(08) 9755 2276;
www.whales-australia.com
10am daily, weather dependent

HIGH COST

During this two- to three-hour cruise, you have the chance of seeing humpbacks and southern right whales, New Zealand fur seals, dolphins and sea birds.

En route from Perth

Big Swamp Wildlife Park in Bunbury
Prince Philip Dr, Bunbury
(08) 9721 8380; bigswampwildlifepark.
mysouthwest.com.au

BUDGET

Hand-feed parrots in a large free-flight aviary, visit kangaroos in a walk-in enclosure and see a display of native fish. There are also barbecues and picnic facilities in the beautiful parkland setting.

Dolphin Discovery Centre
Koombana Dr, Bunbury
(08) 9791 3088;
www.dolphindiscovery.com.au
Seasonal opening times

BUDGET

This is a wonderful opportunity to interact with wild bottlenose dolphins without even getting in a boat. Between 8am and midday, dolphins head in from the sea towards the beach in front of the Dolphin Discovery Centre. You can stand in waist-deep water while they swim around you. There are limited places so it is advisable to book. The centre also operates cruises.

Gnomesville

Junction of Wellington Mill and Ferguson rds, Ferguson Valley

FREE

Kids love this land of little people, which has developed over time as people from all around the world have contributed their own garden gnomes. Make sure you read the humorous labels. Can you find the golf-playing Greg Gnoman? Add your own gnome!

Places to eat

Simmos Ice Creamery and Fun Park

Commonage Rd, Dunsborough
(08) 9755 3745; www.simmos.com.au
Enjoy delicious specialty ice-creams, hot waffles, hot chocolates, coffees and toasted panini. Play in the adventure playground, have a go at mini putt-putt and watch out for Edward, the ice-cream eating emu!

The Goose

Geographe Bay Rd, Busselton
(08) 9754 7700; www.thegoose.com.au
Everyone in the family can enjoy an elegant but relaxed meal. Kids are offered their own 'proper' menu, complete with drink selection, as well as colouring books and pencils. The restaurant is in a fabulous location right on the waterfront, near the Busselton Jetty.

Spaghetti Bowl

117 Bussell Hwy, Margaret River
(08) 9757 2999
This restaurant has a kid-friendly, Italian cafe atmosphere with mud-brick walls and open fireplace. The menu is not limited to spaghetti and includes kids' meals. Local musicians perform on Friday and Saturday evenings.

The Colourpatch Cafe

98 Albany Tce, Augusta
(08) 9758 1295
This large, relaxed cafe claims to be the last eating-house before the Antarctic! Sit and gaze at the water as you eat fresh fish. There is a kids' menu.

Accommodation

A La Plage

Gnarabup Beach (near Margaret River)
0424 257 947; www.beachhousesaust. com/ALP.html
HIGH COST
This luxury five-bedroom, four-bathroom holiday home on three levels is ready for even the smallest guests with barriers for stairs, a cot, change table, highchair and plastic crockery. Facilities include table tennis, a large movie library, games, bikes and a heated pool.

Beachlands Holiday Park

10 Earnshaw Rd, Busselton
(08) 9752 2107 or 1300 232 245;
www.beachlandsresort.com.au
BUDGET TO MID-RANGE
This award winning BIG4 Holiday Park offers camping and caravan sites and self-contained cabins. Ensuite sites are available and all sites have power, water, and even cabling for TV. Facilities include a giant jumping pillow,

heated pool, water playground, bike and pedal-kart hire, and games room. There are also organised kids' activities.

Best Western Augusta Georgiana Molloy Motel

84 Blackwood Ave, Augusta
(08) 9758 1255 or 13 1779; www. georgianamolloy.bestwestern.com.au
MID-RANGE
This motel has family rooms with queen bed, bunk bed (one has a single bed as well), ensuite bathroom, kitchen and dining area, free in-house movies, heating and a patio/veranda seating area outside. Free cots are available.

Riverview Tourist Park

8 Willmott Ave, Margaret River
(08) 9757 2270;
www.riverviewtouristpark.com
BUDGET
Located in a forest clearing by a river, yet walking distance to the

main street, this holiday park offers the best of both worlds. There are caravan sites and various cabins available.

Sheerwater
Lot 126 Windy Harbour Drive, Windy Harbour (between Augusta and Walpole) (08) 9776 7160; www.sheerwater.net.au
BUDGET

In this cottage in the D'Entrecasteaux National Park, you have a chance to experience a real break from the rat-race. There is no mains power, only a generator, but you have cooking facilities, views of the Southern Ocean, and the national park at your door. Bring your own linen.

Another Holiday Idea for Western Australia

Island holiday
Take a tip from the locals and spend a relaxed holiday on Rottnest Island, or 'Rotto' as it's affectionately known. The island is accessible by ferry from Perth, Fremantle or Hillarys Boat Harbour. This is a very special place to visit or stay with kids. There are no cars, so the best way to get around is to hire bikes for all the family

Beach scene at Rottnest Island

(even those still on trainer wheels!) from Rottnest Island Bike Hire; (08) 9292 5105. Alternatively, there is a bus that departs regularly for the most beautiful beaches and bays on the island. You can also take a train ride to see guns and tunnels in a historic military system, play a game of minigolf, go snorkelling, explore the reef in a semi-submersible, or go on a whale-watching cruise. While on the island you'll become well acquainted with the friendly quokkas, furry little marsupials found only in Western Australia.

Find our more from Rottnest Island Visitor Centre (08) 9372 9732; www.rottnestisland.com

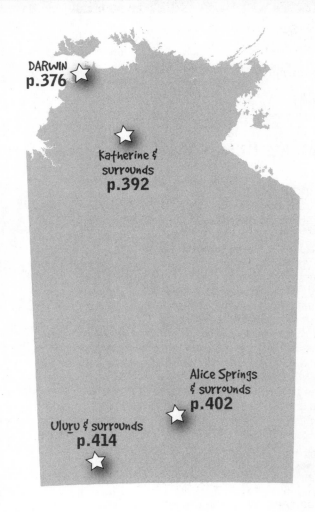

DARWIN
p.376

Katherine &
surrounds
p.392

Alice Springs
& surrounds
p.402

Uluṟu & surrounds
p.414

FAVOURITES_____

Alice Springs Desert Park – taste bush tucker and see an eagle crack open an emu egg with a stick! ***p. 403***

Crocosaurus Cove – swim with crocodiles and 'cuddle' a snake ***p. 377***

Litchfield National Park – take a cooling dip in a leaf-fringed pool beneath a waterfall ***p. 388***

Manyallaluk – visit an Aboriginal community and learn some bush secrets ***p. 395***

Nitmiluk (Katherine Gorge) National Park – glide in a boat down a gorge; look for crocodiles and Aboriginal rock art ***p. 396***

Royal Flying Doctor Service – have a go at an old-fashioned pedal radio and a flight simulator ***p. 405***

Uluru (Ayers Rock) – experience the beauty and spiritual power of this World Heritage icon ***p. 414***

TOP EVENTS

JULY *Meet the Darwin, Katherine or Alice Springs locals and experience an outback show, complete with rodeos and ute challenges* ***pp. 376, 392 and 402***

AUG/SEPT *Make your own 'boat' and join the famous Henley-on-Todd Regatta in Alice Springs* ***p. 402***

DARWIN

Best time to visit is dry season (May–Sept), when temperatures are around 30° C

Wet season (Oct–Apr) brings tropical storms and hot, humid days

WARNINGS Always carry water and wear a hat. It is often too dangerous to swim in the seas or rivers because of crocodiles, sharks or deadly box jellyfish. Protect against mosquitoes and other sources of tropical disease, especially when outdoors in early morning or evening and in wet areas such as Litchfield National Park. Read 'Disease Information for Visitors' at www.health.nt.gov.au/Centre_for_Disease_Control/index.aspx

HIGHLIGHTS

Crocosaurus Cove **p. 377**

Leanyer Recreation Park **p. 381**

Museum and Art Gallery of the Northern Territory **p.382**

Special events

Beer Can Regatta
July

www.beercanregatta.org.au

On this crazy outback family fun day, boats made of beer cans race along the shores of Darwin's Mindil Beach. Other activities include dry boat racing along the sand, sandcastle competitions and soft drink can regattas for kids.

Royal Darwin Show
July

www.darwinshow.com.au

Three days of Top End entertainment includes the Grand Parade, various animal events, cooking competitions, Ford and Holden ute challenges, live music, dancing and children's events.

In town

Crocosaurus Cove
58 Mitchell St, Darwin
(08) 8981 7522; www.crocosauruscove.com
Open daily till early evening
MID-RANGE

You hold up your underwater camera and snap wildly. Your kids wave and grin; just centimetres away, crocodiles longer than *they* are twist and paddle through the water. The kids bob up for air, then dive down again, revelling in the experience of swimming with crocodiles — well, it feels like they are anyway, with only a clear acrylic wall as a barrier. In a few hours your camera will be filled with amazing images. You'll capture the kids holding and patting baby crocodiles, draping snakes over themselves, and watching round-eyed as a python devours two rats.

Keeper feeding reptiles at Crocosaurus Cove, Darwin

INSIDER TIPS

- Allow at least two hours to see everything.

- The crocodiles in the swimming tank are juveniles, and have reached a length of 1–1.5 metres. Make sure the kids bring bathers so they can hop in the water 'with the crocodiles'. This activity runs all day; no extra cost.

- Crocosaurus Cove has much more than crocodiles. There are over 70 species of reptiles from northern Australia on display, as well as a two-storey aquarium filled with huge fish, stingrays, freshwater crocodiles and turtles.

- Bring sunscreen and hats as many activities are in unshaded outdoor areas.

- When you need a break from the heat, move indoors to the air-conditioning.

- Check the program of events (available on the website) to make sure you don't miss anything. The program is different for wet and dry seasons.

- This park is famous for its Cage of Death experience (high extra cost), but the minimum age for this is 15 years. If the adults want to have a go, be aware the crocodiles involved are not usually very active or aggressive.

- If you visit in the evening, you can have the thrill of spotlighting for crocodiles from the viewing platform.

- There is a cafe on site and it remains open for dinner.

 DON'T MISS

- Your chance to hold a baby crocodile – this is available all through the day, just keep an eye out for a staff member in a yellow T-shirt. Have your photo taken, then turn it into a postcard at the Photoshop (extra cost).

- The Fishing for Crocs platform where you experience the excitement of having juvenile crocodiles leap up and snatch meat that you are dangling over an acrylic barrier.

- The Meet the Reptiles activity where you might get the chance to drape a snake around your neck.

- The crocodile feeding times when a handler gets right inside the enclosure with a large 'saltie'!

 FABULOUS FACTS

Crocodiles are the oldest 'living fossil'. They have barely changed in millions of years and their origins can be traced back to the dinosaurs. The largest crocodile skeleton ever found belonged to a 100-million-year-old *Sarcosuchus*. A modern saltwater crocodile can grow to about 6 metres, but this skeleton found in the African Niger Desert was 12 metres long!

Kid Quest

A human's bite force is 20 kilograms. What do you think the bite force of a crocodile might be?

See pp. 640–4 for the answer

Aquascene fish feeding

28 Doctors Gully Rd, Darwin
(08) 8981 7837; www.aquascene.com.au
Check feeding times (dependent on tide)

MID-RANGE

Every day at high tide, wild fish come in from the sea to take advantage of a free feed. You are given bread so you can feed the large fish that come right up to eat out of your hands. There is seating available if you prefer to throw the food or just watch.

Batji Walking Tour

Depart from the interpretive shelter,
end of Esplanade (opposite Holiday Inn),
Darwin
1300 881 186; www.batji.com/tours.html
Departs 10am; check available dates

HIGH COST

Your guide wil be a member of the Indigenous Larrakia people. On this two-hour walking tour, you have the wonderful opportunity to discover a completely different side of Darwin. You'll learn how various plants can be used for food or medicine, and the history and cultural significance of local sites for Aboriginal people.

Aquascene fish feeding, Darwin

Deckchair Cinema

Jervois Rd, off Kitchener Dr, Darwin
(09) 8981 0700;
www.deckchaircinema.com
Nightly Apr–Nov
Box office and kiosk open from 6.30pm;
no bookings

MID-RANGE

Have fun watching a movie together sitting outdoors in deckchairs; bring pillows for extra comfort. If you come early, you can watch the sunset too. Bring a picnic, wear long pants and sleeves, and don't forget the insect repellent.

Duckabout tours

Depart from Darwin Tourism Information Centre, cnr Smith and Bennett sts, Darwin
1300 382 522 or 0403 542 230;
www.duckabout.com.au
Tours depart several times daily
HIGH COST

See Darwin in fun style aboard an amphibious vehicle. Kids love the big splash when you drive into the harbour! Prams cannot be brought on board, and there are no toilets. Tours last one and a quarter hours.

Indo Pacific Marine

29 Stokes Hill Rd, Darwin Wharf Precinct
(08) 8981 1294;
www.indopacificmarine.com.au
Daily Apr–Oct, closed weekday afternoons Nov–Mar
MID-RANGE

The displays at this unique, land-based, living marine centre let you view a real coral reef environment without getting wet. There is a guide to explain everything you see – and point out things you miss! Kids enjoy the low portholes for peeking into the depths, and the magnifying sheets they can use. You can opt for a night tour with evening meal with A Coral Reef by Night (*see* ACCOMMODATION p. 391).

Turtle Tracks Tour

Departs from Stokes Hill Wharf
(08) 8942 3995;
www.turtletrackstours.com
Departs 4pm on selected dates Apr–Oct
Minimum age 6 years
HIGH COST

On this exciting eco-adventure you travel by boat to a remote island beach where you see flatback and olive ridley turtles laying eggs or hatching, depending on the season. The tour includes a meal.

Wave Lagoon

Darwin Waterfront Precinct
www.waterfront.nt.gov.au/darwin-waterfront-precinct/water-recreation/wave-lagoon
Open daily, including Christmas afternoon
BUDGET

This huge, artificial lagoon is fun for the whole family. There is a deep area with artificial waves up to 1.7 metres high, as well as a shallow, still-water section for toddlers. Boogie boards are permitted, but not surfboards.

World War II Oil Storage Tunnels

Kitchener Dr, Darwin Wharf Precinct
(08) 8985 6333;
www.darwintours.com.au/tours/ww2tunnels.html
Open daily May–Sept; limited hours Oct–Apr, closed Dec and Feb
BUDGET

Follow the stairs from the Survivors Lookout down to these tunnels, hidden beneath the cliffs. They were built to keep oil safe from air attacks during World War II, but as water leaked in, they were never used. The eerie tunnels now house photos of life in Darwin during World War II.

Suburbs

Leanyer Recreation Park

Vanderlin Dr, Leanyer
08 8927 4199; www.nt.gov.au/nreta/parks/find/leanyer.html
Recreation park facilities open early till late; water activities open late morning till evening, closed Mon–Tues in school terms

FREE

The kids tumble together into a two-person inflatable tube and go whizzing off, screaming with horror and joy, into the pitch darkness of the red Funderstorm water slide. They shoot out the other end, pick themselves up, and race for the Go Bananas yellow water slide, a long, corkscrewing, narrow tunnel. You look around at other kids skateboarding, playing basketball and riding bikes, at toddlers paddling delightedly under pouring buckets of water, and shooting each other with water cannons, and shake your head, unable to believe that all of this amazing fun is free.

INSIDER TIPS

- Children must be at least 1.1 metres tall to go on the high water slides, but the wonderful water-play area with slippery dips, buckets of pouring water, and water cannons is suitable for all ages.

- There is also a large recreational pool where the water depth varies from shallow to 1.2 metres at the deepest point.

- Lifesavers patrol the water areas, but adults are required to supervise their own children.

- There is also a playground with traditional equipment such as swings and climbing bars.

DON'T MISS

- The shady picnic areas and barbecue facilities – bring your own picnic or buy food from the kiosk (limited opening hours).

- The birdlife – watch for ibis, Burdekin ducks, native doves and plovers, which come in from the surrounding bushland seeking water.

FABULOUS FACTS

In 2009, at the official opening of the water slides, three very excited young girls were the guests of honour. They were the winners of the competition to name the slides, and were the first children to ride on them. Cassie, aged 11 years, had thought up the name 'Funderstorm' for the red slide, 9-year-old Paige had called the yellow slide 'Go Bananas', and Laura, aged 13 years, named the last one 'Blue Blast'.

Kid Quest
Which is your favourite activity in the park?

Museum and Art Gallery of the Northern Territory
Conacher St, Bullocky Point
(08) 8999 8264; www.nt.gov.au/nreta/museums/exhibitions/permanent.html
FREE

One of your kids rummages through objects on a touch trolley, attempting to sort out animal bones and reconstruct dolphin and dugong skeletons. Another one finds books to read, and a picture to colour in, and brings them over to share with you on the couch. A flock of stuffed magpie geese flies overhead and live fish swim around an aquarium. For a while you all relax, enjoying the Discovery Centre for Kids, and then you set off to explore the rest of the museum together.

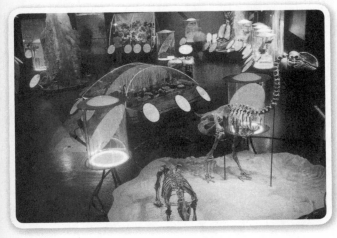

Museum and Art Gallery of the Northern Territory, Bullocky Point

INSIDER TIPS

■ Bags and drink bottles must be left in a locker and you'll need a $2 coin (refundable) to use it.

■ The Cornucopia Museum Cafe is a popular place for locals to brunch and lunch. Daily specials feature local ingredients such as barramundi, mango and dragon fruits. You can join the locals in the cafe or bring a picnic to eat in the landscaped grounds.

■ The cyclone Tracy display (*see* DON'T MISS *below*) includes a pitch-dark room with a loud recording of the real cyclone that might be distressing for small children.

■ When you arrive, check whether there are any special talks of interest.

■ The gallery displaying Australia's deadliest native creatures – including the box jellyfish and redback spider – may make some kids a bit nervous!

■ Parking is free.

DON'T MISS

■ The stuffed 5.1-metre crocodile called Sweetheart, infamous in the 1970s for attacking fishing boats.

■ The megafauna bones – these come from large extinct animals that lived after the dinosaurs.

■ The cyclone Tracy exhibit (*see* FABULOUS FACTS *below*). The display includes a darkened room, film footage, photos, and reconstructions of houses before and after the cyclone.

■ The stories behind the boats in the maritime display. Read the panels and find the boat used by headhunters! Look for the little Indonesian dugout canoe that was blown off course en route to a nearby island – it drifted 330 kilometres to Darwin with six adults and four children on board.

FABULOUS FACTS

Cyclone Tracy was Australia's worst natural disaster. As it approached Darwin on Christmas Eve 1974, the citizens had no idea of what they were about to experience. It struck late at night, destroying virtually every building and killing dozens of people. It was several hours before the rest of Australia, and the world, learnt of the disaster, as all forms of communication were wiped out.

Kid Quest

Dugongs and dolphins are both large marine mammals but they have very different bones. How do they differ?

See pp. 640–4 for the answer

Australian Aviation Heritage Centre

557 Stuart Hwy, Darwin
(08) 8947 2145;
www.darwinsairwar.com.au

MID-RANGE

The main feature here is a massive B-52 bomber, one of only two displayed outside America. The museum reveals Darwin's role in many historic aviation events. Guided tours are available every morning.

Casuarina Coastal Reserve

Via Trower Rd, Casuarina
Parks and Wildlife Office
(08) 8999 4555;
www.nt.gov.au/nreta/parks/find/
casuarina.html

FREE

Play in gorgeous white sand, peer in rockpools and explore World War II artillery observation posts. Watch for birds year-round, and take part in releases of marine turtle hatchlings from May to October. The foreshore is a lovely place for a picnic (barbecues available).

Charles Darwin National Park

Tiger Brennan Dr, Winnellie
Parks and Wildlife Office
(08) 8999 4555;
www.nt.gov.au/nreta/parks/find/
charlesdarwin.html

FREE

In this wetland you can find 36 different mangrove species, shell middens left by Aboriginal people over thousands of years, and bunkers and storage facilities from World War II. There are toilets, barbecues, bushwalking tracks, a bike path and a lookout. Biting insects can be a problem so wear protective clothing and apply insect repellent, especially around sunrise and sunset.

Crocodylus Park

815 McMillans Rd, Berrimah
(08) 8922 4500;
www.crocodyluspark.com

MID-RANGE

See huge 'salties' (saltwater crocodiles), as well as other reptiles, monkeys, big cats, and Australian animals. Pat baby crocodiles, and watch the big ones in action at feeding time. There is a crocodile museum with stuffed specimens, skeletons, skins, and a display illustrating a crocodile's stomach contents!

East Point Reserve

Alex Fong Lim Dr, Fannie Bay
www.darwin.nt.gov.au/live/your-community/parks-and-reserves/east-point-reserve

FREE

This popular family park has a beach, a safe, year-round saltwater swimming lake, picnic areas, barbecues, playgrounds, bushwalking tracks, wallabies and a military museum.

Fanny Bay Gaol Museum

East Point Rd, Fannie Bay
(08) 8999 8201

FREE

It is an eye-opener for kids to see the oppressive conditions inside this gaol, used from 1883 until 1979. It includes sections for children and Aboriginal prisoners, and a gallows. The only bright spot is a display of paintings by some Aboriginal inmates.

Ferry to Mandorah

Departs Cullen Bay Ferry Terminal
(08) 8941 1991; www.seacat.com.au

MID-RANGE

Take a 15-minute ride on a ferry across the harbour and spend a few hours in Mandorah. Play on the beaches, have a bistro meal and swim in the pool at the Mandorah Beach Hotel.

Flight Path Golf and Outdoor Recreation

Vanderlin Dr, Berrimah
(08) 89471257;
www.fpgolfnarchery.com.au

VARIOUS PRICES

Have a game of minigolf (open daily), or try your hand at archery (check operating times, minimum age 8 years).

George Brown Darwin Botanic Gardens

Gardens Rd, Darwin
(08) 8981 1958;
www.nt.gov.au/nreta/parks/botanic

FREE

Highlights include a rainforest gully with waterfall and ponds, a self-guided walk explaining traditional Aboriginal uses of local plants, and the Children's Evolutionary Playground with a three-storey treehouse! There are a few creepy crawlies, so wear closed shoes and apply insect repellent.

Holmes Jungle Nature Park

Holmes Jungle Rd, Karama
(08) 8999 4555;
www.nt.gov.au/nreta/parks/find/
holmesjungle.html

FREE

This is one of the few remaining monsoon rainforests in the Darwin area. It's a shady place to take a wander, with a creek trickling through, and the chance of spotting birds, mammals or reptiles hiding in the jungle. Watch for Territory Parks Alive activities (*see below*).

Jingili Water Gardens

Freshwater Rd, Jingili

FREE

In this attractive tropical garden, kids enjoy clambering around on the boat-themed equipment and rock wall, and splashing in the shallow pools. There are swings and slides, shaded areas and picnic facilities. Warning: the ponds are not fenced.

Territory Parks Alive

Various locations
Parks and Wildlife Service Office
(08) 8999 4555;
www.nt.gov.au/nreta/parks
Various times

FREE

The Northern Territory Parks and Wildlife Service operates fabulous guided walks, campfire talks, slideshows and activities in various parks in and around Darwin. Phone or check the website for details. They also have a great kids' website with fact sheets and colouring-in pictures about animals and plants: www.nt.gov.au/nreta/kids/project/index.html

Day trips

Batchelor Butterfly Farm

8 Meneling Rd, Batchelor
(08) 8976 0199; www.butterflyfarm.net
100 km/1 hr 30 min south
Check opening hours

BUDGET

Wander through tropical gardens where hundreds of butterflies flutter among fruits and flowers, waterfalls and lily ponds. See tropical fruit growing and meet a colony of native turtles. You can also stay in cabins here (*see* ACCOMMODATION p. 390).

Berry Springs Nature Park

Cox Peninsula Rd, Berry Springs
(08) 8999 4555;
www.nt.gov.au/nreta/parks/find/
berrysprings.html
60 km/45 min south
Swimming may be banned Oct–Apr
if conditions unsafe

FREE

Go snorkelling in clear, refreshing pools among native fish. Stroll along the bushwalking track from the shady picnic area – interpretive displays provide information on the wildlife you might see. There is a visitor centre, drinking water, barbecues, kiosk and toilets. The Territory Wildlife Park is located nearby (*see* p. 389).

Howard Springs Nature Park

Howard Springs Rd, Howard Springs
(08) 8999 4555;
www.nt.gov.au/nreta/parks/find/
hsnaturepark.html
30 km/35 min east
Open early morning to evening

FREE

Take a dip in a spring-fed pool surrounded by monsoon forest; there's even a toddler pool. Watch for barramundi and turtles in the main pool and ibis and agile wallabies on the lawns. There is a 1.8-kilometre walking track with interpretive signs about the local plants and animals.

Jumping Crocodile Cruise

Adelaide River, Arnhem Hwy,
Humpty Doo
(08) 8978 9077;
www.jumpingcrocodile.com.au
40 km/1 hr south-east
Depart four times daily

MID-RANGE

During your one-hour cruise on the Alligator River, tour operators dangle meat over the side of the boat, encouraging huge saltwater crocodiles to launch themselves up out of the water. Before the tour, you can cuddle a python (if you're not wearing sunscreen, insect repellent or perfume). Transport is available from town. Window on the Wetlands is located nearby (*see* p. 389).

Lake Bennett

Lake Bennett Wilderness Resort,
Chinner Rd, Winnellie
(08) 8976 0960 or 1800 999 089;
www.lakebennettwildernessresort.
com.au
90 km/1 hr 30 min south

FREE ENTRY

The resort allows public use of the large, artificial freshwater lake, providing an opportunity to swim or hire a canoe without fear of crocodiles! Picnicking is not allowed, but there is a restaurant on site.

Litchfield National Park

Litchfield Park Rd via Batchelor
Batchelor Parks and Wildlife Office
(08) 8976 0282;
www.nt.gov.au/nreta/parks/find/
litchfield.html
130 km/2 hrs 30 min south-west
Swimming may be closed seasonally,
especially Oct–Mar

FREE

This park is the place to come for classic Top End scenery. Take photos next to huge magnetic termite mounds; bring a compass to check that they really do align north–south! Wander through the rainforest and swim in leaf-fringed pools beneath stunning waterfalls. Obtain safety information from the local national parks office, swim only where recommended, and obey all warnings. There is also Litchfield Cafe here (see PLACES TO EAT p. 391).

Swimming at Buley Rockhole, Litchfield National Park

Territory Wildlife Park

Cox Peninsula Rd, Berry Springs
(08) 8988 7200;
www.territorywildlifepark.com.au
60 km/45 min south
Open early till late

MID-RANGE

This is a wonderful opportunity to get up close to animals in natural habitats. Over the day's program, you can feed fish, interact with whiprays (a species of stingray), see a free-flying raptor presentation, and even hold a bird of prey. The walking trails are long, but you can use a shuttle train service. Berry Springs Nature Park is located nearby (*see* p. 387).

Window on the Wetlands

Beatrice Hill, Arnhem Hwy, Humpty Doo
(08) 8988 8188;
www.nt.gov.au/nreta/parks/find/
windowwetlands.html
Visitor centre open early morning
to evening
40 km/1 hr south-east

FREE

The visitor centre offers spectacular views of the surrounding flood plains, and its touch-screen computers give information about wetland animals and local Aboriginal and European history. Free nature walks and activities are offered as part of the Territory Parks Alive program (*see* p. 386). The popular Jumping Crocodile Cruise operates nearby (*see facing page*).

Territory Wildlife Park, Berry Springs

Accommodation

Argus Apartments
6 Cardona Crt, Darwin
(08) 8925 5000;
www.argusdarwin.com.au

HIGH END

Fabulously located in the centre of Darwin, these luxurious, self-contained apartments have dishwashers, two bathrooms, a balcony or patio area and use of an outdoor pool. If your kids don't want to share a queen bed, you will need a three-bedroom apartment.

Batchelor Butterfly Farm
8 Meneling Rd, Batchelor
(08) 8976 0199; www.butterflyfarm.net

MID-RANGE

If you are travelling down south you might want to spend a night at the Batchelor Butterfly Farm (*see* p. 387), one-and-a-half hours from Darwin. There are cabins for families, but these do not have cooking facilities. Food is available at the restaurant on site.

Darwin Free Spirit Resort
901 Stuart Hwy, Berrimah
(08) 8935 0888 or 1800 350 888;
www.darwinfreespiritresort.com.au

BUDGET TO MID-RANGE

Located 15 minutes south of the Darwin city centre, this resort offers three swimming pools, a giant jumping pillow, poolside cafe and bistro, internet kiosks, and guest entertainment during peak season. Choose a camping or caravan site or an air-conditioned, self-contained cabin.

Places to eat

A Coral Reef by Night
Indo Pacific Marine, 29 Stokes Hill Rd,
Darwin Wharf Precinct
(08) 89811 294;
www.indopacificmarine.com.au/
crbn.htm
Limited operating times
Have a seafood meal on a deck
overlooking Darwin Harbour, then
go on a torchlight tour to see
what the corals and marine
animals of Indo Pacific Marine
(*see* p. 380) get up to in the dark
– expect to see some beautiful,
fluorescing effects.

Litchfield Cafe
Litchfield Park Rd via Batchelor
(08) 8978 2077; www.latitude1308.com.
*au/litchfield-national-park/litchfield_*
cafe.html
If you are visiting Litchfield
National Park (*see* p. 388), you
can have a meal here. Sit inside
in air-conditioned comfort, or out
on the veranda or lawn. Meals
include grilled local barramundi,
and kangaroo with salad. Dinner
bookings are essential.

Mindil Beach Sunset Markets
Mindil Beach, Maria Liveris Dr,
Darwin
(08) 8981 3454; www.mindil.com.au
Thurs and Sun evenings, May–Oct
These evening markets are a
favourite with locals and visitors
alike. You can feast on food from
five continents while browsing
craft stalls and enjoying the live
entertainment. There are bands
playing, street performers, cultural
dancers, acrobats and fire shows.
Arrive by about 4pm to enjoy the
famous Darwin sunset.

Stokes Hill Wharf
Darwin
Buy fish and chips or other
takeaway meals from one of the
many food outlets here, then sit
in the fresh air and watch the
sunset over the harbour while
you eat.

Mindil Beach Sunset Markets, Darwin

KATHERINE & SURROUNDS

Katherine is located 300 kilometres south of Darwin

Accessible by coach, car or the famous Ghan train

Dry season (May–Sept) is the most comfortable time to visit. Many attractions close during wet season (Oct–Apr) when the area is prone to flooding and extreme humidity.

WARNING This is an outback region. Carry and drink plenty of water at all times, and familiarise yourselves with other appropriate precautions. You cannot enter Aboriginal land without a permit. Protect against mosquitos and other sources of tropical disease, especially when outdoors in early morning or evening.

HIGHLIGHTS

Manyallaluk **p. 395**

Nitmiluk (Katherine Gorge) National Park **p. 396**

Special events

Katherine Festival
Aug
www.ktc.nt.gov.au/Recreation-Events/Community-Events/Katherine-Festival
Ten days of family fun includes a Teddy Bears' Picnic, live entertainment, fishing competitions, and art and craft activities.

Katherine Show
July
www.katherineshow.org.au
Enjoy live family entertainment, the Holden versus Ford V8 Ute Challenge, novelty competitions, Polocrosse exhibition matches, fireworks and a rodeo.

In town

Freshwater crocodile in the Katherine area

Crocodile Night Adventure
Departs from Springvale Homestead,
Shadforth Rd, Katherine
(08) 8971 9999 or 1800 089 103;
www.travelnorth.com.au
Evenings, May–Oct

HIGH COST, INCLUDES DINNER

The kids are given torches to help spot crocodiles, turtles and catfish as you cruise down the Johnstone River. When you pull over for your campfire meal on the riverbank, you might be joined by a big, friendly freshwater crocodile called Mouse! Watch for the eyes of owls, wallabies and other nocturnal animals glinting out of the darkness, and marvel at the brightness of the stars.

Katherine Hot Springs
Riverbank Dr, Katherine South
(08) 8972 5500
Closed during wet season (Oct–Apr)

FREE

Don't miss this beautiful swimming and picnic spot just a couple of kilometres from the town centre. Surrounded by weeping green foliage, you can take a dip in the clear, bubbling waters of a warm spring, where rock paving allows comfortable and easy access. There is a grassy, shaded barbecue area adjacent to the carpark.

Katherine Museum

Gorge Rd (opposite hospital), Katherine
(08) 8972 3945;
www.katherinemuseum.com

BUDGET

At this historic air terminal from World War II (Katherine no longer has an airport), kids love to watch the video of the devastating 1998 Katherine floods. You can also see Aboriginal artefacts, historic homewares and tools, and a Gypsy Moth plane flown by daring pilot-doctor, Clyde Fenton, who pioneered an aerial ambulance service for the region in the 1930s.

Katherine School of the Air

Giles St, Katherine
(08) 8972 1833;
www.schools.nt.edu.au/ksa
Tours commence 9am, 10am and 11am weekdays; closed Dec–Feb and public holidays

BUDGET

This unique educational facility covers over 800 000 square kilometres of Australia's Outback – 40 times the size of Switzerland! Lessons are conducted via internet, phone, radio or mail and in the one-hour tour you see a long-distance class in action.

Marksie's Stockman's Camp Tucker Night

Katherine Museum, Gorge Rd
(opposite hospital), Katherine
0427 112 806; www.camptucker.com
Operates Mar–Dec, three evenings a week

HIGH COST, INCLUDES DINNER

This is a memorable experience for the whole family. While Marksie entertains you with Aussie yarns, you sit around a campfire eating traditional outback tucker: kangaroo, buffalo, camel, coal-fired vegetables, damper, gem scones with native jams, and gumleaf billy tea. For the kids, there is a scavenger hunt and a billy-spinning competition. Dessert is bush 'ice-cream' – damper is cooked on a stick and the cavity left by the stick is filled with golden syrup. Wallabies appear out of the surrounding shadows, and stars sparkle in the sky, undimmed by city lights.

Mimi Aboriginal Art & Craft

6 Piece St, Katherine
(08) 8971 0036
Open weekdays

FREE ENTRY

At this Aboriginal-owned and operated not-for-profit centre you can view and buy Indigenous art pieces, and you'll often see artists at work.

Springvale Homestead

Shadforth Rd, Katherine
(08) 8971 9999 or 1800 089 103
Tours in dry season May–Oct

FREE

This is the oldest standing homestead in the Northern Territory. Take a free guided tour, indulge in a Devonshire tea, or play on the riverbank under shady Indian raintrees.

Top Didj Cultural Experience, Katherine

Top Didj Cultural Experience

Top Didj Art Gallery, cnr Gorge and Jaensch rds, Katherine
(08) 8971 2751; www.topdidj.com
Three tours daily, Mar – mid-Dec

HIGH COST

Your entertaining Aboriginal guides will show you how to make your own painting in traditional style, how to throw a spear with a woomera, and how to light a fire by rubbing two sticks together. You might also get to pat Edward the pet emu, and meet some orphaned baby kangaroos. This is a unique experience in a beautiful bush location.

In the area

Manyallaluk

Depart from Katherine accommodation or self-drive to Manyallaluk (100 km)
(08) 8972 1253 or 1300 146 743; www.nitmiluktours.com.au
Depart early morning for a whole day tour, Apr–Oct
Minimum age 5 years

HIGH COST

You glance at your kids giggling and chatting with their new Aboriginal friends and marvel at what an amazing day you are all having. You've swum together in a spring-fed pool, eaten kangaroo tail for lunch, learnt to play a didgeridoo, and painted the traditional way using ochres and brushes made out of reeds. Now you are sitting in the shade of a huge mango tree, making string from the bark of a kurrajong tree. Soon you will be learning how to throw spears, and find your own bush foods. This time spent in the heart of an Aboriginal community – sharing their life and culture – is sure to be a highlight of your trip.

INSIDER TIPS

■ Other skills demonstrated on your tour include fire-lighting, weaving pandanus leaves, and how to use plants for medicine and bush tucker.

■ Be sure to bring a hat, sunscreen, insect repellent, walking shoes and a full water bottle.

■ There are facilities for camping if you want to stay overnight.

■ Sometimes tours cannot operate in April due to flooded roads.

DON'T MISS

■ The chance to unwind. Part of your experience will be adjusting to the slow, relaxed Aboriginal lifestyle.

■ Visiting the community store (Monday–Friday), where you can buy paintings on bark or canvas, didgeridoos, pandanus baskets and mats, string bags, beads, small sculptures, clap sticks and fire sticks.

FABULOUS FACTS

The 3000-square-kilometre property of Manyallaluk was a cattle station in the early 1900s, but it has now been returned to the Aboriginal people. This tourism venture provides the community with self-determination and employment. The venture has been so successful it has won three consecutive national tourism awards, gaining a place in the Tourism Hall of Fame.

Kid Quest
Try to learn some Jawoyn Aboriginal words.

Nitmiluk (Katherine Gorge) National Park
Gorge Rd, 30 km north-east of Katherine
National Park Visitor Centre (08) 8972 1253 or 1300 146 743;
www.nitmiluktours.com.au and www.nt.gov.au/nreta/parks/find
May be inaccessible in wet season (Oct–Apr)
FREE ENTRY TO PARK; HIGH COST FOR CRUISES AND CANOE HIRE

As the kids splash around, enjoying the coolness of the water, you float on your back gazing up at the red cliffs that tower above on both sides. Overhead an eagle glides on outstretched wings. Then your swimming time is up. You board the tour boat again, and as it chugs slowly along the gorge, you eagerly follow the guide's pointing finger. He draws your attention to Aboriginal paintings high above the floodline and reveals that a 'knobbly log' is really a freshwater crocodile.

Canoeing at Nitmiluk (Katherine Gorge) National Park

INSIDER TIPS

- Nitmiluk Gorge winds for 12 kilometres through sheer sandstone cliffs, carved out by the Katherine River over millions of years. The gorge actually consists of 13 separate gorges.

- The best way to see the most scenic stretches of the gorge is by boat tour. There are various cruises, and all include easy walks between gorges for a chance to get closer to the plants and wildlife. The longer tours include a swim. Book ahead at the visitor centre to avoid disappointment.

- You can hire one- or two-person canoes at 8am or 1pm each day at the gorge (booking recommended). However, to reach the most scenic stretches you need to paddle for a whole day and camp overnight. Note: the minimum age for canoeing is 6 years.

- There are walking trails leading into the park. To see animals, you need to keep very quiet. Your best chance is early morning or evening.

- If you spot any crocodiles on the river, they are usually freshwater crocodiles. These do not eat humans, but will bite if disturbed.

- You might spot turtles or water monitors (a lizard that grows to 1 metre) swimming or sunning on rocks.

- Picnic facilities and barbecues are available in the grassed area at the gorge.

- It is possible to swim in parts of the gorge, but check warning signs carefully.

- Scenic helicopter flights (high cost) are also available – contact the visitor centre.

- The Sugarbag Cafe in the visitor centre stays open for dinner from June to August (*see* PLACES TO EAT p. 401).

- Several accommodation options are available in the park at Nitmiluk Chalets and Campground (*see* ACCOMMODATION p. 400).

DON'T MISS

- The Nitmiluk Visitor Centre near the entrance to the park. Pick up information, book tours, have a run in the playground, and look at the display for an introduction to the park's flora, fauna, geology, and history. You might also see an artist at work here.

- Swimming beneath Leliyn (Edith Falls) or exploring the surrounds (*see* p. 400).

- The Territory Parks Alive sessions offered here (*see* p. 400).

- The very steep but interesting walk from the jetty up to a cliff-top lookout – allow about two hours return and take plenty of water.

- Bush tucker walks that are occasionally on offer. Enquire at the visitor centre. These are high cost and take about four hours, departing at 8am.

FABULOUS FACTS

Nitmiluk is pronounced Nit-me-look. It is the name used for Katherine Gorge by the local Aboriginal people, the Jawoyn. Nitmiluk means 'Cicada Place' (cicadas make a *nit-nit-nit* sound). The gorge is associated with the Dreamtime, and according to Aboriginal legend, the Rainbow Serpent Bolung dwells in the deep green pools of the second gorge. Out of respect for Bolung, Jawoyn people do not fish in these waters.

Cutta Cutta Caves

Cutta Cutta Caves Nature Park via Stuart Hwy
(08) 8972 1940;
www.nt.gov.au/nreta/parks/find
30 km east of Katherine
Tours depart on the hour, closed Feb–Mar
Entry to caves by guided tour only

MID-RANGE

In the humid underground world of these tropical limestone caves you can marvel at stalactites and stalagmites, gasp at the sight of (harmless) brown tree snakes, and search for the more elusive bats and rare blind shrimps. There is also a free 20-minute woodland walk into the park.

Elsey National Park

110 km south of Katherine
Via Stuart Hwy just south of Mataranka township
(08) 8975 4560;
www.nt.gov.au/nreta/parks/find
May be inaccessible in wet season (Oct–Apr)

FREE

You can swim in a deep, pandanus-fringed waterhole at Bitter Springs, the warm waters of the Thermal Pool (Mataranka Hot Springs), or the shallower Four Mile Hole, which is great for kids. Relax with a picnic, or go for a walk along the Roper River. Various turnoffs from the

Bitter Springs, Elsey National Park

highway lead to the different points in the park.

Leliyn (Edith Falls)

Off Stuart Hwy, 42 km north of Katherine
(follow signposted road for 19 km)
Western side of Nitmiluk National Park
(08) 8975 4852;
www.nt.gov.au/nreta/parks/find
May be inaccessible in wet season
(Oct–Apr)

FREE

Swim in a large, natural pool beneath waterfalls surrounded by pandanus plants. There are short, easy walks in this magnificent location. The park has picnic and barbecue facilities, a grassed area, toilets and kiosk.

Territory Parks Alive

Various locations
(08) 8973 8888;
www.nt.gov.au/nretas/parks
Seasonal

FREE

The Northern Territory Parks and Wildlife Service runs campfire talks, meet-the-ranger sessions, and presentations about Jawoyn culture at Nitmiluk National Park (including Leliyn), and Elsey National Park (*see* p. 399).

Accommodation

BIG4 Katherine Low Level Caravan Park

3649 Shadforth Rd, Katherine
(08) 8972 3962 or 1800 501 984;
www.big4.com.au

BUDGET TO MID-RANGE

This large, scenic park just 3 kilometres from town has shady

campsites and self-contained, air-conditioned cabins. It features a huge swimming pool, bistro and outdoor cinema. Kids enjoy fishing in the river here.

Nitmiluk Chalets and Campground

Nitmiluk National Park via Giles St and Stuart Hwy, 30 km north-east of Katherine
(08) 8972 1253 or 1300 146 743;
www.nitmiluktours.com.au

BUDGET TO MID-RANGE

Stay in the magnificent grounds of Nitmiluk National Park (*see* p. 396), surrounded by bounding kangaroos in the evening and an orchestra of bird calls in the morning. The campground has hot showers and toilets, and a choice of campsites or permanent tent accommodation complete with camp-style beds. The chalets offer self-contained, two-bedroom, air-conditioned accommodation. All have access to a resort pool and the Poolside Cafe.

St Andrews Serviced Apartments

27 First St, Katherine
(08) 8971 2288 or 1800 686 106;
www.standrewsapts.com.au

MID-RANGE

These spacious, two-bedroom apartments are located in the heart of town. They are self-contained and set in landscaped tropical gardens with a pool and barbecue. Cots, highchairs and babies baths are available on request.

Places to eat

Crocodile Night Adventure

Enjoy a campfire meal and a nocturnal river cruise (*see* p. 393 for more information).

Katherine Country Club

Pearce St, Katherine
(08) 8972 1276;
www.katherinecountryclub.com.au
This is a family-friendly bistro with a playground where the kids can have a run around

while you relax. Dinner bookings are essential.

Marksie's Stockman's Camp Tucker Night

Spend an entertaining evening by the campfire (*see* p. 394 for more information).

Sugarbag Cafe

Nitmiluk National Park via Giles St and Stuart Hwy, 30 km north-east of Katherine
(08) 8972 1253 or 1300 146 743;
www.nitmiluktours.com.au
The name 'Sugarbag' comes from a type of bush tucker plant. Enjoy views of the Katherine River and be entertained by cheeky blue-faced honeyeaters flying around while you eat. The cafe serves breakfast, lunch and dinner.

ALICE SPRINGS & SURROUNDS

Alice Springs is located 1500 kilometres south of Darwin; access by air or road

Best time to visit is Apr–Sept; in the height of summer (Dec–Feb) temperatures are regularly around 40° C. Nights and early mornings can be very cold, especially mid-year.

WARNINGS This is an outback region. Before driving, make appropriate preparations, and obtain permits to enter Aboriginal land. If walking, aim for the coolest part of the day, and you will probably want fly nets, which are readily available. Always carry water and wear a hat.

HIGHLIGHTS

Alice Springs Desert Park **p. 403**

Royal Flying Doctor Service **p. 405**

Special events

Henley-on-Todd Regatta
Aug/Sept
www.henleyontodd.com.au
Watch the entertainment, or make your own 'boat' and join in. The boat doesn't have to be watertight as there is no water in the Todd River! A morning parade is followed by a day of races, including a battleship spectacle.

Alice Springs Show
July
www.alice-springs.com.au
This weekend of fun includes animal parades, sand sculpting, kids' entertainment, fireworks, and V8 ute driving exhibitions.

Around town

Alice Springs Desert Park
Larapinta Dr, Alice Springs
(08) 8951 8788; www.alicespringsdesertpark.com.au
Open early morning to evening

MID-RANGE

Your guide plucks something white and sugary-looking off
a leaf and explains how lerp insects exude this sweet substance, used
by Aboriginal people as a bush snack. He asks if anyone wants a taste
and your kids eagerly dive forward. As they eat the bush tucker, you
marvel how far this is from the processed food they demand at home.
Next, they breathe in the scent of the fruit-salad bush, the leaves of
which can be used for perfume. This park is a wonderful showcase for
the diversity and special characteristics of desert flora and fauna.

*Alice Springs
Desert Park,
Alice Springs*

INSIDER TIPS

- Allow at least three hours for your visit.

- The park is divided into different regions so you actually walk
  through and experience woodland habitat, sand country and
  a desert river region.

- Birds and some mammals of the regions are displayed either
  in walk-through aviaries or behind large windows.

- Park maps in Chinese, Japanese, French, German and Italian
  can be downloaded from the website.

- Audio guides are available in English, German, Japanese
  and French.

- There is an air-conditioned cafe in the courtyard.

- Make sure you carry water, but if you need an extra drink, there are coin-operated drink machines and water drinking fountains around the park.

- There is a picnic area with barbecues.

- Strollers can be borrowed (no cost) from the main courtyard area.

- Nocturnal spotlighting tours (extra cost) are offered every weeknight, sometimes followed by a barbecue dinner.

- There are shaded rest areas around the park.

DON'T MISS

- The ranger talks and tours – if possible call ahead to find out the schedule for the day.

- The Nature Theatre presentations, held twice daily, where free-flying birds of prey come in for a feed and demonstrate their natural survival skills. You might even see one of them crack open an emu egg with a stick and drink the contents!

- Tasting food on the Aboriginal bush foods talk.

- The nocturnal mammal house where you can see unusual animals such as the bilby and quoll.

- The early-morning guided birdwatching tours. The tours operate twice a week and binoculars are provided.

- *The Changing Heart* movie, which screens on the hour and explains desert evolution.

FABULOUS FACTS

One of the animals you can see in Alice Springs Desert Park is the mala. This is a small, rabbit-sized wallaby with very shaggy fur. Mala were virtually extinct in mainland Australia, but a successful breeding program is being undertaken here.

Kid Quest
Taste one of the bush tucker foods in the park.

Royal Flying Doctor Service

Stuart Tce, Alice Springs
(08) 8952 1129; www.flyingdoctor.org.au
Open daily, afternoons only on Sun and public
holidays

BUDGET

One of your kids sits in the cockpit, gripping the controls of the plane, knuckles white. Through the large front windows you see the red earth of the desert rushing towards you, closer and closer... Oh no, you are about to crash! Laughing, your young pilot lets go of the controls and jumps up. The flight simulator is abandoned in favour of the next interesting exhibit, a full-sized replica fuselage of a plane with a 'baby' in a humidicrib and a larger 'patient' strapped to a stretcher.

INSIDER TIPS

▓ Allow about an hour for your visit.

▓ In the flight simulator you can fly over Uluṟu and other landmarks in the Red Centre.

▓ There is a cafe on site, but it is closed on Sundays and public holidays.

▓ Whilst the control room here is no longer used for taking calls to the Flying Doctor Service, a map on the wall shows where the planes are being deployed in real time.

DON'T MISS

▓ The guided tours that run every half hour; translated Talk Sheets are available in 14 languages.

▓ Having a meal in the cafe. The food is great, and all proceeds go to the Royal Flying Doctor Service.

▓ The glass cabinet in the museum that displays a typical medical chest kept in remote areas. If you press the button, you can listen to a doctor giving a consultation over the phone.

▓ Trying out the working Traegar Pedal Radio (*see* FABULOUS FACTS p. 406). This is how people in rural Australia communicated with the doctor before telephones were available.

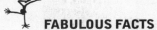

FABULOUS FACTS

The Royal Flying Doctor Service brings emergency and everyday care to people in remote areas of Australia who have no other access to doctors or hospitals. It covers a region of more than 7 million square kilometres – an area larger than Western Europe. It was the first aerial medical service in the world and the inaugural flight on 5 May 1928 was due to the vision and persistence of the Reverend John Flynn. His dream would not have been possible without the pedal two-way radio developed by Alf Traeger, which allowed patients to communicate with the service.

Kid Quest

Find out where the Royal Flying Doctor Service plane is travelling while you are there.

Adelaide House

52 Todd Mall, Alice Springs
(08) 8952 1856;
www.flynntrail.org.au/orgs/
adelaidehouse.html
Closed Sun

ENTRY BY DONATION

Built in 1926, this was the first bush nursing hostel set up by the Reverend John Flynn (*see* ROYAL FLYING DOCTOR SERVICE p. 405). Flynn's vision was to offer medical aid to people in remote areas. See the clever, passive cooling system used in this house, and learn more about Flynn, the vital pedal radio invention, and outback nursing.

Alice Springs Reptile Centre

9 Stuart Tce, Alice Springs
(08) 8952 8900;
www.reptilecentre.com.au

MID-RANGE

This is a great opportunity to see an incredible variety of lizards and snakes close up – and come nose-to-nose with a crocodile on the other side of a viewing window! Don't miss the talk and handling sessions, three times daily. During the cool months (May–August), the reptiles are most active between 11am and 3pm.

Alice Springs School of the Air

80 Head St, Alice Springs
(08) 8951 6834; www.assoa.nt.edu.au
Open daily, afternoons only on Sun and public holidays

BUDGET

Teachers here provide lessons for children scattered over 1 million square kilometres of remote Central Australia. When the service began in 1951, it made use of the Royal Flying Doctor

Alice Springs Telegraph Station Historical Reserve, Alice Springs

Service pedal radios. Now, of course, the internet has made communication much easier. On weekdays you might see real classes in action – and maybe even get the opportunity to participate. At other times, you can watch videos of lessons.

Alice Springs Telegraph Station Historical Reserve
Via Stuart Hwy, Herbert Heritage Dr, Alice Springs
(08) 8952 3993; www.nt.gov.au/nreta/ parks/find/astelegraphstation.html
BUDGET
This old telegraph station is an important part of Australian history. When the mammoth task of constructing the Overland Telegraph through Australia's harsh desert was completed in 1872, messages from London could be relayed around Australia in a matter of hours, instead of the months it took by sea. The restored, refurnished buildings provide a glimpse of outback life in the late 19th century. Watch for wallabies hopping around the surrounding granite country.

Central Australian Aviation Museum
Araluen Cultural Precinct, 8 Memorial Ave, Alice Springs
(08) 8951 1120
BUDGET
Displays include early Royal Flying Doctor Service planes, a restored DC-3 and a diorama telling the tragic story of two pilots who crashed their plane in the desert in 1929 while looking for missing aviators Charles Kingsford-Smith and Charles Ulm (later found stranded with a failed engine).

*Museum of Central Australia,
Alice Springs*

Museum of Central Australia

*Araluen Cultural Precinct, cnr Larapinta
Dr and Memorial Ave, Alice Springs*
(08) 8951 1121
*Open 10am–4pm weekdays, 11am–4pm
weekends*

MID-RANGE

This museum has interpretive displays about the geology and natural history of the Red Centre. The impressive megafauna bones are the top kid-pleasers here.

National Pioneer Women's Hall of Fame

*Old Alice Springs Gaol,
2 Stuart Tce, Alice Springs*
(08) 8952 9006;
www.pioneerwomen.com.au

BUDGET

As this is located in an old prison complex, you can not only see fascinating displays about pioneer women, you can also walk into old prison cells and imagine what it would be like to sleep in those narrow beds and use the exposed toilets!

Olive Pink Botanic Gardens

Tuncks Rd, Alice Springs
(08) 8952 2154; www.opbg.com.au
Open early morning to early evening

ENTRY BY DONATION

There are self-guided walks and interpretive markers so you can go on a hunt identifying trees or finding out about bush tucker and medicinal plants.

Sounds of Starlight Theatre

40 Todd Mall, Alice Springs
(08) 8953 0826;
www.soundsofstarlight.com
Check show times

HIGH COST

Free didgeridoo classes are conducted here twice daily on weekdays. In the evening, this is the setting for spellbinding performances. Didgeridoos, percussion and spectacular imagery evoke Aboriginal culture and the spirit of the outback. At the end, you can join in!

South of The Gap

Earth Sanctuary Star Shows
Earth Sanctuary Homestead, Lot 4005
Colonel Rose Dr, Connellan
(08) 8953 6161; www.earthsanctuary.tv
HIGH COST

View planets, stars, moons and constellations in the night sky while a guide retells ancient creation legends. Earth Sanctuary also runs an eco-tour of their Centre for Sustainable Living. You can add a dinner or sleep-over to the tours if you wish.

Kangaroo Sanctuary
11 Colonel Rose Dr, Connellan
0407 718 409
Check opening hours
Minimum age 6 years
MID-RANGE

Orphaned, tame kangaroos that cannot be released back into the wild find a home in this sanctuary, designed to be as close as possible to their natural environment. Because some of the animals are frightened by squeals and sudden movements, small children are not admitted.

Old *Ghan* Heritage Railway Museum
Norris Bell Dr, Arumbera
(08) 8952 7161;
www.roadtransporthall.com
BUDGET

Located in a 1930s-style railway station, this collection from the Old *Ghan*'s pioneering past, includes locomotives, carriages, dining and sleeping cars. Climb aboard and imagine you are setting off across the outback. The Road Transport Hall of Fame is located next door (*see below*).

Road Transport Hall of Fame
Norris Bell Dr, Arumbera
(08) 8952 7161;
www.roadtransporthall.com
MID-RANGE

Discover some of the amazing vehicles that have traversed this outback region. They are not pristine, but reveal their harsh working lives, including intriguing 'bush engineering' modifications. Also on site is the Kenworth Dealer Museum with its big glossy monsters – heaven for kids who love trucks. The Old *Ghan* Heritage Railway Museum is located next door (*see above*).

In the area

Arltunga Historic Reserve

110 km east of Alice Springs via Ross Hwy
(08) 8956 9770 or (08) 8951 8250;
www.nt.gov.au/nreta/parks/find/arltunga.html
Daily
FREE

There was a gold rush here in the late 19th century, creating the first significant European settlement in the outback. You can wander through the stone residences of this deserted town, and marvel at massive mining machinery that had to be transported hundreds of kilometres across the outback. At the visitor centre, pan for gold and see cultural and historical exhibits. Territory Parks Alive (*see* p. 411) run fun sessions here.

Balloon flights

Pick up from your accommodation in Alice Springs
(08) 8952 8723 or 1800 809 790;
www.outbackballooning.com.au
Pre-dawn pick up
Minimum age 6 years
HIGH COST

As you float in your hot-air balloon, you'll have a wonderful bird's-eye view of the outback landscape and native animals.

Bikeriding

Various locations
VARIOUS PRICES FOR BIKE HIRE

There are several bike-hire places around town and scenic bike paths to locations such as the Alice Springs Telegraph Station Historical Reserve (*see* p. 407). If you are feeling really energetic, you can take the Simpsons Gap Bicycle Path, a 40-kilometre return trip; www.nt.gov.au/nreta/parks/find/simpsonsgap.html. Leave early in the morning to avoid the heat and always carry water.

Emily and Jessie Gaps Nature Park

Ross Hwy 10 km east of Alice Springs
(08) 8951 8250;
www.nt.gov.au/nreta/parks/find/emilyjessie.html
FREE

These rock formations in the Heavitree Range are important spiritual sites for Aboriginal people. Ancient paintings on the rock walls tell the Dreamtime story of the caterpillar beings who created these and other topographic features in the area.

Gemtree

140 km north-east of Alice Springs
Plenty Hwy, Gemtree
(08) 8956 9855; www.gemtree.com.au
Seasonal operating hours

MID-RANGE

Go on a real treasure hunt! Gemtree Tag-Along Garnet Tours provide equipment and instructions, take you to a real gem field to fossick, and appraise all the garnets you find. Alternatively, buy a bucket of garnet-bearing gravel or have a go in Garnet Gully, located in the grounds. Gemtree is also a caravan park, if you wish to stay overnight.

Ochre Pits

110 km west of Alice Springs
Namatjira Dr, West MacDonnell
National Park
(08) 8951 8250; www.nt.gov.au/nreta/parks/find/westmacdonnell.html

FREE

Take an easy boardwalk to view cliffs striped with different coloured ochres. Over thousands of years, Aboriginal people used the ochre from these walls for medical treatment, as a magic charm, and as a decorative paint.

Ormiston Gorge

135 km west of Alice Springs
Namatjira Dr, West MacDonnell
National Park
(08) 8951 8250;
www.nt.gov.au/nreta/parks/find/westmacdonnell.html

FREE

This is a spectacular, scenic gorge with towering red walls. Take a short walk to the waterhole (often suitable for swimming), or a longer walk to Ghost Gum Lookout. Early morning or evening, you might see rock wallabies drinking at the waterhole. Territory Parks Alive (*see below*) runs programs here.

Pyndan Camel Tracks

21259 Jane Rd, White Gums
0416 170 164; www.cameltracks.com
Tours of various lengths run throughout the day; bookings essential

VARIOUS PRICES

Get to know and love camels – the type of transport used by the outback's first European explorers. As you are carried through the White Gums Valley, watch for kangaroos, wallabies, birds and lizards.

Territory Parks Alive

Various locations
Parks and Wildlife Service Office
(08) 8951 8211;
www.nt.gov.au/nreta/parks
Various times, May–Sept

FREE

The Northern Territory Parks and Wildlife Service operates

fabulous guided walks, campfire talks, slideshows and activities in various parks around Alice Springs. Phone or check the website for details. They also have a great kids' website with fact sheets and colouring-in pictures about animals and plants: www.nt.gov.au/nreta/kids/project/index.html

Accommodation

Heavitree Gap Outback Lodge
Palm Circuit, Alice Springs
(08) 8950 4444 or 1800 896 119;
www.auroraresorts.com.au
BUDGET

Located within five minutes' drive from town (shuttle service available), accommodation options include campsites, or kitchenette family rooms in the lodge. There is a restaurant, outdoor pool, playground, and a colony of black-footed rock wallabies that comes for a feed every evening.

MacDonnell Range Holiday Park
Palm Circuit, Alice Springs
(08) 8952 6111 or 1800 808 373;
www.macrange.com.au
BUDGET TO MID-RANGE

Options range from a basic unpowered campsite to a deluxe two-bedroom villa complete with spa bath. This park is about eight minutes out of town. It is a member of BIG4 Holiday Parks and has all sorts of kid-pleasers including an adventure playground, BMX track, half-court basketball, go-karts, bike hire, swimming pools, wading pool, jumping pillows and a recreation room.

Quest Alice Springs
9–10 South Tce, Alice Springs
(08) 8959 0000;
www.questalicesprings.com.au
HIGH COST

These luxurious, modern apartments are close to town and feature fully equipped kitchens, private laundries, balconies and spacious lounge/dining areas. There is a pool on site.

Places to eat

Bojangles Saloon and Dining Room
80 Todd St, Alice Springs
(08) 8952 2873; www.bossaloon.com.au
The eclectic decor includes a life-size replica of Ned Kelly, antique guns, motorbikes, cars, a stuffed wedge-tailed eagle, and a live python. You can taste Territory delicacies such as camel, crocodile, kangaroo and emu.

Gillen Club
Milner Rd, Alice Springs
(08) 8952 3749; www.gillenclub.com.au
This is a sports and family club. There is a Kidzone with computer games and videos, an outdoor playground and a jumping pillow. The bistro has a kids' menu.

Mbantua Dinner by the Campfire Tour
Pick up from your accommodation in Alice Springs
(08) 8952 0327;
www.rttoursaustralia.com.au/4-Mbantua-Dinner-Tour.html
This is a real outback experience as well as a meal. You are taken to the West MacDonnell Ranges to watch the sunset as dinner cooks in a camp oven or on the barbecue. You'll enjoy a gourmet meal made with bush tucker ingredients. This is a high-cost experience.

Memorial Club
Todd St, Alice Springs
(08) 8952 2166;
www.memorialclub.com.au
This family bistro in the middle of town has an outdoor playground with room to kick a football, and a Kids' Club area with videos and computer games.

The Overlanders Steakhouse
72 Hartley St, Alice Springs
(08) 8952 2159;
www.overlanders.com.au
This is a themed restaurant with cattle station decor. There is an imaginative kids' menu that includes a platter of crocodile, kangaroo, emu and camel.

ULURU & SURROUNDS

Uluru is located 440 kilometres south-west of Alice Springs and 2000 kilometres south of Darwin

Accessible by air (Yulara airport) or road

Best time to visit is Apr–Sept; in the height of summer (Dec–Feb) temperatures are regularly around 40° C. Nights and early mornings can be very cold, especially mid-year.

WARNINGS This is an outback region. Before driving, make appropriate preparations, and obtain permits to enter Aboriginal land. If walking, aim for the coolest part of the day, and you will probably want fly nets, which are readily available. Always carry water and wear a hat.

HIGHLIGHTS

Uluru   *p. 414*

Around Uluru

Uluru, Uluru–Kata Tjuta National Park

Uluru

Uluru–Kata Tjuta National Park
(08) 8956 1128;
www.environment.gov.au/parks/uluru
Open sunrise to after dark

MID-RANGE

There is a lot to take in on any first-time visit to Uluru and your kids are sure to have lots to say. Astonished comments will tumble from their mouths: Uluru is even bigger than they expected, and they thought the surface was going to be smooth, and they didn't think plants would be growing all around it – isn't this supposed to be the desert? Your tour guide leads you around the base of Uluru, pausing in front of painted ochre diagrams on the wall of a cave. Hundreds of years ago, this cave was a classroom where men gave lessons to boys. Your kids whisper that it would be fun to have lessons in a cave, and you realise this is not just a tourist visit, but a spiritual and cultural experience for all of you.

INSIDER TIPS

■ The Anangu people are the traditional owners of Uluru–Kata Tjuta National Park. Uluru and Kata Tjuta are sacred sites.

■ Climbing Uluru is offensive to the Anangu people, and it is also dangerous – Uluru is the height of a 90-storey building.

■ Uluru was called 'Ayers Rock' by European settlers and you are likely to hear this name used sometimes.

■ The best way to experience Uluru is to walk around the base. It is preferable (though not compulsory) to do this with a guide, who can make sure you do not view, enter or photograph important sensitive areas and will teach you some Anangu law and culture.

■ There are free ranger tours for the Mala Walk – partway around the base – that operate every morning (seasonal start times). Phone ahead or check the website for other walk options.

■ If you go out for a dawn or dusk viewing of Uluru, rug up for warmth. Temperatures in the evening can be extremely cold, no matter how hot it is during the day.

■ Visitors over 16 years of age must buy a national park pass, valid for three consecutive days; the same pass is valid for the whole park including Kata Tjuta (*see* p. 417).

■ There are toilets, a cafe and picnic facilities near the base of Uluru at the Uluru-Kata Tjuta Cultural Centre (*see* p. 417).

■ If you see dingoes in the park, you are advised not to feed them.

DON'T MISS

■ The chance to find a peaceful place where your family can experience the spirit of Uluru alone.

- Visiting one of the waterfall areas about an hour before sunset. Many birds come there to drink, and at dusk, the microbats appear, snatching insects out of the air.
- Talinguru Nyakunytjaku viewing area (*see facing page*).

FABULOUS FACTS

Anangu people believe the landscape was created by ancestral beings who were part animal, part human. One of the most important is Mala Man (Mala is the Anangu name for the rufous hare-wallaby). Rufous hare-wallabies used to be abundant in this area, but became extinct in the 1950s. A small colony was reintroduced in 2005 and is breeding successfully — so watch out for them on your Mala Walk.

Kid Quest
The natural colour of Uluru is actually grey, but high iron content makes the exposed areas go rusty. When you are up close, look for bits where the rust has chipped off to reveal the grey underneath.

Anangu Aboriginal Tour
Pick up from your hotel or meet at the Touch Wall at Uluru
(08) 8950 3030;
www.ananguwaai.com.au
Various times
HIGH COST

These tours are led by the traditional owners of the land. You will learn Dreamtime legends and gain skills such as how to

make kiti (bush glue), throw a spear, or carry a piti (food bowl) on your head.

Dot Painting Workshop
Pick up from your hotel or meet at Uluru–Kata Tjuta Cultural Centre
(08) 8950 3030;
www.ananguwaai.com.au
Afternoons
HIGH COST

This is an eye-opening and fun experience. You find out the meaning of the symbols in the dot paintings then create your own artwork to take home — either individual pieces or a combined work that relates your family's story.

Kata Tjuṯa

Uluṟu–Kata Tjuṯa National Park,
40 km from Uluṟu
(08) 8956 1128;
www.environment.gov.au/parks/uluru
Open early morning to evening

MID-RANGE

You have a choice of two walks among these spectacular red rocks (some even higher than Uluṟu). You can take the Walpa Gorge Walk, which is easier and shorter, or you might go partway along the more difficult Valley of the Winds Walk. You will see lots of birds at the creek bed if you wait quietly. Toilets are provided at the Sunset Viewing carpark but there is no kiosk, so bring food and drink. Don't forget your fly nets (ignore the kids' protests), and allow plenty of time to get back from your walk and drive out before the park closes.

Talinguru Nyakunytjaku

Uluṟu–Kata Tjuṯa National Park
(08) 8956 1128;
www.environment.gov.au/parks/uluru
Open early morning to evening

MID-RANGE

Viewing platforms here offer stunning outlooks over Uluṟu and Kata Tjuṯa. Make sure you climb up high and look down to see how the landscape of bushes scattered among vibrant coloured sands resembles a dot painting. There are also short self-guided walks through the sand dunes, with signs explaining how to play Aboriginal children's games, how to collect and process bush foods, and how to make tools.

Uluṟu Camel Tours

Various locations, times and prices
(08) 8950 3030;
www.ananguwaai.com.au
Minimum age 5 years

VARIOUS PRICES

Find out what it is like to ride on one of these 'ships of the desert' that helped explorers and settlers traverse the outback. You can take a short ride around the camel farm (budget) or tour the desert for a couple of hours (high cost), taking in spectacular views of Uluṟu and Kata Tjuṯa.

Uluṟu–Kata Tjuṯa Cultural Centre

Uluṟu–Kata Tjuṯa National Park
(08) 8956 1128;
www.environment.gov.au/parks/uluru
Open early morning to evening

FREE ENTRY WITH NATIONAL PARKS PASS

Necklaces made from native plants at the Uluṟu–Kata Tjuṯa Cultural Centre

This is a great starting point for your visit to Uluru and Kata Tjuta. Look for writing and painting displays by Junior Rangers (local school kids). Watch a video on Anangu people passing on their Creation story through painting, singing and dancing. See local people preparing bush tucker or working on traditional art and craft (most weekday mornings) or take a guided mid-afternoon plant walk (during the cooler months).

En route from Alice Springs

Watarrka (Kings Canyon) National Park
(08) 8951 8250;
www.nt.gov.au/nreta/parks/find/watarrka.html
FREE

Take one of the walking tracks and explore this national park, famous for its rugged red ranges and rockholes. The two easier trails, both 2.6 kilometres return, have signage along the way explaining Aboriginal culture. One leads to the picturesque Kathleen Springs waterhole and the other follows Kings Creek. If you can cope with a 6-kilometre difficult trek, involving a climb up 500 steps and a lot of clambering over large rocks, take the Canyon Rim Walk. Your rewards are spectacular views down into Kings Canyon, and a rest stop midway at the Garden of Eden waterholes. There are toilets and picnic areas but no kiosk. Food and accommodation are available at the nearby Kings Canyon Resort.

Accommodation

Campground, Ayers Rock Resort
Yulara Dr, Yulara
(08) 8957 7001 or 1300 134 044;
www.ayersrockresort.com.au
BUDGET

Choose a shady site for a tent or caravan, or an air-conditioned two-bedroom cabin with shared bathroom facilities. There are two tennis courts and a swimming pool on the grounds.

Emu Walk Apartments, Ayers Rock Resort
Yulara Dr, Yulara
(08) 8957 7714 or 1300 134 044;
www.ayersrockresort.com.au
HIGH COST

Ayers Rock Resort encompasses the campground (*see facing page*), several hotels, and the Emu Walk Apartments. The two-bedroom apartments have air-conditioning, kitchens and either a balcony or veranda. Single beds for the kids are available on request, and guests can access several swimming pools and two tennis courts.

Places to eat

Bough House Restaurant
Outback Pioneer Hotel,
Yulara Dr, Yulara
(08) 8957 7605
Children aged 12 years and under eat free here, so make the most of the buffet spread, which includes traditional Australian tucker and local delicacies.

Pioneer BBQ and Bar
Outback Pioneer Hotel,
Yulara Dr, Yulara
(08) 8957 7605
This relaxed dining area is popular with families. Buy your meat at the BBQ Bar and cook it yourself. Kids can join in singing and dancing with the live band that performs nightly.

Another Holiday Idea for the Northern Territory

Attend a real corroboree
Spend an incredible weekend living with a Jawoyn (pronounced Jar-win) Aboriginal community in a remote corner of Arnhem Land. Share indigenous foods, Dreamtime stories, dancing ceremonies, and didgeridoo-making at the Barunga Festival in June, www.barungafestival.com.au; or attend a traditional corroborree at a sacred site, joining in with dances, stories, and songs at the Walking with Spirits festival in late July or early August, www.djilpinarts.org.au/spirits/index.html. Bring your own camping equipment and a bit of food, and enjoy this special opportunity in a wilderness location.

QUEENSLAND

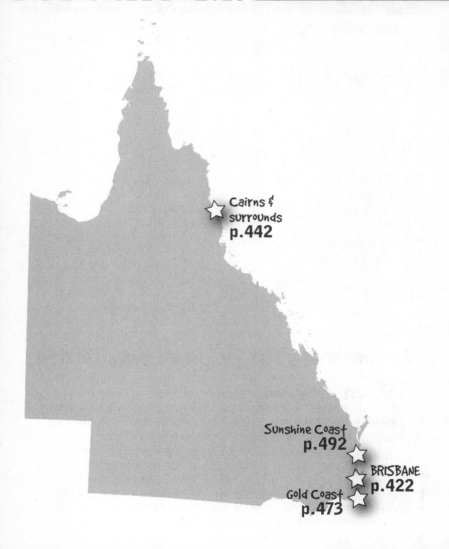

Cairns &
surrounds
p.442

Sunshine Coast
p.492

BRISBANE
p.422

Gold Coast
p.473

FAVOURITES

Buderim Ginger Factory – see who can catch the Gingerbread Man! *p. 495*

Gold Coast theme parks – stunt drivers, dancing dolphins and some of the biggest thrill rides in the world *p. 473*

Green Island – snorkel among the corals and brilliantly coloured fish of the Great Barrier Reef *p. 448*

Hartley's Crocodile Adventures – gasp at jumping crocodiles, and pat kangaroos *p. 461*

Mossman Gorge, Daintree National Park – creep through the rainforest jungle and look for 'dragons' *p. 466*

Queensland Museum South Bank – giant cockroaches, giant dinosaurs and a giant strangler fig *p. 425*

Tjapukai Aboriginal Cultural Park – taste bush tucker, learn to throw spears and boomerangs, and find out how to play the didgeridoo *p. 444*

TOP EVENTS

JUNE (EVEN YEARS) *One week of fabulous theatre and craft fun for under-9s at Brisbane's Out of the Box Festival* **p. 422**

JUNE *Count the roadside scarecrows on Tamborine Mountain and enjoy a weekend of family entertainment at the Scarecrow Festival* **p. 473**

OCT *Find out how to pan for gold and identify gemstones at the week-long Gympie Gold Rush Festival* **p. 492**

BRISBANE

Special events

The Ekka
Aug
www.ekka.com.au
Brisbane's annual show – known to locals as 'The Ekka' (Brisbane Exhibition) – runs for nine days. It's kids' heaven, with an animal-petting nursery, rides, showbags, live entertainment, competitions, pony grooming, milking demonstrations, parades and more.

Out of the Box Festival
June (even years)
www.outoftheboxfestival.com.au
This biennial week-long festival is produced by the Queensland Performing Arts Centre (QPAC) especially for under-9s and their families. The huge program includes workshops and performances – and most of them are free!

Panyiri Festival
May
www.paniyiri.com
Join the Greek community for three days of delicious food, Zorba dancing, amusement rides and games.

In town

Batty Boat Cruise
Departs from Mowbray Park Jetty,
East Brisbane
(07) 3221 0194
Late afternoon, warmer months
MID-RANGE

The cruise takes you down the
Brisbane River to Indooroopilly
Island. On the boat, you can
buy snacks, hear a running
commentary, and sometimes
meet an orphaned bat. At dusk,
thousands of black, grey-headed
and little red flying foxes take off
noisily from their roosts on the
island. You see them skim the
river to take sips of water and fly
off to feed on flowering trees in
the Brisbane suburbs.

Commissariat Store
115 William St, Brisbane
(07) 3221 4198;
www.queenslandhistory.org.au/
CommissariatStore.html
Tues–Fri
BUDGET

This little-known museum is a
piece of Brisbane history. It was
built by convicts and whatever
time you arrive there will be a
guide to tell you about convict
life and show you real leg irons
and other convict artefacts.

Ferry ride
13 1230;
*www.translink.com.au/howto_*
usetheferry.php
Hop on a CityCat or CityFerry
(which is smaller and makes
more stops) and catch a view of
Brisbane from the river. This is
a fun way to reach destinations
such as South Bank (see below).

MacArthur Museum Brisbane
Level 8, MacArthur Chambers,
201 Edward St, Brisbane
(07) 3211 7052;
www.macarthurmuseumbrisbane.org
Limited opening hours
BUDGET

This building was the
headquarters of the Allied Forces
in the South-West Pacific during
World War II. Stand in General
MacArthur's real office, which is
just the way it looked when he
was here in control, and listen
to his voice. See toys children
played with during the war
and the identity discs they had
to wear.

Queensland Police Museum

Queensland Police Headquarters,
200 Roma St, Brisbane
(07) 3364 6432;
www.police.qld.gov.au/aboutUs/
facilities/museum
Open weekdays
Suitable for ages 10+

FREE

Kids who enjoy a challenge (and something a bit grisly) love the simulated murder scene complete with clues to help them solve the crime. There are also displays on the Dog Squad and police investigative techniques.

Riverlife Adventure Centre

Naval Stores, Lower River Tce,
Kangaroo Point
(07) 3891 5766; www.riverlife.com.au
Minimum age 8 years

VARIOUS PRICES

This terrific centre, offering a range of outdoor activities, is located virtually in the heart of town! You can abseil or climb the nearby cliffs, hire bikes and ride through South Bank (*see facing page*), or hire kayaks to use on the Brisbane River. Family packages cover various combinations of activities and meals. Aboriginal Cultural Experiences are sometimes offered as well.

Roma Street Parkland

1 Parkland Blvd, Brisbane
(07) 3006 4545;
www.romastreetparkland.com

FREE

This huge, subtropical garden includes a playground, picnic and barbecue areas, water features and stepping stones. Before you go, download the kids' activity sheets from the website so the whole family can have fun together finding the answers to the discovery trails.

Having a barbecue at Roma Street Parkland, Brisbane

South Bank

Queensland Museum South Bank
Cnr Grey and Melbourne sts, South Brisbane
(07) 3840 7555; www.southbank.qm.qld.gov.au

FREE; EXTRA COST FOR SOME SPECIAL EVENTS AND EXHIBITIONS

This is a place where your kids will rush from one exhibit to another, excited to explore, then call you over to share their discoveries. They'll eagerly place insect slides – and their own hands – under a giant microscope to see them magnified on a computer screen. They'll make the parts of a car engine work by turning a handle. Their favourite, though, will probably be ENERGEX Playasaurus Place, where they can test the size of their own feet against giant dinosaur footprints, join in a dinosaur dance, and gaze up in awe at full-size replicas of prehistoric beasts.

INSIDER TIPS

■ The website has lots of interesting information and fun, educational games.

■ The wide-ranging exhibitions include a 'zoo' with animals from prehistoric times to the present (from the tiniest insect to the biggest whale), a transport display which includes the smallest boat ever to sail the world, and an exhibit about soldiers awarded the Victoria Cross which has a sound and light show on life in the trenches in World War I.

■ If you have 3–8 year olds, the best time to visit is a weekday morning for the *What's Inside?* activities, such as puppets, books and games, which are set up for littlies in various exhibition spaces.

■ There is a cafe open from mid-morning to mid-afternoon.

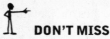

DON'T MISS

- The Inquiry Centre on Level 3, where you can touch specimens, see living animal exhibits – including the largest cockroaches in the world, a python and huge stick insects – and ask experts questions about animals, rocks, fossils and people.

- Sciencentre on the Lower Level of the same building (extra cost, *see* p. 428).

- The giant strangler fig in the Discover Queensland exhibit. How many creatures can you find hiding in it?

- The pictures of dinosaurs and insects with cut-out faces, where kids can pose for photos.

- The Story of Energy display in ENERGEX Playasaurus Place, where you can find out about energy sources and how to help the environment.

- The chance to test your strength, running speed, reflexes and throwing accuracy in the Body Challenge area in Body Zone.

FABULOUS FACTS

The life-size replica of tyrannosaurus rex in ENERGEX Playasaurus Place is not quite correct! It was made and shipped out from America in 1978. Since then, palaeontologists have discovered new information about this dinosaur. Look at the small, new model and see if you can pick the differences.

Kid Quest

*Play the ENERGEX Playasaurus Place Energy Game
and choose ways you could save energy and help
the environment.*

Aquativity

Next to Streets Beach at South Bank
South Bank Visitor Centre
(07) 3867 2051
Seasonal, open late in summer

FREE

This interactive water-play park with its fun water jets and fountains also has an environmental theme, and children can learn about native sea creatures, clouds, storms and the importance of rivers.

Children's Art Centre

Queensland Art Gallery and Gallery of Modern Art, Stanley Pl, South Bank (07) 3840 7303; www.qag.qld.gov.au/kids

FREE; EXTRA COST FOR SOME SPECIAL EXHIBITIONS

To encourage kids to interact with (and understand) the art on display in the galleries, there are special workshop areas with themed activities – anything from designing supermarket packaging to building paper houses. You'll find that kids are well catered for throughout the galleries with activity trails and engaging signage. If your kids are aged from 18 months to 4 years, don't miss Toddler Tuesday morning sessions with activities and movement based around art (bookings required). To find out about tours or special events aimed at older kids, phone ahead or check the website.

The Corner, State Library of Queensland

Cultural Centre, Stanley Pl, South Bank (07) 3840 7810; www.slq.qld.gov.au Suitable for under-8s 10am–3pm

FREE

In this wonderful space, kids can read books, play educational and imaginative games, or join an art team (10am–12pm) on a creative adventure, which might be in yoga, sculpture, cooking or song.

Queensland Maritime Museum

Southern end of South Bank Parklands, next to Goodwill Bridge (07) 3844 5361; www.maritimemuseum.com.au

BUDGET; EXTRA COST FOR DRY DOCK

The highlight for kids is climbing aboard *Diamantina* in the Dry Dock. This is a Royal Australian Navy frigate from 1945. Kids can explore the whole ship: bridge, engine room and the cramped quarters where the crew slept and ate.

Sciencentre, South Brisbane

South Bank Parklands, South Bank

Sciencentre

Lower Level, Queensland Museum
South Bank, cnr Grey and Melbourne sts,
South Brisbane
(07) 3840 7555;
www.southbank.qm.qld.gov.au/
sciencentre

MID-RANGE

There are levers to lift, tunnels to explore, puzzles to solve and lots of scientific surprises. Kid favourites are the bike that turns them into skeletons, the Wonky Walk challenge and the Spinning Chair.

South Bank Parklands

South Bank
South Bank Visitor Centre
(07) 3867 2051;
www.visitsouthbank.com.au

FREE

All the attractions of South Bank are linked by an oasis of beautiful parkland, fountains, eateries and performance spaces. Follow the winding, bougainvillea-draped arbour from one end to the other, or wander the riverside promenade. Look for the ornate Nepalese Peace Pagoda, buskers and street performers, the Rainforest Walk, weekend craft markets, and concerts in the Suncorp Piazza. Phone ahead or check the website for special events.

Streets Beach

Middle of South Bank Parklands
South Bank Visitor Centre (07) 3867 2051;
www.visitsouthbank.com.au

FREE ENTRY

This man-made beach in the middle of the city has become a landmark in its own right, with lifeguard towers and a stand of date palms. It has white sand, sparkling clean water without waves or dangerous rips, picnic areas, pebbled creeks for padding, and lifeguards patrolling seven days a week.

Wheel of Brisbane

Cultural Forecourt, Russell St,
South Bank
South Bank Visitor Centre
(07) 3867 2051;
www.southbankcorporation.com.au/
wheel-brisbane
Open from morning till late

MID-RANGE

This huge ferris wheel will take you to a height of 60 metres, providing a 360-degree view of the river and city. At night, it twinkles like fairyland with thousands of LED lights.

Suburbs

Alma Park Zoo
Alma Rd, Dakabin
(07) 3204 6566; www.almaparkzoo.com.au

MID-RANGE

As you wend your way through the bushland setting of this zoo, dry leaves crunch underfoot and the air is filled with eucalyptus scent and the ring of bird calls. You step into a walk-through enclosure to find kangaroos and wallabies lazing all around you on the ground. One kangaroo lumbers to its feet, and hops forward. Hastily, you pour some

Alma Park Zoo, Dakabin

animal feed into your kids' hands, and they squeal as the kangaroo grips their fingers with its little black paws and nuzzles the food out of their palms.

INSIDER TIPS

■ The zoo has all the Australian favourites, as well as many exotic animals including lemurs, monkeys, camels and red pandas.

■ Food for the kangaroos, deer and farm animals can be purchased at low cost.

■ The best time to visit is on a weekday when the zoo is quiet.

■ This is a small, manageable-sized zoo for kids to explore.

■ Raised viewing areas are provided for littlies.

■ There are picnic lawns and free barbecue facilities as well as a cafe.

■ You can book a special encounter with red pandas or marmosets, where you actually handfeed and pat the animals (high extra cost, minimum age 8 years).

■ Check the daily schedule online or when you arrive to make sure you don't miss any opportunities.

■ Pram hire is available, but it is advisable to book ahead.

DON'T MISS

- The Friendship Farm where kids can pat and feed the animals.

- The keeper talks throughout the day, especially the koala presentation (twice daily) where you can line up afterwards to pat a koala.

- The Koala, Snake and Crocodile Experiences (extra cost), which follow the keeper presentations. You have a cuddle (yes, you can even cuddle a baby crocodile), and receive a photo as a memento. Pre-purchase these encounters at Palm Cafe when you arrive.

- The Creepy Crawly Display with giant burrowing cockroaches, rainforest tarantulas and giant millipedes.

FABULOUS FACTS

The black-capped capuchins you see at the zoo are the only monkeys that naturally make use of 'tools' such as stones to open fruit and nuts. They come from the Amazon Basin area of South America where they are hunted for food.

Kid Quest
Which animals have finger prints, just like humans?
See pp. 640–4 for the answer

Brisbane Botanic Gardens Mount Coot-tha
Mount Coot-tha Rd, Toowong
(07) 3403 2532; www.brisbane.qld.gov.au
FREE

You all set off on the Hide 'n' Seek Children's Trail, peering eagerly into the undergrowth. One child lets out a shout, spotting the replica panda hidden inside the clump of bamboo, then asks eagerly what they have to find next. It's a race now to the Dragon Bridge to look for dragons…well, dragonflies anyway. The trail brochure says that 3 million years ago, dragonflies grew as big as your outstretched arms. The kids zoom off, pretending to be giant insects. A moment later they are crouched quietly, examining the fern frond embedded in a fossil rock and comparing it with the living king fern growing beside the creek.

INSIDER TIPS

- You can download the Hide 'n' Seek Children's Trail from the website or pick one up in the garden. The trail leads you into the shady Exotic Rainforest.

- Meals are available in the gardens at either a fully licensed restaurant or a cafe.

DON'T MISS

- The Bonsai House (limited opening hours). Kids are fascinated by the tiny fig trees, conifers, camellias, azaleas and maples.

- The adjoining Mount Coot-tha Forest, where you can take a walk to the J. C. Slaughter Falls.

- The picturesque Japanese garden with its ponds and mysterious winding paths.

- The Sir Thomas Brisbane Planetarium (*see* p. 433).

- The self-guided Aboriginal Plant Trail (download leaflet), which teaches you the hidden uses of the plants you see.

- The Fragrant Plant and Herb Garden, where kids may gently touch the plants to release and inhale the scents.

FABULOUS FACTS

Some of the plants you see on the Aboriginal Plant Trail are poisonous if eaten, but Aboriginal people have discovered ways to make them edible. The seeds of the candlenut tree can be eaten after they are roasted in a fire, but the chestnut-like seeds of the black bean tree need a long process of pounding, roasting and soaking in running water before they can be safely consumed.

Kid Quest

See how many birds, lizards, turtles and eels you can find in the Bamboo Grove Lagoon.

Lone Pine Koala Sanctuary

Jesmond Rd, Fig Tree Pocket
(07) 3378 1366; www.koala.net
Open daily including Christmas Day;
closed Anzac Day morning

MID-RANGE

A flock of loudly screeching rainbow lorikeets descends from the skies, and the kids laugh and squeal as the mass of coloured birds eagerly pecks food from their outstretched hands. This is quite a contrast to the peaceful time you have just enjoyed with a huggable, sleepy koala.

Lone Pine offers a multitude of opportunities to interact with animals. Apart from koalas and lorikeets, you can hold owls, eagles, snakes and baby freshwater crocodiles, cuddle baby chickens and guinea pigs, and handfeed kangaroos, wallabies and emus.

INSIDER TIPS

■ Kangaroo food is available for purchase (low cost).

■ An interesting way to reach the sanctuary is along the Brisbane River on a Mirimar Wildlife Cruise (high cost), which departs from the centre of town. You pass good examples of the old 'Queenslander' style timber houses and Indooroopilly Island with its fruit bat colony squabbling and flapping in the trees. See www.mirimar.com for more information.

■ If you want to cuddle a koala, do this early in the day to avoid the queues.

■ Some animal encounters are only at particular times, so check the daily schedule.

DON'T MISS

■ The opportunity to cuddle a koala. You can do this any time during the day for free, but if you want photos (even with your own camera) there is an extra cost.

■ Feeding the catfish in the Brisbane River (October–March). Purchase fish food at the sanctuary then head for the jetty at 11am, when crowds of catfish turn up, mouths gaping for food.

- The eastern water dragons (a type of large lizard) that wander freely around the grounds.

- The entertaining and informative sheepdog show, held three times daily.

- The birds of prey show, twice daily, where you get very close to these spectacular creatures.

 FABULOUS FACTS

Koalas are among the most famous of Australian animals and are known for their habit of sitting in eucalypt trees where they do nothing but eat and sleep. Despite their widespread notoriety, koalas are only found in small areas on Australia's eastern coast, and are very particular about the type of eucalypt leaves they eat. These leaves also provide their drinking needs, but do not supply much energy, which is why koalas sleep most of the day.

Kid Quest

Is it true that lorikeets have hair on their tongues?

See pp. 640–4 for the answer

Australian Woolshed

148 Samford Rd, Ferny Hills
(07) 3872 1100;
www.auswoolshed.com.au

VARIOUS PRICES

This recreated outback sheep station is a popular tour group destination. You can pat animals (including koalas) and bottle-feed lambs. There are four shows daily where you can view sheep shearing and see sheep dogs at work. There are also water slides (open in summer), bungee trampolines and minigolf.

Sir Thomas Brisbane Planetarium

Brisbane Botanic Gardens
Mount Coot-tha, Mount Coot-tha Rd,
Toowong
(07) 3403 2578;
www.brisbane.qld.gov.au/planetarium
Closed Mon, check show times other days

MID-RANGE

During the day you can see shows about the universe, including fun kids' shows with titles such as *Secret of the Cardboard Rocket*, and on Saturday nights you can join an astronomer for a live viewing and explanation of the night sky (suitable for children aged 6 years and over).

Note: this city, as well as the planetarium, is named after Sir Thomas Brisbane, a Governor of New South Wales in the 1820s and an eminent astronomer who helped map the southern skies.

Connect with Nature
Various locations
1300 130 372; www.derm.qld.gov.au/
*parks_and_forests/activities_in_parks_*
and_forests/index.html
Weekends, public and school holidays
VARIOUS PRICES
Queensland Parks and Wildlife Service runs children's activities, family discovery walks and theatre performances in parks around Brisbane. Phone ahead or check the website to find out what's on offer.

Daisy Hill Koala Centre
Daisy Hill Rd, Daisy Hill Conservation Park, Daisy Hill
(07) 3299 1032;
www.derm.qld.gov.au/parks/daisy-hill
FREE
This is a chance to see koalas up close (though you are not allowed to touch them). There are displays about a koala's life cycle and how animals in Australia have changed since the time of the dinosaurs. Climb the treetop tower to spot koalas in the adjacent conservation park. Better still, visit the park and look for red-necked wallabies as well as koalas, have a picnic, and take a walk along the short trails and read the interesting interpretive signs.

Enchanted Forest Park
Via a tiny driveway off Frasers Rd, Ashgrove
www.ourbrisbane.com/suburbs/north/
enchanted-forest-park
FREE
The playground equipment here includes a fort reached by a spider web, a small-size shop front, and a toadstool that tells stories! The under-10s will relish this opportunity for climbing and imaginative play.

Iceworld Olympic Ice Rinks
1179 Beaudesert Rd, Acacia Ridge
(07) 3277 7563
2304 Sandgate Rd, Boondall
(07) 3865 1694; www.iceworld.com.au
Various public times
MID-RANGE
Burn off a bit of energy and have fun. Phone ahead or check the website for public skating times.

Kingston Park Raceway

20 Mudgee St, Kingston
(07) 3826 2222;
www.kingstonpark.com.au
Minimum age 5 years

VARIOUS PRICES

Claiming to be the largest and most technically advanced go-karting and amusement centre in Australia, this venue offers a variety of go-karts and tracks so even kids as young as 5 years can drive (in a dual cart with an adult). There are also amusement rides and computer games.

Newstead House

Newstead Park, Breakfast Creek Rd, Newstead
(07) 3216 1846 or 1800 061 846;
www.newsteadhouse.com.au
Check opening hours

BUDGET

Brisbane's oldest residence has been beautifully restored in full Victorian-era splendour. Look for the collection of olden-days dolls displayed in the haunted bedroom. Newstead Park has picnic areas and a fabulous Alice-in-Wonderland themed playspace for kids.

Rocks Riverside Park

Counihan Rd, Seventeen Mile Rocks
www.brisbane.qld.gov.au

FREE

This is the largest riverside park in Brisbane with plenty of room for running around. There are big sandpits with toddler toys, a water-play zone, a great climbing web and flying fox, a bushwalking trail and barbecues. Note: there is not much shade.

Tinchi Tamba Wetlands

Wyampa Rd, Bald Hills
www.our.brisbane.com/suburbs/local-guide-6

FREE

Keep an eye out for kangaroos, crabs, frogs, lizards, and unusual birds, some of which migrate all the way from Alaska. You can also enjoy great playground equipment, eat a picnic and go fishing in the river.

Walkabout Creek Wildlife Centre

South D'Aguilar National Park, 60 Mount Nebo Rd, The Gap
(07) 3300 2558;
www.walkaboutcreek.com.au/wildlife.htm

BUDGET

Meet a platypus, wombat, rainforest birds, reptiles and nocturnal marsupials in glassed enclosures in the centre, then take a walk in the national park to see if you can find any animals in the wild. Look for short-necked turtles by the creek, large lace monitor lizards in the trees, and listen for the *tink-tink* of bellbirds.

Moreton Bay

Brisbane Whale Watching

Depart from the jetty at Redcliffe
(07) 3880 0477;
www.brisbanewhalewatching.com.au
Daily Jun–Nov, boarding time 9.30am
HIGH COST, INCLUDES MEALS

As you cruise the clear waters of Moreton Bay in a high-speed catamaran, you'll sight dolphins, green turtles and loggerhead turtles. Best of all, there's a chance of a close-up encounter with humpback whales. The cruise returns mid-afternoon.

Moreton Island

40 km offshore from Brisbane
Moreton Island Visitor Centre
1300 667 386; www.derm.qld.gov.au/
parks/moreton-island
VARIOUS PRICES

Most of this huge sand island is a national park. Sandboard down the dunes, swim in the Blue Lagoon, visit a historic lighthouse, or look for humpback whales (June–November), dugong and shorebirds. For a chance to handfeed wild dolphins, stay overnight at Tangalooma Resort, 1300 652 250; www.tangalooma.com. Note: the only way to get around is by taking a tour, or bringing or hiring a four-wheel drive vehicle.

Ferry operators that service the island are:
- Micat car and passenger barge, Lytton, (07) 3909 3333; www.moretonventure.com
- Tangalooma Flyer passenger ferry, Pinkenba (07) 3637 2000 or 1300 652 250; www.tangalooma.com

North Stradbroke Island

Reached by water taxi or ferry
from Cleveland
Visitor centre (07) 3415 3044;
www.stradbroketourism.com
VARIOUS PRICES

Swim in freshwater lakes, play on perfect beaches, take a four-wheel drive eco-tour, go fishing, bushwalking or snorkelling, or watch for whales, dolphins and other marine life. You might decide to stay for a holiday instead of just visiting.

St Helena Island Tour

A B Sea Cruises, Manly
(07) 3893 1240;
www.sthelenaisland.com.au
Check tour times

HIGH COST, INCLUDES MEALS

This is a wonderful immersive journey into Australia's convict past. Travel by catamaran to see real old prison buildings on St Helena Island and take part in a fascinating re-enactment of convict life. Take a day tour or late-night ghost tour.

Settlement Cove Lagoon

Redcliffe Pde, Redcliffe
www.moretonbay.qld.gov.au/discover.
aspx?id=16353

FREE

This is a water-play park patrolled by lifeguards. It has a large lagoon-style swimming pool, waterfalls, slides, ship-themed play equipment and a fenced toddler pool with fun things that squirt and drip. Bring a picnic or head for one of the many cafes over the road.

Snorkel Moreton Bay

Departs from Redcliffe Jetty, Redcliffe
(07) 3880 4444;
www.dolphinwild.com.au
Departs every morning

HIGH COST, LUNCH INCLUDED

The fun includes a ride in a boom-net, playing on a perfect island beach, a guided snorkel tour among coral and sub-tropical fish (some fish are tame enough to eat from your hands), and a chance to see dolphins, huge turtles, dugongs and humpback whales (June–November). Tours return mid-afternoon.

Wynnum Foreshore

Off Wynnum Esplanade, Wynnum

FREE

You can build castles on the white sands of Pandanus Beach, splash around in the Water Park, climb and slide in great playgrounds, paddle in the Wynnum Wading Pool, or wander a mangrove boardwalk and spot crabs in the mud.

Wading pool at Wynnum Foreshore, Wynnum

Ipswich

Children's Gallery
Ipswich Art Gallery, d'Arcy Doyle Place,
Nicholas St, Ipswich
(07) 3813 9222;
www.ipswichartgallery.qld.gov.au
FREE

This gallery runs a wonderful program of workshops for kids of all ages – from tie-dyeing T-shirts to creating artwork to eat. Some activities incur a small charge for materials. Phone ahead or check the website to find out what's on.

Ipswich River monsters
River Heart Parklands,
via Roseberry Pde, Ipswich
FREE

This must be the most carefully hidden tourist sight in Australia. As darkness falls, and the security lights come on, head down the path to the river – and don't tell the kids what they are about to see! Position yourselves on the second viewing platform and look down. Out of the dark water, endearing, mythical River Creatures will suddenly appear, swimming in the river. Note: look for the fun little statues and waterfalls in the parklands as well.

Queens Park
Goleby Ave, Ipswich
(07) 3810 6666
Seasonal hours for Nature Centre
FREE; ENTRY TO NATURE CENTRE BY DONATION

Play in a terrific, shaded playground, wander a Japanese garden, and visit a walk-through aviary. See wombats, brush-tailed rock wallabies, and bilbies in the Nature Centre.

The Workshops Rail Museum
North Street, North Ipswich
(07) 3432 5100;
www.theworkshops.qm.qld.gov.au
MID-RANGE

This is a fabulous place for kids. There are levers to pull, a workshop filled with steam and sparks to visit, mini vehicles to ride, the largest model railway set in Queensland to watch, simulators to drive, full-size trains to gape at, and much more!

The Workshops Rail Museum, North Ipswich

Day trips

Caboolture Historical Village

280 Beerburrum Rd, Caboolture
(07) 5495 4581;
www.historicalvillage.com.au
50 km/1 hr north
Closes mid-afternoon

BUDGET

As you explore the restored buildings of this village, you might come across a blacksmith, wood-turner or potter at work, or see gems being polished. There is usually more activity on weekdays when school groups visit.

Caboolture Warplane Museum

Hangar, 104 McNaught Rd, Caboolture
(07) 5499 1144;
www.caboolturewarplanemuseum.com
50 km/1 hr north
Closes mid-afternoon

BUDGET

Kids who like planes will love the flight simulator, the restored World War II aircraft, and the displays depicting famous aviation disasters.

Glow worm Caves

Cedar Creek Estate, 104–144 Hartley Rd,
North Tamborine
(07) 5545 1666 or 1300 CEDAR CREEK;
www.cedarcreekestate.com.au
70 km/1 hr south
Entry by tour, half-hourly

MID-RANGE

Your tour begins in a display cave, complete with artificially created stalagmites, stalactites, and water features. You watch an audiovisual display about glow worms then progress to another cave specially built to house them. All around you in the darkness is a fairyland of tiny, glowing creatures. Cedar Creek Estate is also a vineyard and winery, so adults might like to sample the wines.

See also Gold Coast (p. 473), Sunshine Coast (p. 492)

Accommodation

Brisbane City YHA

392 Upper Roma St, Brisbane
(07) 3236 1004;
www.yha.com.au/hostels/qld/brisbane-surrounds/brisbane-city

BUDGET

Family rooms in this backpacker hostel have double beds, bunks and private bathrooms. Kids enjoy the relaxed atmosphere, the company of young people, a rooftop swimming pool and games room.

Brisbane Holiday Village

10 Holmead Rd, Eight Mile Plains
(07) 3341 6133;
www.brisbaneholidayvillage.com.au

BUDGET TO MID-RANGE

This holiday village is just ten minutes drive from the city centre. Accommodation options range from campsites to five-star, self-contained cabins with two bathrooms. Facilities include two swimming lagoons, minigolf, a Temple of the Terrors play area, toddler playground, tennis court and cafe.

Mantra South Bank Brisbane

161 Grey Street, South Bank
(07) 3305 2500 or 1300 554 632;
www.mantra.com.au

HIGH COST

Fabulously located next to the delights of South Bank (*see* p. 425), you can have a luxury, self-contained apartment with two bedrooms and a balcony. There is a heated lap pool on site. Note: both rooms have double beds; separate beds for the kids are available on request.

Oaks Charlotte Towers

128 Charlotte St, Brisbane
(07) 3027 8400 or 1300 663 477;
www.oakshotelsresorts.com/oaks-charlotte-towers

MID-RANGE

Enjoy the convenience of a two-bedroom apartment, complete with kitchen, laundry and balcony, in the heart of the city. Guests have use of a sundeck and plunge pool. Note: both rooms have double beds; separate beds for the kids are available on request.

Places to eat

Chinatown
Around Ann St, Fortitude Valley
You will find lots of atmosphere and choice here, and it is not just Chinese food on offer – there are Thai, Malaysian, Vietnamese, Cambodian, Japanese and Laotian restaurants as well.

Morgans Seafood
Bird of Passage Pde, Scarborough
(07) 3203 5744;
www.morganseafood.com.au
Gaze out over the harbour as you eat seafood straight from the boats. For easy dining, buy takeaway to eat in the outdoor tropical garden or the playground over the road. On Thursday nights, indulge in a seafood smorgasbord with kids' prices – bookings essential.

South Bank Parklands
South Bank
South Bank Visitor Centre
(07) 3867 2051;
www.visitsouthbank.com.au
There are lots of places to eat in this lovely setting (*see* p. 428), and you are likely to find ibis (big native water birds) running around your table.

CAIRNS & SURROUNDS

Cairns is 1700 kilometres north-west of Brisbane and has its own international airport; Port Douglas, another popular holiday base, is a further 70 kilometres north

Best time to visit is dry season (May–Nov); Dec–Apr is hot and rainy

WARNINGS Wear protection from the sun, even in winter. Venomous stingers (box jellyfish) are present in the sea Oct–June. Cyclone season is Jan–Mar.

HIGHLIGHTS

Cairns Tropical Zoo *p. 442*

Hartley's Crocodile Adventures *p. 461*

Green Island *p. 448*

Low Isles *p. 450*

Mossman Gorge, Daintree National Park *p. 466*

Rainforestation Nature Park *p. 453*

Skyrail *p. 455*

Tjapukai Aboriginal Cultural Park *p. 444*

Wildlife Habitat *p. 463*

Around town

Cairns Tropical Zoo
Captain Cook Hwy, Palm Cove (27 km north of Cairns)
(07) 4055 3669; www.cairnstropicalzoo.com.au
HIGH COST, TICKETS VALID FOR THREE DAYS

Cairns Tropical Zoo, Palm Cove

The kids stare transfixed through the mesh of the fence as the crocodile keeper jiggles a hunk of meat. You can all see the large shadow of a 5-metre crocodile gliding through the water towards its keeper. Suddenly, the large beast erupts out of the pool, and snaps at the meat. Your kids gasp as the keeper backs away, holding the prize higher instead of letting go. He keeps backing as the crocodile advances, but at last he throws the meat into the crocodile's gaping jaws, and the beast pauses to eat. Bursting into relieved, excited chatter, your kids haul you away to the next exhibit.

INSIDER TIPS

- You can purchase tickets that combine entry to this zoo with Hartley's Crocodile Adventures (*see* p. 461) and Kuranda Koala Gardens (*see* p. 459).

- This is a small, manageable zoo; allow two to three hours for your visit.

- Most of the animals are more active in the morning.

- Check the daily schedule so you don't miss any shows.

- There is a cafe with views of the zoo's lovely tropical gardens.

- Koala cuddles are available (extra cost).

DON'T MISS

- The kangaroo enclosure, where you can pat and handfeed tame eastern grey kangaroos.

- The birds of prey walk-through aviary. Some of the birds, such as tawny frogmouths, are masters of disguise, so move slowly and see how many you can spot.

- The free-flight bird show, which includes the wedge-tailed eagle, the barn owl and several cockatoos.

- The snake show, where you might get a chance to pat the stars!

- The crocodile show, when the keeper enters the enclosure to feed a huge, 300-kilogram 'saltie'.

FABULOUS FACTS

One of the birds on display is the southern cassowary, an endangered resident of the rainforests. These birds are famous for vicious behaviour, as they have killed several people with their knife-like claws. Despite their attacking abilities, they are not large meat-eaters. They feed mainly on fruit, occasionally picking up a small mammal, bird or lizard. The purpose for the hard 'casque' on their heads is not known!

Kid Quest

Find out which bird of prey is capable of detecting the heartbeat of a mouse at a distance of 10 metres!
See pp. 640–4 for the answer

Tjapukai Aboriginal Cultural Park, Caravonica

Tjapukai Aboriginal Cultural Park

Cairns Western Arterial Rd, Caravonica (13 km north of Cairns)
(07) 4042 9900;
www.tjapukai.com.au

VARIOUS PRICES

All eyes are on your Aboriginal guide, poised with a boomerang in his hand. Against the backdrop of creek and bush, his bare, muscled arm striped with traditional paint, he is a timeless figure. The weapon flies out of his hand and loops through the air. He catches it with a grin, and your kids' eyes light up. Now it is their turn. They have already had a go at throwing spears at a kangaroo (painted on a haystack), and now they are going to try to make a boomerang return.

INSIDER TIPS

■ Tjapukai Aboriginal Cultural Park works like a theme park – you move from zone to zone for different experiences. Keep an eye on the timetable so you reach each zone in time for a scheduled show.

■ Allow at least half a day for your visit.

■ The restaurant buffet becomes crowded with tour groups at lunchtime. Plan to eat early or bring your own food.

■ Shows are performed in both English and the Tjapukai language.

■ The cheapest way to visit is to drive yourself and bring lunch, but there are various packages available that include transfers from Cairns and the buffet lunch (all high cost).

■ Dinner shows are also offered through Tjapukai by Night (*see* PLACES TO EAT p. 470).

■ Tjapukai Aboriginal Cultural Park is located in a beautiful rainforest setting, so in parts you will be walking on rough ground. Wear comfortable walking shoes.

■ Buying goods from the gallery shop supports the local Aboriginal community.

■ The park is adjacent to the base of Skyrail (*see* p. 455).

DON'T MISS

■ The free extra activities for kids – paint your own boomerangs, or decorate message stones for good luck and protection.

■ The Cultural Village – take lessons in spear and boomerang throwing, taste bush tucker and find out how to play the didgeridoo.

■ The Dance Theatre performance – learn how to move like a brolga (a native dancing bird) or a kangaroo.

■ The Magic Space – have your face painted in traditional style.

- The Creation Theatre, where you are immersed in the dreamtime story of the Tjapukai people through live performance and holograms.

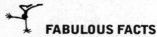

FABULOUS FACTS

In the 19th and 20th centuries, Europeans tried to extinguish a culture that had survived for tens of thousands of years. Children were removed from Aboriginal homes to be brought up by European missionaries. They were banned from speaking their language or learning from Aboriginal elders. However, local Indigenous culture was not lost, and you can experience some of its riches at Tjapukai Aboriginal Cultural Park.

Kid Quest

Learn some Tjapukai words.

Cairns Esplanade and Lagoon

The Esplanade, Cairns
www.cairnsesplanade.com.au
Open early till late; closed Wed morning
FREE

The lagoon is a vast, salt-water swimming pool patrolled by lifeguards. It's free from the stingers (box jellyfish) and saltwater crocodiles that are found in the sea around this area. The Esplanade is a venue for Saturday markets and live concerts. There are sandy shores, grassed areas and a boardwalk. Use the telescope provided to watch seabirds – there's also an information board to help with identification.

Cairns Wildlife Dome

On top of Reef Hotel Casino,
cnr Wharf and Abbott sts, Cairns
(07) 4031 7250;
www.cairnsdome.com.au
MID-RANGE

This is a great opportunity to meet a few Australian animals right in the heart of town – and undercover! Tickets are valid for five days, so if you're staying in town you can make full use of the entertainment on offer. There's a walk-in aviary, free shows and tours throughout the day, and the chance to have a photo with a koala (extra cost).

Flecker Botanic Gardens and Centenary Lakes

Collins Ave, Edge Hill
(07) 4032 3200;
www.botanicfriendscairns.com.au
FREE

See spectacular and weird exotic plants from around the world, look for turtles in the water, learn about rainforest plants along the Gondwanan Heritage Trail, visit a traditional shelter in the Aboriginal plant-use garden, or follow the Red Arrow Trail and look for brush turkeys in the rainforest of Mount Whitfield (pick up a trail booklet from the shop in the main gardens). Note: you will need insect repellent around the wet areas of the gardens and lakes.

Muddy's Playground

The Esplanade, Cairns
www.cairnsesplanade.com.au/
SwimPaddlePlay
Open early till late; closed Tues morning
FREE

This playground for under-10s features a water-play area with pumps, channels and jumping jets, and a dry area with a flying fox, sound chimes, a rope bridge, slides, playhouses, storytelling areas and puzzle games. Bring a picnic or buy a snack at the cafe.

Reef Teach

2nd Floor, Mainstreet Arcade,
85 Lake St, Cairns
(07) 4031 7794;
www.reefteach.wordpress.com
Tues–Sat evenings, except public holidays
MID-RANGE

Learn all sorts of amazing facts about the reef, and touch a wide range of corals and other marine specimens, including some dangerous (dead) ones. This is a fabulous introduction to the Great Barrier Reef.

Royal Flying Doctor Service Visitor Centre

1 Junction St, Edge Hill
(07) 4053 5687
Closed Sun
BUDGET

The highlight here is being able to climb aboard a decommissioned Royal Flying Doctor Service plane complete with equipment. Kids can imagine being pilots, patients or doctors involved in an emergency dash.

Great Barrier Reef___

Green Island

45 min east of Cairns by fast catamaran
Depart from Reef Fleet Terminal,
end of Spence St, Cairns
(07) 4044 9944;
www.greatadventures.com.au

HIGH COST

Your kids jump off the snorkelling boat, still babbling with excitement about the sights they have seen: spiky corals with long, delicate branches, entrancing hawksbill turtles, flashes of brightly-coloured fish, round corals in bunches like flowers, and schools of silvery fish. One of them eagerly waves the underwater camera, thrilled to have captured so many wonderful images. The other one is talking about a huge grey shape – was it a stingray or maybe a shark? But it's not long before the other delights of the island claim their attention – the soft, white sand to play in, the rainforest to explore, the swimming pool ...

Snorkelling around Green Island

INSIDER TIPS

- Green Island is the most accessible place for exploring the Great Barrier Reef.

- Having an island for a base is ideal for families because you can alternate water activities with sand play and rainforest walks. This is the only coral cay on the reef with rainforest growing on it.

- The best way to view the reef is to take a snorkelling trip by boat (extra cost). It is possible to step straight off the beach to snorkel, however snorkelling areas are not patrolled by lifeguards (swimming areas are patrolled).

- The cruise ticket may include snorkel equipment, wetsuits, snorkelling trips or glass-bottomed boat tours, depending on the package you choose.

- Great Adventures (the main cruise operator on the island) operates three departure times to the island daily, which means you can go out for just half a day if you wish.

- There is a hire facility on the beach for canoes, beach umbrellas, and volleyball equipment.

- The optional extras of scuba diving and underwater walking tours are restricted to those aged 12 years and over.

- There is a range of eating places on the island.

- Accommodation is available on the island at the luxury Green Island Resort (*see* ACCOMMODATION p. 472). If you're on a Great Adventures cruise you are entitled to use the resort's swimming pool.

DON'T MISS

- The Great Barrier Reef! This is your main reason for visiting Green Island. Kids who are not old enough to swim in the sea and snorkel can view the reef from a glass-bottomed boat.

- The easy, self-guided walk around the island. You can download information brochures from the website in several languages, or pick up a brochure at the information desk in the resort.

- The many different birds. In the forest, look for emerald doves or buff banded rails foraging among leaves on the ground, and listen for the cooing of Torres Strait pigeons. On the shore, watch for seabirds diving for fish.

- The underwater observatory (extra cost) located at the end of the jetty. It was a world-first when it opened in 1954. Look through the portholes for a deeper view of the sea without going scuba diving.

- Marineland Melanesia (extra cost), located next to the resort. See turtles and huge saltwater crocodiles and hold baby crocodiles; (07) 4051 4032; www.marinelandgreenisland.com.

FABULOUS FACTS

Green Island is located on the famous Great Barrier Reef, a World Heritage area. It is the most extensive coral reef in the world, and the only living thing on earth that is visible from space. There are more than 400 different types of coral on the reef, over 1500 species of tropical fish, 200 types of birds, and 20 types of reptiles.

Kid Quest

Where does the name Green Island come from?
Clue: it has nothing to do with the vegetation.
See pp. 640–4 for the answer

Low Isles

Depart from Marina, Wharf St, Port Douglas
(07) 4099 4772 or 1800 085 674; www.sailawayportdouglas.com
Departs every morning for a full-day trip

HIGH COST, INCLUDES LUNCH

You look at the white sails of the catamaran billowing, and the kids laughing with excitement as they ride in the nets, and you know you are going to have a fun day. On the island, the kids are keen to pull on their wetsuits and follow your guide into the sea. They grab hold of the coloured 'noodles' to help them float, and kick off happily. A huge green turtle swims past, right underneath you, and moments later you are all gazing down with awe on the wonderful corals, giant clams and colourful fish of the reef.

INSIDER TIPS

- The trip is done by sail, and takes about an hour each way, depending on the wind.

- When the catamaran reaches Low Isles you are ferried to shore by smaller boats and are then based on land for the next few hours, which means kids have room to run around. There is a heritage walk and a lighthouse on the island.

- The sand on the island is quite sharp underfoot and can get very hot, so make sure you all have shoes that are suitable for keeping on the whole time.

- Nervous swimmers are well looked after by the guide, and non-swimmers have the option of a glass-bottomed boat tour instead of snorkelling.

- Sailaway takes a maximum of 30 people, so attention is very personalised. An alternative is Quicksilver Cruises, which takes larger groups to the island, is family-friendly and offers a guided walk of the beach with a marine biologist; (07) 4087 2100; www.quicksilver-cruises.com/wavedancer.htm

- Low Isles is less spectacular than the outer reef, but a trip to an island is often a better option for kids than snorkelling off boats or a pontoon for a few hours (*see* OUTER REEF PONTOON TOURS p. 452).

- Be aware that soft drinks are not included in your package and will cost extra.

- Wetsuits are provided. They are an optional extra out of season, but they are a good idea all year round as they stop you from getting cold, help with buoyancy, and protect against stingers (box jellyfish) and sunburn.

- Snorkel gear is included, but kids sometimes prefer their own swimming goggles to larger masks. If possible, buy snorkels and masks beforehand (look for cheap ones in discount shops), so they can practise in a bath or pool before the trip.

DON'T MISS

- The morning snorkel led by a guide. Sailaway is the first cruise boat to reach the island each morning, so take advantage of this opportunity to snorkel in clearer water before the next (much larger) tour group arrives. Your guide takes you to the best viewing places and provides a wonderful commentary.

- Swimming with the sharks after lunch! Once the meal is over, you head out in a glass-bottomed boat and drop the food scraps into the water. This starts a feeding frenzy of reef sharks (not dangerous!) and large fish, and you are welcome to hop in and swim amongst them. Non-swimmers have fun too, watching the fish and sharks mill around the boat.

- The chance to help sail – sometimes the captain lets the kids help, so make sure you ask.

■ The walk around the island. Interpretive signs explain the history of the island including what it was like to live in the lighthouse, and the ecosystems of the beach, mangroves and headland.

 FABULOUS FACTS

Low Isles, just 15 kilometres north-east of Port Douglas, is one of the closest points to land in the Great Barrier Reef. In the late 1920s, it was the site for the first detailed study of a coral reef anywhere in the world. The information gathered in that study is used today to measure human impact on the Great Barrier Reef.

Kid Quest

Have a look at pictures of reef fish and coral before your visit. How many you can spot and recognise?

Outer Reef Pontoon Tours

90 min east of Cairns or Port Douglas by fast catamaran
Depart from Reef Fleet Terminal, end of Spence St, Cairns, or from Marina Mirage, Port Douglas

HIGH COST, LUNCH INCLUDED

Various operators conduct full-day tours to the outer reef where you have the best chance of viewing high quality coral and meeting a diversity of marine life. From a floating platform with safety rails, you can snorkel (with or without a guide) in sheltered coral lagoons, or non-swimmers can view the reef from semi-submersible reef viewers, glass-bottomed boats or underwater observatories. Operators include:

■ Sunlover Reef Cruises
(07) 4050 1333 or
1800 810 512;
www.sunlover.com.au

■ Reef Magic Cruises
(07) 4031 1588 or
1300 666 700;
www.reefmagiccruises.com

■ Quicksilver Cruises
(07) 4087 2100;
www.quicksilver-cruises.com

Sprint and Snorkel

Depart from end of the slipway jetty,
Wharf St, Port Douglas
(07) 4099 3175 or 0408 870 965;
www.reefsprinter.com.au
Departs three times daily
Minimum age 5 years
HIGH COST

An exhilarating speedboat ride takes you to the reef in 15 minutes. Moored at the Low Isles, you can snorkel (gear provided) or view the reef from a glass-bottomed boat. You return a couple of hours later.

Hinterland

Rainforestation Nature Park
Kennedy Hwy, Kuranda
(07) 4085 5008; www.rainforest.com.au
Various prices

The Army Duck (*see* FABULOUS FACTS p. 454) rattles and bumps over the uneven ground of the ancient rainforest. Suddenly a river appears between the arching fronds of tall tree ferns. The kids clutch the metal sides of the truck, their eyes wide. Is the Army Duck really going to drive into the water? It rumbles forward. Will it float? Yes! It glides over the murky water like a boat, the engines turning the propellers. The guide points out a snapping turtle sunning itself on a log, then you chug into a narrow creek where overhanging branches crowd over your heads.

INSIDER TIPS

■ During the Army Duck Tour, your guide provides information about the animals and plants around you.

■ The Army Duck Tour departs hourly on the hour, and commentary sheets are available in many languages.

■ There are several attractions at Rainforestation (*see* DON'T MISS p. 454). You can purchase tickets for these separately, or buy a package.

DON'T MISS

- The traditional Aboriginal dances performed three times daily against the rainforest backdrop.

- The Dreamtime walks where you watch spear throwing, learn how to throw a boomerang, and discover other secrets of Aboriginal culture.

- The Koala and Wildlife Park where you can handfeed free-roaming kangaroos, and meet many other Australian favourites. There are talks throughout the day, and opportunities to hold koalas and baby crocodiles (extra cost).

- The Tropical Fruit Orchard, where you can see over 40 different types of exotic tropical fruit growing, including jackfruit, paw paw, lychees, mango, cocoa and star apple. You can taste them at the Tropical Treats Juice Bar.

FABULOUS FACTS

The Army Ducks at Rainforestation Nature Park are old army vehicles. They were built during World War II to help ferry men and cargo between warships and beaches. The designers took normal General Motors trucks, substituted waterproof hulls for standard bodywork, and added propellers and rudders for operating in the water.

Kid Quest

Why do the Army Ducks have their steering wheels on the 'wrong' side?

See pp. 640–4 for the answer

Skyrail

Travels between Caravonica (13 km north of Cairns) and Kuranda

(07) 4038 1555; www.skyrail.com.au

Check timetable

HIGH COST

Initially, the kids are more fascinated by the cable car than the view, peering up to see the mechanism, and pointing at gondolas travelling in the opposite direction. But as you float out over the rainforest, they press their faces to the windows, exclaiming in awe. They point out the fig trees with long aerial roots, and the patches of white cloud drifting like smoke among the lush greenery. And then they catch their first glimpse of the Barron Falls, an avalanche of white water thundering down the mountainside.

INSIDER TIPS

- Each Skyrail gondola seats six people.

- The trip takes an hour and a half one way, so take advantage of the two stops en route to let the kids run around (and go to the toilet).

- The cable car travels 7.5 kilometres over unspoilt tropical rainforest. You glide a few metres above the forest canopy and then descend into the rainforest at each of the mid-stations.

- There are plenty of things to do in Kuranda, at the end of the Skyrail journey (*see* Kuranda attractions listed on pp. 456–9).

- You can take the Skyrail in one direction and Kuranda Scenic Railway (*see* p. 459) in the other. For more flexibility with departure times from Kuranda, do the return journey by Skyrail. Even if you book ahead, departure times can usually be changed.

- Caravonica terminal is adjacent to Tjapukai Aboriginal Cultural Park (*see* p. 444).

DON'T MISS

- The chance to photograph Barron Falls. As you approach the Skyrail station at Barron Falls, have the cameras ready!

- The interactive education centre at the Barron Falls station, where you can find out about the plants and wildlife of the rainforest, watch brief informative videos and take a short walk into the forest.

■ The ten-minute tour offered at Red Peak station, where you learn how to notice and identify things in the rainforest.

FABULOUS FACTS

The rainforests of Tropical North Queensland's coastline are the oldest continually surviving rainforests on earth. This means the landscape of this World Heritage area looks much the same as it did in the time of the dinosaurs. There are 3000 different plant species growing here, including nearly 400 rare or threatened plants, and some trees more than 3000 years old.

Kid Quest

Do rainforests really have a lot of rain?
See pp. 640–4 for the answer

Atherton Birds of Prey
Atherton Chinatown,
86 Herberton Rd, Atherton
(07) 4091 6945; www.birdsofprey.com.au
Closed Feb, Mar and Nov
Check show times

MID-RANGE

Watch and join in a spectacular free-flight birds of prey show. Afterwards, meet a saltwater crocodile and a spotted-tailed quoll, or experience the thrill of holding a magnificent wedge-tailed eagle (extra cost, limited numbers).

Australian Butterfly Sanctuary
8 Rob Veivers Dr, Kuranda
(07) 4093 7575;
www.australianbutterflies.com

MID-RANGE

Wander among 1500 rainforest butterflies – and if you are dressed in bright-coloured clothes, they are likely to land on you! Free guided tours take you into the breeding laboratory to see the different stages of the butterfly life cycle.

Australian Venom Zoo
8 Coondoo St, Kuranda
(07) 4093 8905; www.tarantulas.com.au

MID-RANGE

This is a collection of the most venomous snakes and spiders in the world – not for people with a fear of spiders! The venom is used in medical research, and on most days you can watch live venom extractions at around 1pm.

Barron Gorge National Park
Via Barron Falls Rd from Kuranda
www.derm.qld.gov.au/parks/
barron-gorge

FREE

Various walks are available in this World Heritage area of ravines, forest and waterfalls.

If you move quietly, you are likely to see brush turkeys scratching among the leaves, and early in the day you might spot a musky rat kangaroo or cassowary. The Barron Falls Lookout is a popular destination, and you can also take tours of Barron Gorge Hydro-Power Station; (07) 4036 6955.

Birdworld
Heritage Markets,
Rob Veivers Dr, Kuranda
(07) 4093 9188;
www.birdworldkuranda.com
MID-RANGE

Meet and handfeed hundreds of birds from around the world. They are housed in a giant, free-flying habitat landscaped to replicate their natural environment. See stilts, herons and black swans in a lake beneath a waterfall, or blue, gold and scarlet macaws among rainforest trees.

Cairns Wildlife Safari Reserve
Kennedy Hwy, Kuranda
(07) 4093 7777;
www.cairnswildlifesafarireserve.com.au
MID-RANGE

See lions, tigers, cheetahs, hippopotamuses, rhinoceroses and other safari animals. Don't miss the keeper talks and feed times scheduled through the day.

Crystal Caves and Fascinating Facets
69 Main St, Atherton
(07) 4091 2365;
www.crystalcaves.com.au
Closed Feb
MID-RANGE

Provided with helmets, lights and maps you explore underground caves to discover a vast array of crystals, minerals and fossils. You can also visit the glowing, purple amethyst room, and gaze entranced at The Empress, the 3-metre high amethyst geode, the biggest in the world. Perhaps best of all, you can purchase a whole geode in the shop and crack it in half to reveal the thousands of glittering crystals inside!

Curtain Fig National Park
Via Gillies Hwy, Atherton Tablelands
www.derm.qld.gov.au/parks/curtain-fig
FREE

From the carpark, follow the raised boardwalk to the amazing spectacle of a 500-year-old fig tree with a curtain of aerial roots dropping 15 metres to the forest floor. If possible, visit in the evening with a low wattage torch and see if you can spot any rare Lumholtz's tree-kangaroos in the surrounding forest.

Gallo Dairyland, Atherton

Davies Creek National Park
Via Kennedy Hwy and Kuranda,
Cairns and Tropical North Visitor
Information Centre (07) 4051 3588;
www.derm.qld.gov.au/parks/davies-
dinden-bare-hill

FREE

Two kilometres past the Davies Creek National Park campground is a carpark with a marked 1.1-kilometre loop track. This leads to a lookout over the magnificent Davies Creek Falls and a walk along the creek where you can paddle, climb on smooth granite boulders and look for platypus. A different turn-off from the Kennedy Highway takes you to nearby Dinden National Park and the easy Clohesy Walk to see a huge, impressive fig tree and interpretive signs about the rainforest.

Gallo DairyLand
Malanda Rd, Atherton
(07) 4095 2388;
www.gallodairyland.com.au

FREE

At this entertaining dairy farm, kids can pat baby animals in the nursery, see cows being milked (3–4.30pm), view cheese-making (most mornings), and watch a chocolatier hand-craft beautiful chocolates in the cafe/restaurant.

Granite Gorge Nature Park
11 Harrigan Rd, Mareeba
(07) 4093 2259;
www.granitegorge.com.au

BUDGET

Wander through a natural landscape of huge, weirdly shaped volcanic boulders, interspersed with creeks and foliage. Handfeed wallabies and turtles, go swimming or fishing, clamber over rocks and try to spot formations that look like animals.

Hallorans Hill
Via Louise St, Atherton
www.derm.qld.gov.au/parks/
hallorans-hill

FREE

A walking track (3-kilometres return) starts at the environmental park next to Atherton Hospital and leads up this extinct volcano. Look for a curtain fig tree, miniature waterfalls, rockpools, brush turkeys and tree-kangaroos on the way up, and spot Mount Bartle Frere, the tallest mountain in Queensland, from the top. The kids can enjoy the play equipment in the park on your return.

Kuranda Koala Gardens
Heritage Markets, Kuranda
(07) 4093 9953; www.koalagardens.com
MID-RANGE
Feed kangaroos and wallabies, cuddle a koala (extra cost), and venture into a walk-through snake enclosure — if you dare!

Kuranda Scenic Railway
Travels between Cairns, Freshwater and Kuranda Stations
(07) 4036 9333; www.ksr.com.au
Check timetable
HIGH COST
Take a winding rainforest train ride past waterfalls, through tunnels and high over gorges. You can listen to a commentary as you travel. There are various tour options, including taking part of the trip by Skyrail (*see* p. 455). The travel time between Cairns and Kuranda is about two hours. Remember to request window seats.

Kuranda Scenic Railway

Lake Eacham
Lake Eacham Rd, Crater Lakes National Park
www.derm.qld.gov.au/parks/lake-eacham
FREE
Swim in a beautiful blue lake, or walk the Lake Circuit (3-kilometre/1-hour return) and watch out for saw-shelled turtles, eastern water dragons, musk rat-kangaroos and over 180 bird species. Information signs explain Aboriginal connections with this area.

MakoTrac GoKart Action
Spring Rd, Mareeba
(07) 4092 5788; www.makotrac.com
Closed Mon
HIGH COST
Go-karts are available in sizes to suit all ages. Children as young as 4 years can ride their own little Bambini Karts (available by booking only). The centre also has a minigolf course.

Malanda Falls Conservation Park
Park Ave, Malanda
Malanda Falls Visitor Centre
(07) 4096 6957;
www.derm.qld.gov.au/parks/malanda-falls/about.html
FREE
Swim in the falls, have a picnic, or pick up a map from the visitor centre and take a short, self-guided walk. Keep an eye out for platypus, Lumholtz's tree-kangaroos and green ringtail possums. Rainforest Dreaming

walks led by an Aboriginal guide can be booked through the visitor centre.

Malanda Mosaic Trail
Various locations
www.malandafalls.com/documents/
mosaics.pdf
FREE

Print out a mosaic trail brochure from the website and discover the history of the Malanda area through nine mosaics created by local artists. Can you find the blue butterfly hidden in each mosaic?

Mareeba Tropical Savannas and Wetlands
Pickford Rd, Biboohra
Visitor Centre (07) 4093 2514;
www.mareebawetlands.org
VARIOUS PRICES

This wetland sanctuary is home to kangaroos, wallabies and numerous bird species including emus and brolgas. You can take a

self-guided walk, hire a canoe and paddle amongst the birds and lilies, or join a guided tour (April–December). Safari-style accommodation is available at Jabiru Safari Lodge; 1800 788 755; www.jabirusafarilodge.com.au

Whitewater rafting
Lake Placid via Cook Hwy
1800 801 540; www.foamingfury.com.
au/barron-river-family-rafting.php
Minimum age 6 years
HIGH COST

Kids aged from 6 to 12 years can participate in the thrill of a half-day rafting adventure specially designed for families. You ride in both an eight-seater raft and a two-person raft at different stages of the journey. Time is spent paddling on a beautiful lake surrounded by rainforest.

Around Port Douglas

Hartley's Crocodile Adventures
Captain Cook Hwy, Wangetti Beach
25 km south of Port Douglas
(07) 4055 3576; www.crocodileadventures.com
Opens early

MID-RANGE

The guide dangles a lump of meat on a string over the side of the boat. The kids press their faces to the glass walls, waiting. The next instant, a huge saltwater crocodile explodes out of the lagoon and everyone on board shrieks with delight. This cruise is the finale in a string of adventures you've had at Hartley's. The kids have already held a snake, fed dangerous cassowaries and watched a crocodile attack show in which a keeper waded into the water and used bait to entice a crocodile to demonstrate the death roll.

Hartley's Crocodile Adventures, Wangetti Beach

INSIDER TIPS

- Allow plenty of time as there is a lot to do here – or come back on the same ticket for another visit.

- Boat cruises depart several times daily. You will be allotted your time when you arrive, but check other tours, performances and feeding times (available from the website) and plan your visit around them.

- Strollers are available for hire, and it is a very easy park to get around with wheels.

- The cafe restaurant is surrounded by lovely scenery and a pond full of crocodiles! You can taste crocodile here if you like.

- You will be doing a lot of walking outdoors, so wear appropriate shoes, a hat and sunscreen.

DON'T MISS

- The morning crocodile feeding show where you find out about crocodile feeding and habits.

- The afternoon crocodile attack show – a heart-stopping performance!

- The boat cruise. Get close to crocodiles behaving as they would in the wild – lazing on a riverbank, building nests, and interacting with each other.

- The crocodile farm tour (twice daily). Learn how eggs are collected, and take the opportunity to hold a baby crocodile – if you want!

- Feeding the cassowaries (twice daily). This is a rare chance to get a good view of these dangerous, large birds.

- The walk-through enclosure with kangaroos and koalas. If you are lucky, some of the koalas may even be awake and moving around the trees.

- The snake show – find out what to do if you get bitten! Holding a snake is an extra cost.

- The green, square audio boxes outside selected displays, which you can activate to hear surprising facts and stories.

- The MacAlister Education Centre with interpretive display panels, touch tables and live exhibits on smaller animals like fish and bugs.

- The Plant Discovery Walk, a self-guided trail where you discover ancient dinosaur food and learn why some plants are valuable to Aboriginal people.

FABULOUS FACTS

Saltwater (or estuarine) crocodiles are commonly known as 'salties'. They can control their own heart rate, slowing it down to one beat every thirty seconds or so. They are able to hold their breath for several hours under water, and they can see in water using built-in 'goggles' – a protective translucent eyelid. At night, if you shine a light on them, their eyes glow red.

Kid Quest

What sort of nest does a saltwater crocodile build?

See pp. 640–4 for the answer

Wildlife Habitat

Cnr Captain Cook Hwy and Port Douglas Rd, Port Douglas
(07) 4099 3235; www.wildlifehabitat.com.au
Open from early morning

MID-RANGE

'Look at the joey!' cries one of the kids, pointing at a cute, furry face with big dark eyes peeking inquisitively out of it mother's pouch. Eagerly, the kids proffer handfuls of food, and the mother kangaroo bounds towards them. She stretches forward, delicately nuzzling the palm of each hand for food, and allowing her devoted admirers to stroke her soft fur. A moment later, there are kangaroos and wallabies of all shapes and sizes, and two tall emus, crowding in, all eager for a feed.

INSIDER TIPS

- The park is divided into three habitats. In the wetlands there are black-necked storks and many different coloured parrots and various free-flying birds. In the rainforest, look for cassowaries (huge, flightless birds), forest dragons (a type of lizard) and brightly coloured eclectus parrots. The grasslands habitat is a favourite with kids because it is here that they meet and feed kangaroos, wallabies and emus. Representatives of the world's only successful captive breeding colony of Lumholtz's tree-kangaroos can also be seen here.

- You can wander through the park on your own, take a free guided tour or attend informative animal presentations.

- Strollers are available for hire.

- Allow at least two hours for your visit. If you wish to return, tickets are valid for three days.

- You can buy a 4 Park Pass which includes entry to Rainforestation Nature Park (*see* p. 453), Cairns Wildlife Dome (*see* p. 446), and Australian Butterfly Sanctuary (*see* p. 456).

- For an extra cost you can have a photo taken holding a koala, snake or baby crocodile.

- Head for the grasslands habitat early in the morning or late in the afternoon when the kangaroos and wallabies are most active and hungry.

- Snacks are served at Curlew Cafe until 2pm. For an extra cost, you can have Breakfast with the Birds or Lunch with the Lorikeets among colourful free-flying birds (*see* p. 471).

- A fun way to reach the park is to hire a bike in town and ride (*see facing page*).

- Until recently, this attraction was named The Rainforest Habitat Wildlife Sanctuary.

DON'T MISS

- The free guided and feeding tours of each habitat where you learn more about the animals. Reception will let you know the tour times on arrival. Try to plan your visit around these tours.

- The signposts and Wildlife Keeper's Notes with extra information about the animals (including young animals) and plants.

FABULOUS FACTS

The birds you meet at Wildlife Habitat have many interesting characteristics. Stone curlews can carry their baby birds or eggs under their wings to remove them from predators. Emerald doves feed their babies 'pigeon milk' which is produced in a muscular pouch near the throat. Rose-crowned fruit doves build loosely woven nests so that tropical rains do not fill them up with water.

Kid Quest

Most kangaroos hop because they can only move both feet together. What type of kangaroo can move its legs independently?

See pp. 640–4 for the answer

Bike hire

Port Douglas Bike Hire,
cnr Wharf and Warner sts, Port Douglas
(07) 4099 5799;
www.portdouglasbikehire.com

VARIOUS PRICES

A great way to get around this beautiful, quiet town is by bike. You can ride along 12 kilometres of bike track, including beachside paths, without going on a road.

Four Mile Beach

End of Macrossan St, Port Douglas

FREE

The sand is a bit hard for making sandcastles, and it is not safe to swim here most of the year, but there is a great playground and kids have fun finding crabs and starfish in little pools at low tide.

Hire a pontoon boat

Port Douglas Boat Hire,
Marina Mirage, Port Douglas
(07) 4099 6277 or 0439 067 812

MID-RANGE

Pontoon boats are great fun for families. Kids can move around while the boat stays safe and stable. Putter around the creeks and mangrove forest looking for wildlife – you may even spot a crocodile. The boats have shade canopies and some have barbecues. You'll be supplied with instructions on how to drive the boat and a map showing creeks and fishing spots – you can also hire fishing gear. Remember to use insect repellent.

Horseriding

Port Douglas Horse Riding,
6613 Captain Cook Hwy, Port Douglas
(07) 4098 4101;
www.portdouglashorseriding.com.au

HIGH COST

Families are well catered for at Port Douglas Horse Riding. You are taught how to handle your horse, and younger kids can be led when you go for a ride. Wear long pants and closed shoes.

Kuku Yalanji Cultural Habitat Tours

The Esplanade, Cooya Beach
(20 km north-west of Port Douglas)
(07) 4098 3437; www.bamaway.com.au/
KukuYalanji.aspx
Two tours daily; bookings essential
Suitable for ages 4+

HIGH COST

Four Mile Beach, Port Douglas

Spend two hours with an Indigenous Kuku Yalanji family in their daily hunting and gathering. Find out how to track, stalk and throw a spear to find food on the beach, mudflat and mangroves.

Lady Douglas River Cruises
Depart from Marina Mirage,
Port Douglas
(07) 4099 1603 or 0408 986 127;
www.ladydouglas.com.au
Seasonal
MID-RANGE

Meander through mangrove channels while listening to an entertaining commentary and looking for saltwater crocodiles and birdlife.

Swim with whales
Depart from Marina Mirage,
Port Douglas
June–Sept
HIGH COST

Humpback and dwarf minke whales visit Port Douglas during their annual migration. Several cruise operators offer the amazing opportunity to swim with the dwarf minkes – and the whales seem to enjoy the encounter too!

The Daintree

Mossman Gorge, Daintree National Park
Gorge Rd, via Mossman
www.derm.qld.gov.au/parks/daintree-mossman-gorge
FREE

Sun sparkles on the cool, rippling water of the gorge and all around you is the lush green of the rainforest. The kids call excitedly as they spot a turtle sitting on a giant, rounded boulder in the river. They run

ahead over the suspension bridge, almost missing the sight of a huge jungle perch gliding through the water below. You've given them the task of spotting the first information board – by following the boards you'll find out how surrounding plants are used by the Indigenous Kuku Yalanji people.

INSIDER TIPS

■ The Department of Environment warns against entering the river because of dangers from swift currents, flash flooding and slippery rocks.

■ Read Jeannie Baker's *Where the Forest Meets the Sea*, a beautiful and thought-provoking picture book about this area.

■ Mossman Gorge National Park is an easily accessible introduction to tropical rainforest.

■ Try to arrive early in the morning while the birds are calling and before too many people arrive. Hot summer afternoons draw the crowds, especially on weekends.

■ Watch out for stinging trees. They have large, heart-shaped leaves with serrated edges and grow to 4 metres high. The stings are extremely painful.

■ There is a picnic area with toilets near the carpark. Watch for Australian brush turkeys that come scavenging for food.

■ The two walks leading from the Mossman Gorge carpark connect up with each other. The one on the right leads to the river (watch for a short track that takes you down to a sandy beach). If you cross the suspension bridge, you'll find the track with information signs that takes you on a one-hour circuit through the forest.

DON'T MISS

■ The guided walks on Aboriginal life in the rainforest. These leave from the entrance to Mossman Gorge four times daily (except Sundays), and take an hour and half. Visit culturally significant sites and learn about cave paintings, see traditional bark shelters and cool rainforest streams, learn how to find bush tucker, and have a taste of damper; Kuku Yalanji Dreamtime; (07) 4098 2595; www.yalanji.com.au/walks.html

■ Other Daintree attractions a bit further north, such as Cape Tribulation, Daintree Discovery Centre and Jungle Surfing (*see* pp. 468–9).

FABULOUS FACTS

One of the animals found only in the rainforests of north-eastern Queensland is Boyd's forest dragon. The colourful markings on this spiky, prehistoric looking lizard include a mustard yellow pouch beneath the chin, and bright patches of yellow, black and white on its olive body. Surprisingly, these serve as camouflage in the rainforest.

Kid Quest

Look for dragons! Well, a Boyd's forest dragon anyway. They cling to tree trunks waiting for tasty beetles, spiders and ants to crawl past, so check any bump you see on a tree.

Cape Tribulation, Daintree National Park

Via Bailey Creek Rd, Lower Daintree
www.derm.qld.gov.au/parks/daintree-cape-tribulation

BUDGET

A ferry crossing to reach Cape Tribulation operates from 6am to midnight. Two-wheel drive access is possible, but high clearance is useful and caravans are not recommended on this narrow, winding road. There are four short boardwalks into the rainforest at Cape Tribulation. Walk quietly and try to spot rare animals such as Bennett's tree-kangaroos, Daintree River ringtail possums and southern cassowaries. The Dubuji Trail commencing near the picnic area at Myall Beach, south of the cape, has signs about survival strategies used by rainforest plants and animals. Safety warnings: keep your distance from cassowaries, which are large, dangerous birds; stingers

Green tree frog,
Daintree National Park

(box jellyfish) are present in tidal and coastal waters year-round; and saltwater crocodiles can lurk in all waterways.

Daintree Discovery Centre
Cnr Cape Tribulation and Tulip Oak rds, Cow Bay
(07) 4098 9171;
www.daintree-rec.com.au
Open from early morning
MID-RANGE

Follow boardwalks that meander through the rainforest. Do a self-guided tour with the help of an audio recording and a comprehensive guide book (included in adult entry fee), or take a guided tour. Climb a tower for spectacular views, and use indoor touch screens to learn about the creatures unique to this area. There is a ferry crossing to reach the Daintree Discovery Centre (*see* CAPE TRIBULATION DAINTREE NATIONAL PARK, *on facing page*).

Jungle Surfing
Tours depart from the pharmacy and accommodation places,
Cape Tribulation
(07) 4098 0043;
www.junglesurfing.com.au
Several tours daily
Minimum age 3 years
HIGH COST

Fancy flying through the rainforest? At Jungle Surfing you are harnessed to cables and experience the exhilaration of 'flying' from tree to tree.

Places to eat

Australian Muster Experience
Kingston Rd, Whyanbeel Valley
(07) 4098 1149;
www.australianmusterexperience.com
The sounds and activities of stockmen droving cattle – clattering of horses' hoofs, cracking whips, yapping cattle dogs and bellowing cattle – are turned into live outdoor entertainment while you eat an Aussie barbecue meal. There is musical entertainment as well.

Fasta Pasta
68–72 Shields St, Cairns
(07) 4041 0388; www.fastapasta.com.au
The extensive, reasonably priced Italian menu is not limited to pasta, and the kids' menu includes a small pizza as well as pastas and other kids' favourites.

Flames of the Forest
Mowbray River Rd, Mowbray Valley
(07) 4099 3144;
www.flamesoftheforest.com.au
Out in the magical setting of the rainforest, you not only have a wonderful meal, but you are immersed in a candlelit drama

prawns late in the afternoon and kids can have fun feeding the scraps to the fish living under the restaurant. At about 5pm on most evenings there is great excitement when a giant groper called George swims up for a feed. When you're ready for dinner, the kids' menu includes tempura fish with green salad – and a picture to colour in.

of Aboriginal storytelling and music. This wonderful experience is available three nights a week; bookings essential.

Iron Bar Saloon
5 Macrossan St, Port Douglas
(07) 4099 4776
The huge drawcard here is the cane-toad races, held every night (small charge to watch). So enjoy your dinner in the outback-themed restaurant, then join in the fun.

Marina Mirage
Wharf St, Port Douglas
There's something for everyone from the range of diverse restaurants at the Marina Mirage. Enjoy the waterfront views, and watch the boats coming in.

On the Inlet Seafood Restaurant
3 Inlet St, Port Douglas
(07) 4099 5255;
www.portdouglasseafood.com
This restaurant is built right over the water. Enjoy a bucket of

Sizzlers
532 Mulgrave Rd, Earlville
(07) 4033 1676; www.sizzler.com.au
With a soup, salad, pasta, fresh fruit and dessert bar, and a wide choice of mains, this is an easy, casual night out for the family. Kids can order small-size steaks.

Skippers Cafe
The Esplanade, Cairns
(07) 4044 3715
Located right in the middle of Muddy's Playground (*see* p. 447), this cafe is a favourite for family dining. Meal portions are large and reasonably priced, and the atmosphere is relaxed.

Tjapukai by Night
Tjapukai Aboriginal Cultural Park, Cairns
Western Arterial Rd, Caravonica
(07) 4042 9900; www.tjapukai.com.au
Dine on a sumptuous buffet dinner, enjoy an Aboriginal cultural show, and have your face painted in traditional Aboriginal style. Find out more about Tjapukai Aboriginal Cultural Park (*see* p. 444).

Wildlife Habitat

**Cnr Captain Cook Hwy and
Port Douglas Rd, Port Douglas
(07) 4099 3235;
www.wildlifehabitat.com.au**

Fancy breakfast with the birds or lunch with the lorikeets? At the wonderful Wildlife Habitat (*see* p. 463) you can enjoy a delicious buffet while cockatoos, curlews, parrots, herons and other birds wander freely around. You are discouraged from feeding them your own food, but they might drop down to steal a peck at your fruit or juice.

Accommodation

Coconut Holiday Resort

**Cnr Bruce Hwy and Anderson Rd, Woree
(07) 4054 6644 or 1300 262 668;
www.coconut.com.au**

BUDGET TO HIGH COST

Set up a tent or caravan in the shady, scenic grounds, or rent a cabin or luxury self-contained villa. Facilities include Splash Waterpark, two large resort pools with water slides, wading pool, various ball sports, a huge adventure playground, jumping pillows and a giant chess set. The resort is ten minutes drive south of central Cairns.

Coral Sands Resort

**65 Vasey Espl, Trinity Beach
(07) 4057 8800; www.coralsands.com.au**

MID-RANGE

Set in lovely landscaped gardens and close to a beach, these four-star apartments are self contained with balconies and two bathrooms. There is a huge lagoon pool with a waterfall.

Glengarry Tourist Park

**Mowbray River Rd, Port Douglas
(07) 4098 5922 or 1800 888 134;
www.glengarrypark.com.au**

BUDGET TO MID-RANGE

This BIG4 park is located on a bus route, just 7 kilometres south of town. You have a choice of self-contained, air-conditioned family villas, and various styles of campsites, all set in lush tropical gardens with a lagoon-style pool, and a TV room. Go fishing or crabbing in nearby Mowbray River.

Green Island Resort

Green Island
(07) 4031 3300 or 1800 673 366;
www.greenislandresort.com.au

HIGH COST

Green Island is a little spot of paradise on the Great Barrier Reef, 26 kilometres off the coast of Cairns (*see* p. 448). Guests have the island to themselves when the last day trippers depart at 4.30pm. The price of the room includes transfers from Cairns, and activities such as snorkelling, guided walks, fish feeding, beach volleyball and canoeing. Accommodation is luxury hotel style. If kids don't want to share a double bed you need to book adjoining rooms or pay for a roll-away bed.

Reef Gateway

239 Lake Street, Cairns
(07) 4052 1411 or 1800 067 966;
www.reefgateway.com

MID-RANGE

These self-contained apartments in the heart of Cairns have a saltwater swimming pool and are walking distance to Muddy's Playground (*see* p. 447). Indicate if you require separate beds for the kids when booking.

Verandahs

7 Davidson St, Port Douglas
www.verandahsportdouglas.com.au

MID-RANGE

These spacious apartments are easy walking distance to cafes and the beach. The apartments are well set up for families, and some have two bathrooms. There is a heated pool with a shallow area, and there are even toys for use here or at the beach.

GOLD COAST

This region is located 80 kilometres south of Brisbane; regional airport at Coolangatta

Suits day trip from Brisbane or extended holiday

Year-round destination

HIGHLIGHTS

Currumbin Wildlife Sanctuary   *p. 484*

Dreamworld   *p. 474*

Sea World   *p. 476*

Thunderbird Park   *p. 488*

Warner Bros. Movie World   *p. 478*

Special events

Gold Coast Show
Aug
www.goldcoastshow.com.au
This weekend of classical entertainment offers something for everyone, with show bags, sideshows, an animal nursery, live entertainment, wood chopping, equestrian events as well as competitions.

Scarecrow Festival
June
www.tamborinemountainscarecrow festival.com.au
Follow the Scarecrow Trail – by car or on foot – through 14 kilometres of lovely mountain scenery. Spend the weekend in North Tamborine and enjoy non-stop entertainment by dancers, buskers and street performers. There's even a special kids' pavilion.

North of Surfers Paradise

The Giant Drop at Dreamworld, Gold Coast

Dreamworld

Dreamworld Parkway, Gold Coast
(07) 5588 1111 or 1800 073 300;
www.dreamworld.com.au
Open till late in holiday seasons
HIGH COST

The front of the queue is in sight ... You are about to board the Tower of Terror, a ride that is touted to be the tallest, the fastest, the scariest in all the world. You are going to rocket upwards at a speed of 160 kilometres an hour, then plunge vertically, face down, the height of a 38-storey building – in just six seconds! You take your seat, heart in your mouth; beside you, the kids are bursting with anticipation. They grip your hands as the harness is lowered. Your ride is about to begin!

INSIDER TIPS

- There are height restrictions for many of the thrill rides (120–200 centimetres for the Tower of Terror), but some, including the Rocky Hollow Log Ride, are suitable for small kids.

- For very little people, Wiggles World and Nickelodeon Central offer attractions such as spinning-teacup rides and a theatre show where slime and cream pies are flung at the audience!

- Various ticket options are available, including combinations with other theme parks or two-day passes.

- There are plenty of food outlets, but if you have a ticket to WhiteWater World as well, bring your own food and take advantage of the shaded picnic facilities next door.

- Before boarding the thrill rides, put small valuables such as keys and glasses into zipped pockets so they don't fly out and get lost.

- Strollers are available for hire.

- As well as rides, this theme park has wonderful opportunities to meet animals (*see* DON'T MISS *below*) and operates an animal conservation and breeding program.

- Weekends and school holidays are the busiest times, so go during the week if possible.

- To avoid long queues, you can hire a Q4U, a small handheld device that allows you to make ride reservations from anywhere in the park. Enjoy yourselves with other attractions while Q4U holds your place in a queue! Available at the Q4U shop next to IMAX.

- Another option to avoid crowds is an Early Entry Pass (extra cost, limited numbers available each day), which can be booked online and allows entry an hour before usual opening time.

- Make sure you pick up a Daily Shows Timetable when you arrive so you can plan your day. Arrive at each show 15 minutes early for the best seats.

- Pre-purchase your tickets so you don't have to queue up just to get in.

- Try to arrive early and head over to the furthest popular points before the crowds reach there.

DON'T MISS

- Tiger Island, where Bengal and Sumatran tigers play and swim with their handlers. There are up-close presentations during the day.

- The Australian Animal Presentations, for the chance to get up close to koalas, crocodiles, critically endangered bilbies, and other Australian wildlife.

- The steam train ride, which gives your feet a rest and takes you to Australian Wildlife Experience.

- The Oakey Creek Farm Show – see live sheep shearing.

- The optional animal encounters (high extra cost, minimum age 10 years). If the dream of a lifetime for your kids would be to cuddle a baby wombat, or pat a tiger, this is your opportunity.

FABULOUS FACTS

The endearing little bilby with its long ears is a threatened species with only a few hundred left in the wild. Dreamworld is conducting a breeding program, releasing bilbies into areas such as the remote Currawinya National Park where a predator-proof fence protects them from feral cats and foxes. The vision for the future is to be able to increase the free-roaming wild population outside fenced areas.

Kid Quest

Humans are not the only ones who like thrills here. You can see one animal leap from a height of 8 metres – that's higher than a two-storey building! Which animal is it?

See pp. 640–4 for the answer

Sea World

Seaworld Dr, Main Beach
(07) 5591 0000; www.seaworld.com.au

HIGH COST

A motor dinghy roars into the pool, grabbing the audience's attention. Leaping in graceful arcs beside it come the stars of the show – the beautiful dolphins. Soon the air fills with gasps and cries, and your kids watch transfixed. The dolphins put on a stunning display of synchronised swimming. In time to music, they twirl, somersault and leap, clap their fins and dance on their tails. They shoot up vertically from the water as if they are being shot from cannons, and give their keepers zooming rides across the pool, even launching them into the air.

Touching a dolphin at Sea World, Main Beach

INSIDER TIPS

- Various ticket options are available, including combinations with other theme parks.

- The main attraction here is the animals. Don't go for the rides. The queues can be extremely long and although there are ride options for very little folk, and some really challenging thrills, there is not much in between.

- There are various food outlets in the park. You are asked not to bring in your own food, unless you have allergies.

- Sections of the park are frequently closed for maintenance, but there is always plenty to see and do.

- There is an extra cost for some activities, including the water-play area, which has a shallow kids' pool.

- Some shops and rides are only open from midday until 4pm.

- If you've ever wanted a helicopter ride this is your chance (high extra cost). Rides as short as five minutes are available. There is a minimum of three adults per ride.

- If you are participating in an animal encounter in the water (*see* DON'T MISS *below*) you will be supplied with a rash vest and board shorts or wet suit, but you'll need your own swimwear underneath, and you must remove all jewellery and hair clips.

- Sea World Nara Resort is right next door and is attached by monorail.

DON'T MISS

- The Dolphin Show described above.

- The touch pool at Shark Bay, where you can pat starfish, sea cucumbers, sea urchins, hermit crabs and baby sharks.

- An Animal Adventure (extra cost), if you would like to get 'up close and personal' with the sea creatures in the park. Children 5 years old and over (and a minimum height of 110 centimetres) can cuddle a seal, hop in a pool with dolphins, or ride in a glass-bottomed boat over a lagoon filled with sharks. Children 10 years old and over can snorkel with the sharks! Book ahead to avoid disappointment; (07) 5519 6200 or 13 3386.

- The sea lion theatre, where humans in costume and sea lions put on a performance together.

- Meeting the stars of Network Ten's national cartoon show *Toasted TV*. This show is filmed on location at Sea World. Phone (07) 5588 2222 to find out when you can watch the filming.

FABULOUS FACTS

Sea World staff are on call 24 hours a day to rescue sick, injured and stranded animals in the wild. The cost of providing the necessary resources, specialised equipment, boats, helicopters and staff can be very high, but the costs are all met by Sea World – so your entry fees are going to a good cause.

Kid Quest
Do seals chew their food?
See pp. 640–4 for the answer

Warner Bros. Movie World, Oxenford

Warner Bros. Movie World
Pacific Motorway, Oxenford
(07) 5519 6200 or 13 3386;
www.movieworld.com.au
HIGH COST

The huge screen counts down to the beginning of the show: ten ... nine ... eight ... With tyres screeching and smoking, car after car revs into the arena, spinning around in an amazing display of precision driving. Your kids slide to the edge of their seats, eyes glued to this live-action stunt show. Actors bounce onto the set, adding humour and human interest as they pretend to film an action movie. The camera view is beamed up on the screen, and the kids grin and point as their own faces appear. Then all eyes return to the stunt cars as they skid across the set on two wheels!

INSIDER TIPS

- Hollywood Stunt Driver (described above) is very popular, so go to the morning performance or arrive early in the afternoon to avoid disappointment. If you have little kids, be aware that this show ends with startlingly loud explosions and clouds of fire.

- The only real filming done here is for Channel Nine's *Kids' WB*; phone ahead or check the website to find out times.

- If possible, visit on a weekday out of school holidays, otherwise the queues will be so long you will probably only manage three to five rides in a whole day. Crowd numbers are lower in winter than summer.

- Check the website for scheduled maintenance closures for the rides.

- When you arrive, you receive a park map with show times for the day.

- There are strict height restrictions for the thrill rides.

- You are not permitted to bring in your own food unless you have special needs (and your bags will be searched at the entrance). People who arrive by car can get around this by asking for a pass-out and going back to their cars to eat.

DON'T MISS

- The Batwing Spaceshot – for thrillseekers! This is an extreme ride where you are launched up a 60-metre-high tower at high speed, and then dropped. The minimum height for participants is 123 centimetres.

- The family rides in the WB! Fun Zone. A favourite is the Road Runner Rollercoaster; minimum height 100 centimetres.

- The Star Parade – littlies will be thrilled to see their favourite Loony Tunes characters.

- Having your photo taken with Scooby Doo and the other characters wandering around (no extra cost).

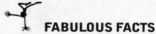

FABULOUS FACTS

People can organise to have parties, or even weddings, at Warner Bros. Movie World. Picture a wedding photograph with a huge Bugs Bunny posing between the bride and groom, or a birthday party in Spooky Castle, with Scooby-Doo, fire jugglers and bongo drummers for entertainment. Or how about a party in a saloon from the Western movie *Blazing Saddles*, complete with cowboys!

Kid Quest

If you could have a party here with characters acting out a show for you, what theme would you choose?

Australian Kayaking Adventures

Depart from Marine Pde, Labrador
0412 940 135;
www.australiankayakingadventures.com.au
Every morning
Minimum age 5 years
HIGH COST, INCLUDES BREAKFAST

On this half-day kayaking tour you play on secluded island beaches and snorkel in pristine waters. In addition, there's a chance of sighting bottlenose dolphins, turtles and stingrays. Whales can also be spotted in season (June–November). Equipment and kayaking lessons are included.

Jet boating

Paradise Jet boats, Jetty C, Mariner's
Cove Marina, Main Beach
(07) 5526 3190 or 1300 538 2628;
www.paradisejetboating.com.au
Depart on the hour
HIGH COST

Cruise past millionaires' yachts, helicopters and float planes, then hold your breath as the boat revs up and you spin, turn, slide and fishtail at almost 80 kilometres per hour. Rides last 30 or 45 minutes.

Paradise Country

Entertainment Rd, Oxenford
(07) 5573 3999 or 13 3386;
www.paradisecountry.myfun.com.au
MID-RANGE

Experience farm life and outback adventure in a theme park. See sheep shearing and stockmen rounding up sheep, learn how

to crack a stockman's whip, throw a boomerang, or milk a cow. Watch horsemanship displays, taste damper and billy tea, have a camel ride, and meet kangaroos and koalas.

South Stradbroke Island day trip

VARIOUS DEPARTURE POINTS AND PRICES

It is about a half-hour trip across the water to South 'Straddie' (as the island is affectionately known). You can travel with one of the cruise operators and have the use of a day resort (high cost) or just take a water taxi. Activities on the island include sandboarding, water sports and sharing meals with the locals – kangaroos and birds!

Wet'n'Wild Water World

Pacific Motorway, Oxenford
(07) 5556 1660 or 13 3386;
www.wetnwild.com.au

HIGH COST

As the name suggests, this is the place to come for lots of water fun: twisting water slides, pools, and Buccaneer Bay, an under-10s water-play area. On select Saturdays in summer you can watch a movie while floating in a pool at Dive'n'Movies. Pools are heated during the cooler months.

Whitewater World

Dreamworld Parkway, Coomera
(07) 5588 1111;
www.whitewaterworld.com.au
Extended hours in summer

HIGH COST

Wet'n'Wild Water World, Oxenford

You'll find amazing water slides, a water-powered roller coaster, and a wave pool here – grab an inflatable ring to ride on or bring your own. Perhaps best of all is the Nickelodeon Pipeline Plunge which has interactive water activities including blaster cannons and a massive bucket that dumps a thousand litres of water on everyone below. Whitewater World is suitable for all ages, and the pools are heated during winter.

Zorb Gold Coast

232 Old Pacific Hwy, Pimpama
(07) 5547 6300; www.zorb.com.au
Minimum age 6 years

HIGH COST

Zorbing is an imaginative spin on water fun. Try free-rolling down a hill inside a huge, clear plastic ball, sloshing around with water! Up to three people can ride together and the water is heated in winter. There are also dry rides available for people 153 centimetres and over.

Surfers Paradise

Adrenalin Park
6 Palm Ave, Surfers Paradise
(07) 5570 2700; www.funtime.com.au
Open till late

VARIOUS PRICES

Hear the screams as you approach! The giant slingshot flings riders 80 metres into the air, and the Vomatron spins them around at high speed. The minimum height requirement for these rides is 110 centimetres, but littlies are catered for with minigolf, simulated helicopter and car-racing rides and bungy trampolines.

Aquaduck
Departs from Centre Arcade,
Surfers Paradise Blvd
(07) 5539 0222; www.aquaduck.com.au
Check tour times

HIGH COST

Your bus takes you on a tour of the Gold Coast as you listen to an entertaining commentary, and then you splash into the sea and the vehicle turns into a boat. Kids can have a turn at driving on the water (under supervision) and receive a certificate.

Bungy trampolines
Cypress Ave, Surfers Paradise
(07) 5539 0474; www.flycoaster.com
Open till late

VARIOUS PRICES

Fly through the air on a bungy trampoline or opt for a game of minigolf.

Carrara Markets
Cnr Gooding Dr and Manchester Rd,
Carrara
(07) 5579 9388;
www.carraramarkets.com.au
Weekends from early morning

FREE ENTRY

This is not 'just another market'. There is a Family Fun Lane which offers face painting, pony rides, a merry-go-round and a roaming clown with balloons. Market stalls have plenty for the kids too, with superhero and fairy costumes, pets and toys.

Dracula's Haunted House
3177 Surfers Paradise Blvd,
Surfers Paradise
(07) 5592 5534;
www.draculashauntedhouse.com.au
Open till late
Suitable for ages 10+

MID-RANGE

Welcome to five floors of horror! Come face-to-face with a 3-metre funnel-web spider, get attacked by a white pointer, and meet numerous blood-soaked ghosts ... If all of this sounds too terrifying, there are some fun thrills in the shop out the front.

QDeck Experience,
Surfers Paradise

Infinity

**Chevron Renaissance Shopping Centre,
Surfers Paradise Blvd, Surfers Paradise
(07) 5538 2988; www.infinitygc.com.au
Open till late
Suitable for ages 8+**

MID-RANGE

Get lost in a mind-blowing,
infinite maze of darkness and
illusion. You'll be dazzled by a
dynamic show of sounds, lights
and sensory effects.

King Tutts Putt Putt

**Cnr Surfers Paradise Blvd and
Pandanus Ave, Surfers Paradise
(07) 5570 2277;
www.kingtuttsputtputt.com.au
Open till late**

MID-RANGE

Come face-to-face with
dangerous dinosaurs or an
ancient Egyptian mummy's tomb
in three themed indoor and
outdoor minigolf courses, or try
your skills in the shooting gallery.

QDeck Experience

**Level 77, Q1, Surfers Paradise Blvd,
Surfers Paradise
(07) 5582 2700 or 1300 473 325;
www.qdeck.com.au
Open till late**

MID-RANGE

Take the express lift and reach
Level 77 in less than 43 seconds.
Take in breathtaking 360-degree
views from one of the highest
points in Surfers Paradise while
you wait for your stomach to
catch up! The high-powered, coin-
operated binoculars allow you to
locate key points of interest down
below. The deck is glass-enclosed.

Ripley's Believe It Or Not Museum

**Soul Centre, Cavill Mall,
Surfers Paradise
(07) 5592 0040;
surfersparadise.ripleys.com
Open till late**

MID-RANGE

See the world's smallest car,
a replica of the world's tallest
man, a shrunken head, and many
more incredible or magical
exhibits and illusions.

Timezone

Level 1, Centro Surfers Paradise,
Cavill Mall, Surfers Paradise
(07) 5539 9500;
www.timezonegoldcoast.com.au
Open till late

MID-RANGE

This is the biggest Timezone centre in the world, offering minigolf, laser skirmish, kiddie rides, air hockey, dodgem cars, a shooting gallery, bowling and lots of video games.

Wax museum

56 Ferny Ave, Surfers Paradise
(07) 5538 3975;
www.waxmuseum.com.au
Open till late

MID-RANGE

Enter the World in Wax to meet realistic wax replicas of famous people and mythical characters. If you dare, visit the Chamber of Horrors to see dioramas of medieval torture devices and other horrors.

South of Surfers Paradise

Currumbin Wildlife Sanctuary, Currumbin

Currumbin Wildlife Sanctuary

28 Tomewin St, Currumbin
(07) 5534 1266 or 1300 886 511;
www.cws.org.au
Opens early

HIGH COST

'You hold it!' The dish of lorikeet food is thrust into your hand as a mob of colourful, screeching birds descends on you. Laughing, you try to hold the dish steady as two birds land on your hands and start to peck. You can feel a third one treading on your head. For a moment, the kids just watch, apprehensive of these noisy feathered creatures with their bright green backs and wings, blue heads and red and yellow chests. Finally, one child plucks up the courage to take the dish, and grins with delight as the birds follow.

INSIDER TIPS

■ The lorikeet feeding takes place at the beginning and end of the day. There is a small extra cost for the bowl of lorikeet food.

■ The cafe is open from breakfast until dinner time.

■ Strollers are available for hire.

■ There is a miniature railway for getting around this large park.

■ Do not touch the Eastern Water Dragons (big, colourful lizards) that sunbake on the pavers. These are wild animals and may bite.

■ Check the timetable and plan your day so you don't miss out on keeper talks and feeding times.

■ The Sanctuary animal hospital is the largest wildlife hospital in the Gold Coast region and accepts up to thirty sick, injured or orphaned animals every day!

■ Allow plenty of time to meet all the different animals and see the shows, which include didgeridoo and Aboriginal dance performances, snake and crocodile encounters, and a free-flight wild raptor show.

DON'T MISS

■ The Dingo Talk, where you sometimes have the chance to pat a dingo.

■ The koala and wombat show – a rare chance to see a koala awake! For an extra cost you can hold a koala.

■ The Green Challenge high ropes adventure course (extra cost) woven through the eucalypt and rainforest treetops. Keep an eye out for koalas in the trees.

■ A Wildnight Adventure (separate ticket) if you would like to see nocturnal animals feeding, hunting and playing. You'll even get to touch some of them. There is a maximum of twenty guests for each guided, two-and-a-half-hour night tour. A buffet dinner is included, and bookings are essential.

- Handfeeding the free-ranging kangaroos (food can be purchased for a small charge).

FABULOUS FACTS

The rainbow and scaly-breasted lorikeets you see in the sanctuary are wild birds that drop in for a feed. In fact, the whole sanctuary was started when a beekeeper and flower-grower named Alex Griffiths began feeding wild lorikeets to prevent them from eating his prized blooms, way back in 1947. This developed into a tourist attraction, and the sanctuary was born. Fewer birds come to the sanctuary during spring and summer when native trees are in full bloom, providing plenty of food.

Kid Quest
What food is in the lorikeets' dish?
See pp. 640–4 for the answer

Best beaches

FREE

Greenmount Beach and Coolangatta are both great sheltered beaches for families, with white sand and beautiful views. From Greenmount, walk around to Rainbow Bay and Snapper Rocks. Palm Beach near Burleigh Heads is a popular golden-sands beach, winner of Cleanest Beach Award, and Tallebudgera, north of Palm Beach, is a lovely beach that offers both estuary and ocean swimming.

Catch a crab

Lot 685, Birds Bay Dr, West Tweed Heads (just over the border in NSW)
(07) 5599 9972;
www.catchacrab.com.au
Tours every morning

HIGH COST

On your tour you feed fish, handfeed friendly wild pelicans, see a wild raptor show, pump for yabbies, fish in the Tweed River, visit an oyster farm and, of course, catch (and cook) mud crabs. There is an optional lunch (extra cost) at the end of your tour.

Catch a crab, West Tweed Heads

David Fleay Wildlife Park

West Burleigh Rd, Burleigh Heads
(07) 5576 2411 or 1300 130 372;
www.derm.qld.gov.au

MID-RANGE

Native animals are displayed here in a beautiful natural environment that includes a nocturnal house. You can see endangered cassowaries, crocodiles, platypus, Lumholtz's tree-kangaroos, mahogany and yellow-bellied gliders, wedge-tail eagles, snakes and the endangered greater bilby. Don't miss the daily presentations, or the chance to pat a koala (extra cost).

Paramount Adventure Centre

38 Hutchinson St, West Burleigh
(07) 5593 6919;
www.paramountadventures.com.au
Check opening hours

VARIOUS PRICES

You can do indoor rock climbing, or have a go at kayaking, mountain biking or a learn-to-surf program.

Putt Putt Golf

2492 Gold Coast Hwy, Mermaid Beach
(07) 5575 3381;
www.puttputtgolf.com.au
Open till late

MID-RANGE

Test your skills on three themed, 18-hole putting courses set amongst tropical gardens, lakes and waterfalls. Plastic putters are provided free for toddlers. There are also video games.

Superbee Honey World

35 Tomewin St, Currumbin
(07) 5598 4548; www.superbee.com.au

FREE

Get an amazing peek into a bee's life through glass bee hives. Can you pick the queen? A bee keeper will reveal some secrets, show how honey is extracted and encourage you to taste the different honeys.

Hinterland

Thunderbird Park

Cnr Tamborine Mountain Rd and Cedar Creek Falls Rd, Tamborine Mountain
(07) 5545 1468; www.thunderbirdpark.com

VARIOUS PRICES

Oblivious of the hot sun and the dust, the kids hammer away with their picks at the hard, rocky ground. There are shouts of glee as each lump is clawed out and rattles into the tin bucket. At last the bucket is full, and eagerly picking it up, they hurry back through the forest and over the creek to the rock cutting shop. They stretch up on their toes, watching with anxious eyes as the electric saw slices through their largest find, then there are cries of delight as the thunderegg splits in half and they see the crystals inside.

INSIDER TIPS

▪ There are numerous activities besides fossicking available in Thunderbird Park, including an adventure course and horseriding (*see* DON'T MISS *on facing page*).

▪ Children doing fossicking must be accompanied by a paying adult over 18 years of age.

▪ You are given instructions and a safety talk before fossicking.

▪ You can take home as many thundereggs as you can fit inside your bucket, and you will receive a miner's permit as an extra souvenir. Cutting is a small extra cost.

▪ Fully enclosed footwear must be worn for most activities in the park.

▪ The mine closes in wet weather.

▪ Various styles of accommodation are available at Cedar Creek Lodges in the park; (07) 5545 1468.

▪ Picnics are not permitted in this private park, but meals are available at the Rainforest Restaurant.

▪ The park is adjacent to Tamborine National Park (*see* p. 490).

DON'T MISS

- Thunderbird Park Mine (mid-range cost), where you can fossick for thundereggs, (07) 5545 7999.

- Adventure Parc (high cost, minimum age 6 years), which offers amazing rope and adventure courses of varying levels of difficulty. Try the flying foxes, swinging ropes, trapezes and single beams suspended from ancient towering eucalypts; 1300 881 446; www.adventureparcaustralia.com

- Tamborine Mountain Trail Rides offer horse rides through beautiful mountain scenery (high cost, minimum age 6 years) or led pony rides for the littlies; (07) 5545 3505; www.horseridingqld.com

- Laser skirmishes (high cost, minimum age 6 years), available most Saturdays if there are enough players. Put on your camouflage gear and play at soldiers in a real forest! Bookings are essential; 0432 058 910 or 1300 666 559; www.laserskirmish.com.au

- The bushwalks (no cost) amongst giant fig trees, eucalypts, tree ferns, palms and waterfalls – keep an eye out for koalas and kangaroos.

FABULOUS FACTS

Thunderbird Park has the largest deposit of thundereggs anywhere in the world. You have to wait until they're cut open to find out what colours and patterns of crystals have formed inside. It is believed that thundereggs are bubbles of gas that were trapped in lava 200 million years ago during volcanic upheavals.

Kid Quest

Find your own beautiful thunderegg.

Bushwalking in Tamborine National Park

the Lamington National Park on the Tree Top Walk, feed wild birds (small cost), or take a guided walk (mid-range cost). Accommodation is available at O'Reilly's Rainforest Retreat, (07) 5502 4911 or 1800 688 722.

Tamborine National Park
Main Western Rd via Mount Tamborine
www.derm.qld.gov.au/parks/tamborine
FREE

This park offers various picturesque bushwalks through subtropical rainforest. The 3-kilometre circuit walk to Witches Falls takes you past giant strangler figs and seasonal lagoons where you can look for frogs.

O'Reilly's
Lamington National Park Rd via Canungra
Discovery Centre (07) 5544 0569;
www.oreillys.com.au
FREE ENTRY

Climb a ladder and wander through the rainforest canopy of

Places to eat_____

Alfresco Italian
2991 Gold Coast Hwy, Surfers Paradise
(07) 5538 0395; www.welovealfresco.com
This relaxed, family-friendly restaurant has an extensive Italian menu, including dishes for the kids.

Australian Outback Spectacular
Entertainment Dr, Oxenford
(07) 5573 3999 or 13 3386;
www.outbackspectacular.myfun.com.au

The venue is themed like an outback landscape and the meal includes beef steak with Kakadu plum sauce, Aussie damper, pavlova and billy tea. There is stunning live entertainment – stunt riders on horseback, wild colts, stampeding cattle, high speed quad bikeriding, and even a helicopter – all happening right in front in front of you as you eat dinner!

Accommodation

Couran Cove Island Resort
South Stradbroke Island
(07) 5509 3000 or 1800 268 726;
www.couran.com

MID-RANGE

This is a different style of Gold Coast accommodation. Set on a beautiful island, 40 minutes by boat from the mainland, you have a choice of eco-friendly lodges or rooms, both with cooking facilities. Use of sporting facilities, bikes, kayaks, catamarans, unlimited ferry transfers and guided rainforest tours is all included. A kids' club runs most of the year.

Paradise Resort Gold Coast
122 Ferny Ave, Surfers Paradise
(07) 5579 4444 or 1800 074 111;
www.paradiseresort.com.au

MID-RANGE

This resort is set up for families with an outdoor adventure playground, swimming pool and year-round organised kids'

activities. If you feel like a break there's even a kids' club where you can leave the children for the day. It is a short stroll to the centre of town or the main surf beach. Some rooms have basic cooking facilities and separate TVs and PlayStations for the kids.

Treasure Island Holiday Park
117 Brisbane Rd, Biggera
(07) 5500 8666 or 1800 339 966;
www.treasureisland.com.au

BUDGET TO MID-RANGE

Located ten minutes north of Surfers Paradise, this BIG4 park offers a choice of campsites and self-contained villas. Kids enjoy the water slide, wading area and kids' pool, as well as the giant jumping pillow, playground, minigolf course and ball play areas. The buggies you can hire to drive around inside the park are a real hit! There are organised family activities during school holidays.

SUNSHINE COAST

The Sunshine Coast is located 100 kilometres north of Brisbane Airport at Maroochydore with regular flights from major cities
Suits extended holiday or long day trip from Brisbane
Year-round destination

HIGHLIGHTS

Australia Zoo **p. 493**

Buderim Ginger Factory **p. 495**

Underwater World **p. 501**

Special events_____

Gympie Gold Rush Festival
Oct
www.goldrush.org.au
This week-long program includes gold-panning competitions, gemstone displays, a spectacular float parade, amusements for kids and live music.

Woodford Folk Festival
Dec/Jan
www.woodfordfolkfestival.com
A special children's festival and spectacular fire event are part of this six-day festival with a relaxed hippy vibe. The program has an environmental theme and takes place on a scenic park in the hinterland.

Hinterland

Australia Zoo

1638 Steve Irwin Way, Beerwah
(07) 5436 2000; www.australiazoo.com.au

HIGH COST

Your child tentatively holds out one hand, offering a carrot. The elephant's long, grey trunk snakes forward, snatches it up, and promptly transfers it to its gaping mouth. Shining eyes turn towards you and an awed voice says, 'The elephant ate from my hand!' Australia Zoo gives kids some very special opportunities for getting close to animals. Kids spend hours at the Tiger Temple's unusual underwater viewing area where they can watch the tigers swimming. They love meeting the animals going for walks with keepers through the zoo grounds, and patting and feeding the kangaroos in their free-roaming enclosure.

INSIDER TIPS

■ Although it is called Australia Zoo, animals from all over the world are on display.

■ Ask the keepers if you can pat the animals being walked through the grounds.

■ Wear a hat, sunscreen and comfortable walking shoes, although there are plenty of shaded areas.

■ Make use of the website to plan your visit. There are several shows through the day.

■ All the shows are accompanied by information about animal conservation (and opportunities for donations).

Bindi Irwin, affiliate of
Australia Zoo, Beerwah

- The zoo is very spread out, which gives the animals plenty of space, but means you have to walk a lot. Luckily, you can hop aboard a free shuttle if you get tired!

- Queues to feed the elephants tend to be shorter in the afternoon. If there is a queue, it generally moves quickly.

- You can bring your own picnic to enjoy on the lawn, or purchase meals from the huge undercover food court which has plenty of choices, including some healthy options.

- Mosquitoes can be a problem in the wetland section and the nearby kangaroo enclosure, so bring insect repellent.

- You can reach the zoo by a free coach that departs from various Sunshine Coast points every morning; phone the zoo to book your seats.

- There are various animal encounters, and even Wildlife Hospital Tours, available for an extra cost; various age restrictions.

- Kids can take a break from animal-viewing in the shaded playgrounds, the jumping castle, and the free rides.

- Prams and red pull-along wagons are available for hire.

DON'T MISS

- The elephant feeding, twice daily (no extra cost).

- Hand-feeding the free-roaming red and grey kangaroos (small charge for food).

- The Wildlife Warriors performance in the 5000-seat Crocoseum. You'll see a crocodile feeding, but the highlight is watching the birds fly over the heads of the audience. Terri, Bindi and Robert Irwin sometimes appear in these shows.

- The tiger show – see how playful tigers can be! They play with toys, wrestle with keepers and dive into their pool. Show times vary each day, so check the time on your arrival.

- The wildlife photo studio where you can have a photo taken with various animals (extra cost); see the website for timetable.

- The Kids Zoo where kids can pat and feed baby animals; small charge for food.

- The koala walkthrough, where you can pat a koala at any time; (no extra cost).

- Bindi's pony trail, where there are free pony rides for little ones under 127 centimetres tall.

- Farmyard Fun encounter (extra cost) where under-10s can get right inside the animal enclosures. Give the keepers a hand with cleaning, brushing, cuddling and feeding.

FABULOUS FACTS

The wombat is the closest relative to the koala. Females have a pouch that faces backwards so their babies don't get dirt in their faces when mum digs the burrow! They usually move slowly but are capable of amazing speeds. They eat grasses and roots. Their powerful claws are for digging, and if predators enter their burrows they tend to crush them with their backsides.

How do elephants drink?
See pp. 640–4 for the answer

Buderim Ginger Factory

50 Pioneer Rd, Yandina
(07) 5446 7100 or 1800 067 686; www.gingerfactory.com.au

FREE ENTRY; VARIOUS PRICES FOR ACTIVITIES

As the 'rowboat' chugs around the moat, the kids giggle and point at the hilarious antics of the Gingerbread Man and all the other puppets involved in an imaginative chase around the world. When the ride comes to an end, they clamber out, eager to reach the little train that is tooting merrily in the background. The station is located in the midst of tropical gardens. You take your seats, the kids looking around with interest at the spectacular plants with spiky leaves and brightly coloured blooms, and the quaint cottages selling toys and souvenirs, then the trains toots, and you're off.

INSIDER TIPS

- There is free entry to the complex, including the gardens and food areas, but there are various costs for tours, shows and rides.

- On the 'Taste of Ginger' tour you get a worm's-eye view of growing ginger from an artificial underground location, then learn about the production of fresh ginger, and taste some ginger products. You also view the factory floor.

- If you want to see the factory in action, you need to take the 'Taste of Ginger' tour during the week as the factory does not operate on weekends.

- On the Superbee Live Bee Show a beekeeper removes a frame from a hive and reveals all sorts of intriguing information about bees as you watch them through a clear panel in the hive. You're also invited to taste a range of different honeys.

- The ginger tour and live bee show both commence on the hour every hour in the morning and on the half hour in the afternoon. Each lasts 40 minutes.

- The ginger train ride departs every half hour and lasts 15 minutes.

- The *Overboard* puppet show runs continuously and the ride lasts 15 minutes.

DON'T MISS

- Posing the kids next to one of the giant gingerbread men for a photo.

- The ginger and cinnamon ice-cream.

- Exploring the beautiful tropical gardens.

- The ride through the garden and rainforest in an original century-old cane train with open sided carriages.

FABULOUS FACTS

The use of ginger dates back at least 5000 years. It was brewed into a tea in ancient China and India and drunk after meals to aid digestion. It is still used today as a herbal remedy and is believed to cure nausea, indigestion, fever and infection. It provides flavouring and scent for multiple products, from gingerbread men to cosmetics.

Kid Quest
Which is your favourite honey flavour?

Aussie World

**Ettamogah Pub Complex,
73 Frizzo Rd, Palmview**
(07) 5494 5444;
www.aussieworld.com.au

MID-RANGE

A rollercoaster, dodgem cars, bucket-loads of water balloons to throw, laughing clowns, remote-controlled boats ... Aussie World has rides for all sizes and tastes.

Bellingham Maze

13–19 Main Creek Rd, Tanawha
(07) 5445 2979; www.bellmaze.com

MID-RANGE

Go on a dwarf hunt in a hedge maze, try to solve some brain-teasing puzzles, and count the birds in the walk-through aviary.

Big Kart Track

Steve Irwin Way, Landsborough
(07) 5494 1613; www.bigkart.com.au

HIGH COST

Those who are 12 years or over (and over 153 centimetres tall), can drive on one of the biggest

The Big Pineapple Complex, Woombye

go-kart tracks in Australia. Littlies have a special junior track so they don't have to miss out, while very little ones can share a ride in a double-seater.

The Big Pineapple Complex

Nambour Connection Rd, Woombye
www.bowdensown.com.au

VARIOUS PRICES

The 16-metre fibreglass pineapple is a heritage-listed landmark. Inside the complex you can indulge in tropical fruit parfaits, tour the pineapple plantation and tropical fruit orchards by mini-train, or get close to baby animals in the wildlife nursery. There is also a new, interactive automotive museum with an amazing collection of sport and racing cars.

Big Kart Track, Landsborough

Buderim Forest Walk

Via Quorn Close, Buderim
www.buderim.com/forest.htm

FREE

A boardwalk leads to a spectacular waterfall with a clear pool, log bridge, stepping stones and picnic facilities.

Eumundi Markets

73 Memorial Dr, Eumundi
(07) 5442 7106;
www.eumundimarkets.com.au
Wed and Sat, early morning to early afternoon

FREE ENTRY; VARIOUS PRICES FOR ACTIVITIES

Have your fortune told and check out the toy stall at this huge market. There are also live performers, merry-go-rounds, a jumping castle and slot cars.

Gold Mining Museum

215 Brisbane Rd, Gympie
(07) 5482 3995;
www.goldmuseum.spiderweb.com.au

BUDGET

This is a park displaying buildings and life-like dioramas from Gympie's gold rush era. Kids enjoy the schoolhouse, railway and light-horse displays, and are fascinated by glimpses of outdated technology such as a telephone switchboard and old typewriters.

Mapleton Falls National Park

Obi Obi Rd, Mapleton
1300 130 372;
www.derm.qld.gov.au/parks/mapleton-falls

FREE

Short, easy trails lead into rainforest and eucalypt forest. On the Mapleton Falls Lookout walk, keep an eye out for roosting peregrine falcons (August–September). On the Wompoo Circuit, listen for the *wallock-a-woo* call of the wompoo fruit-dove and read information signs about the surrounding landscape features.

Maroochy Bushland Botanic Garden

Via Palm Creek Rd, Tanawha
www.sunshinecoast.qld.gov.au

FREE

Lovely short walks will take you to a lagoon, a rockpool (with frogs), and a sculpture garden. A favourite with families is the Whipbird Gully Walk where you can look for hidden creatures, including giant spiders and butterflies.

Mary Cairncross Scenic Reserve

148 Mountain View Rd, Maleny
(07) 5429 6122;
www.mary-cairncross.com.au

ENTRY BY DONATION

Kids love the realistic dinosaur diorama in the Education Centre, showing how the rainforest looked millions of years ago. Pick up a fact sheet about the reserve, and take a self-guided tour along the boardwalk. See how many birds, mammals, reptiles – or dinosaurs – you can spot in the forest.

Mary Valley Heritage Railway
Depart from Old Gympie Station,
Tozer St, Gympie
(07) 5482 2750;
www.thevalleyrattler.com

VARIOUS TIMES AND PRICES

Take a ride on a steam train or a 'Red Rocket' railmotor on winding tracks through the scenic Mary Valley. See cows grazing and plantations of pineapples and macadamias.

Nutworks
37 Pioneer Rd, Yandina
(07) 5472 7777;
www.nutworks.com.au
Weekdays

FREE

You can watch chocolates and confectionery being manufactured and sample the products at the shop and cafe.

Opals Down Under
11 Ballantyne Crt, Palmview
(07) 5494 5400;
www.opalsdownunder.com.au

BUDGET

Go on a real treasure hunt! The whole family can have fun fossicking for gemstones in the Scratch Patch. You can also see opals being cut (bookings essential), or watch a DVD about opal mining, cutting and valuation.

Noosa

Best beaches

FREE

Noosa Main Beach is good for beginner surfers, is patrolled by life-savers every day of the year, and has toilets and showers. Little Cove is popular with families, but it is not patrolled. Peregian Beach, located about 8 kilometres south of Noosa, is a quiet beach with sand sloping gently into the water, but it is also a surf beach so be sure to swim between the flags in the section near the shops.

Looking for seashells on Noosa Main Beach, Noosa

Bikeriding

**Bike On Australia,
various locations
in Noosa
(07) 5474 3322;
www.bikeon.com.au**
VARIOUS PRICES

Hire bikes and
ride along the
beach or on the
many tracks
around Noosa, or try a mountain
bike adventure tour.

Camel safaris

**Beach Rd, Noosa North Shore
0408 710 530;
www.camelcompany.com.au
Minimum age 5 years**
HIGH COST

Board your 'ships of the desert'
for an interesting journey along
the beach or through the bush.
Safaris last one to two hours and
bookings are essential.

Horseriding on the beach

**Beach Rd, Noosa North Shore
(07) 5474 2665; www.equathon.com
Tours twice daily
Minimum age 10 years**
HIGH COST

Take a one-and-a-half-hour ride
along the beach, or a two-hour
ride through beach and bush.

Noosa National Park

**Via Hastings St and various other
access points around Noosa,
(07) 5447 3522;
www.derm.qld.gov.au/parks/noosa**
FREE

In this easily accessible section of
coastal rainforest there are lovely
beaches and a network of walking
trails. You have a chance of
spotting lace monitors (a type of
large lizard) and koalas, and of
glimpsing of humpback whales
(June–November). Remember
to stay on the trails and keep
away from cliff edges. The
beaches are great for exploring
and the bushland comes right
down to the sand, providing
plenty of shade. Note: the water
is not patrolled here and
swimming can be dangerous
(*see* BEST BEACHES p. 499 for safer
options).

Surf lessons

**Noosa Learn to Surf, Noosa Main Beach,
west of the first rock wall
0418 787 577; www.learntosurf.com.au
Group lessons twice daily
Minimum age 7 years**
HIGH COST

This beach is exceptionally safe
for learning to surf. You'll be
supplied with special soft
surfboards and start in waist-
deep water with the coaches right
beside you. You must be able to
swim 25 metres.

Maroochydore to Caloundra

Underwater World
Parkyn Pde, Mooloolaba
(07) 5458 6280; www.underwaterworld.com.au

MID-RANGE

The kids are thrilled by the many opportunities to get up close to creatures of the sea. They stand on the travelator gazing in awe at giant rays, moray eels and sharks swimming all around as they are slowly carried through the clear tunnel of the Oceanarium. They eagerly dip their arms in the touch pool to pick up and pat the starfish and sea cucumbers, listening wide-eyed to the keeper's talk. Best of all, they love the big, fishy kisses they receive from the stars at the end of the seal show.

Underwater World, Mooloolaba

INSIDER TIPS

- Allow three to four hours for your visit.

- Arrive early for the otter show as there is not a lot of room for spectators.

- There is a cafe in a pleasant wharf area. You can purchase boxed kids' meals and healthy options here.

- There are wonderful seal and otter encounters available for a high extra cost.

- Check the website for the daily schedules of keeper talks and feeds.

 **DON'T MISS**

- The seal show, which is not just fun but has an environmental message.

- The touch tank, which may have small sharks in it as well as sea stars and sea cucumbers.

- The Honda SUV transformed into an aquarium!

- The opportunity for a seal kiss – available at extra cost following each seal show.

- The stingray feeds – rays nearly climb out of the pool just in front of you in their eagerness to be fed.

- The Crawly Creatures exhibit, where you can get up close to some very large crabs and lobsters.

 FABULOUS FACTS

One of the most popular residents of the Crawly Creatures exhibit is the giant Japanese spider crab. These crabs can grow up to nearly 4 metres in size from claw tip to claw tip – that's bigger than many kids' bedrooms. Most of this size is in the length of their long, thin, spider-like legs. However, with the male, most of its leg is actually a claw, which can open to a width of 3 metres!

Kid Quest

See if you can find a cow fish, lionfish, stonefish, and rabbit-fish.

Best beaches

Mooloolaba beach has a wide sand area popular with families. Kings Beach at Caloundra has a sea-water swimming pool with a kids' swimming area and giant water fountain, and extensive parklands with a flying fox and free barbecues. At Cotton Tree, kids can swim in the Maroochy River, and play on its sandy shores and in the playground.

Blue Water Kayak Tours

Depart from two locations, Caloundra
(07) 5494 7789;
www.bluewaterkayaktours.com
Phone for tour times
Minimum age 8 years
HIGH COST

Paddle your kayaks across Pumicestone Passage, admiring the fish and the pelicans, to Bribie Island. Here you can walk around looking for more birds, or relax on the glorious beach.

Flying Trapeze Lessons

Mudjimba Beach, Mudjimba
1300 791 793;
www.adrenalin.com.au/trapeze-learn-to-fly-the/qld-sunshine-coast/land/12375
Thurs–Tues afternoons
Minimum age 6 years

HIGH COST

During the 90-minute outdoor lesson you learn safety procedures and basic body positions before putting on your safety harness. Once you're comfortable swinging on the trapeze, you have a go at flying!

Queensland Air Museum

Caloundra Airport, 7 Pathfinder Dr, Caloundra
(07) 5492 5930; www.qam.com.au

BUDGET

Anyone interested in planes will love this huge display of historic aircraft.

Ski 'n Skurf cable ski park

367 David Low Way, Bli Bli
(07) 5448 7555;
www.suncoastcablewatersports.com
Seasonal
Minimum age 10 years (over 35 kg)

HIGH COST

Learn how to waterski, kneeboard, skurf, and wakeboard,

all on the end of a cable instead of being dragged along by a boat. No prior experience is required.

Sunshine Castle

292 David Low Way, Bli Bli
(07) 5448 4477; www.sunshinecastle.com

MID-RANGE

In this medieval-style castle, kids can climb turrets, look over battlements, hunt for treasure, meet a knight in shining armour, and see a moat, a pillory and a dungeon. There are also fairytale dioramas, a model train and dancing dolls. Try to visit on the first Saturday morning of the month when the castle comes alive with market stalls and is peopled by knights and merchants from a re-enactment group.

Top Shots Fun Park

2 Allora Dr, Maroochydore
(07) 5452 7007;
www.topshotsmaroochydore.com
Open till late Fri, Sat and school holidays
Rides suitable for ages 4+

VARIOUS PRICES

Kids can have hours of fun here, with arcade games, a vertical trampoline, an inflatable water slide, rock climbing, minigolf, and blaster boats for dousing friends and enemies.

Accommodation

BIG4 Maroochy Palms Holiday Village
319 Bradman Ave, Maroochydore
(07) 5443 8611 or 1800 623 316;
www.maroochypalms.com.au

BUDGET TO MID-RANGE

Choose a camping or caravan site, or one of the luxury, self-contained villas. Located on the Maroochy River, 5 kilometres from central Maroochydore, this village has a huge playground, a swimming pool complex with a water playground, a games room, minigolf, and a lake with boardwalks where you can feed waterbirds, fish and eels. There are extra activities during school holidays, including a kids' club.

Mantra
Cnr Mooloolaba Espl and Venning St, Mooloolaba
(07) 5452 2600;
www.mantramooloolababeach.com.au

HIGH COST

These self-contained apartments, available with one, two and three bedrooms, are located on the waterfront, close to shops and restaurants. All have balconies with ocean or garden views, and guests have use of an outdoor lagoon-style pool or indoor heated pool.

Pandanus
Cnr Smith and Walan sts, Mooloolaba
(07) 5457 8989 or 1300 787 668;
www.pandanusmooloolaba.com.au

MID-RANGE

These spacious, three-bedroom, self-contained apartments are in a quiet location a short distance from both beach and shopping precinct. Each has a balcony, two bathrooms (no arguments!) and use of a heated pool.

Places to eat

Ettamogah Pub
73 Frizzo Rd, Palmview
(07) 5494 5444;
www.aussieworld.com.au
The quirkily shaped building is based on a pub that first appeared in cartoon drawings in the 1950s. It is attached to Aussie World (*see* p. 497) and offers kids' meals in the restaurant.

Noosa Head Surf Club
69 Hastings St, Noosa Heads
(07) 5474 5688;
www.noosasurfclub.com.au
This family-friendly restaurant has casual dining on a deck overlooking the water. There are lots of seafood choices as well as burgers and a kids' menu.

Panda's Playland and cafe
1 Gateway Dr, Noosaville
(07) 5470 2999;
www.pandasplayland.com.au
If your kids are 10 years old or under, this is a great place to have lunch. While the kids enjoy the indoor play equipment, you can have a relaxed meal. The cafe serves light hot meals, and prepares picnic boxes for the kids.

Another Holiday Idea for Queensland

Stay on outback stations
Instead of clinging to the coast, take the long journey inland, staying on sheep and cattle stations. Head for Longreach and Winton and discover spectacular red mesa country, dinosaur footprints, opal mines, Aboriginal art sites, the original Qantas hangar, pristine World Heritage rainforest, and the Stockman's Hall of Fame. You can take this journey by Queensland Rail, 1300 131 722; www.queenslandrail.com.au.

Find out more about outback destinations from Outback Queensland Tourism Association, 1800 247 966; www.outbackholidays.info

TASMANIA

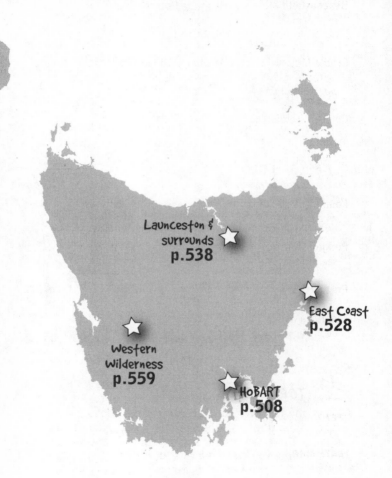

Launceston &
surrounds
p.538

East Coast
p.528

Western
Wilderness
p.559

HoBART
p.508

FAVOURITES_____

Beaconsfield Mine and Heritage Centre – have a go at noisy old mining machinery, and walk in the footsteps of a mining accident rescue   *p. 549*

Cradle Mountain–Lake St Clair National Park – be enchanted by the magic and mystery of the Tasmanian wilderness   *pp. 559 and 569*

Devils@Cradle – are Tasmanian devils really devilish? Meet them and find out!   *p. 562*

Gordon River Cruise – step ashore and find a 2000-year-old tree in a dinosaur forest   *p. 564*

Louisa's Walk – find out what it was really like to be transported as a convict   *p. 516*

Penguin Tours at Bicheno – get so close to little penguins you can see inside their burrows   *p. 528*

Port Arthur – experience the day-to-day life of a convict   *p. 522*

Tasmazia and the Village of Lower Crackpot – amazing cubby houses, intriguing mazes and an enchanting miniature village   *p. 556*

TOP EVENTS

FEB Enjoy the colonial ambience of Evandale Village Fair and see if you can spot Mulga Bill in the penny-farthing races!   p. 538

LATE MAR A weekend of imaginative activities around river and town at Focus on Franklin   p. 508

EARLY MAY Get a taste for Tasmanian country life at Agfest just south of Launceston   p. 538

HOBART

HIGHLIGHTS

Alpenrail Swiss Model Village and Railway **p. 514**

Battery Point **p. 509**

Tasmanian Museum and Art Gallery **p. 510**

Special events

Australian Wooden Boat Festival
Feb, odd-numbered years
www.australianwoodenboatfestival.
com.au
This free, four-day event is
a celebration of wooden boats
– historic, replica and modern.
Children's activities include
live entertainment and a chance
to make little wooden boats
to sacrifice to the 'Ship
sinking pond'.

Focus on Franklin
Late Mar
www.focusonfranklin.org
The highlight of this event in
the town of Franklin, south of
Hobart, is the spectacular sound
and light show on Saturday night.
The weekend offers lots of fun
activities for kids such as a
jumping castle, musical hay-
bales, pizza throwing, a tea-party
relay race, apple bowling, tug-of-
war, hay-bale fort building,
storytelling, live concerts, fire
department drills and displays,
dragon boats, ferry boat rides
and remote control yacht races.

Hobart Doll Show
Late Aug
0421 024 798;
www.chooseit.org.au/hobartdolls
This is doll-lovers' heaven, with
displays of handmade porcelain
dolls, antique toys, and teddy
bears, and stalls selling doll
accessories and miniatures.

Richmond Village Fair
Mar
www.richmondvillagefair.com

Dress up in your best colonial wear and participate in a fair that has been taking place in this picturesque village north-east of Hobart since 1828. This unsophisticated, country-style event includes Punch and Judy shows, live music, stalls, and vintage fire-engine displays.

Around town

Battery Point
Battery Point, Hobart
www.batterypoint.net

FREE

As you set foot in this historic area of Hobart you feel as if you are stepping back in time. It's like a little Cornish village, complete with a village green encircled by quaint cottages. You keep expecting a pirate with a cutlass or a lady in a hooped skirt to suddenly appear. The kids play on the swings in a village green, puff and pant their way to the top of a 'secret' set of steps, and captain an adventure ship in a playground perched high on a hill.

INSIDER TIPS

- The playground with the adventure ship is Princes Park Playground, Castray Esplanade, Battery Point; there is a historic semaphore station in the corner of the park.

- The 'secret steps' are Kelly's Steps, located at the end of Kelly Street. They were built by adventurer James Kelly in 1839 to connect Battery Point with Salamanca Place. A market is held in Salamanca Place every Saturday (*see* p. 513).

- There are plenty of eating places in the Battery Point area.

- The village green can be found in Arthurs Circus.

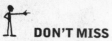

DON'T MISS

■ The ghost tours of the area, if you're game (extra cost, *see* p. 512).

■ The chance to see inside one of the historic houses, at Narryna Heritage Museum (extra cost, *see* p. 513).

■ A delightful, old-fashioned lolly shop, Bahr's Chocolate Shop and Milk Bar, at 95 Hampden Road; (03) 6223 6771. There are jars of lollies in the windows, and delicious handmade chocolates inside.

FABULOUS FACTS

Battery Point is named after the battery of guns that was installed here in 1818 to protect Hobart from enemy ships that might sail up the Derwent River. The guns are long gone, but you can still see houses built by the first European settlers as homes for local mariners and officers of the garrison. The semaphore station and signal mast on the edge of Princes Park once signalled to ships entering the harbour and relayed messages via a chain of other stations to Port Arthur (*see* p. 522).

Kid Quest
Count your way to the top of Kelly's Steps.

Tasmanian Museum and Art Gallery
40 Macquarie St, Hobart
(03) 6211 4177;
www.tmag.tas.gov.au
FREE

The wonderfully interactive Antarctica exhibition, Islands to Ice, gives an insight into an amazing place that few people visit. Your kids will hover, intrigued over a map of Antarctica made out of ice, just like the real place, and eagerly use the compass provided to locate the magnetic South Pole (surprisingly, in the ocean off East Antarctica). You will all have fun putting on 3-D glasses to watch the projections of glass lantern slides from Sir Douglas Mawson's 1911–13 expedition. But then you will gaze soberly at the bubbles in a 300-year-old core of ice – physical evidence of changing CO_2 levels and the warming of our planet.

Tasmanian Museum and Art Gallery, Hobart

INSIDER TIPS

- This museum and gallery complex is relatively small and easy to explore, but has an interesting, eclectic mixture of exhibits.

- Download a Mystery Trail brochure and kids can have fun finding the answers.

- The art gallery has changing displays and a significant collection of Australian colonial paintings.

- The Courtyard Cafe serves snacks and lunches.

DON'T MISS

- Ningenneh Tunapry – the Tasmanian Aboriginal Gallery – where you can see a traditional bark hut and the first bark canoe built in over 170 years. The beautiful shell jewellery and basket-ware in this space reveal the vibrancy of contemporary Aboriginal culture.

- The extinct animals display in the zoology gallery – particularly the information on the thylacine (Tasmanian tiger).

- The Young Collectors exhibit, where kids' own collections are put on display, labelled in correct museum style.

- The mobile Art Cart and Museum Cart, which have changing hands-on activities for kids.

FABULOUS FACTS

The museum site itself is of great historical significance. Archaeological evidence has revealed that it was occupied by Aboriginal people for more than 40 000 years. The museum is composed of several buildings, and the Commissariat Store, built in 1810, is one of the oldest buildings in Australia.

Anglesea Barracks and Military Museum of Tasmania

Davey St, Hobart
(03) 6237 7160;
www.militarymuseumtasmania.org.au
Open Tues and Thurs morning

BUDGET

These are the oldest continually occupied military barracks in Australia, and some of the buildings were constructed in 1814. The old military gaol houses the museum. Peep in the cells for glimpses of lifelike displays such as a soldier firing a machine gun and a prisoner on his stretcher bed.

Faerie Shop

Shop 11, Salamanca Arts Centre,
77 Salamanca Pl, Hobart
(03) 6224 8731; www.faeries.com.au

FREE

Watch your little kids' delight as they step through the sparkling pink entrance into fairyland! Sometimes there are story sessions or faerie and pixie school (extra cost).

Ghost tours

Depart from The Bakehouse,
Salamanca Sqr
0439 335 696;
www.ghosttoursofhobart.com.au
Depart at dusk; bookings essential
Suitable for ages 8+

MID-RANGE

Explore the narrow alleys and stairways of Battery Point or Hobart's historic city centre and meet ghosts of convicts, bushrangers, whalers, cannibals and criminals. The tour guides promise to take you only to genuinely haunted sites on this spine-chilling two-hour tour!

Salamanca Market, Hobart

Narryna Heritage Museum

103 Hampden Rd, Battery Point
(03) 6234 2791; www.narryna.com.au
Open daily, afternoons only on weekends
and public holidays

BUDGET

In this beautifully restored historic home the highlights for kids are the nursery with its antique toys and magnificent dolls' house, and the collection of clothes, including children's wear.

Penitentiary Chapel Historic Site

Cnr Brisbane and Campbell sts, Hobart
Day tours (03) 6231 0911, evening ghost
tours 0417 361 392;
www.penitentiarychapel.com
Entry by tour only; check times

BUDGET

This site offers a fascinating and gruesome insight into Tasmania's past. Originally intended as a chapel for convicts, this building became a place of horror with the addition of underground solitary confinement cells, an execution yard and gallows. If you are game, ghost tours — by flickering lamplight — are available most evenings!

Royal Tasmanian Botanic Gardens

Queens Domain, Tasman Hwy, Hobart
(03) 6236 3075; www.rtbg.tas.gov.au

FREE

Highlights for kids are the Japanese Garden with its red, arched bridge and the misty Subantarctic House where they can see plants from subantarctic islands and hear sounds of wind, birds and seals.

Salamanca Market

Salamanca Pl, Hobart
Hobart City Council (03) 6238 2843;
www.salamancamarkethobart.com.au
Open Sat till mid-afternoon

FREE

This lively outdoor market with a backdrop of historic sandstone warehouses is a popular tourist attraction. Be entertained by buskers and browse the colourful stalls selling food, jewellery, art and craft.

TrikeMania Adventure Tours

Murray St Pier, Hobart
0408 655 923;
www.discovertasmania.com
Check times
Minimum age 4 years

VARIOUS PRICES

Fancy roaring around on the back of a motorbike? TrikeMania offers

TrikeMania Adventure Tours, Hobart

rides on a motor-trike – a motorbike with a back seat, complete with seatbelts. Take a 15-minute thrill ride or book a personalised tour of Hobart. Helmets and warm clothes are supplied. Note: only three passengers can be accommodated.

Suburbs

Alpenrail Swiss Model Village and Railway
82 Abbotsfield Rd, Claremont
(03) 6249 3748; www.alpenrail.com.au
Closed Tues
MID-RANGE

Alpenrail Swiss Model Village and Railway, Claremont

As the tiny trains chug their way around the mountains, the kids run from one end of the display to the other, pointing and exclaiming at each new, entrancing detail they discover. They find buttons to push and are thrilled when the church bells ring and the bus horns toot. The realism of this miniature Swiss landscape impresses both adults and kids. Everyone has their own favourite detail – tunnels, lakes with boats, a wedding party arriving at the church... And there are more delights still to explore, with a fairy garden outside the door!

INSIDER TIPS

- The display is an accurate scale model of the mountains and rail system of the Bernese Alps area in Switzerland.

- There are wings available to wear while you wander in the fairy garden.
- Tea and biscuits are available in a chalet in the Fairy Garden.
- The Cadbury Visitor Centre is nearby (*see below*).

DON'T MISS

- The night scene with glowing train headlights, internally lit carriage windows, and sky streaked with lightning.
- The cows coming down from their summer pastures. Listen for the alphorn and the clanking of the cowbells.
- The tiny figures seated inside the trains.
- The Fairy Garden where you can find elves and goblins as well as fairies, and entrancing fairy houses.
- The video presentation about the construction of the model.
- Extra displays that are specially designed for little ones, where they can control Thomas the Tank Engine and the Smurf trains themselves.

FABULOUS FACTS

Alpenrail covers an area of 200 square metres – the size of two average houses. It has about 350 metres of 0-scale track and took 7 years to construct. Like any good model railway, it's a work-in-progress with constant modification.

Kid Quest

See if you can spot a tiny figure waving from the window of one of the trains!

Cadbury Visitor Centre
100 Cadbury Rd, Claremont
1800 627 367;
www.cadbury.com.au/about-cadbury/
cadbury-visitor-centre.aspx
Closed weekends and public holidays,
shortened hours in winter
BUDGET
There are no tours of the actual factory, but you listen to a short talk, watch a DVD about how Cadbury chocolates are made

and receive samples to taste. Factory seconds are sold in the shop (not accessible without the tour).

Female Factory Historic Site
16 Degraves St, South Hobart
(03) 6233 6656;
www.femalefactory.com.au
Closed weekends and public holidays
Phone ahead to check tour times
MID-RANGE

In the late-18th and early-19th centuries, many British prisoners were sentenced to transportation to Australia. Female convicts sent to Hobart either worked as servants or lived in this female 'factory' doing washing, mending and sewing for the gentlefolk. Some of them had children, who were imprisoned with their mothers. The rooms are now bare, but the guided tour, which lasts just over an hour, gives you an insight into the convicts' lives. Better still, take Louisa's Walk tour (*see below*).

Hobart Paddle
Depart from Marieville Espl, Sandy Bay
www.freycinetadventures.com.au/
hobart-sea-kayaking
Twice daily; bookings essential
Minimum age 8 years
HIGH COST

In stable, double sea kayaks, you explore Hobart's interesting historic wharf areas. All equipment is provided, including life jackets and weatherproof jackets, and a hot fish and chip snack is included. No experience or swimming ability is required.

Kangaroo Bluff Historic Battery
Cnr Gunning St and Fort St, Bellerive
www.parks.tas.gov.au
FREE

This historic fort with cannons was built in the late-19th century, to support several others along the coast. At that time there was a fear that the Russians were going to invade Australia. You can play in the fort and have a picnic in the surrounding park.

Long Beach Reserve
Via Beach Rd, Sandy Bay
FREE

This area offers lovely sandy beaches, an adventure playground, and picnic and barbecue facilities. Wander around to Blinking Billy Point to watch the racing yachts.

Louisa's Walk
Depart from Cascade Brewery,
Cascade Rd, South Hobart
(03) 6229 8959 or 0437 276 417;
www.livehistoryhobart.com.au
Every afternoon; bookings essential
Suitable for ages 5+
MID-RANGE

This is a unique and unforgettable experience. As two actors lead you through the gardens of Cascade Brewery and in through the gates of the forbidding prison walls of the Female Factory Historic Site (*see above*) they immerse you in the story of

Irish convict Louisa Regan, transported to Van Diemen's Land in 1841 for stealing a loaf of bread. Have your tissues ready!

Mount Wellington Descent Bike Ride

Pick up from your hotel or Tasmanian Travel and Information Centre, 20 Davey St, Hobart
(03) 6228 4255;
www.mtwellingtondescent.com.au
Two tours daily
Minimum age 8 years
(and 140 centimetres tall)

HIGH COST

Travel by van to the top of Mount Wellington and then enjoy a scenic three-hour mountain ride, downhill all the way! A guide will lead you and give you the opportunity for off-road cycling if you like. The tour finishes at Salamanca Place in the heart of Hobart.

Putters Adventure Golf

10 Main Rd, Moonah
(03) 6228 0099; www.putters.com.au
Open daily, till late Fri and Sat
MID-RANGE

There are two challenging and fun adventure minigolf courses here. The outdoor course is set in landscaped gardens with waterfalls, pools and sand traps. Indoors, you have to chase balls up and down a cascade and water wheel. There is also a great playground and a cafe.

Shot Tower

Channel Hwy, Taroona
(03) 6227 8885; www.parks.tas.gov.au
BUDGET

In the late 19th century, shot for firearms was made by pouring molten lead through colanders at

Shot Tower, Taroona

the top of this tower. The droplets cooled as they fell to the bottom, landing in a tub of water and forming roughly round pellets. Kids will love the challenge of climbing and counting the 259 steps to the top.

Tasmanian Cricket Museum and Bellerive Oval Tours

18 Derwent St, Bellerive
(03) 6282 0433;
www.tascricket.com.au/library_and_museum
Limited opening hours
BUDGET

Discover Tasmania's cricketing history through videos and interactive displays. Tours of Bellerive Oval are offered Tuesday mornings, except on match days and public holidays.

Tasmanian Transport Museum

Anfield St, Glenorchy
(03) 6272 7721;
www.railtasmania.com/ttms
Open weekend and public holiday afternoons
BUDGET

Kids (and adults) who enjoy big things on wheels will love the trains, trams, buses and vintage fire trucks here. Train trips are offered on the first and third Sunday of the month.

Tasmanian Transport Museum, Glenorchy

Kingston

Australian Antarctic Division
Channel Hwy, Kingston
(03) 6232 3212
Closed weekends
FREE
Kids with an interest in Antarctica will be thrilled to visit the real location where all equipment, fresh fruit and vegetables are organised for Australian Antarctic research expeditions. You can view photographs and models of Antarctic activities.

Kingston Beach
Osborne Espl, Kingston Beach
12 km/15 min south
FREE
This is a safe swimming beach in a pleasant cove on the shores of the D'Entrecasteaux Channel.

Day trips

Bonorong Wildlife Park
593 Briggs Rd, Brighton
(03) 6268 1184; www.bonorong.com.au
30 km/30 min north

MID-RANGE
Don't miss the free 45-minute tours on offer twice a day. You'll meet and pat wombats and koalas, and find out all about Tasmanian devils. The private night tours (extra cost) are even better. The keeper takes you right inside the enclosures and you get to hand-feed animals such as echidnas, quolls, tawny frogmouths, golden possums and, if you dare, the Tasmanian devils! Bookings are essential for night tours.

Bruny Island
Visitor Centre (03) 6267 4494;
www.brunyisland.org.au
85 km south/1 hr by land and sea

VARIOUS PRICES
This is a wild, scenic spot with large areas of unspoilt bush and an abundance of wildlife. There is a car ferry service available from Kettering, (03) 6273 6725, www.brunyislandferry.com.au, but not all hire car companies allow their vehicles on the island. Alternatively, several operators offer day tours from Hobart, providing commentary and the opportunity to view the marine world from underwater submarines. A large part of the island is a national park. You can go for bush and beach walks looking for various animals,

including seals and whales (June–October) and find ruins of whaling stations. In the evening, you can watch little penguins come ashore. There are plenty of places to eat and to stay overnight. Other attractions on the island include:

- Bruny Island Berry Farm, 526 Adventure Bay Road, Adventure Bay; (03) 6293 1055
- Alonnah Paddle Boats and Kayaks, 31 William Carte Drive, Alonnah; (03) 6293 1547
- Bligh Museum of Pacific Exploration, 876 Main Road, Adventure Bay; (03) 6293 1117

Curringa Farm Tours
5831 Lyell Hwy, Hamilton
(03) 6286 3332;
www.curringafarm.com.au
75 km/1 hr north-west
Open Sept–Apr; bookings essential
HIGH COST

Visit this working farm to see sheepshearing and cropping, meet new little lambs, watch the sheep dogs at work and find out about caring for the land. There is also accommodation available if you'd like more time to enjoy the bush and participate in farm activities.

Devil Jet Rides
The Esplanade, New Norfolk
(03) 6261 3460; www.deviljet.com.au
35 km/45 min north-west
HIGH COST

Spend half an hour speeding around the picturesque upper reaches of the Derwent River. Lifejackets and other gear are provided for all sizes.

Hastings Caves State Reserve
Hastings Cave Rd via Geeveston
(03) 6298 3209; www.parks.tas.gov.au
125 km/1 hr 30 min south
Check tour times for the cave
THERMAL POOLS BUDGET ENTRY;
CAVE TOURS MID-RANGE

Swim in a pool filled naturally by a warm, bubbling spring, go for short forest walks to look for platypus, trout, eels, quolls and birds, and take a guided tour of the spectacular Newdegate Cave with its stalactites and stalagmites.

Tangara Trail Rides
1960 South Arm Rd, Sandford
0400 113 482;
www.tangaratrailrides.com.au
15 km/20 min south
VARIOUS PRICES

Just a short distance from central Hobart you can enjoy scenic rides along bushland trails and beaches. Kids usually need to be 8 years old to go on a trail ride, but younger ones can enjoy a led-ride on a pony.

Hastings Caves State Reserve

Huon Jet
The Esplanade, Huonville
(03) 6264 1838; www.huonjet.com
30 km/40 min south-west

HIGH COST

Enjoy the exhilaration of zooming around in a fast jet boat on the Huon River, alternating with pauses to admire reflections of Huon pines in the water. Lifejackets and other gear are provided for all sizes. Tours last 35 minutes.

Ida Bay Railway
Depart from Lune River Station,
328 Lune River Rd, Lune River
(03) 6298 3110;
www.idabayrailway.com.au
100 km/1 hr 30 min south
Check timetable

MID-RANGE

Take a scenic trip on this historic train to Deep Hole Bay, a large, white secluded swimming beach accessible only by rail. You are welcome to hop off, have a picnic or barbecue, go for a bushwalk and enjoy the beach before returning on a later train (just be sure to let the driver know). This is a two-hour return trip.

Mount Field National Park
Lake Dobson Rd via the town
of National Park
Road conditions (03) 6288 1319,
snow reports (03) 6288 1166;
www.parks.tas.gov.au
90 km/1 hr 30 min north-west

BUDGET

You can take short walks to the spectacular Russell Falls or into the fern forest where you can see swamp gums, the world's tallest flowering plants. A nature walk brochure is available from the visitor centre. Continue 16 kilometres to the higher Lake Dobson section where there is usually snow suitable for skiing and tobogganing from June to September.

Old Hobart Town Model Village
23 Bridge St, Richmond
(03) 6260 2502;
www.oldhobarttown.com
30 km/30 min north-east

MID-RANGE

Be amazed by the accuracy and detail of this small-scale reconstruction of the Hobart of 1820. Built outdoors, it is surrounded by an appropriate landscape complete with small rivers and trees. Little model figures of convicts and overseers bring the scene to life.

Port Arthur
Tasman Peninsula
(03) 6251 2310 or 1800 659 101;
www.portarthur.org.au
100 km/1hr 20 min south-east

VARIOUS PRICES

This former convict settlement is Tasmania's top tourist attraction. You can wander through the grounds and buildings on your own or take a guided tour. There are lots of imaginative and kid-friendly displays to help you learn about the convicts' lives. See the restored officers' houses and the convict dormitories, prison cells, hospital and church. Visit the dockyard and coal mines operated with convict labour and board the MV *Marana* to tour the boys' prison or the Isle of the Dead. Ghost tours are available in the evening (extra cost). Note: if doing the ghost tour, plan to stay overnight in the area as it is a windy route back to Hobart with lots of wildlife on the road. Day passes are valid for two consecutive days.

Richmond Bridge
www.environment.gov.au/heritage/
places/national/richmond
30 km/30 min north-east

FREE

This much-photographed landmark with its sandstone arches was built by convicts in the 1820s. It is supposed to be haunted by the ghost of George Grover, a vicious overseer, who used to whip the convict workers until they caught him drunk one night and threw him over the side. Richmond Colonial Gaol is nearby (*see below*).

Richmond Colonial Gaol
37 Bathurst St, Richmond
(03) 6260 2127
30 km/30 min north-east
BUDGET

Built in 1825, this is the oldest intact gaol in Australia. Kids love seeing the flogging yard and having a go in the solitary confinement cells. One of the most infamous residents of the gaol was Ikey Solomon, who was transported from England. He is immortalised in Bryce Courtenay's *Potato Factory* and is possibly the model for Charles Dickens' character Fagin in *Oliver Twist*.

Ride the Rail
Maydena Adventure Hub,
Gordon River Rd, Maydena
(03) 6288 2288 or
1300 720 507;
www.adventureforests.com.au/
maydena/128
85 km/1 hr 15 min west
Oct–Mar; bookings essential
Minimum age 5 years
HIGH COST

Pedal your own Rail Riders along the old Maydena railway track. You travel 2.5 kilometres through the beautiful Derwent Valley, passing historic railway artefacts. The return trip takes about an hour.

Sorell Fruit Farm
174 Pawleena Rd, Sorell
(03) 6265 2744; www.sorellfruitfarm.com
30 km/30 min north-east
Nov–May
VARIOUS PRICES

Experience picking and tasting fruit straight off the tree – or

Port Arthur

vine. Depending on the season you can pick various berries, cherries, apricots, nectarines, peaches and apples. Visit in early October before any fruit are ripe to enjoy the enchanting cherry blossoms (no cost).

Southern Design Centre
11 School Rd, Geeveston
(03) 6297 0039;
www.southerndesigncentre.com
60 km/1 hr south-west
FREE

If your kids are interested in art and craft, pop in here on your way to the Tahune Forest Reserve (*see below*) or Hastings Caves State Reserve (*see* p. 520). You can often catch an artisan at work spinning wool, creating artworks out of fabric pieces, wood-turning or making linocuts.

Tahune Forest Reserve
Arve Rd, Geeveston
(03) 6295 7111;
www.adventureforests.com.au/tahune
60 km/1 hr south-west
VARIOUS PRICES

This is one of the most accessible places in Tasmania to view the famous Huon pines. Tracks lead you to giant trees that are 2000 years old. It is amazing to stand in front of something that has been living for so long and realise how much the world has changed over its lifetime! If you like heights, try the AirWalk which takes you into the treetops for

spectacular views, or experience the thrill of flying with Eagle Glide cable hang-gliding.

Tasman National Park
Several access roads via Arthur Hwy
(03) 6214 8100; www.parks.tas.gov.au
100 km/1 hr 30 min south-east
BUDGET

Be amazed by soaring cliffs and other natural features along this wild stretch of coastline. The rock formations of Tasman Blowhole, Devils Kitchen and Tasmans Arch can be accessed easily at the northern end of the park near Eaglehawk Neck. Remarkable Cave, a tunnel carved into the rock face by the Southern Ocean, is on a surfing beach on the southern tip of the Tasman Peninsula. See if you can spot examples of the rare euphrasia flowers found only in this national park; check the Tasman National Park 'Highlights' section of the website before you go. The park is a popular stop en route to Port Arthur (*see* p. 522).

Tasmanian Devil Conservation Park
Arthur Hwy, Taranna
(03) 6250 3230;
www.tasmaniandevilpark.com
85 km/1 hr south-east
Extended summer hours
MID-RANGE

This park offers fascinating encounters with various native animals. You can watch

Tasmanian devils feeding (with a great show of snarling and crushing-up of bones), hand-feed kangaroos and follow a 1.5-kilometre trail to the Kings of the Wind free-flight bird show. The park's breeding program for Tasmanian devils is vital to animal conservation, as devils in the wild are rapidly dying out from a facial tumour disease. The park is en route to Port Arthur and near Tasman National Park (*see* p. 524).

Tinderbox Marine Reserve
Via Tinderbox Rd, Tinderbox
(03) 6233 6560; www.parks.tas.gov.au
25 km/30 min south
FREE
This is a great area for beginner snorkellers, although a wetsuit is recommended for comfort at most times. Look for the dozens of different seaweeds, beautiful weedy sea dragons, pipe fish and seahorses, as well as starfish, squid, octopus, sponges and other fish.

Woodbridge Hill Hand Weaving Studio
229 Woodbridge Hill, Woodbridge
(03) 6267 4430;
web.clearnetworks.com.
au/~handweaving
40 km/40 min south
Phone ahead for opening hours
FREE
Watch a weaver at work on a handloom and touch the different soft fibres used for the weaving – including Collie dog hair!

Tasmanian Devil Conservation Park, Taranna

ZooDoo Wildlife Park
620 Middle Tea Tree Rd, Richmond
(03) 6260 2444; www.zoodoo.com.au
30 km/30 min north-east
MID-RANGE

Play in the animal nursery, laugh at the monkeys, meet miniature ponies, walk amongst kangaroos and wallabies, take a safari bus to feed emus and camels... there are lots of different types of animals to encounter in this interactive zoo.

Accommodation

Discovery Holiday Parks – Hobart
673 East Derwent Hwy, Hobart
(03) 6243 7185 or 1800 030 044;
dhp-hobart.tas.big4.com.au
BUDGET

Just ten minutes' drive from town, you can camp, stay in a caravan or take a two-bedroom cabin with full-size kitchen, all in natural bushland. Facilities include beach volleyball, minigolf, tennis court and playgrounds for big and little kids.

St Ives Hobart
67 St Georges Tce, Battery Point
(03) 6221 5555;
www.stivesmotel.com.au
MID-RANGE

This motel and apartment complex is a few minutes' walk from Hobart's city centre and waterfront and Battery Point (*see* p. 509). The spacious two-storey apartments have kitchen and living areas downstairs and two bedrooms and bathroom upstairs.

White Beach Tourist Park
White Beach Rd, Nubeena South
(03) 6250 2142;
www.whitebeachtouristpark.com.au
BUDGET

If staying overnight near Port Arthur, you can enjoy this quiet beachfront location surrounded by white ghost gums and overlooking the clear, blue water. There is also a playground. Choose a camping or caravan site or a self-contained two-bedroom cabin.

Places to eat

Captain Fell's Historic Ferries
Franklin Wharf, Hobart
(03) 6223 5893;
www.captainfellshistoricferries.com.au
Have dinner on a boat cruise and enjoy a spectacular view of Hobart's twinkling lights. Very reasonably priced family packages are available.

Drunken Admiral
17 Hunter St, Hobart
(03) 6234 1903;
www.drunkenadmiral.com.au
Kids enjoy the cosy, nautical-themed decor. The appropriately fish-focussed menu includes fish and chips, always a favourite with small fry.

Mures Lower Deck
Victoria Dock, Hobart
(03) 6231 2121;
www.mures.com.au/lower_deck
This family-friendly bistro has a dinghy for the kids to play in, puzzles and drawing materials, booster seats and highchairs. Meals are simple, reasonably priced and freshly cooked. Seafood is a specialty and you can watch the fishing boats being unloaded while you eat.

Blue Skies Cafe Bar and Restaurant
Murray Street Pier, Hobart
(03) 6224 3747;
www.blueskiesdining.com
Kids have their own real menu here, which includes items such as 'Penne pasta tossed through a light tomato sauce with green peas, mild salami, fresh herbs and parmesan cheese' and even their own list of mocktails. This is a relaxed venue on the waterfront of a working dock.

Richmond Maze and Tea Rooms
13 Bridge St, Richmond
(03) 6260 2451;
www.sullivanscove.com/towns/richmond/maze
Richmond is a picturesque historic village. There are two timber mazes to explore (budget cost), so you can visit the tea rooms for lunch or afternoon tea, and tell the kids to get lost! The menu includes simple kids' party snacks and Witches' Brew.

EAST COAST

Bicheno, located 180 kilometres north-east of Hobart and 160 kilometres south-east of Launceston, is a popular base for exploring the East Coast

Year-round destination, but some attractions close over winter

Bicheno

Penguin Tours

Depart from Penguin Tour Kiosk, Tasman Hwy, central Bicheno
(03) 6375 1333; www.bichenopenguintours.com.au
Every evening at dusk

MID-RANGE

From your vantage point in the middle of the penguin rookery, you enjoy an intimate view of the little penguins waddling past en route to their burrows. You're close enough to see two penguins pause and squabble before disappearing into separate dark doorways among the rocks and bushes. A fluffy round ball of a chick squeaks impatiently outside its home and you all giggle with amused sympathy as it tries to grab a bite to eat from every penguin that passes. At last the real mum and dad arrive, bringing supper in their beaks.

INSIDER TIPS

- You are taken by bus, a trip of five minutes, to a private property where the one-hour tour takes place.

- Departure time varies according to season, from 5.30pm in mid-winter to 9pm in mid-summer.

- During the tour you walk through the rookery to various observation points overlooking the beach, watch the penguins come in from their day of feeding at sea, and see them return to their burrows – and their chicks.

- Chicks can be seen at various stages of development between the months of August to December.

- Over the winter months, there may be as few as five birds appearing.

- Wear warm clothing and covered footwear – sometimes the penguins bite toes!

- You are not allowed to take photographs.

- The tour takes place in the dark with only a very faint glow from the guides' low emitting torches.

- The paths you walk on are the penguins' natural highways, widened slightly.

DON'T MISS

- The opportunities to see right inside the penguin burrows. There are a few man-made wooden burrows with lids, and the guides can raise the lids for you to peek inside.

- The night sky – in this area without lights, the view of the stars is spectacular.

- The chance to ask questions of knowledgeable guides.

FABULOUS FACTS

Little penguins (sometimes called fairy penguins) are the smallest penguins in the world, not much more than 30 centimetres high. Their activities change according to season. At the beginning of the breeding season, you see males dragging grasses into the burrows to build comfortable nests, and calling loudly, advertising for mates. During courtship, penguins may waddle around the burrow in circles. Once eggs are laid, both parents take turns to sit on the nest, and when the chicks hatch the feeding begins.

Kid Quest
How do you tell the difference between male and female penguins?
See pp. 640–4 for the answer

Bicentennial Foreshore Footway
Around the Bicheno foreshore
FREE
Start from the blowhole, with its orange-tinted rocks, blue ocean vistas and jets of white spray, and follow a 3-kilometre path along the rocky foreshore (watch out for large waves). On the way, you pass The Gulch, a tiny, picturesque harbour for the local fishing fleet. Walking maps are available from the Tourist Office, 41 Foster St, Bicheno.

Bicheno Aquarium
Gulch Rd, Bicheno
0418 300 620;
www.bichenoaquarium.com.au
Seasonal
BUDGET
This small, changing display of sea creatures from the Southern Ocean includes seahorses, jellyfish and sharks. A little touch pool for the kids has starfish and hermit crabs.

Glass Bottom Boat Tour
Depart from The Gulch,
The Esplanade, Bicheno
(03) 6375 1294 or 0407 812 217
Twice daily Sept–Apr, depending on weather
MID-RANGE
This is a great way to see the beautiful sea life in this magnificent bay – ideal for kids who aren't safe in the water yet. Tours last about 40 minutes. Dress warmly!

Waubs Bay Beach
Waubs Bay, Bicheno
FREE; SNORKELLING EQUIPMENT HIRE
HIGH COST
This beach has soft sand, and safe water for swimming. Kids can try snorkelling too – there are fish, sea dragons and seahorses to spot just by stepping off the beach. Wetsuits and other snorkelling equipment are available for hire from Bicheno Dive Centre, 2 Scuba Ct; (03) 6375 1138; www.bichenodive.com.au.

North of Bicheno____

East Coast Natureworld

18356 Tasman Hwy, Bicheno
(03) 6375 1311; www.natureworld.com.au

MID-RANGE

As soon as you walk into the grounds, the free-ranging kangaroos come hopping towards you. The kids fill their hands with food, thrilled to find the kangaroos' soft, furry faces eating right out of their palms. Suddenly, there's a loud honking as two Cape Barren geese race up and start nipping at the kangaroos to chase them away. A moment later, two beaks are prodding at the food too. You all laugh and move on. There is a lot more here to see: the nocturnal house, Tasmanian devils, snakes, ostriches ...

INSIDER TIPS

- Natureworld covers a large area so allow several hours.
- Devils Den Cafe has a budget-priced kids' menu and a great view out over the grounds and the free-ranging kangaroos and birds.
- Natureworld serves as an important rescue, breeding and rehabilitation centre and returns a large percentage of animals to the wild.
- Check the schedule of feeding times and keeper talks. The snake feeding is an unusual sight, but does not take place every day.

DON'T MISS

- The big walk-through aviaries, where rainbow lorikeets zoom and dive around your heads; the regent parrot might even land on you.
- Devil World, where you not only get a close-up view of Tasmanian devils through windows, but kids can have a go at lots of fun, educational exhibits. Look for the displays of real animal droppings and learn how to identify the droppings you see in the bush.
- Old McDonald's Farm, where the kids can pat and feed domesticated animals such as a pony, ducks and goats.

- The big playground, which is out the back, past the emus and ostriches.

- The coal mine heritage display where you can go inside a replica mine and see a huge display of mining equipment.

- The nocturnal house (*see* FABULOUS FACTS *below*).

FABULOUS FACTS

If you visit the nocturnal house soon after Natureworld opens in the morning, you will see time going backwards twelve hours. The sun sets, and real conditions of the preceding night – temperature, light and sounds – occur again. This technology makes the nocturnal animals wake up and behave naturally and comfortably during daylight hours when they would normally be asleep. You can see animals in Nocturnal World that you rarely get a chance to meet, such as sugar gliders, bettongs, bandicoots, quolls and golden possums.

Kid Quest
Do Tasmanian tiger snakes lay eggs?
See pp. 640–4 for the answer

Bay of Fires
Via Binalong Bay Rd from St Helens
FREE

An easily accessible part of the famous Bay of Fires is the southern section, stretching from Binalong Bay to The Gardens. This is one of the most spectacular, secluded beaches you will ever see: miles of pure white sand, turquoise water and huge granite boulders covered with bright orange lichen. Explore the rockpools, and don't forget the surrounding conservation area where you can look for coastal wildflowers, wallabies, wombats, echidnas, kangaroos and Tasmanian devils. There are various sheltered little coves with calm water, but the beaches here are not patrolled, so stay alert.

Douglas Apsley National Park
Via Rosedale Rd, west of Tasman Hwy
Parks and Wildlife Office (03) 6256 7000;
www.parks.tas.gov.au
BUDGET

From the Apsley Waterhole carpark, a short easy track leads through open forest to a lookout platform. You can climb down to the waterhole via the campground (although it's a bit steep), and kids can have fun hopping over the stones and paddling.

South of Bicheno

Wineglass Bay, Freycinet National Park

Freycinet National Park and Wineglass Bay
Via Coles Bay Rd
Visitor Centre (03) 6256 7000; www.parks.tas.gov.au

BUDGET

You are standing on the edge of a cliff, looking out over what has to be one of the most spectacular views in the world. To one side you have a glimpse of the famous Wineglass Bay, and a hundred metres below your feet, the sea is so clear you can see the fish swimming in the water. Beside you rises the white, glistening tower of Cape Tourville Lighthouse, which warns ships away from this treacherous, rocky point. Out at sea, a graceful shape leaps into the air, and then another – two dolphins playing in the waves.

INSIDER TIPS

- Freycinet National Park begins just south of Bicheno, but a good place to start exploring is from the visitor centre located in the Coles Bay area of the park (about half an hour from Bicheno). You can obtain information here about the different walks and beaches. Most of the activities you will want to do are close to this visitor centre.

- The Cape Tourville Lighthouse is accessed by a 600-metre circuit boardwalk. There are information boards to help you locate landmarks and explain the flora and fauna.

- Picnic facilities, barbecues, water and toilets are available near the visitor centre and at Honeymoon Bay.

- During summer, park rangers offer a variety of activities.

- Camping is available in the park, but it is so popular that a ballot system operates for the peak summer and Easter periods.

- The perfect sands of famous Wineglass Bay can be reached by an 11-kilometre hike. An easier way is on a Freycinet Paddle tour (*see* p. 535).

- The Wineglass Bay Cruise (*see* p. 536) sails inside the bay.

DON'T MISS

- The famous view of Wineglass Bay. The lookout is accessed by a steep one-hour return walk.

- Honeymoon Bay, which is a lovely sheltered swimming spot that is ideal for learning to snorkel. In the clear water you might catch sight of a stingray or some scallops. You need to bring your own snorkelling equipment. There are also rockpools to explore here.

- Muirs Beach, a sheltered, safe beach with soft sand, suitable for playing and swimming. Muirs Beach is accessed from The Esplanade, Coles Bay.

- The white-breasted sea eagles, which are sometimes seen flying around the park. Their wing span can exceed two metres!

FABULOUS FACTS

Oddly, the beaches within Freycinet National Park do not share the same type of sand. This is because each one has been created by the erosion of a different kind of rock. Honeymoon Bay is fine gravel, recently created from pink feldspar pebbles from The Hazards above it, while the sand at Friendly Beaches (in the northern part of the park) squeaks when you walk on it because it has a high content of pure, rounded grains of silica – it is literally squeaky clean.

Kid Quest
What is the gruesome origin of the name Wineglass Bay?
See pp. 640–4 for the answer

All4Adventure

Depart from cnr The Esplanade
and Freycinet Dr, Coles Bay
(03) 6257 0018;
www.all4adventure.com.au
Two to three tours daily
Unsuitable for children who require a car
seat

HIGH COST

Bump and roar your way through the Freycinet National Park! Kids ride in the back of a 3-seater All Terrain Vehicle with one adult, while other adults ride quad bikes. Your guide leads you up and down tracks through the bush and out to the coast for breathtaking views.

Around Swansea

FREE

There are lovely safe swimming beaches in the sheltered inner shores of Great Oyster Bay, and about 7 kilometres south of town you'll find Spiky Bridge — a strange-looking stone bridge built by convicts in the 1840s. Nobody is quite sure of the purpose for the vicious spikes of stone sticking up from the walls.

Bark Mill Museum

96 Tasman Hwy, Swansea
(03) 6257 8094;
www.barkmilltavern.com.au

BUDGET

As you step through the door, lights come on, sounds start up and you are transported back in time. See an old working mill that used to crush bark for tanning leather, and discover interesting stories about this region's history. You can buy meals from the Bark Mill Tavern (*see* PLACES TO EAT p. 537) and there is a playground outside.

Freycinet paddle

Muirs Beach, The Esplanade, Coles Bay
(03) 6257 0500;
www.freycinetadventures.com.au
Daily, Nov–Apr

HIGH COST

This full-day tour includes paddling in stable, double sea kayaks around Coles Bay, a stop on a secluded beach for lunch, a trip by Aqua Taxi to Hazards Beach in Freycinet National Park, and a self-guided thirty-minute walk from there to the famous Wineglass Bay. (This is one of the easier ways to access Wineglass Bay.) For families with kids, the adventure can be undertaken over two days. There is also the option of just a three-hour kayak tour, which is offered twice daily throughout the year.

Maria Island National Park

Via ferry from Triabunna
Park ranger (03) 6257 1420,
www.parks.tas.gov.au
Ferry 0419 746 668;
www.mariaislandferry.com.au
Seasonal ferry timetable; other boats
can be chartered

HIGH COST

This island has forests, fern gullies, fossil-studded cliffs, deserted beaches, safe swimming, convict and industrial ruins, and lots of wild animals. There are no cars or shops (except a visitor centre), so this is an interesting experience for the kids (and you)! Bring your own food and water (water is limited), and start exploring. Camping is available and there is some basic accommodation (book ahead through park ranger).

Wineglass Bay Cruise
Depart from the jetty at the end of Jetty Rd, Coles Bay
(03) 6257 0355;
www.wineglassbaycruises.com
Every morning, Sept – late-May
HIGH COST

On this four-hour cruise you sail right into beautiful Wineglass Bay. In the clear water you can see whale vertebrae, left over from the days when whales were slaughtered here. Watch for live whales (October–November), sea eagles, dolphins and albatross. When the boat anchors, you can swim or snorkel. Highlights for kids are the charts for ticking off wild animals they see, shucking oysters with the captain, hopping on a box to help steer the boat, and Rastus the dolphin-spotting dog.

Accommodation

Bicheno East Coast Holiday Park
4 Champ St, Bicheno
(03) 6375 1999;
www.bichenoholidaypark.com.au
BUDGET TO MID-RANGE

Opposite beach and shops, and right in the centre of town, you have a choice of camping and caravan sites or a self-contained cabin. There is also a playground and recreational room.

Bicheno Gaol Cottages
Cnr Burgess and James sts, Bicheno
(03) 6375 1266;
www.bichenogaolcottages.com
MID-RANGE

How would you like to stay in a historic gaol, complete with original cells and cell doors? The cottage has been renovated in period style and has a queen bed and two singles, a kitchen, lounge with open fire and dining room.

Bicheno Hideaway
179 Harveys Farm Rd, Bicheno
(03) 6375 1312;
www.bichenohideaway.com
MID-RANGE

Set in ocean-front bushland, 3 kilometres from central Bicheno, these self-contained chalets have stunning ocean views, private decks and barbecues. Kids love the duckpond and the hand-reared Bennett's wallaby that arrives to be fed at dusk, as well as the chooks (and fresh eggs) and all the local possums, bandicoots, and wombats. Books, DVDs and fishing gear are available for loan.

BIG4 Bicheno Cabin Park
Cnr Tasman Hwy and Murray St, Bicheno
(03) 6375 1117 or 1800 789 075;
www.bichenocabins.com.au
BUDGET
This BIG4 park does not have camping or caravan sites, but offers various styles of cabins to suit a family, all with lounge areas, ensuite bathrooms and kitchens. The park is walking distance to the town centre and beaches and has its own playground.

Places to eat

Bark Mill Tavern
96 Tasman Hwy, Swansea
(03) 6257 8094;
www.barkmilltavern.com.au
Kids enjoy the wood-fired pizzas and the big open fireplace. You can have a sit-down meal in the tavern or buy a quick snack from the bakery. If you come here during the day, you can visit the Bark Mill Museum (*see* p. 535).

Beachfront Tavern
Best Western Beachfront,
232 Tasman Hwy, Bicheno
(03) 6375 1111
This relaxed, child-friendly venue serves traditional pub meals. Kids can make their own selections at the salad bar or order from the kids' menu.

Kate's Berry Farm, Swansea

Kate's Berry Farm
12 Addison St, Swansea
(03) 6257 8428;
www.katesberryfarm.com
Anyone with a sweet tooth will love the home-made berry ice-creams and chocolates. On a sunny day, sit outdoors and admire the view over the berry plants and down to Freycinet Peninsula.

LAUNCESTON & SURROUNDS

Launceston is located 200 kilometres north of Hobart and has its own airport

Overnight ferry (via Devonport) from Melbourne

Year-round destination, though many attractions close over winter

HIGHLIGHTS

Beaconsfield Mine and Heritage Centre **p. 549**

Cataract Gorge **p. 539**

Hollybank Treetops Adventure **p. 545**

Platypus House **p. 550**

Queen Victoria Museum and Art Gallery **p. 541**

Special events

Agfest
Early May
www.agfest.com.au
One of the more entertaining and unusual events at this agricultural fair staged near Oaks (south of Launceston) is a fashion competition for clothes made entirely of recycled farmyard junk! There are also the more traditional sheep dog trials, equestrian events, craft competitions and lots of stalls.

Evandale Village Fair
Feb
www.evandalevillagefair.com
The village of Evandale, just south of Launceston, reverts to its past with penny-farthing bicycles returning to the streets and residents in 19th-century dress. The main feature of this one-day event is the National Penny Farthing Races, meanwhile market stalls and live entertainment create the ambience of a colonial country fair.

Royal Launceston show
Oct
www.launcestonshowground.com.au
You'll find all the fun of a
traditional agricultural show here
with show jumping, animal
competitions, wood chopping, dog
trials, fairground rides, sideshows,
live entertainment and fireworks.

Around town

Cataract Gorge
Basin Rd, West Launceston
(03) 6331 5915; www.launcestoncataractgorge.com.au
Chairlift operates daily, including Christmas Day

FREE ENTRY; CHAIRLIFT MID-RANGE

It's early morning and most attractions are still closed, but Cataract
Gorge is open at any hour. The kids are having a great time racing
across the suspension bridge and causing it to rock. You stand in the
middle, hanging onto the side, and take in the scent of eucalypt and the
magnificent view. The South Esk River winds below, its dark waters
cascading over rocks, the jagged cliffs towering on either side.
Suddenly the kids call out in excitement – they've spotted a wallaby.
It's hard to believe this peaceful, scenic spot is only a short walk from
the centre of town.

INSIDER TIPS

- The walk from the city centre is a pleasant 15 minutes along the
  banks of the Tamar River.

- On the northern side of the gorge is Cliff Grounds, a Victorian-era
  garden with ferns, exotic plants and a picturesque historic
  rotunda.

- First Basin on the southern side of the gorge has a free, unheated
  swimming pool and a wading area that are great for hot summer
  days. There is also a playground.

- Wallabies can often be seen at early morning or dusk. Iridescent blue peacocks strut around all day and come begging for food at the restaurants and kiosks.

- There are eating places on both sides of the gorge, as well as picnic areas and barbecues.

- There are tracks to follow on both sides of the gorge. The Zig Zag Track on the southern side is more difficult, and can become muddy and slippery in wet weather. The Gorge Walk on the other side is an easy 1-kilometre sealed path.

- In winter the gorge will sometimes flood and it is an amazing sight to see from the suspension bridge.

- A trail leads to the historic hydro-electric power station (*see* FABULOUS FACTS *below*), but it is a challenging trek with lots of climbing over rocks and takes about two hours return.

- You can take a Cataract Gorge cruise (*see* p. 543).

DON'T MISS

- The chairlift journey from one side of the gorge to the other. You do not sit in enclosed capsules, but in open two-person chairs held in by safety rails. As you travel slowly and sedately over the river, you feel like a gliding bird.

- The rotunda in Cliff Grounds — while the kids are playing in this large, elaborate 'cubby house' you can read the interesting information about the building of Kings Bridge (the alternative to the suspension bridge).

- The Fairy Dell, also in Cliff Grounds, a pretty concave in the hills with a magical atmosphere.

FABULOUS FACTS

In December 1895, Launceston became the first city in the Southern Hemisphere to have electricity produced by water power. It was generated by a hydro-electric power station further up the South Esk River. You can visit the historic Duck Reach power plant buildings, and if you do, you will be astounded to realise that the great floods of 1929 reached up to this height.

Queen Victoria Museum and Art Gallery

Invermay Rd, Inveresk Precinct, Launceston
(03) 6323 3777; www.qvmag.tas.gov.au

FREE; SOME TEMPORARY EXHIBITIONS AND THE PLANETARIUM EXTRA COST

The kids laugh and lurch from side to side, unable to keep their balance on a perfectly stationary, straight walkway – curved walls, painted with rainforest scenes, are rotating around them, causing sensory confusion. Still giggling, they stagger out of the Perception Tunnel and rush for the next exhibit.

The Phenomena Factory in this museum is full of fun, interactive activities designed to demonstrate scientific principles. Kids relish the chance to pull levers and transform a drink bottle into a rocket, see how much electricity they can generate by pedalling, and test their bowling speed with a radar gun.

INSIDER TIPS

■ There is usually a free educational film showing in the Nuala O'Flaherty Auditorium if you want to take some weight off your feet for a while.

■ Exhibits are constantly changing, so some of the activities described here may have been replaced by something even better!

■ Light meals are available in Choose Cafe, which has indoor and outdoor seating – and you can even dine aboard a stationary train.

■ Several exhibition spaces in the museum, including The Phenomena Factory, have both indoor and outdoor activity areas.

■ The Planetarium (*see* DON'T MISS p. 542) does not operate every day. Check the website for the latest timetable.

DON'T MISS

- The new Tasmanian Connections exhibition, which has dinosaurs, artefacts from shipwrecks and convicts, and other intriguing displays.

- The Planetarium (budget, minimum age 5 years), where you can watch shows about space exploration, stars and planets projected onto a vast dome. Astronomical concepts are demonstrated in a way that is both dramatic and scientifically accurate.

- Replay: Sporting Life in Tasmania. You might find out some curiosities about sport that you never knew before!

- Playgroup (budget), if you have kids aged from 2 to 6 years of age. This takes place on the second and third Wednesday morning of the month and involves storytelling, craft activities and games based around museum exhibits. Bookings are essential, (03) 6323 3798.

FABULOUS FACTS

One of the main exhibits here is the museum itself! It is the site of the historic Launceston railway workshops, used in the late 19th century when a passenger train service operated in Launceston. Nowadays, the only passenger trains in Tasmania are heritage ones for tourists. In the exhibition Transforming the Island you discover Tasmania's rail history, see old workshops (left as if the workers have just walked out), and climb around on old trains.

Kid Quest
What is vigoro?
See pp. 640–4 for the answer

Cable Hang Gliding, Trevallyn

Cable Hang Gliding
Reatta Rd, Trevallyn
0419 311 198;
www.cablehanggliding.com.au
Check opening hours

MID-RANGE

If your kids enjoy flying foxes in playgrounds, then let them have a go at leaping off an 18-metre cliff and soaring for 200 metres (attached to the end of a cable). This attraction is located in a nature reserve, so you can also go for bushwalks here and maybe even spot a wombat.

Cataract Gorge Cruise
End of Home Point Pde, Home Point
(03) 6334 9900;
www.tamarrivercruises.com.au
Check tour times

MID-RANGE

Cruise past the towering, spectacular cliffs of Cataract Gorge (*see* p. 539) while enjoying an entertaining commentary and the ambience of a quaint, 1890s-style vessel. This cruise lasts 50 minutes. Longer cruises that include meals are available at a higher cost (*see* TAMAR RIVER CRUISES p. 558).

City Park
Cnr Cimitiere and Tamar sts, Launceston
Launceston Council (03) 6323 3000;
www.launceston.tas.gov.au
FREE

This is a popular green space in the middle of town. Kids can let off steam in the playground and enjoy the antics of a resident group of Japanese macaque monkeys (kept in a large enclosure). There are free concerts on Sunday afternoons in summer.

Franklin House
413 Hobart Rd, Franklin Village
(03) 6344 7824;
www.nationaltrusttas.org.au
Open daily, closed Sun mornings
BUDGET

This beautifully restored Victorian house was also a private boarding school in the 19th century. Highlights for kids include the children's trail in the garden (download a brochure from the website), the original schoolroom, and the kitchen garden.

Ghost Tours
Depart Royal Oak Hotel,
16 Brisbane St, Launceston
0421 819 373;
www.launcestoncityghosttours.com
Every evening; bookings essential
Suitable for ages 8+
MID-RANGE
On this 90-minute tour through the alleyways and inner laneways of Launceston, you will hear true tales of murder and hangings.

Kids Paradise
1 Waterfront Dr, Riverside
(03) 6334 0055;
www.kidsparadise.net.au
Closed Mon during school term
BUDGET
This fantastic indoor playground really is kids' paradise – and even adult 'kids' are encouraged to join in. There are computer games, ball games, inflatables to romp around on, play-acting rooms such as a hair-dressing salon and pirate's lair, and a special soft play area for under-5s. The Tailrace Cafe is on site (*see* PLACES TO EAT p. 558).

Kingsway Crazy Golf
22 The Kingsway, Launceston
(03) 6333 0388
Open till late
MID-RANGE
This 18-hole minigolf course is fun for all the family. Go crazy chasing balls through the mirror maze, and try to find them in the glow-in-the-dark challenge!

Launceston Aquatic Centre
18A High St, Launceston
(03) 6323 3636;
www.launcestonaquatic.com.au
Opens early daily
BUDGET
There are indoor and outdoor swimming pools, but the highlights for kids are the giant outdoor water slide and the colourful indoor water-play area with water slide and a huge bucket that dumps water.

Launceston Tramway Museum
City end of Invermay Rd, Launceston
(03) 6394 3078; www.ltms.org.au
Sat only
BUDGET
All aboard! Kids enjoy the rattly rides that are offered on these historic trams throughout the day.

National Automobile Museum
86 Cimitiere St, Launceston
(03) 6334 8888; www.namt.com.au
MID-RANGE
Rev-heads will adore this collection of classic and historic cars and motorcycles including Rolls-Royces and Ferraris.

Old Umbrella Shop
60 George St, Launceston
(03) 6331 9248;
www.nationaltrusttas.org.au
Open weekdays and Sat morning
FREE ENTRY
This quaint shop looks like something out of a storybook. It has survived, largely intact,

Old Umbrella Shop, Launceston

from the early 20th century. It is fun just to step inside and see the display of antique umbrellas and the old-fashioned till, but you can also purchase umbrellas and souvenir items.

Tamar Island Wetlands Reserve
West Tamar Hwy, Riverside
(03) 6327 3964; www.parks.tas.gov.au

BY DONATION

Kids have fun crossing the boardwalk over the river to reach Tamar Island. The wetlands

offer great opportunities to spot wildlife, including black swans (sometimes with cygnets), pademelons, swamp rats, frogs, echidnas, platypus and even Tasmanian devils. There is a great interpretive centre where you can find out more about the wetlands.

Tasmania Zoo
1166 Ecclestone Rd, Riverside
(03) 6396 6100;
www.tasmaniazoo.com.au

MID-RANGE

This is the biggest wildlife park in Tasmania and has exotic as well as native animals. The highlight is the Tasmanian devil feeding, three times daily, which includes a chance to pat a baby devil. You can also do Down and Dirty buggy rides (high cost), which involve a 17-kilometre ride in an open buggy through mud and water.

East Tamar Valley

Hollybank Treetops Adventure
Hollybank Forest Reserve, 66 Hollybank Rd, Underwood
(03) 6395 1390; www.treetopsadventure.com.au
Last tours leave mid-afternoon; bookings essential
Minimum age 3 years

HIGH COST

Picture yourself tramping through the forest following the guides, your safety harnesses, straps and buckles clanking and jangling. One by one, the group climbs the ten steps to a 2-metre-high platform. The kids

take off first, flying towards the nearest 'cloud station'. They scream with exhilaration as the ground drops away beneath them. A moment later, you follow. Any fears are swept aside by the magical sensation of flying. You are gliding through the treetops and it's like nothing you have experienced before.

Hollybank Treetops Adventure, Underwood

INSIDER TIPS

- It is imperative to check in 15 minutes before your confirmed tour time.

- The guides on this zip-line tour are expert at calming people who are afraid of heights.

- The harnesses are designed to provide the sensation of sitting in a big seat – you don't even need to hold on.

- Each group has two guides and is limited to a maximum of 12 participants.

- There are six 'cloud stations' where you stop and rest en route.

- The tour lasts up to three hours including harnessing up, safety checks, training on a simulator and a short walk through the forest to and from the course.

- Every child under 13 must be accompanied by an adult guardian, and kids less than 8 years old (or lighter than 36 kilograms) are required to 'fly' in tandem with an adult.

- Loose objects such as jewellery, watches, hats and mobile phones need to be removed. There are secure lockers for storage.

- Wear enclosed, comfortable sports or hiking shoes. In winter you'll need warm clothes and a weather-proof jacket.

- There are barbecue and picnic facilities, and a kiosk selling snacks.

- A bus shuttle is available from Launceston (extra cost).

DON'T MISS

- Checking out your photos at the visitor centre before you leave. You cannot take your own cameras on the trip, but the guide takes photos of highlights of your experience and these will be ready for you to purchase if you wish.

- Exploring Hollybank Forest Reserve. Hollybank was one of the earliest private plantations in Tasmania, and some of the European trees planted here were for wood to make cricket bats. The deciduous trees are very picturesque in autumn. There are various walking trails, as well as space to run around – or play a game of cricket.

FABULOUS FACTS

The full length of the cable adventure is almost 1 kilometre and once your pulley is attached to the wire it cannot be removed from the cable until you finish your ride approximately one-and-a-half hours later! However, you do have stops along the way, so the journey is broken up into spans ranging from 15 to 400 metres. (The first is a short one.) You travel from heights of 4 to 50 metres above the ground.

Kid Quest

What is the fastest possible speed you can reach on the tour?

See pp. 640–4 for the answer

Bass and Flinders Centre

8 Elizabeth St, George Town
(03) 6382 3792;
www.bassandflinders.org.au

BUDGET

Step on board a full-size replica of the wooden sailing sloop, the *Norfolk*, which re-enacted George Bass and Matthew Flinders' 1798–99 circumnavigation of Tasmania. You can take a guided tour to learn about the exploits of these two famous maritime explorers.

George Town Watch House

Macquarie St, George Town
(03) 6382 4466
Check opening times

BUDGET

Built as a prison in 1847, this building now houses a model village of early George Town along with various local history displays.

Lilydale Falls

Lilydale Falls Reserve, Golconda Rd, Lilydale

FREE

These two small waterfalls are easily reached in a short walk through fern and eucalypt forest from the carpark. There is a picnic area near the carpark, along with a playground and toilets.

Low Head Lighthouse

Low Head Rd, Low Head
Sun at noon

FREE

Late on a Sunday morning you can usually see volunteers fire up the restored foghorn engines in preparation for the two-tone blast of the foghorn! Look for the replica semaphore masts nearby. Messages were sent by semaphore between Low Head and Launceston until 1858. There is no access to the lighthouse.

Low Head Maritime Museum

399 Low Head Rd, Low Head
(03) 6382 1143;
www.museum.lowhead.com

BUDGET

In 1805 a pilot service was set up to guide ships past dangerous rocks in the Tamar River. The pilot service is still in operation, but the convict-built cottages of early pilots now house this museum. Exhibits include an old whaling harpoon, a diving suit, shipwreck artefacts and a display about the work of pilots. If you visit on a Sunday, continue down the road to the Low Head Lighthouse (*see above*).

Low Head Penguin Tours

486 Low Head Rd, Low Head
0418 361 860;
www.penguintours.lowhead.com
Nightly at sunset, including
Christmas Day

MID-RANGE

Meet endearing little penguins, only 30 centimetres tall, as they return from foraging at sea. They will waddle around your feet and you can visit their burrows, where you might catch a glimpse of baby chicks (December–February).

West Tamar Valley___

Beaconsfield Mine and Heritage Centre
West St, Beaconsfield
(03) 6383 1473; www.beaconsfieldheritage.com.au

MID-RANGE

Eyes are glued to the screen as you follow the harrowing story of the mine disaster and rescue that took place just a few metres away in April 2006. And now you can experience it for yourselves... You worm your way along a narrow concrete pipe, just like the miners did when the earthquake triggered the mine collapse. Popping up through a gap in the pipe you see a replica of the tiny cage where miners Brant Webb and Todd Russell waited fourteen long days for rescuers to reach them.

INSIDER TIPS

- Allow a couple of hours to view the museum. The disaster and rescue exhibit is only one of many interesting and highly interactive displays (*see* DON'T MISS *below*).

- After watching the rescue video, keep your eyes open when walking around town. You just might spot one of the heroes featured on screen.

- You can buy a Tamar Triple Pass which includes entry to Beaconsfield Mine and Heritage Centre along with Seahorse World (*see* p. 553) and Platypus House (*see* p. 550).

- Much of the museum is out of doors, so dress appropriately.

- There is no cafe on site, but there are cafes nearby and there's a park over the road with picnic and barbecue facilities.

DON'T MISS

- The accounts of the heroic efforts of the rescuers. The kids may not want to read these, but you can tell them the salient points.

- The walkway that leads to the old grubb shaft. At the end you'll find all sorts of noisy old machinery – the kids can have a go at working pump rods, a waterwheel and a battery stamper.

- The observation platform where you can view the working mine right next door. You might see the miners going up and down the shafts into the ground — it was in a similar shaft that the miners were trapped, 1 kilometre under the earth.

- The Life and Times display. Have a go at weaving a rag rug, riding in a vintage wheelchair, writing with a quill and trying on old-style clothing.

- The opportunity to try out a whole range of old machinery — look for the yellow hand symbols. The kids will love sorting and packing apples with the apple-grading machine and making phone calls using a 1950s public telephone and switchboard.

- The hologram of a mine — a captivating re-creation of the real thing.

- The model working mine where kids can wind the cage up and down.

- The gold mining activity, where kids can have fun mucking around with mud, water and a pan (or cradle) — and find shavings of 'gold'.

 FABULOUS FACTS

In the late-19th century, Beaconsfield was one of the richest gold towns in Tasmania with over 50 working mines. As time passed, the mining technology became uneconomical and mines closed one by one. From 1914 to the early 1990s they all lay silent. Then the price of gold increased, technology improved, and the mines reopened. The mine you see operating next door produces thousands of ounces of gold every week.

Kid Quest
See if you can locate the figurines of animals hidden all through the museum.

Platypus House
Inspection Head Wharf, 200 Flinders St, Beauty Point
(03) 6383 4884; www.platypushouse.com.au
Entry by guided tour only

MID-RANGE

It is a rare treat to see platypus as close as this, active and in the light. These strange, furry creatures with long bills paddle through the water, webbed feet churning. Your kids could spend ages watching them through the glass as they feed, dive down and bob up for air, but there's another monotreme waiting around the corner. The tour guide leads you inside the echidna garden, and invites you to kneel on the ground. To the kids' delight, echidnas are soon waddling into their laps on the way to trays of mush, which they lick up with long, earthworm-like tongues.

INSIDER TIPS

- Allow about an hour for your visit. Tours last 35 minutes and depart regularly throughout the day, half-hourly in summer. It is advisable to book.

- The exhibits are all indoors.

- There is an interpretive centre that explains the biology of the platypus and echidna, both egg-laying mammals.

- There is also a 15-minute film on platypus to watch in the theatrette.

- You can buy a Tamar Triple Pass which includes entry to Platypus House along with Beaconsfield Mine and Heritage Centre (*see* p. 549, and Seahorse World (*see* p. 553).

- There is a cafe on site.

DON'T MISS

- The website – it has lots of intriguing information about platypus and echidnas.

- All the great photo opportunities. You are even allowed to take flash photos of the platypus as their eyes are closed underwater.

- Seahorse World (see p. 553), which is just nearby.

FABULOUS FACTS

With its eyes, nose and ears tightly closed when it dives, a platypus has to find food by using electrical receptors in its bill. It gulps in yabbies, crayfish and anything else it finds, storing the food in cheek pouches until it comes up for air (every minute or so). The platypus then 'chews' its food by grinding it between horny plates inside its bill. Although platypus babies have teeth, these fall out after a few months.

Glengarry Bush Maze

48 Jaydee Rd, Glengarry
(03) 6396 1250

BUDGET

Have fun finding your way through a hedge maze in a lovely bushland setting. You can also have a snack in the tearoom and play with big wooden puzzles.

Lavender House

690 Rowella Rd, Rowella
(03) 6394 7559; www.lavender-lady.com

VARIOUS PRICES

See the different types of lavender plants grown here (in bloom November–February), watch the process of manufacturing lavender cosmetics, and taste lavender ice-cream and lavender scones in the tearoom. You can take a self-guided tour (budget) or make a booking for a guided tour (mid-range).

Narawntapu National Park

Via Bakers Beach Rd
Parks and Wildlife Office
(03) 6428 6277;
www.parks.tas.gov.au

BUDGET

The main entrance at Springlawn has interpretive displays and provides picnic and toilet facilities. You have a great chance of seeing native animals in the wild, including common wombats, Bennett's wallabies, pademelons and lots of birds. Some of the wild animals here are quite tame, but you are asked not to feed them as this can cause disease. There are lovely walking tracks, and Bakers Beach is generally safe for swimming.

Notley Fern Gorge State Reserve

Notley Gorge Rd, Notley Hills
(03) 6336 2678; www.parks.tas.gov.au

FREE

Take a short bushwalk to a creek in a ferny glade and look for Brady's Tree – this burnt-out tree was a bushranger's hideout. On West Tamar Highway, Rosevears, you can see Brady's Lookout where the bushrangers used to watch for their victims.

Seahorse World, Beauty Point

Seahorse World
Inspection Head Wharf,
200 Flinders St, Beauty Point
(03) 6383 4111;
www.seahorseworld.com.au

MID-RANGE

Take a 45-minute guided tour behind the scenes of this seahorse-breeding farm and see every fascinating stage of the seahorse life cycle. There is also a touch pool and aquariums with sea dragons, pipefish, deadly blue-ringed octopuses, stingrays and giant Australian cuttlefish. Platypus House (*see* p. 550) is nearby.

Supply River Mill Reserve
Via Deviot Rd, Deviot

FREE

This is a fun place to go for a gentle, scenic bushwalk and picnic. Follow the bank of Supply River and you'll find a waterfall and the ruins of a water-driven flour mill from 1825, now covered in periwinkles. Bushrangers used to attack the people at this mill and it is said to be haunted.

Tamar Valley Resort
7 Waldhorn Dr, Grindelwald
(03) 6330 0400 or 1800 082 627;
www.tamarvalleyresort.com.au

VARIOUS PRICES

This is a recreated Swiss village, complete with chalets and quaint shops. Enjoy a game of 18-hole minigolf, a pirate-themed playground, bike hire and lakeside activities. You can also stay here (*see* ACCOMMODATION p. 557).

In the area

41 Degrees South Aquaculture

323 Montana Rd, Deloraine
(03) 6362 4130;
www.41southtasmania.com

BUDGET

This is a salmon farm and ginseng producer. Feed the fish in the ponds (food supplied), and wander round the wetlands in the grounds to view waterbirds. Free tastings of salmon and ginseng products are available.

Brickendon Historic Farming Village

236 Wellington St, Longford
(03) 6391 1251; www.brickendon.com.au
Open Tues–Sun; closed July and Aug

MID-RANGE

This working farm offers a gentle, old-fashioned family outing. You can pat and feed farm animals, romp around the heritage gardens, hire a fishing rod and try your luck in the river, and have a go at colonial-style games such as horse-shoe throwing. The historic farm buildings are there to be explored – you can hammer on the blacksmith's anvil or play the organ in the chapel. And there are always activities to watch on the working farm. Accommodation is available (*see* p. 556).

Imaginarium Science Centre

19–23 MacFie St, Devonport
(03) 6423 1466;
www.devonport.tas.gov.au
Closed Sun

MID-RANGE

This museum showcases travelling exhibitions that teach everyday science in an interactive and fun way.

Marakoopa and King Solomons Caves

Mole Creek Karst National Park,
via Liena Rd, Mayberry
(03) 6363 5182; www.parks.tas.gov.au
Check tour times

MID-RANGE

You are spoilt for choice in these wonderful caves. At King Solomons you see amazing shawls, stalactites and stalagmites. At Marakoopa, where you see myriads of enchanting glow-worms, there are two tour options. Tour the lower chamber to see sparkling crystals and reflective pools of stalactites, and hear the tinkle of underground creeks, or visit the Great Cathedral to see delicate formations in beautiful colours. Tickets for all tours are purchased at the visitor centre on your way into the park.

Ross

Tourist Information Centre, 48 Church St
(03) 6381 5466; www.visitross.com.au

FREE

This little convict-built village on the banks of the Macquarie River was settled in 1812. The convicts who carved the beautiful sandstone bridge were given a free pardon for their work. See if you can find the carving reputed to show the drunken face of Governor George Arthur. In the adjacent Tasmanian Wool Centre you can see and touch different types of wool, including the superfine merino this region is famous for.

Skulduggery mystery tour games

Longford
(03) 6254 1212;
www.heritagehighway.com.au/
skulduggery

BUDGET

This game, which the whole family plays together, unravels a real mystery from the 1820s. Skulduggery game packs are available online or from various Longford locations, including Brickendon Historic Farming Village (*see* p. 554) and the council offices at 13 Smith Street. The aim of the game is to help Convict Field Policeman John James solve an authentic case of Vandiemonian skulduggery. The pack contains clues that lead you through historic Longford as you solve the mystery. Packs are also available for Oatlands and Ross.

Ross Bridge,
Ross

Tasmazia and the Village of Lower Crackpot
500 Staverton Rd, Promised Land
(03) 6491 1934; www.tasmazia.com.au

MID-RANGE

As well as the most amazing mazes, including one for toddlers with a Fairy Princess' Castle, there is a miniature village, a Cubby Town (with fire station, pancake parlour and supermarket) and many secrets to uncover.

Topiary tour
Railton
www.townoftopiary.com.au

FREE

Have fun wandering around this town to find all the plants that have been grown and clipped into shapes – can you find the train, elephant, crocodile and koala? Topiary maps are available from shops in town or you can download one from the website.

Accommodation

BIG4 Kelso Sands Holiday Park
86 Paranaple Rd, Kelso
(03) 6383 9130 or 1800 664826;
www.kelsoholidaypark.com.au

BUDGET TO MID-RANGE

In a rural location 40 minutes from Launceston, on the west bank of the Tamar River, you have a choice of caravan or camping sites or self-contained two- or three-bedroom cabins. There is a pool for summer, a jumping pillow, a playground and an 'enchanted forest' where lots of native wildlife can be found, including wombats and Tasmanian devils.

Brickendon Historic Farming Village
236 Wellington St, Longford
(03) 6391 1251; www.brickendon.com.au

MID-RANGE

Only half-an-hour's drive from Launceston, this enchanting working farm has a variety of self-contained cottages. Enjoy open fires and deep old-fashioned baths, and see what you can find in the tin trunk of toys. For information on what to see and do on the farm, see p. 554.

Elphin Villas

29A Elphin Rd, Launceston
(03) 6334 2233;
www.elphinvillas.com.au

MID-RANGE

These self-contained villas are spacious with private courtyards. They have two or three bedrooms and some have two bathrooms. They are in a quiet location, adjacent to a shopping centre and walking distance to the centre of town.

Tamar Valley Resort

7 Waldhorn Dr, Grindelwald
(03) 6330 0400 or 1800 082 627;
www.tamarvalleyresort.com.au

HIGH COST

Ten minutes north of Launceston, these self-contained, two-bedroom chalets are a home away from home. Facilities include a heated indoor pool, wading pool, jumping pillow, tennis court, huge playground, games arcade, lakes with trout, ducks and swans. You can hire canoes, pedal-go-carts and mountain bikes. *See* p. 553 for more details.

Places to eat

Burger Got Soul

243 Charles St, Launceston
(03) 6334 5204

Pick up a fresh burger, selecting from twenty or so combinations, with big chunky chips. It won't be as quick as a fast-food burger, but you will taste the difference.

Chocolate Studio

2 Cuisine La, Launceston
(03) 6334 7878;
www.taschocolate.com.au

This is chocolate lovers' heaven, but it also serves a great breakfast or lunch, and has a kids' play area. Make sure you taste the hot chocolate!

Fish 'N Chips

30 Seaport Blvd,
Old Launceston Seaport
(03) 6331 1999

This modern seafood restaurant is child-friendly and has indoor and outdoor dining right on the waterfront. Meals are fast, and there is a blackboard to keep the kids entertained.

Tamar River Cruises, Home Point

Tailrace Cafe
1 Waterfront Dr, Riverside
(03) 6327 3542;
www.kidsparadise.net.au
This cafe is located in Kids Paradise (*see* p. 544), so you can enjoy a burger or pizza lunch as well as a romp in the indoor playground.

Tamar River Cruises
End of Home Point Pde, Home Point
(03) 6334 9900;
www.tamarrivercruises.com.au
Cruise down the magnificent Tamar River watching the passing scenery and looking for native waterbirds while you eat.

Cruises last from three to four hours. The vessel is a large, open-plan catamaran so the kids can move around.

Rosevears Waterfront Tavern
215 Rosevears Dr, Rosevears
(03) 6394 4074
This historic tavern, built in 1831, is located on the west bank of the Tamar River. It is child-friendly and serves typical pub meals. Choose a window seat or eat outdoors and watch the boats and birdlife on the water.

WESTERN WILDERNESS

Cradle Mountain (145 kilometres from Launceston) and Strahan (290 kilometres from Hobart) are the main tourist centres in this large region; suits driving holidays
Many attractions close over winter

HIGHLIGHTS

Cradle Mountain–Lake St Clair National Park (north) **p. 559**

Devils@Cradle **p. 562**

Gordon River cruises **p. 564**

Cradle Mountain

Cradle Mountain–Lake St Clair National Park (north)

Via Cradle Mountain Rd
Visitor Centre (03) 6492 1110 or
(03) 6492 1133; www.parks.tas.gov.au

MID-RANGE

You gaze at the immensity of the wilderness stretching around you: the mystical Dove Lake, the famous Cradle Mountain reaching to the sky, its peaks wreathed in mist... The peace, quiet and beauty are indescribable. Even your kids are silent and awed. This trip, away from television, telephones, crowds and computers, is immersing you all in the simple

Pademelon in Cradle Mountain–Lake St Clair National Park

pleasure and beauty of nature. You've seen wombats, wallabies and possums, and now, soft white snowflakes start drifting down.

INSIDER TIPS

- Cradle Mountain–Lake St Clair National Park covers a vast area. Cradle Mountain is in the northern section of the park and there is no direct link to Lake St Clair in the south (*see* p. 569).

- Take care when you drive around the park, especially at night, as many animals share the road with you.

- Before entering the park, stop at the visitor centre to pick up information, buy tickets and board the shuttle bus. Visitors are encouraged to leave their cars here and make use of the shuttle service (extra cost) to Lake Dove and other destinations en route to reduce traffic in the park.

- The ranger station, located within the park, has toilets, picnic shelters, electric barbecues and safe drinking water. Any water from other sources needs to be treated before drinking.

- There is a cafe next door to the visitor centre, and meals are also available at Cradle Mountain Lodge.

- Rangers run guided activities in summer, departing from the ranger station. Ask for details at the visitor centre.

- There can be rain, sleet, snow or driving winds at any time of the year. Weather conditions are generally most stable in late summer or autumn.

- Staying overnight in the park gives you a greater chance to spot animals, which are more active at night. *See* p. 570 to find out about some of the places you can stay.

- Tasmanian National Parks have entry fees. If you plan to visit several national parks, keep costs down by purchasing a Holiday Pass, available from visitor centres.

DON'T MISS

- The short, easy walks near the ranger station. The Enchanted Walk takes you along the banks of Pencil Pine River, where you can try to spot platypus. The Waterfalls Walk leads to Pencil Pine

Falls – a spectacular but very chilly swimming spot – and Knyvet Falls. The Rainforest Walk only takes about ten minutes and gives you a view of the Pencil Pine Falls.

- The animals – keep your eyes open for echidnas, wombats and pademelons, especially in the early morning or evening. There are also numerous birds.

- The walk around Dove Lake (about two hours). You take a track from the Dove Lake carpark and travel clockwise on a raised boardwalk around the lake. You'll pass quartzite beaches with sparkly (prickly) sand, and a much-photographed old boat shed, before a short uphill climb for views back across the lake.

- The boardwalk that runs all the way from the ranger station to Dove Lake. The full walk takes about two hours one way, but if you get tired you can hop on the shuttle bus (purchase tickets in advance).

- Devils@Cradle (*see* p. 562), located about 500 metres from the entrance to the park.

FABULOUS FACTS

Millions of years ago, Tasmania was part of a super continent, Gondwana, and was attached not only to mainland Australia, but to South America, New Zealand, Africa, India and Antarctica. Many ancient plants you'll see in Cradle Mountain–Lake St Clair National Park, such as deciduous beech trees, and the King Billy pines and pencil pines, bear evidence of these Gondwanan origins. In 1982, the park became part of the Tasmanian Wilderness World Heritage Area.

Kid Quest

Why is it called Cradle Mountain?
See pp. 640–4 for the answer

Devils@Cradle

3950 Cradle Mountain Rd,
Cradle Mountain
(03) 6492 1491; www.devilsatcradle.com

MID-RANGE

A little hand eagerly reaches out to stroke the charcoal-black fur of a Tasmanian devil. When you pat these little creatures, it is hard to believe they are the same animals that look so vicious when they feed and have play-fights with their mates. A moment ago, the kids were watching in horrified fascination as the devils

Devils@Cradle, Cradle Mountain

tore at an animal carcass with their sharp teeth. But this one is soft and cuddly, and curled up in the ranger's arms like a kitten.

INSIDER TIPS

- Devils@Cradle is located about 500 metres from the entrance to Cradle Mountain–Lake St Clair National Park.

- Feeding time can be a bit gruesome as the devils are fed a recognisable animal carcass, not just pieces of meat.

- Be aware it can snow here in winter and the area remains extremely cold into spring. Rug up warmly, especially if you are doing the night feeding tour.

- The visitors centre has a number of educational displays and allows you the convenience of viewing a devils' den from the warmth and comfort of indoors. You can also view them from the sheltered outdoor viewing deck.

- Not only are the devils' enclosures as close to a wild setting as possible, but the whole park is largely undeveloped, blending into the surrounding forests and grasslands and providing important alpine habitat for wild Tasmanian devils and other native marsupials.

- Day tours run hourly. If you want to do the night feeding tour, it is a good idea to book ahead, especially in busier months.

- During daylight saving time, the night feeding tour takes place while it is still light, which makes it easy to view the other animals in their enclosures.

- The park runs an important breeding program for the endangered Tasmanian devils.

DON'T MISS

- The wild animals living around the park. As soon as you step out of your car, start to watch out for wombats and other animals that might be ambling around, especially if you come for the night tour.

- The other carnivorous marsupials on display: the eastern quoll and spotted-tail quoll.

- The guided tours on offer. The guides give an informative talk about the devils' life cycle, problems and threats, but best of all you usually get to pat one of these animals. Day tours are cheaper, but in the night feeding tours the animals are more active.

- The hidden, automatic cameras on the outskirts of the park used to monitor wild devils. The cameras are enclosed in plastic containers, painted in camouflage colours and mounted on wooden posts. Every day, the noise of the captive devils feeding attracts other devils to come in from the wild. Park rangers leave titbits for them near the cameras – not enough to stop the devils foraging for themselves, but to delay them in order to photograph them. Devil Facial Tumour Disease is rapidly killing off devils in the wild and these cameras help the rangers monitor their health.

FABULOUS FACTS

Tasmanian devils often feed on road kill. When they eat, they gorge themselves until their tummies are so swollen they can only waddle. Because they are carnivorous, they give the impression of being bold, but they are actually very timid. When you walk in the bush, devils will keep out of sight, but you can watch for signs that they are around. Their greyish droppings can be easily differentiated from those of herbivorous Australian animals, such as wallabies and wombats, because they contain bits of bones or fur!

Kid Quest

Do devils have pouches like kangaroos?

See pp. 640–4 for the answer

Cradle Mountain to Strahan

Dr Frankenstein's Museum of Monsters

12 Whyte St, Zeehan
(03) 6471 6580
Check opening hours

BY DONATION

This home-made house of horrors located in a suburban backyard might give your kids some creative ideas.

Montezuma Falls

Via Williamsford Rd, Williamsford

FREE

This is the highest waterfall in Tasmania and you get a stunning view of it from a swing bridge.

To reach it, leave your car in the carpark at Williamsford and set off on a three-hour return walk along a disused tramway into the rainforest.

West Coast Pioneers' Museum

Main St, Zeehan
(03) 6471 6225;
www.westcoastheritage.com.au

BUDGET

Kids can marvel at minerals, explore a replica mining tunnel, find out how metals are made, climb an old locomotive, and play at being judge – or criminal – in a real old courthouse.

Around Strahan

Gordon River cruises

Gordon River Cruises, depart Strahan Wharf, The Esplanade, Strahan
1800 084 620; www.gordonrivercruises.com.au
Depart every morning including Christmas Day, twice daily in peak
World Heritage Cruises, depart Strahan Wharf, The Esplanade, Strahan
(03) 6471 7174; www.worldheritagecruises.com.au
Depart every morning, Sept–June, twice daily in peak

HIGH COST

Your vessel glides along and you gaze spellbound at the reflections of trees in the mirror-calm waters. The boat moors at Heritage Landing, and as you step into the rainforest, you jokingly warn your kids to watch out for dinosaurs. Widening eyes reveal that they almost believe you. Moving along the boardwalk, with thick, ancient jungle pressing in from both sides, it's not difficult to imagine. The next stop is Sarah Island, with its convict ruins and associated stories. Here the peace and beauty of the trip is temporarily shattered as your guide vividly reveals the lives of convicts who lived here when it was a dreaded penal colony.

INSIDER TIPS

■ The cruise takes you to Hells Gates (where Macquarie Harbour meets the ocean), salmon and trout farms, Sarah Island, the Gordon River and the rainforest at Heritage Landing.

■ Tours last about six hours, so you might want to bring some quiet activities for the kids when they have had enough of gazing at scenery. The vessels provide play areas.

■ A buffet lunch or dinner is included.

■ Seats are allocated (in different sections according to price) but there is plenty of room on the decks to move around.

■ Window seats cost extra, but you can always get a good view by going out on deck.

■ Avoid touching the old trees along the walk, as this removes the protective bark and moss.

■ There is an entertaining commentary during your cruise.

DON'T MISS

■ The 2000-year-old Huon pine that is the highlight of your walk from Heritage Landing.

■ The signs along the rainforest boardwalk that explain some of the plants and animals you can see.

■ Tasmanian pademelons, which might be hopping around the boardwalk. Do not feed them as processed food can cause disease and a slow, painful death.

FABULOUS FACTS

In the 1980s, the Tasmanian State Government tried to build a dam just downstream of the junction of the Gordon and Franklin rivers to generate hydro-electricity. Conservationists, horrified at the plan to destroy this wilderness area, created a surge of protest worldwide. The area was declared a World Heritage area, and the Federal Government used its powers to stop the building of the dam.

Bonnet Island Experience
Depart from Strahan Wharf,
The Esplanade, Strahan
(03) 6471 4300 or 1800 420 155;
www.bonnetisland.com.au
Seasonal tour times
Minimum age 5 years
HIGH COST

At twilight, journey to a tiny island to see little penguins and short-tailed shearwaters return to their burrows after a day fishing at sea. Standing beside the historic lighthouse and the remains of the keeper's cottage, learn about the harsh life of lighthouse keepers and hear tales of storm, shipwreck, rescue and survival.

Four-Wheeler Motorbike Tours
Depart from Henty Sand Dunes
Picnic Area
0419 508 175;
www.4wheelers.com.au
Bookings essential
Minimum age 5 years
HIGH COST

Enjoy a thrilling forty-minute, bone-shaking ride up and down the Henty Sand Dunes. There's a three-seater buggy to take an adult driver with two kids in the back, and extra adults ride their own four-wheeler motorbikes.

Henty Dunes
Via Henty Rd, Strahan
FREE

These huge, 30-metre high sand dunes are great fun to tumble around and slide on. Board hire is available from The Shack, The Esplanade, Strahan; (03) 6471 7396.

Hogarth Falls

People's Park,
via The Esplanade, Strahan

FREE

A 40-minute-return walk follows a freshwater stream into magnificent rainforest and leads you to an enchanting waterfall. Look for tracks in the muddy banks of the stream and see if you can guess which animals left them. It could be wallabies, possums, quolls, yabbies or platypus.

Kayaking

The Shack, The Esplanade,
Strahan
(03) 6471 7396;
www.wildriversjet.com.au
Minimum age 3 years

VARIOUS PRICES

Hire some double kayaks and take off to explore the Macquarie Harbour on your own, or take a guided kayaking tour. Safety gear is provided.

Morrison's Mill

The Esplanade, Strahan
(03) 6471 7235
2.45pm daily, Sept–May

FREE

See a 100-year-old sawmill cut a log of Huon pine and hear a talk about the history and uses of this timber. Huon pine items and off-cuts are available for sale. Only salvaged logs are used.

Ocean Beach

Ocean Beach Rd, Strahan
Parks and Wildlife Service
(03) 6471 7122

FREE

Head out here in the early evening to watch the sun sink into the Southern Ocean. As it grows dark, you'll see thousands of shearwaters (muttonbirds) return to their burrows in the sand dunes after a day of food gathering (October–March). They circle overhead and then land, often right at your feet! Every evening in peak holiday season, a park ranger gives a free talk about the birds. Before dark, look for large piles of shells on the beach, but don't disturb them. These middens show where Aboriginal people have eaten on the beach over thousands of years. Note: swimming is unsafe here due to strong currents.

Ship That Never Was

Strahan Amphitheatre,
The Esplanade, Strahan
(03) 6471 7700; www.roundearth.com.au
5.30pm daily, Sept–May

MID-RANGE

This is a humorous and lively theatre production based on a true story from 1834. The play revolves around a group of convicts who stole a boat, escaped from imprisonment on Sarah Island and sailed all the way to Chile.

Strahan Woodworks

12 The Esplanade, Strahan
(03) 6471 7244;
www.strahanwoodworks.com.au
FREE

Call in here if the kids are interested in woodwork as you will often catch a wood-turner or cabinet maker at work.

West Coast Wilderness Railway

Travels between Strahan and Queenstown
(03) 6225 7000 or 1800 420 155;
www.westcoastwildernessrailway.com.au
Check timetable
HIGH COST

You will marvel at the people who created this 35-kilometre track in the late-19th century, hewing tunnels by hand and bridging deep gorges in the wilderness. The historic train runs one direction each day and you are taken back to your starting point by coach. At stops along the way you can take short rainforest walks and have a taste of local honey. If you depart from Queenstown, you might even get a chance to try gold-panning. The total trip takes a full day and lunch is included.

West Strahan Beach

FREE

This beach, just ten minutes' walk from the town centre, is safe for swimming and has sheltered barbecue and picnic facilities and a small playground.

Wild Rivers Jet

The Shack, The Esplanade, Strahan
(03) 6471 7396;
www.wildriversjet.com.au
Minimum age 4 years
HIGH COST

Fancy a speed boat tour around Macquarie Harbour? During your fifty-minute thrill ride you'll see spectacular harbour and mountain views and historic remnants of mining operations.

West Coast Wilderness Railway

Special event

Mount Lyell Picnic
Australia Day, Jan
Strahan
West Strahan Beach becomes the centre of festivities for a day with various children's and adult races and novelty events.

Strahan to Hobart

Cradle Mountain–Lake St Clair National Park (south)
Via Lyell Hwy
Visitor Centre (03) 6289 1172
or (03) 6492 1133;
www.parks.tas.gov.au
BUDGET

Lake St Clair is the deepest lake in Australia and is the headwaters of the Derwent River, which flows to Hobart. At the visitor centre you can see a hologram of the extinct thylacine and pick up a walks brochure. The Figure of Eight track (4.8 kilometres, about one-and-a-half hours) takes you through four different types of vegetation and passes the spectacular meeting point of two rivers. Look for wildflowers (late spring and summer) and interpretive signs about Aboriginal culture and local flora. See p. 559 for more information on Cradle Mountain–Lake St Clair National Park.

Franklin–Gordon Wild Rivers National Park
Via Lyell Hwy
Lake St Clair Visitor Centre
(03) 6289 1172; www.parks.tas.gov.au
MID-RANGE

Easy walks into this national park are located just off the highway. From the Franklin River picnic area, a short stroll takes you to views of deep gorges and the formidably wild Franklin and Surprise rivers. Closer to Queenstown, the 20-minute-return Nelson Falls Nature Trail leads you between tall tree ferns

and over little creeks to an impressive waterfall. Watch for information panels about the ancient forest and the animals that live here.

Iron Blow Lookout
Via Lyell Hwy, Gormanston

FREE

Is anyone in the family fond of heights? Try standing on a cantilevered viewing platform – like a diving board with rails – out over the middle of the Iron Blow, a disused open-cut mine.

Accommodation

Cradle Mountain Lodge
Cradle Mountain–Lake St Clair National Park, Cradle Mountain Rd, Cradle Mountain
(03) 6492 2100 or 1300 806 192; www.cradlemountainlodge.com.au

HIGH COST

This lodge consists of comfortable cabins located close to the ranger station and several short walking tracks. Family cabins have one or two rooms, a fridge and tea-making facilities – but no televisions! Lodge staff offer year-round guided tours and other activities in the national park.

Strahan Bungalows
Cnr Andrew and Harvey sts, Strahan
(03) 6471 7268; www.strahanbungalows.com.au

MID-RANGE

These self-contained, two-bedroom bungalows are conveniently located in the tourist town of Strahan, two minutes' walk from a safe swimming beach. A cot, highchair, board games and cards are available.

Waldheim Cabins
Cradle Mountain–Lake St Clair National Park, Cradle Mountain Rd, Cradle Mountain
(03) 6491 2271; www.parks.tas.gov.au

BUDGET

This simple wilderness accommodation is located 5 kilometres within the national park. Each cabin has four to eight single bunk beds, gas heating and basic cooking facilities. Linen can be supplied for an additional cost. There is a separate amenities block with showers and toilets. Native animals wander around the cabins, especially at dusk.

Places to eat

Ol' Jack's Cafe and Gallery
32 Agnes St, Rosebery
(03) 6473 3097; www.oljacks.com.au
This cafe surrounded by rainforest and mountains has a warm, casual atmosphere. Pick up a bite to eat and wander around a display of artwork by local artists while the kids enjoy the play area.

Schwoch's Seafoods
The Esplanade, Strahan
(03) 6471 7500
There's something for everyone here. You can get top quality fish and chips, fresh crayfish and great pizzas. Dine in or take your meal away and eat by the harbour.

Tavern Bar and Bistro
Cradle Mountain Lodge, Cradle Mountain–Lake St Clair National Park
(03) 6492 2100 or 1300 806 192;
www.cradlemountainlodge.com.au
This is the more casual dining option at Cradle Mountain Lodge. The bistro-style meals have a good range of choices and you can sit by a log fire while you eat.

Another Holiday Idea for Tasmania

Sea trip to Devonport
Mainlanders jokingly talk about Tasmania as being 'overseas', but why not enjoy the novelty of this. Kids love the experience of travelling overnight by car ferry from Melbourne to Devonport, and from here you can experience many of the delights of Tasmania within an hour or two's drive. Discover forests, gorges and caves, meet little penguins and have fun in the mazes at Tasmazia.

For information about ferries contact Spirit of Tasmania; 1800 634 906; www.spiritoftasmania.com.au

GENERAL INDEX

For index entries by theme, see p. 606

T

World War II Oil Storage Tunnels,
Darwin Wharf Precinct NT 380
WOW Wilderness Cruise, Walpole Jetty
Area WA 339
Wynnum Foreshore Qld 437
Wyungara Nature Sanctuary, Lakes
Entrance Vic. 173

Y

Yadgalah Mini Golf, Denham WA 357
Yallingup Maze WA 364
Yallingup Shearing Shed WA 364
Yanchep National Park WA 328
Yarra Bend Park, Fairfield Vic. 147
Yarra Valley Railway, Healesville Vic.
151

Yarrabin, O'Connell NSW 104
Yarrawonga Holiday Park Vic. 202
Ye Olde Lolly Shoppe, Margaret River
WA 366

Z

Zig Zag Railway, Clarence NSW 28
Zip Circus School, Coffs Harbour
NSW 65
Zoo Roar'n Snore, Parkville Vic. 152
ZooDoo Wildlife Park, Richmond Tas.
525
Zorb Gold Coast, Pimpama Qld 481

INDEX BY THEME

Themes Legend

Aboriginal culture (e.g. bush tucker, Indigenous culture), p. 607

Adventure plus (e.g. abseiling, canoeing, bikeriding, rock climbing, surfing), p. 608

Animal encounters (e.g. wildlife parks, wildlife-watching, animal farms, zoos, aquariums), p. 610

Arts and crafts (e.g. galleries, craft workshops, literary encounters, author residences), p. 615

Big is best (e.g. tall trees, giant-sized objects, towers, megafauna displays), p. 615

Brain food (e.g. technology centres, science centres, puzzle centres, museums, mazes), p. 616

Close to nature (e.g. gardens, picnic spots, national parks, World Heritage areas, treetop walks, waterfalls, beaches), p. 617

Combat (e.g. forts, war museums, military vehicle displays), p. 621

Dinosaur roar! (e.g. dinosaur skeletons, models and fossils), p. 621

Factory at work (e.g. mint tours, steelworks, car factories, manufacturing tours), p. 621

Fairies and fantasy (e.g. fairy shops, fantasy displays), p. 622

Flight (e.g. military and civilian planes, hot-air balloons, Flying Doctor bases, flying tours), p. 622

Getting wet (e.g. water parks, swimming beaches, surfing, kayaking, rafting, snorkelling), p. 622

High life (e.g. towers, hot-air balloons, treetop walks, rock climbing), p. 624

Just for fun (e.g. playgrounds, theme parks, play centres, minigolf), p. 624

Lost in space (e.g. planetariums, observatories, moon-rock displays), p. 626

Mini-world (e.g. miniature animals, model villages, model railways), p. 626

Sail away (e.g. boats, naval vessels, submarines, maritime museums, shipwrecks, lighthouses), p. 626

School with a difference (e.g. School of the Air, circus lessons, art workshops, surf lessons), p. 628

Aboriginal culture

Adventure plus

Arts and crafts

Big is best

Brain food

Close to nature

Wineglass Bay Cruise, Coles Bay Tas.
536

School with a difference

Showtime

Spine-tingling places

Sports crazy

Time travel

Trails

Underground

Wheels

ABOUT THE AUTHOR

Anna Ciddor's work is loved by children and parents around the world. She has written over fifty books, on topics as diverse as travel, toilets and Australian history, but she is most well known for her popular Viking Magic trilogy, *Runestone, Wolfspell* and *Stormriders*. Anna Ciddor's writing always delights with its fresh, unique approach, for which she has won Children's Book Council Notable Book Awards and an Australia Council Literature Board Grant. In *1000 Great Places to Travel with Kids in Australia*, she combines her understanding of what kids find fun and entertaining, with her passions for travel, history and all the jewels (and hidden gems) that make up Australia.

ACKNOWLEDGEMENTS

The publisher would like to acknowledge the following individuals and organisations:

Publications manager
Astrid Browne

Project manager
Melissa Krafchek

Editor
Heidi Marfurt

Cover design
Elissa Ciddor

Internal design
Leonie Stott

Layout
Mike Kuszla, J&M Typesetting

Illustrations
Anna Ciddor and Elissa Ciddor

Cartography
Bruce McGurty

Photo selection
Melissa Krafchek

Pre-press
PageSet Digital Print & Pre-press

Photography credits
New South Wales: All images are courtesy of Tourism New South Wales, except for p. 4 (Hamilton Lund/Tourism New South Wales), p. 5 (Phillip Quirk/Tourism New South Wales), pp. 6 and 10 (Hamilton Lund/Tourism New South Wales), p. 13 (Sally Mayman/Tourism New South Wales), p. 15 (Courtesy of Oceanworld Manly), p. 16 (Hamilton Lund/Tourism New South Wales), p. 23 (Sally Mayman/Tourism New South Wales), p. 37 (Hamilton Lund/Tourism New South Wales), p. 26 (Courtesy of Jenolan Caves), p. 40 (Courtesy of Byron Bay Arts Studio), p. 44 (Courtesy of Tropical Fruit World), p. 46 (Stuart Owen-Fox/Tourism New South Wales), p. 65 (Hamilton Lund/Tourism New South Wales), p. 54 (Courtesy of Australian Reptile Park), p. 56 (Courtesy of TreeTop Adventure Park), p. 63 (Courtesy of Pet Porpoise Pool), p. 67 (Grahame McConnell/Tourism New South Wales), p. 76 (Explore Australia Publishing), p. 78 (Don Fuchs/Tourism New South Wales), p. 83 (Courtesy of Budamurra Aboriginal Corporation), p. 86 (Paul Blackmore/Tourism New South Wales), p. 88 (Dee Kramer), p. 91 (Stuart Owen-Fox/Tourism New South Wales), p. 94 (H.R. Clark), pp. 95 and 98 (Pip Blackwood/Tourism New South Wales), p. 105 (Perisher)
Australian Capital Territory: All images are courtesy of Australian Capital Tourism, except for p. 110 (Courtesy of the Australian War Memorial), p. 118 (National Zoo & Aquarium), p. 120 (Tourism New South Wales)
Victoria: All images are courtesy of Tourism Victoria, except for p. 135 (Courtesy of the National Sports Museum), p. 138 (Courtesy of Eureka Skydeck 88), p. 144 (James Geer/Museum Victoria), p. 156 (Courtesy of Sovereign Hill Museums Association), p. 185 (Courtesy of Sand Sculpting Australia), p. 193 (Matthew Walsh/Tourism Victoria), p. 224 (Courtesy of the National Wool Museum)
South Australia: All images are courtesy of the South Australian Tourism Commission, except for p. 242 (Courtesy of the City of Port Adelaide Enfield), p. 243 (Julie Smith/Courtesy of the City of Port Adelaide Enfield), p. 244 (Milton Wordley/Courtesy of the City of Port Adelaide Enfield), p. 256 (National Motor Museum), p. 259 (Courtesy of Old Timers Mine), p. 263 (Densey Clyne/AUSCAPE), pp. 273 and 275 (Fleurieu Peninsula Tourism), p. 283 (Tourism Australia), p. 299 (Nick Rains/Explore Australia Publishing), p. 303 (Murraylands Tourism Marketing),
Western Australia: p. 306 (Christian Sproge), p. 310 (© photolibrary. All rights reserved.), p. 313 (Jiri Lochman/Lochman Transparencies), p. 315 (Courtesy of the Western Australian Birds of Prey Centre), p. 319 (© photolibrary. All rights reserved.), p. 324 (Courtesy of the Aquarium of Western Australia), p. 331 (Courtesy of Whale World), p. 334 (© photolibrary. All rights reserved.), p. 336 (Courtesy of Pentland Alpaca Farm), p. 342 (© photolibrary. All rights reserved.), p. 345 (Australian Geographic), p. 348 (© photolibrary. All rights reserved.), p. 352 (Courtesy of Ocean Mia Photography), p. 355 (David Parer and Elizabeth Parer-Cook/AUSCAPE), p. 356 (Australian Geographic), pp. 360 and 361 (www.busseltonjetty.com.au), p. 364 (Stephen Blakeney), p. 369 (Courtesy of Yallingup Surf School), p. 373 (Ian Beattie/AUSCAPE)
Northern Territory: All images are courtesy of the Tourism NT, except for p. 377 (Peter Eve/Tourism NT), p. 395 (Courtesy Top Didj & Art Gallery)
Queensland: All images are courtesy of the Tourism Queensland, except for p. 438 (Courtesy of The Workshops Rail Museum), p. 458 (Courtesy of Gallo Dairyland), p. 461 (Courtesy of Hartley's Crocodile Adventures), p. 474 (Courtesy of Dreamworld), p. 486 (Courtesy of Catch a Crab Tours), p. 493 (Courtesy of Australia Zoo)
Tasmania: p. 511 (Courtesy of the Tasmanian Museum and Art Gallery), p. 512 (Rick Eaves/Explore Australia Publishing), p. 513 (Courtesy of TrikeMania Adventure Tours), p. 514 (Courtesy of Alpenrail Swiss Model Village and Railway), p. 517 (Richard Eastwood/Tourism Tasmania), p. 518 (Grant Dixon/Lonely Planet Images), p. 521 (Tourism Tasmania), p. 523 (Simon Birch/Port Arthur Historic Site Management Authority), p. 525 (Melissa Krafchek), p. 533 (Nick Rains/Explore Australia Publishing), p. 537 (Nick Osborne/Tourism Tasmania), p. 543 (Chris McLenna/Tourism Tasmania), p. 545 (David Wall/Lonely Planet Images), p. 546 (Courtesy of Hollybank Treetops Adventure Pty Ltd), p. 553 (Nick Osborne/Tourism Tasmania), p. 555 (Geoff Murray/Tourism Tasmania), p. 558 (Courtesy of Tamar River Cruises and Cataract Cruises), p. 559 (Garry Moore/Tourism Tasmania), p. 562 (Courtesy of devils@cradle), p. 568 (Pure Tasmania)

Explore Australia Publishing Pty Ltd
85 High Street
Prahran, Victoria 3181, Australia

Explore Australia Publishing Pty Ltd is a division of Hardie Grant Publishing Pty Ltd

Published by Explore Australia Publishing Pty Ltd, 2011

Concept, maps, form and design © Explore Australia Publishing Pty Ltd, 2011
Text © Anna Ciddor, 2011

ISBN-13 9781741173406
10 9 8 7 6 5 4 3 2 1

Printed and bound in Australia by McPherson's Printing Group

Publisher's note: Every effort has been made to ensure that the information in this book is accurate at the time of going to press. The publisher welcomes information and suggestions for correction or improvement. Email: info@exploreaustralia.net.au

Publisher's disclaimers: The publisher cannot accept responsibility for any errors or omissions. The representation on the maps of any road or track is not necessarily evidence of public right of way. The publisher cannot be held responsible for any injury, loss or damage incurred during travel. It is vital to research any proposed trip thoroughly and seek the advice of relevant state and travel organisations before you leave.

The maps in this publication incorporate data copyright © Commonwealth of Australia (Geoscience Australia), 2006. Geoscience Australia has not evaluated the data as altered and incorporated within this publication, and therefore gives no warranty regarding accuracy, completeness, currency or suitability for any particular purpose.

Disclaimer: While every care is taken to ensure the accuracy of the data within this product, the owners of the data (including the State, Territory and Commonwealth governments of Australia) do not make any representations or warranties about its accuracy, reliability, completeness or suitability for any particular purpose and, to the extent permitted by law, the owners of the data disclaim all responsibility and all liability (including without limitation, liability in negligence) for all expenses, losses, damages, (including indirect or consequential damages) and costs which might be incurred as a result of the data being inaccurate or incomplete in any way and for any reason.

ANSWERS TO KID QUESTS

New South Wales

Sydney
- Australian Museum, p. 3: Kangaroo tooth

- Australian National Maritime Museum, p. 8: The *Vampire* is named after a V-class destroyer from World War I. All the V-class destroyers were given names that started with 'V', and sounded aggressive!

- Sydney Aquarium, p. 9: Saltwater crocodile

- Taronga Zoo, p. 12: Echidna

Byron Bay & surrounds
- Macadamia Castle, p. 44: Carpet pythons are not venomous and are not dangerous to humans

Central Coast
- Tuggerah Lake, p. 51: A deep growling sound

Coffs Harbour & surrounds
- Muttonbird Island, p. 63: Early settlers said that the shearwaters tasted like mutton (old sheep), so they called them muttonbirds

- Pet Porpoise Pool, p. 65: Dolphins come to the surface and breathe through a blowhole in the top of their head

Port Macquarie & surrounds
- Billabong Koala and Wildlife Park, p. 72: The female cassowary

Southern Highlands & South Coast
- Booderee National Park, p. 82: Harriet Parker, the daughter of a lighthouse keeper. She was accidentally shot by the daughter of another lighthouse keeper who was fooling around with a loaded firearm.

Western Plains
- Old Dubbo Gaol, p. 96: A horse kicked him in the face

- Western Plains Zoo, p. 99: Dark blue–black

Australian Capital Territory

Canberra
- National Museum of Australia, p. 113: Washing gold. Cradles

like these were used by hundreds of miners during the 1850s to extract gold from dirt.

- Canberra Deep Space Communication Complex, p. 122: American Pete Conrad

Victoria

Melbourne
- Fitzroy Gardens, p. 132: When this area was occupied by Indigenous people hundreds of years ago, they carved a shield or canoe out of the bark

- Melbourne Aquarium, p. 133: The keepers hide the tablets inside the fish. The penguins are fed only one fish each per day.

- Melbourne Museum, p. 135: When two ants meet, they give each other drops of sweet liquid as a way of communicating information

- Scienceworks, p. 146: Slimy bacteria and fungi

Ballarat and surrounds
- Blood on the Southern Cross, p. 156: The flag was blue with a pattern of the white stars of the Southern Cross

Mornington Peninsula
- Cape Schanck Lighthouse, p. 179: 59 steps

- Fort Nepean, p. 180: When World War I began, a German freighter was at Victoria Dock in Melbourne. As it tried to leave Port Phillip Bay, the gun at Fort Nepean fired a shot across its bows and it surrendered. Just after World War II broke out, a small Bass Strait freighter failed to identify itself on entering Port Phillip Heads and a warning shot was fired from Fort Nepean.

- French Island, p. 182: The main language is English, the same as the rest of Australia. In 1802 French explorers circumnavigated the island and named it 'Ile de France' (Island of France), but the first Europeans to settle here were British.

The Murray
- Port of Echuca, p. 193: The row boat is on display on the railway platform

- Swan Hill Pioneer Settlement, p. 197: There was a brand of 1856 washing machine called a Bullet, and you can see one on display behind Towaninnie Homestead

- Army Museum Bandiana, p. 198: A shark

Phillip Island
- Penguin Parade, p. 205: Dark blue

South Australia

Adelaide

- Adelaide Gaol, p. 231: Contraband items such as alcohol were often smuggled into the prison hidden inside dirty nappies destined for the laundry

- Adelaide Zoo, p. 234: The superb lyrebird. The zoo's lyrebird is known as 'Chook' and is famous for his ability to imitate not only other bird sounds, but anything he hears, such as mobile phone ring tones or a truck's reversing beep.

- South Australian Maritime Museum, p. 242: You had to knock out the weevils, a type of insect that lived in the biscuits!

Coober Pedy

- Old Timers Mine, p. 261: A safe for storing opals

- Josephine's Gallery and Kangaroo Orphanage, p. 262: Some go back to the wild and some go to sanctuaries

Fleurieu Peninsula

- Granite Island Penguin Centre, p. 269: When little penguins moult, they are not waterproof, so they need enough fat to sustain them for three weeks until they have grown new feathers and can go out to sea again to find food

- Granite Island Penguin Tour, p. 271: Their wings are very hard; they use them to dig their burrows

- South Australian Whale Centre, p. 272: A shark

Kangaroo Island

- Flinders Chase National Park, p. 284: Yes, unlike other seals such as leopard seals

- Seal Bay p. 287: A humpback whale

Mount Gambier & Limestone Coast

- Admella Discovery Trail, p. 297: From combining the first couple of letters of each of her trading ports – ADelaide, MELbourne and LAunceston

- Naracoorte Caves National Park, p. 299: They were too big to fit through most of the cave entrances

Western Australia

Perth

- Shipwreck Galleries, p. 321: Commander Palsaert, who had gone off in a small boat to fetch a rescue party, returned and discovered what had happened. He arrested the mutineers and immediately tried them for their crimes. Seven were hung, two cast away on the mainland, and the others flogged and taken to the *Batavia* for further punishment. Palsaert retrieved the loot.

■ Maritime Museum, p. 323: Because it has sunk a ship – an old Australian Navy ship – which it used for target practice

Great Southern
■ Whale World, p. 333: 22 metres long!

Shark Bay
■ Monkey Mia dolphin interaction, p. 352: The dugong

■ Ocean Park, p. 353: Hot water! Call 000 for an ambulance, then apply the hottest water the patient can tolerate, as this will start to break down the venom.

Northern Territory

Darwin
■ Crocosaurus Cove, p. 379: The bite force of a 5-metre crocodile is approximately 3.4 tonnes – that's 3400 kilograms!

■ Museum and Art Gallery of the Northern Territory, p. 384: Dugongs have large, dense, heavy bones while dolphins have light, fragile bones

Queensland

Brisbane
■ Alma Park Zoo, p. 430: Primates and koalas

■ Lone Pine Koala Sanctuary, p. 433: Yes, they have brush-tipped tongues for feeding on nectar and soft fruits

Cairns & surrounds
■ Cairns Tropical Zoo, p. 444: The barn owl

■ Green Island, p. 450: When Captain Cook sighted the island on his voyage of discovery in 1770, he named it after Charles Green, the chief astronomer on board his ship, *Endeavour.*

■ Rainforestation Nature Park, p. 454: Because they were built and designed in America, where vehicles are driven on the right side of the road

■ Skyrail, p. 456: Yes, Australian tropical rainforests have 1.2–3 metres of rain a year, and most of it falls in the summer months, December–March

■ Hartley's Crocodile Adventures, p. 463: A large mound nest made of reeds, grasses, leaf litter and mud near the water's edge. The eggs are left to incubate inside this mound.

■ Wildlife Habitat, p. 464: The tree kangaroo

Gold Coast

- Dreamworld, p. 476: The tiger

- Sea World p. 478: No, seals swallow their food whole

- Currumbin Wildlife Sanctuary, p. 486: A commercially produced powdered lorikeet and honey-eater food, which is mixed with water and honey to form a sticky porridge. Try not to spill it on your clothes!

Sunshine Coast

- Australia Zoo, p. 495: Elephants use their trunks to suck up water and then pour it into their mouths

Tasmania

Hobart

- Tasmanian Museum and Art Gallery, p. 512: In 1936 – you can see a film of it in the zoology gallery

East Coast

- Penguin Tours, p. 530: With great difficulty. The guides say there is a slight difference between the size and shape of the beaks, but this is not always reliable. Luckily, the penguins can tell the difference!

- East Coast Natureworld, p. 532: No, they carry their eggs inside them and give birth to live young. That is why tiger snakes are able to survive in Tasmania, where the weather would be too cold and unpredictable for reliable incubation of eggs.

- Freycinet National Park and Wineglass Bay, p. 534: When the bay was used as a whaling base, the slaughtering of the whales used to stain the sea the colour of red wine

Launceston & surrounds

- Queen Victoria Museum and Art Gallery, p. 542: It is a local sport that is a cross between baseball and basketball

- Hollybank Treetops Adventure, p. 547: 93 kilometres per hour, depending on friction, an individual's weight, wind direction and speed

- Platypus House, p. 552: When echidnas use their beaks to search for ants and termites, they get dirt inside, which has to be blown out so they can breathe and continue to seek food

Western Wilderness

- Cradle Mountain, p. 561: Because the jagged, double peak is shaped like a cradle – some say like a gold miner's cradle, used to separate the precious ore from dirt

- Devils@Cradle, p. 563: Yes, and they often raise four babies at once, which live in the pouch together for about 16 weeks